Default Printed Page

Left margin

Right margin

4

76

Line number

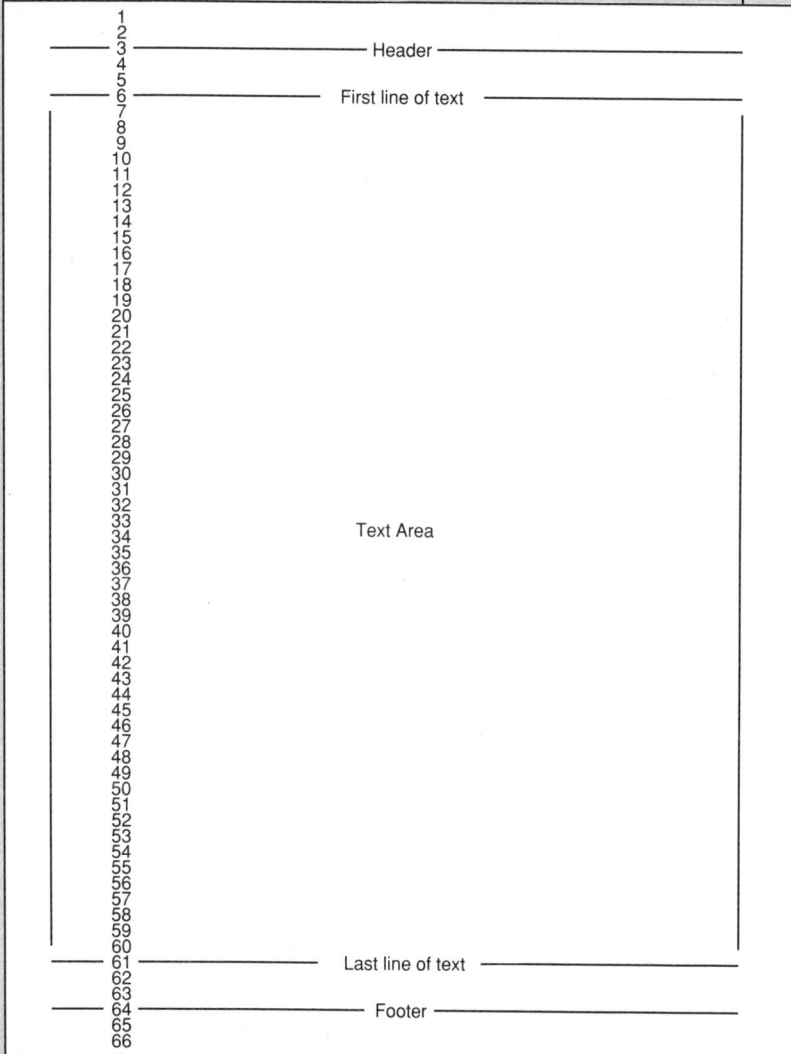

1		
2		Top margin - 2 lines
3	Header	
4		Two blank lines
5		
6	First line of text	
7		
8		
9		
10		
...	Text Area	
60		
61	Last line of text	
62		Two blank lines
63		
64	Footer	
65		Bottom margin - 2 lines
66		

Lotus 1-2-3 Tips and Tricks

LOTUS 1-2-3® TIPS AND TRICKS

◆ ◆ ◆

Second Edition

Gene Weisskopf

SYBEX®

San Francisco • Paris • Düsseldorf • London

Acquisitions Editor: Dianne King
Supervising Editor: Joanne Cuthbertson
Copy Editor: Ami Knox
Technical Editors: Maryann Brown and Dan Tauber
Word Processors: Deborah Maizels, Chris Mockel, and Scott Campbell
Book Designer: Eleanor Ramos
Chapter Art and Layout: Joe and Miriam Roter
Screen Graphics: Delia Brown
Typesetter: Elizabeth Newman
Proofreader: Winnie Kelly
Indexer: T.G. McFadden
Cover Designer: Thomas Ingalls + Associates
Cover Photographer: Victor Budnik
Screen reproductions produced by XenoFont

Epson is a registered trademark of Epson Corporation.
Hercules is a trademark of Hercules Computer Technology.
IBM, IBM PC, PC/XT, XT, AT, and PC-DOS are trademarks of International Business Machines
Corporation.
Intel is a registered trademark of Intel Corporation.
LaserJet is a trademark of Hewlett-Packard Inc.
Lotus, 1-2-3, Learn, and Speedup are trademarks of Lotus Development Corporation.
Microsoft is a registered trademark of Microsoft Corporation.
XenoFont is a trademark of XenoSoft.

The Browse program is copyright 1986 by Ziff-Davis Publishing Company.
The LIST program is copyright 1987 by Vernon D. Buerg.

SYBEX is a registered trademark of SYBEX, Inc.

TRADEMARKS: SYBEX has attempted throughout this book to distinguish proprietary
trademarks from descriptive terms by following the capitalization style used by the manufacturer.

SYBEX is not affiliated with any manufacturer.

Every effort has been made to supply complete and accurate information. However, SYBEX
assumes no responsibility for its use, nor for any infringement of the intellectual property rights of
third parties which would result from such use.

Library of Congress Card Number: 88-51991
ISBN 0-89588-668-5
Manufactured in the United States of America
10 9 8 7 6 5 4 3 2 1

To my father, Alex, who taught me that it's okay to guide your life by the stars, as long as you carry a sextant

ACKNOWLEDGMENTS

◆ ◆ ◆

The author's name is a prominent feature on a book's cover, but this book would not have been possible without the many people who worked to produce it and inspire it.

First and foremost, I must give thanks and recognition to all the members of the Sacramento PC Users Group. From them comes a tremendous body of ideas, questions, problems, and interest in microcomputers that is truly astounding, and is reflected to some degree on every page of this book.

Special thanks go to John Skelly, whose insight and interest make him one of the grand masters of 1-2-3 and the PC. Our friendship over the years and the chili omelets at Eppies were a major motivation for this book.

Much is owed to the wonderful talents of Tony Barcellos, the editor, production crew, and publicist of *Sacra Blue*, the newsletter of the Sacramento PC Users Group. Over the past four years he has ensured that my monthly column appeared in every issue, accurate and intact. In Tony's capable hands, the 80-page newsletter wrapped my contribution in a tasteful, informative, and sometimes even humorous package, which has gained national recognition.

At Sybex, I must first thank Dianne King, acquisitions editor, for her interest, enthusiasm, and support in bringing me into the Sybex fold. Her perusing of *Sacra Blue* says much about her attention to her job.

Lyn Cordell, the developmental editor for the first edition, deserves particular praise for guiding this project through to a first-rate finish. Her skill with the red pencil, her simple but to-the-point suggestions, and her pleasant and reassuring voice on the phone are much appreciated.

Ami Knox gets my thanks for her work as editor on this, the second edition. Her comments were helpful and kept the scope of the work in perspective.

My gratitude goes to Mark Taber for his job as technical editor on the first edition. He maintains a good outlook in all things, and it made my job easier to know that he was going over each page of the manuscript.

And to those in the computer industry, I would like to thank:

Intel Corporation for supplying me with an Above Board 286; it's amazing how fast you find uses for an extra 2 megabytes of memory (soon to be 4 megabytes).

Lotus Development Corporation for providing me with a beta copy of 1-2-3 Release 2.2, and offering a wealth of information that will ensure that this book is timely and relevant.

John Friend, for having created PC-Outline and GrandView, two programs which make the mechanics of writing not only feasible, but also a real pleasure.

Jim Savercool at the phone company in Roseville, who is a wonderful mix of systems designer and accountant. His call for 1-2-3 applications has proved to be an exhilarating challenge.

And I extend my warmest appreciation to those who are closest to me and participated in this book through their inspiration and motivation:

Mom, for showing such finesse when pointing out "just a small grammatical error" the first time I showed her the manuscript.

My grandmother Passya, for gently tempering my interest in computers with her stories of life before the time of automobiles, airplanes, and telephones.

My brother Alan, for keeping me in touch with the larger picture as this project progressed.

Peter and Heidi, for being too young to really know what life was like before pocket calculators.

And finally, my appreciation and love to Carol, my wife and companion for years and years, who can now stop reminding me that the term *author* is reserved for those who have actually published a book.

◆ CONTENTS AT A GLANCE _____

TABLE OF CONTENTS

◆ ◆ ◆

INTRODUCTION
◆ ◆ ◆

IF YOU USE LOTUS 1-2-3 RELEASE 2.01 OR 2.2 ON A REGULAR BASIS, you have probably come to expect that any problem you bring to your computer can be solved with this spreadsheet. Lotus has served you in countless ways, and the more complex the task, the more satisfying the results when you hit the {calc} key for the final time. Sometimes, however, these high expectations can lead to frustration.

◆ BEYOND THE REFERENCE MANUAL

You might be certain that you can construct a worksheet to meet a particular need, but after a dozen attempts and repeated trips to the manual, you may still be missing the key. If luck is with you, a friend or coworker will look over your shoulder and point out the solution, a solution that always seems too simple to have missed.

Lotus 1-2-3 Tips and Tricks is designed to supply you with just such timely pointers, as well as with shortcuts, words of caution, and tips on good worksheet habits. Pick a chapter, or a topic in a chapter. You'll discover a thorough discussion that demystifies a particular aspect of Lotus, revealing merits, tricks, and pitfalls previously taught only by experience. You will be on your way to successful applications built on solid knowledge of the spreadsheet.

This book covers both Releases 2.01 and 2.2, and those topics that are new with Release 2.2 are flagged in the margin with a symbol like the one next to this paragraph. If you use Release 2.2, look for these symbols, because solutions presented for Release 2.01 might be handled differently in Release 2.2. Or, there may be a new feature in Release 2.2 that supplies a more direct solution to an otherwise circuitous one. Read the text that is flagged, and you will be assured of having the information you need to master Release 2.2.

Although numerous resources are available for learning the commands and functions of 1-2-3, readers are often left with a full complement of tools and almost no idea of how to use them. *Lotus 1-2-3 Tips and Tricks* provides a complete guidebook to the "must see" features of Lotus, and also flags any patches of "thin ice" you may encounter. It acts as your guide to the productive use of 1-2-3, discussing Lotus features and techniques in light of their role in building strong, consistent applications. Along the way, you'll find special, neglected, or little-known powers of the spreadsheet illustrated with examples that are highlighted as Tips and Tricks. In addition, from the other end of the spectrum, you'll find Cautions that warn you away from potential hazards. A Tip is sound advice on productive but safe working habits that ensure success with your worksheets. Here is an example:

> **TIP** ◆ *Range names enhance the readability of formulas, and any variables that are referred to frequently should be given names. This formula may not be very meaningful:*
>
> +$B$16*(1+$H$29)
>
> *But with appropriate range names, its meaning springs to the surface:*
>
> +$RETAIL*(1+$SALES_TAX)

A Trick, on the other hand, may be a shortcut that is not readily apparent to most users, or an interesting combination of Lotus components that produces surprising results. Some features of 1-2-3 are so underused that the demonstration of their utility is also classified as a trick. For example:

> **TRICK** ◆ *Although 1-2-3 cannot print graphs directly from the worksheet, you can use the System command to access the PrintGraph program in only two short steps:*
>
> /s
> pgraph

A Caution illuminates the darker side of the topic under discussion, revealing any hidden dangers that even experienced users may encounter. Some Cautions are quite specific, while others warn you away from bad work habits that could potentially weaken or damage your worksheet.

> **CAUTION** ◆ *Never use the spacebar to erase a cell. If you do, the cell will look empty but will contain the space character and so be included in the count of a counting function, whereas a truly empty cell would not. This practice also defeats the efficient use of the End key to move about the worksheet and sprinkles the worksheet with RAM-eating space characters. If you want to return a cell to a blank state, use the Range Erase command.*

♦ WORKING INTO THE FUTURE _____

Since Release 2 of 1-2-3 entered the market at the end of 1985, it has been the spreadsheet standard. With over five million copies sold worldwide, it is a phenomenon among personal computer programs.

When Lotus Development Corporation unveiled 1-2-3 Release 3 in mid-1989, they also announced a second new version of the spreadsheet, Release 2.2. Where Release 3 would offer many new features in what was essentially a completely rewritten program, this second version was designed as an incremental upgrade to the widely popular Release 2.01.

Release 3 requires more sophisticated hardware, runs slower, cannot use Release 2.01 add-ins, and in several ways branches off the tremendous "highway" of Lotus after-market products, training, and support. Instead of confronting their millions of users with this all-or-nothing upgrade offer, Lotus Corporation instead offers Release 2.2.

This book follows that same philosophy. It is directed to Release 2.0, 2.01, and 2.2; topics specific to Release 3 are not included. However, most of the subjects in this book will also prove valuable in Release 3, just as most of what you learn in Release 2 (2.0, 2.01, or 2.2) of 1-2-3 will be useful knowledge if you move to Release 3.

But if you look at the list of new features in Release 3, and the new way in which old features are treated, you will see that to mix both versions in the same book could be quite an undertaking. From your own perspective as a reader who uses Release 2, you would want to skip over all the topics specific to Release 3. In the same way, those who use Release 3 might not want to read about a technique (however innovative or valuable) that is needed in Release 2, but can be circumvented through the new features of Release 3.

Therefore, this book is addressed to the multitude of users who each day build solutions with the Lotus 2 spreadsheet. It will help you tap the potential of the spreadsheet while avoiding its hazards. If a time comes when you choose to move to Lotus 3, you will have honed your skills and tapped the full potential of Release 2.

♦ WHAT THIS BOOK COVERS _____

Lotus 1-2-3 Tips and Tricks explains and demonstrates those features of Lotus that should be mastered by all users. The topics covered are balanced with consideration of the Lotus programming environment as a whole. The book consists of three sections: "Control and Performance," "Analysis," and "Making Connections."

PART 1: CONTROL AND PERFORMANCE

Part 1 emphasizes various features, techniques, and skills that will assist you in creating reliable worksheets quickly and easily.

Chapter 1, "Tapping the Power of Lotus with Macros," demonstrates the power of macros and how they enhance all worksheet applications for users of any skill level. If you are not familiar with macros, you will be introduced to the surprisingly simple process of creating them. This is followed by discussions of macro etiquette, debugging techniques, recording macros, and dynamic macros that can change themselves.

Chapter 2, "Using Range Names for Clarity, Speed, and Accuracy," is a must for worksheet applications that are reliable and easy to revise and debug. You can use range names instead of cell coordinates to simplify all worksheet routines, decrease addressing errors, provide worksheet documentation, and ensure that macros always address their intended cells.

Techniques for the successful completion of a Lotus worksheet are covered in Chapter 3, "Building Worksheets That Work." These include the use of variables, locating different types of data within the worksheet, building formulas that work, and controlling the size of the worksheet.

Chapter 4, "Debugging the Spreadsheet," looks at ways to uncover the problems that can arise both during and after worksheet construction. These include the built-in documentation tools of the Lotus spreadsheet, tracking down formula errors, and correcting numbers mistakenly entered as text.

Hard disks are the norm, but many Lotus users do not optimize their working routines to take advantage of their hard disk. Chapter 5, "Integrating 1-2-3 with Your Hard Disk," starts by explaining how to organize your programs and data files on your hard disk. Then, you'll learn how to build the Lotus Gateway, an application that automates your use of 1-2-3 from the DOS prompt to the final Quit command, and includes DOS batch files, the AUTO123 worksheet, the \0 auto-invoking macro, and a macro-driven worksheet that allows you to change to any of your worksheet subdirectories.

Chapter 6, "Living in the Lotus Environment," covers topics that are outside of Lotus but affect your use of the spreadsheet—specifically your computer's hardware and the DOS environment. The chapter closes with an automated application for transferring worksheet data to another program for further processing.

PART 2: ANALYSIS

The chapters in Part 2 concern specific Lotus features that are used in the course of analyzing worksheet data.

Chapter 7, "Cell Contents versus Cell Display," covers the often subtle relationship between what is displayed in a cell and what it actually contains.

Chapter 8 is called "Dealing with Dates, and Some Notable @ Functions." Date arithmetic is an important part of many worksheets, and this chapter unveils all the mysteries of Lotus dates. Also covered are a group of @ functions that are frequently misused or underused.

Chapter 9, "Manipulating Text with String Arithmetic and @ Functions," demonstrates the great potential of string arithmetic. Included are the @ functions that play a major role when you manipulate text in the worksheet.

Chapter 10, "Navigating a Database," covers the topics of building and operating a database within the worksheet. When you structure your data within the framework of a database, a whole new range of analysis techniques becomes available. The @d data functions, perhaps the most powerful of all the @ functions, are also covered in this chapter.

Chapter 11, "Graphs That Speak for Themselves," looks at the graphing capabilities of Lotus from three angles: first, organization of the worksheet data from which graphs are built; second, the graph commands used to build a graph; and third, the PrintGraph program that formats graphs for printing.

PART 3: MAKING CONNECTIONS

Part 3 deals with the movement of data. This includes moving data from Lotus to your printer, moving it within and between worksheets, and between the worksheet and the DOS environment.

Chapter 12, "Printing Your Worksheets," discusses the recurring task of sending worksheet data to the printer. The format of the Lotus printed page is covered first, followed by ways to manipulate the worksheet format before printing. Solving printer problems is given special attention, as is the topic of printing to disk files, a valuable and frequently ignored Lotus feature. Finally, the spreadsheet-publishing add-in Allways is discussed.

Chapter 13, "Transferring Data Where You Need It," looks at the many ways to move data in the Lotus environment. The various commands for moving data within the worksheet are discussed first, including the Data Sort command. The File commands, used for transferring data between worksheets, come next, and that discussion includes worksheet consolidations. Following that, the linking formulas of Release 2.2 are covered as a new way to transfer data from one worksheet to another. Then, data transfer by means of text files is considered as a tool for importing data from or exporting data to other programs, such as your word processor. Finally, the Data Parse command is demonstrated as the last link in importing data into the worksheet.

Because add-in programs can affect literally every aspect of the Lotus spreadsheet, the subject of add-ins is at once both too large to include in this book and too important to neglect. Therefore, the essentials of installing and using add-ins are covered in Appendix A, which also discusses the types of add-in programs that are available.

The various incarnations of 1-2-3 Release 2 have been on the market since the end of 1985. There are over five million owners of the program worldwide, and an equal or greater number who use it on the job. Appendix B is included to help you make the decision of whether or not you will upgrade to Release 3. If you have already upgraded to Release 2.2, then it may be a moot issue, but at some point in the future you will find yourself again considering the option. Appendix B highlights the major new features of Release 3, and discusses the hardware your equipment must have. It also points out some of the compatibility issues you will confront if you do make the change.

This book is designed to supplement, not replace, the Lotus user's manual—you will not find every command and function in 1-2-3 listed in these pages. If you require a more detailed explanation of a basic feature, consult your other Lotus resources: the manual, magazines, or Lotus reference books. Better still, take some time to experiment with the topic on your computer, use the Lotus help screens, and explore.

◆ WHO CAN USE THIS BOOK

Although this book is aimed at users with some knowledge of the Lotus spreadsheet, you will find topics of value in *Lotus 1-2-3 Tips and Tricks* no matter what your level of experience.

THE 1-2-3 NOVICE

On the surface it seems that only those with some knowledge of 1-2-3 would be interested in a compendium of useful techniques, shortcuts, and cautionary advice. But even if you are still building your fundamental skills, there is much in *Lotus 1-2-3 Tips and Tricks* that will be of value to you.

You will learn about the important features in Lotus that should not be overlooked during the learning process. Commands or methods are explained in reference to their best use or to problems that are commonly experienced. Thus, you'll benefit from an experienced point of view that will add new insight to your understanding of the spreadsheet.

THE INTERMEDIATE USER

If you have been using Lotus for some time, you have probably climbed far enough on the learning curve so that you are no longer a beginner. Although the trail may have been steep at times, you have discovered many tools and techniques that allow you to build worksheets while continuing to learn.

For the same or less effort you'll reap far greater gains as you proceed through this book. The 1-2-3 commands and features that are stressed and the style that is emphasized will enlarge your perspective on the Lotus worksheet, and you will move in directions that you have considered closed to you until now.

You may have assumed, for example, that you can live without macros until you master the spreadsheet commands. One of the fundamental ideas stressed in this book is that the sooner you begin to use macros, the faster and farther you will develop your worksheets. Using macros offers enormous immediate and long-term benefits, as well as immense satisfaction, for a relatively small investment in learning.

THE ADVANCED USER

If you are an experienced user of 1-2-3, you undoubtedly have your own bag of tricks at the ready, filled with practical methods, solutions, and timesavers. Here you'll find another kit of Lotus remedies, surprises, and hints, along with a healthy sprinkling of cautions and sound advice to compare with and add to your own. The broad picture presented here may also cast an interesting new light on the spreadsheet environment.

A subtle shift occurs when you progress from a skilled user to one who programs the worksheet. This book will help you through that transition by providing an inside look at the spreadsheet and the methods you can use to create strong, reliable applications with 1-2-3.

THE LOTUS PROGRAMMER

Those of you who have been productive with Lotus for some time have certainly mastered the worksheet commands, functions, and macro language. When you have reached this point, you begin to use the Lotus spreadsheet as a powerful programming tool to create applications for yourself and especially for others.

If you are one of these experts, consider this book a tour through another user's worksheet experience, and enjoy the perspective it presents. You may find quite a few tidbits to enhance your own repertoire.

◆ CONVENTIONS USED IN LOTUS 1-2-3 TIPS AND TRICKS _____

The terms *worksheet* and *spreadsheet* are used interchangeably.

In the interest of clarity, all worksheet or macro examples are kept as brief and to the point as possible. If macros are not yet a part of your everyday vocabulary, be assured that demonstrations are concise and should be quite readable with a little practice. Try typing out the macro keystrokes on the keyboard to see how they operate.

This book is written for Lotus 2.01 and 2.2, and some of the examples (such as a few that use string arithmetic) will not work correctly in Lotus 2.0. In general, though, the term Lotus 2 refers to versions 2.0, 2.01 and 2.2, unless one or the other is specifically noted.

Lotus keywords are enclosed in brackets, such as F2 {edit} for the edit function key.

Cell addresses and range names appear in all caps, while Lotus @ functions are in lowercase letters: @avg(JAN_TOTAL)+A3. Macros, too, follow this pattern. Cell coordinates or range names are all caps, while Lotus menu commands or macro keywords are lowercase. For example:

```
{blank TOTALS}{goto}TOTALS ˜
/fcceFILENAME ˜
```

In 1-2-3, all macros that are invocable from the keyboard are range-named with a backslash, \, and a single letter of the alphabet, such as \A. For clarity, in this book range names for other macros that cannot be called from the keyboard will also begin with a backslash, so that \PRINT_SUMMARY or \MENU1 both refer to macros, and not to data ranges in the worksheet.

Remember that, in a macro, braces, {}, are reserved by Lotus and always represent a macro command: {right}, {branch}, {menubranch}, {if}, {home}, and so on. The tilde, ˜, stands for Enter, as in {goto}A5 ˜ .

PART ONE:

Control and Performance

THE CHAPTERS IN PART 1 ADDRESS TWO CRITICAL FACTORS in worksheet development: control and performance. The two are considered together because they cannot really be separated; control produces worksheets that meet your needs and expectations, and good performance ensures that your worksheets will be responsive and a breeze to use.

Some people consider macros a topic for advanced users only, one that belongs in the back of the book. Here, macros are placed prominently in Chapter 1 because, as you will see, they are the key to control and performance for users at every skill level.

Chapter 2 highlights range names, a feature that is often neglected or underused, but is crucial for smooth worksheet operation.

Control and performance have to be built-in; they can't be added on. Chapters 3 and 4 present techniques and good habits for the complementary processes of building and debugging worksheet applications.

Chapter 5 puts you in control of Lotus and your hard disk— a vital union for top-notch performance.

Being in command of Lotus requires that you also control the environment where Lotus resides. Chapter 6 views Lotus from the perspective of the program's total environment—your computer and disk operating system.

ONE:

Tapping the Power of
Lotus with Macros

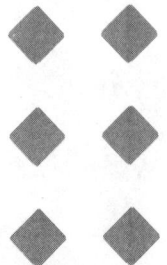

1

◆ ◆ ◆

IN THE WORLD OF COMPUTERS, A MACRO IS A SINGLE DESIGNATED keystroke that executes many others. This also describes macros in Lotus, but only partially. Macro capabilities in the 1-2-3 worksheet have grown far beyond simply repeating keystrokes to producing large, complex, and dynamic programming applications. Of all the features in 1-2-3, macros do the most to extend the versatility and scope of a spreadsheet.

This chapter starts by describing the many benefits that macros bring to a worksheet. Next comes a short review of writing macros and a section on good habits that should be developed when writing them. The important subjects of testing and debugging are covered, followed by the Lotus add-in, Learn, and its equivalent built-in feature in Release 2.2. The power of macros that can change themselves is then shown, along with some techniques that put that power to work. Finally, the virtues of the Macro Library Manager of Release 2.2 are discussed.

◆ MACROS: THE "4" IN 1-2-3 _____

Automated keystroke sequences can be used in a wide variety of situations by any 1-2-3 user. If you consider yourself a Lotus "programmer," then you already have a full stable of macro routines built into your spreadsheet applications. Without macros, many of your worksheets could not perform their intended function.

Those who have experience with macros also know that it is almost impossible to write applications or templates to be used by others without macros. By utilizing the extended macro programming language, you can make worksheets that are simple and easy to use, even for computer novices.

If you are a raw beginner, do not consider macros a tool that is only for advanced users. Learn the basics of macros at an early stage, and you will find that they improve almost every worksheet that you develop. The benefits will be noticeable even when you write a short macro in the simplest worksheet.

If you are a long-time Lotus user who does not use macros extensively, this chapter will help you get in gear. When worksheet control and performance are the issue, macros are the answer.

CONSISTENCY

Being in control of a Lotus worksheet means that you get consistent results, even to the extent of "garbage in, garbage out"! While you strive for correct answers, macros ensure that your answers are also consistent.

Macros are ideal for repetitious worksheet tasks. Printouts produced by macro-driven routines always have the same components and the same look. Margins, headers and footers, column titles, or the number of blank lines between different print ranges are always the same.

A consistent look or function can be carried across any number of worksheets simply by using the same macro in all of them.

ACCURACY

Not only do macros perform consistently, but when they are written correctly, their results are always correct. They eliminate random spelling errors and stray typos. When you use a macro, a sequence of commands will always be repeated in exactly the right order.

When you sort a range of cells, if you leave one column out of the data range, the scrambled records that result may be critical. With a macro doing the job, the proper columns will always be included so that such disasters are thwarted.

SPEED

Although control must always be the primary concern, who wants to be in control of an application that would lose a race with a snail? Because macros execute many times faster than the fastest typist can type, they will enhance the performance of almost any worksheet.

As users of worksheet applications increase their demands for solutions, and as spreadsheet developers increase their skills with Lotus, worksheets continue to grow and become more and more ponderous. Without macros, most large, complex worksheets would never be used—no one would have the time.

SIMPLICITY AND CONVENIENCE

As a worksheet becomes more complex, the tasks needed to run it are best handled by macros, at the touch of a key. Users at all skill levels will appreciate not having to read long instructions for each step in the normal worksheet routine.

With macros, novices need not understand the commands that are called when, for example, data is extracted and printed. Experts can breeze through the routines without having to remember each setting and sequence of commands. The extracted data they want will appear at the press of a button.

Difficult routines can be captured with a single key, and repeated as often as desired. Multiple routines can be accessed from within a macro without resetting the normal command options manually. The macro can include all the settings necessary for printing, creating graphs, database queries, sorting, and so on.

Because macros can simplify long, involved routines, they are the perfect adjunct to the add-in Allways. As you use Allways more and more to enhance the output of your worksheets, you will find that macros will provide you with valuable shortcuts and can automate much of the formatting process.

POWER FOR COMPLEX TASKS

No matter how expert a user is, at some point (and usually quite early) the normal tasks within a worksheet become too complex to perform easily by hand. Consider the number of user instructions that would be needed to complete the following tasks without macros (and consider the odds that all the steps would be done correctly):

◆ Enter data into the worksheet with error checking and data validation

◆ Enter specific information only for certain codes

◆ Extract records to specified locations in the worksheet

◆ Print several ranges with appropriate spacing, and include the proper border rows and columns, setup codes, headers, and so on

◆ Branch to other routines, depending on criteria within the worksheet

◆ Temporarily exit to DOS to run another program, and then return to 1-2-3 and continue macro execution

◆ Create a graphics slide show by using the {graphon}, {wait}, and {graphoff} commands

Unless you have sadistic tendencies, you would never expect another user (or yourself) to accomplish so many complex tasks successfully and in a reasonable amount of time. Macros can do it all and everyone will be ahead.

2.2 ◆ ——

WORKSHEET DOCUMENTATION

Macros can turn an otherwise drab and lifeless worksheet into an active and dynamic programming environment. They get the job done well and quickly, but one of their most important functions, spreadsheet documentation, is frequently overlooked.

Even without any clarifying comments, the macros in a worksheet describe the *overall* flow of the worksheet, as well as each specific task it performs: printing, sorting, extracting data, and so on.

Figure 1.1 shows several macros in a typical spreadsheet application. The macro names are in column A. The corresponding macros occupy columns B through F. Most of the macro code has been left out for demonstration purposes, so that only the "shell" is left with a few actual macro commands. The menus are also abbreviated to make their story clear.

Although this screen may look daunting if you are a beginner, after a little experience its meaning will be clear. Let's take it step-by-step.

The first macro has two names, \0 and \A (backslash zero and backslash A). It is automatically invoked by Lotus when the speadsheet is retrieved. (You'll learn more about the auto-invoked \0 macro later in this chapter. For now it is enough to say that it is extremely useful.) This \0 macro is stored in cell B1. When the worksheet is retrieved \0 automatically calls another macro named \STARTUP, which is stored in another part of the worksheet that is not visible on this screen.

```
A2: [W12]                                                        READY

        A           B           C           D           E           F
 1   \Ø, \A     {\STARTUP}{branch \M}
 2
 3   \M         {menubranch \MENU1}
 4
 5   \MENU1     Data_Entry  View        Compile     Print       Save
 6   Main                                           Choose from print menu
 7                                                  {menubranch \MENU4}
 8
 9   \MENU2     Data        Report_1    Report_2    Summary
10   View
11
12   \MENU3     Report_1    Report_2    Summary     All
13   Compile
14
15   \MENU4     Data        Report_1    Report_2    Summary     All
16   Print      Print records in list
17              {\PRINT_DATA}{branch \M}
18
19   \PRINT_DATA /ppcarDATA_LIST~oml1Ø~mr132~s\Ø15~
20              f!Page #~qagpq{return}
```

Figure 1.1 ◆ *Macros can document every worksheet routine*

When \STARTUP is completed, control returns to the \0 macro, which then branches to the macro \M. This macro calls \MENU1, which is the main menu. On the main menu you can see the choices Data_Entry, View, Compile, Print, and Save. This menu covers all the normal tasks in this worksheet. It can always be reached by pressing Alt-M.

Below this menu are three submenus that are called from the choices on the main menu. The View menu allows users to jump to special areas in the worksheet. The Compile menu runs through the necessary steps to produce the desired output. The Print menu has options for printing every existing report. Each of these menus contains other choices that control your use of the worksheet.

For example, the first choice on the Print menu, Data, branches to a subroutine named \PRINT_DATA. This macro can be seen on line 19, and would normally be one of many such routines. The keystrokes in this macro show the exact steps to follow to print the range DATA_LIST. These two lines of code tell all there is to know about this print job.

◆ ABCs OF WRITING MACROS

This section is a short introduction to writing macros. Those who already use macros can consider it a refresher course in macro basics.

DIFFERENTIATING THE PARTS OF A MACRO: TEXT AND LOCATION

There are only two parts to any macro: the *text* of the macro itself, and the *location* where Lotus can find the macro and execute it. With these two components, you can write a macro.

The macro *text* simply consists of the characters that will be executed when the macro is called up. You type the characters into a worksheet cell like any other text, where they can later be invoked as a macro. You can enter as many as 240 characters in each cell of a macro, but good practice dictates a more reasonable maximum of 50 or 60 characters.

> ⊗ **CAUTION** ◆ *Lotus makes no distinction between macro text and any other text in the worksheet. It simply executes the characters that are in the named macro cell. It is up to you to be sure that the text in that cell is correct.*

A macro can be just one cell, or a series of cells down a column. When the characters in one cell have been executed in the macro, Lotus tries to continue in the next cell down. It stops the macro and returns to the Ready mode if one of these three things occurs:

1. It finds a macro Quit command: {quit} or /xq

2. It reaches a blank (or nontext) cell

3. It encounters an error in the macro

Macros must be text, not numbers. If you mistakenly include a cell with a numeric value in your macro, the macro will simply quit when it reaches that cell.

Note that string values satisfy the macro text requirement. By using string formulas to write macro code, you can perform some powerful programming tricks. This will be explained in detail later in this chapter in the section called "Enhancing Your Macros with Self-Modifying Code."

To invoke a macro, you must first identify its location with a name. This is done by assigning a *range name* that defines at least the first cell of the macro code. (See Chapter 2 if you are not familiar with range names; they are key players in the worksheet.) You have 26 choices for macro names: any of the letters A to Z, prefaced with a backslash (\). For example, a macro can be named \C.

To invoke the named macro, you simply hold down the Alt key and press the letter of the macro name: Alt-C.

> **TIP ◆** *Macros can call up other macros, and a macro that is called in this way need not be given a name that uses the \-letter sequence. Any range name can be used (you can even use the actual cell address, although that is not good practice). In theory, you only need one keyboard-invocable macro to run all the other macro routines in the worksheet.*

2.2 ◆ ———

You can bypass the naming process in Release 2.2 by using the Run key, Alt-F3, which is very much like the Name key (F3). In response to any 1-2-3 command that prompts you for a range, such as the Go To command (F5), you can press the Name key and pick a range name from the list of all the range names in the worksheet.

On the other hand, you use the Run key only from the Ready mode. Highlight a macro's range name on the list and press Enter, and 1-2-3 will invoke the macro. Or, press Escape and then point to the macro cell you wish to invoke. The Run key is probably the most convenient method of invoking new macros for testing, because it saves you from having to give a macro a backslash name that would be used only temporarily.

> ⊗ **CAUTION** ◆ *The Run key can be a convenience, but it can also create problems and lead to poor working habits. All range names appear on the list when you press Alt-F3, not just macro names, and it is all too easy to mistakenly pick the wrong name from the list, thereby creating a "macro monster" of a cell that you never intended to be a macro.*
>
> *Also, don't think you need to use the Run key if you have too many macros and not enough backslash names for them all. A simple solution is discussed later in this chapter in the section called "Always Use Menus."*

KEYSTROKE MACROS

Knowing the two basic parts of a macro, you can now create one by entering text into the worksheet and giving that cell a name. Try this one. In cell B2, type the phrase *Lotus Tips and Tricks*. That will be the text of the macro. With the cell pointer still on that cell, give the cell the name \Z. Use the commands Range Name Create, enter \Z as the name, and then press Enter to accept B2 as the macro location.

Now move the cell pointer to a blank cell, such as B4, and invoke the macro by holding down the Alt key and typing Z. Your screen should look like the one in Figure 1.2. Lotus has executed the text in the macro \Z, cell B2, as you can see in the edit window at the top of the screen. This is the most basic macro, a *keystroke macro*, which enters the keystrokes just as though you had typed them in from the keyboard.

Although this macro is rudimentary, it perfectly demonstrates the major advantages of using macros: consistency, accuracy, speed, convenience, and spreadsheet documentation.

The macro you just created types out the phrase and then stops—it does not enter the text into the cell. To include an Enter in the macro, you must use the tilde (˜), which Lotus interprets as the keystroke Enter. Press Escape to clear the Edit window. Now edit the macro and add the tilde as the last character, so the macro looks like this:

Lotus Tips and Tricks ˜

Again, move the cell pointer to a blank cell and invoke the macro by typing Alt-Z. This time, the macro will type the phrase and enter it into the cell. Just

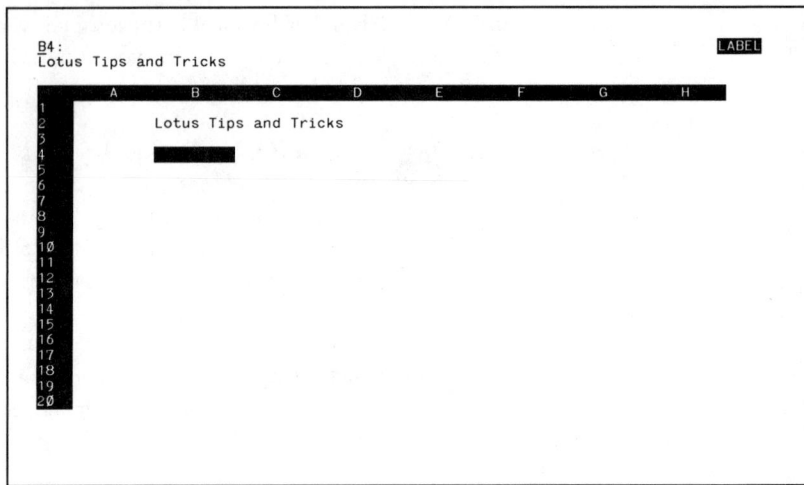

```
B4:
Lotus Tips and Tricks                                          LABEL
        A       B       C       D       E       F       G       H
1
2              Lotus Tips and Tricks
3
4              ████████████
5
6
7
8
9
10
11
12
13
14
15
16
17
18
19
20
```

Figure 1.2 ◆ *A simple keystroke macro*

about all the keys on the keyboard can be addressed in a macro; the noncharacter keys are enclosed in braces—{right}, {left}, {insert}, {home}, and so forth. See the inside back cover of this book for a complete listing of them.

The true power of keystroke macros becomes evident when they include commands from the Lotus menu. Using the slash key (/) in the macro will call up the Lotus menu (assuming that Lotus was at the READY mode when the slash key was encountered). Follow it with the characters of each command that you want to access. When writing a macro that starts with the slash command key, remember to preface it with a label prefix, such as an apostrophe (') or caret (^); otherwise the slash will simply call up the Lotus menu instead of typing that character into the cell.

⊗ **CAUTION** ◆ *1-2-3 has a second menu key that can be used instead of the slash key—the less than symbol, <. This extra menu key serves as a safety valve if, for example, a memory-resident program you are running disables the slash key; you will still be able to call up the Lotus menu with the < key. However, this feature can be a minor irritant when you try to enter text that begins with <. For example, to enter <TOTAL>, you would have to attach a label prefix to avoid the Lotus menu.*

If you forget the label prefix, < can have a deadly effect in a macro. Try the first macro shown here and watch the sparks fly.

{goto}A5 ˜ <Here I am> ˜

Now run this one, which has a label prefix included:

{goto}A5 ˜ '<Here I am> ˜

Although you can choose Lotus menu items by using the "point-and-shoot" method (highlight the item and press Enter), you should never do this within a macro. One obvious reason is that macros that were written for Lotus 1A could fail under the revised menus of Lotus 2.0 or 2.01, and those written for 2.01 could fail under 2.2. And then there is also Lotus 3.0 to consider. Always specify the first letter of the menu item you wish to choose; it's the easiest and safest method.

Using the first letter method also makes macros shorter and more readable. Here is a print macro that uses the point-and-shoot method of choosing Lotus commands:

/{right 5} ˜ ˜ {right 4} ˜ ˜ {left} ˜
{right 2} ˜ ˜ 10 ˜ ˜ {right} ˜ 132 ˜ {end} ˜
{right 2} ˜ {right} ˜ {right} ˜

Compare this long and unreadable macro to the following one, which uses the first letter of each command:

/ppcaoml10 ˜ mr132 ˜ qagq

Avoiding the point-and-shoot method is especially important when you are performing file operations, because the order of file names on the Retrieve menu changes as files are added to or deleted from the directory. Always spell out the name of the file in the macro for complete accuracy, as shown here:

/fcceFILEONE ˜

Remember, to cancel a macro that is running, you need only press Ctrl-Break—hold down the Ctrl key and press Break.

COMMAND LANGUAGE MACROS

Keystroke macros can be used to automate many tasks in the worksheet. Printing routines are perhaps the most common ones that benefit from macro execution, but all other chores can also be handled by macros. Macros become a programming language with the addition of the Lotus Command Language.

As in BASIC and other higher-level languages, the Command Language in Lotus has a variety of programming tools that control the flow of the macro code. The Lotus 1A language consisted of the /X commands, such as /xg for

GoTo, /xm to call a menu, and /xq for Quit. In Lotus 2, the language is built around the *keyword* commands, which are enclosed in braces: {branch}, {menubranch}, {quit}, and so on.

> **TIP** ◆ *Although the /X commands that were used in Lotus 1A perform just as well under Lotus 2, they execute more slowly than the keyword commands. This is because they literally write their commands to the menu line as they execute, whereas the keywords execute internally and therefore faster. Except in certain circumstances, you should try to use only the keyword commands of Lotus 2.*

The Command Language keywords make up a diverse and extensive set of commands, which form a powerful complement to the keystroke macros. Among the many enhancements to the Lotus 1A command macros is the looping macro {for}, which is used to call a macro subroutine a given number of times. The {let} statement assigns a value (numeric or text) to a cell, and is a simple but very useful function. Menus can be called as a subroutine with {menucall}, so that control is returned to the calling macro when the subroutine menu is completed or a {return} command is encountered.

The {beep} command adds a beep to any macro. The screen can be tidied up with {windowsoff} and {paneloff}, which also speed up macros by eliminating the need to refresh the screen.

2.2 ◆ ─────

In Release 2.2, the {frameoff} command hides the row number and column letter identifiers in the inverted L frame. Although it does not allow more rows or columns of data to show, it does help to unclutter the screen. Note that you can also use the command {bordersoff} to produce the same effect.

You can prevent anyone, including yourself, from stopping a macro with the {breakoff} command. It should always be used cautiously, however, and should never be used during the testing process. You can recalculate a range of the worksheet with the {recalc} macro statement, which can save a tremendous amount of time in a large worksheet.

An additional benefit of the Command Language is that multiple cell pointer movements can be combined in one keystroke. That means you can move the cell pointer four cells to the right by writing {right 4}, so this is a real time and space saver.

> **TRICK** ◆ *A feature that went undocumented in Lotus 2.01, but is now part of the Release 2.2 manual, is the ability to further shorten cell pointer movement commands by using just the first*

letter of the command. You can shorten the phrase {right} to {r}, and {left 4} to {l 4}. The same is true for {up} and {down}. But until you are adept at writing and interpreting macros, you might want to stick with full words.

GETTING OFF TO A FAST START WITH THE \0 MACRO

A macro given the name \0 (backslash zero) is the *auto-invoke* macro in a worksheet. It is unique in that it will automatically be invoked by Lotus whenever the worksheet that contains the macro is retrieved. This feature provides complete macro control of any worksheet application from the moment the file is retrieved. The uses for this tool are endless; the task that it performs depends only on the type of worksheet that it appears in.

> **TIP** ◆ *The \0 macro cannot be invoked from the keyboard by pressing Alt-0; only Lotus can invoke it when the file is retrieved. Therefore, always give the macro a second name, such as \A, so that you can invoke it at any time for testing.*

When a worksheet is retrieved, you can avoid the \0 macro in one of two ways. The macro STEP mode, discussed in the section "Reining in Macros with the STEP Mode," will force the macro into single-step execution, from which it can easily be stopped with Ctrl-Break. Or you can press Ctrl-Break while the file is being loaded, Lotus will read that keystroke as soon as the worksheet has been retrieved, and the macro will be terminated.

> **TIP** ◆ *If an auto-invoke macro will be used in a worksheet, but is not needed during the development stage, do not name it \0 until the worksheet is completed. This may save you the trouble of avoiding the macro each time the worksheet is retrieved.*

2.2 ◆ ─────

Because the need to disable the \0 macro occurs frequently enough, the ability to do so has been built into Release 2.2. The Worksheet Global Default Autoexec command has the options Yes and No that allow you to enable or disable the macro when a worksheet file is retrieved. Don't forget to use the Worksheet Global Default Update command if you want your selection to be current the next time you run 1-2-3.

The auto-execute macro can be tailored to the worksheet it controls. You may find that there are some recurring chores for which the \0 macro will prove invaluable, as the following examples demonstrate.

Setting Up the Display

Probably the best use for the \0 macro is to position the cell pointer in the proper area of the worksheet. Although this is not necessary in worksheets where the cursor should remain in the cell it last occupied when saved, it is a wonderful timesaver for most other worksheets. Users who rarely retrieve a particular worksheet will be ready to go as soon as the \0 macro places them in the proper working location:

```
/wwc/wtc{goto}START ˜ /wtb{quit}
```

In this example, the macro first clears any worksheet windows and titles, then moves to the range named START, where it sets the worksheet titles and quits. Each time the worksheet is loaded, the user will be presented with the same screen.

Setting Up the Data

In some worksheets, the data may need to be brought up to date each time it is used. For example, in a master inventory list, there may be one work area that should be erased at the start of each session. Then, worksheet files containing subsets of the inventory may need to be brought into the master list. Perhaps the list must be sorted before the normal routines can be run. The following \0 macro could perform all those steps:

```
/reWORK_AREA ˜ /reSUB_LIST_AREA ˜
{goto}SUB_LIST_AREA ˜
/fcceSUBLIST1 ˜ {end}{down 2}
/fcceSUBLIST2 ˜ {end}{down 2}
/fcceSUBLIST3 ˜ {end}{down 2}
/dsrdLIST ˜ pSORT_COL1 ˜ a ˜ sSORT_COL2 ˜ d ˜ g
{goto}START ˜ {quit}
```

Controlling Access to a Worksheet

Although Lotus offers password protection for its worksheets, sometimes a less stringent means of control is needed. Here is a useful validation macro for a worksheet that must not be used unless the data within a secondary worksheet is current. The \0 macro brings in a cell named DATE_CELL from the other worksheet (SUBFILE), checks the date in that cell, and responds accordingly:

```
{goto}DATE_INPUT ˜ /reDATE_INPUT ˜
/fccnDATE_CELL ˜ SUBFILE ˜
{if DATE_INPUT<@now--7}{branch \INVALID_DATA}
{branch \CONTINUE}
```

If the date that is brought in from DATE_CELL is less than seven days from the current date, the macro branches to a routine named \INVALID_DATA. In that routine, the user can be reminded that the other worksheet must first be brought up to date. At that point, the current worksheet could be erased.

Offering a Menu

If several users share the same system, you may want to supply a menu of their names, where each choice branches appropriately. If Susan, Corky, and Dwayne all need to access different portions of the worksheet (or even retrieve a different worksheet), the appropriate macro might look like the one in Figure 1.3.

In Chapter 5, you will see how the \0 macro can help automate a Lotus menu of file directories on a hard disk.

◆ MACRO ETIQUETTE

Programming with Lotus macros is an amazingly simple process that can produce tremendous results. As with all programming, though, good habits that are developed early ensure good results.

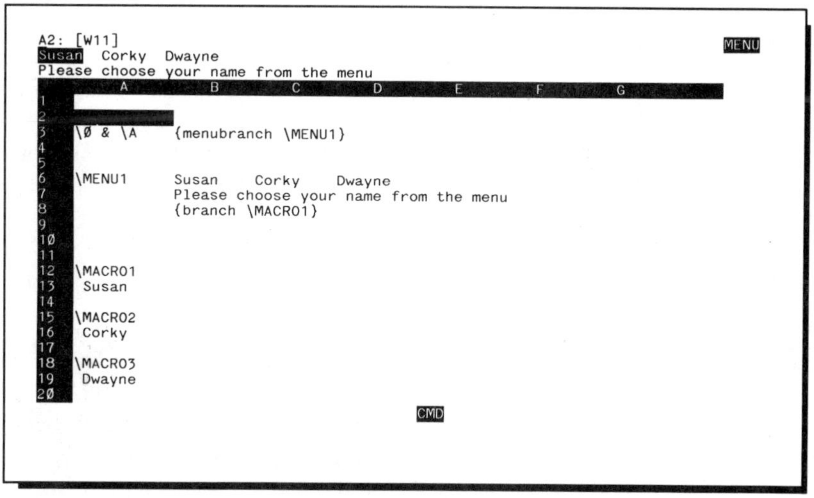

```
A2: [W11]                                                        MENU
Susan  Corky  Dwayne
Please choose your name from the menu
          A          B          C          D       E      F      G
1
2
3    \Ø & \A     {menubranch \MENU1}
4
5
6    \MENU1       Susan     Corky     Dwayne
7                 Please choose your name from the menu
8                 {branch \MACRO1}
9
10
11
12   \MACRO1
13    Susan
14
15   \MACRO2
16    Corky
17
18   \MACRO3
19    Dwayne
20                                          CMD
```

Figure 1.3 ◆ *A \0 menu to provide macro routines for each user*

AVOID DISASTER: NEVER REFERENCE CELL COORDINATES

The "prime directive" for writing macros is never to reference cell coordinates. Macros are nothing but text in the worksheet, and they are therefore static and unchanging. They are not like formulas, which are "aware" of cell movements within the worksheet. If you refer to a cell address in a macro, you are only courting disaster. Here is a simple and seemingly harmless macro that erases one cell:

/reB16 ˜

How would it operate after a row is inserted at row 14? It would still erase B16, even though the cell that it originally addressed at B16 is now at B17. The macro is unusable.

Except in the earliest stages of writing and testing, a macro should never be *hard-coded* with actual cell addresses. Instead, always use a range name to reference a location in the worksheet:

/reMY_CELL ˜

Or, once a range of cells is fixed in its layout, use a range name to reference other nearby cells:

{goto}MY_CELL ˜ {right 3}{down 2}/re ˜

As rows are inserted or deleted, the macro can still find MY_CELL. If MY_CELL is moved, the macro can still find it and perform as expected.

This rule also applies to the locations of other macros that are called. Never reference a hard-coded cell address to branch to another macro—always be sure that the other routines are named. The last thing you want is to have your macro branch to a location that is occupied by some unrelated text.

The exception to this rule applies to macros that are formulas, as will be explained later in this chapter.

ALWAYS USE MENUS

When first writing macros, the new user tends to give each routine its own keyboard-invocable name: \P for Print, \S for Save, \G for Go To, and so on.

This is fine in the earliest testing stages, but once a worksheet is completed, the multiple backslash names will create confusion. Is \I for inserting a column or a row? Or is it the one that includes the secondary worksheet? Macro menus eliminate the need for multiple keyboard-invocable macros, and reduce if not eliminate your need for the Run key, Alt-F3.

You can use several strategies to enhance your macros with menus: offering choices with menus, creating a top-down macro structure with menus, and supplementing documentation to your worksheet with menus.

Offer Choices with Menus

A finished worksheet usually has some sort of a normal working routine. All the steps for this routine should be included on a macro menu.

> *TIP ◆ Make it a custom for any worksheet with macros to have one keyboard-invocable macro named \M that calls up a menu. From this main menu, users can choose the other macro routines. If you follow this practice, all users of any experience will be able to access your macro-driven applications.*

With all the necessary macros listed in one or more menus, users can breeze through any worksheet duties and are less likely to forget one of the normal steps. A typical main menu might contain these choices:

Data_Entry	View	Compile	Print	Save

From this menu, either macro routines or other menus would be called. Only one keyboard-invocable macro is used, and a lot of instruction and potential confusion are eliminated.

Menus that call submenus can be written so that the Escape key takes the user back to a previous menu. This is not a built-in macro device. Whenever Escape is pressed within a macro menu, Lotus returns to the command following the {menubranch}, {menucall}, or /xm command that invoked the menu in the first place.

Here is a macro named \M that includes a branch to a menu, followed by a beep command:

```
{menubranch \MENU2}{beep}
```

If Escape is pressed while \MENU2 is active, Lotus returns control to \M and executes the next command—in this case, {beep}. To return control to another menu—\MENU1, for example—the macro would look like this:

```
{menubranch \MENU2}{menubranch \MENU1}
```

Now control returns to another menu command, and this time branches to \MENU1. Using this method, several menus can be chained together so that pressing Escape always returns you to the previous menu.

When the macro that invokes the main menu is written as shown below, pressing Escape while in the main menu always recalls that menu. The user is prevented from leaving the menu except by making a choice from it. In this example, \M is the macro that invokes \MENU1, the primary menu:

{menubranch \MENU1}{branch \M}

If \M calls the main menu, then the following sequence of menu calls would step the user back from submenu \MENU3 one menu at a time as the Escape key is pressed, all the way up to the main menu:

{menubranch \MENU3}{menubranch \MENU2}{branch \M}

> ⊗ **CAUTION ◆** *Whether you use this method or not, do not forget that Escape still always returns control to the command that follows the call to the menu. If you neglect this fact, you may be surprised by the results when that command immediately executes at the touch of the Escape key.*

Create a Top-Down Macro Structure with Menus

Relating Lotus macros to top-down, structured programming may seem to stretch the point, but good macro coding practice can be enforced by the use of macro menus. As you develop a worksheet routine, include a menu choice for it on the main menu. Need another routine? Just write the routine and add the new choice to the menu. If you end up with several related macros, such as various print routines, you can place all of them as choices on one menu, and have that menu called from the main menu.

When you later need to follow the threads of the routines, you need only look to the main menu, and from there trace all the steps for each item, down through any submenus until you reach the final {quit} or {return}.

Add Documentation to Your Worksheet with Menus

One of the benefits of macros mentioned earlier in this chapter is their function as worksheet documentation. If all the normal worksheet routines are included in macro menus, then they are all available for inspection by you or other interested users. In the sample macros shown in Figure 1.1, the four menus included all the macro routines needed and showed how the worksheet is normally used.

INCLUDE A VIEW MENU

If a worksheet is to be automated, you need not force the user (or yourself) to spend time searching for a certain area in which to enter data or check some totals. Create a View menu subordinate to the main menu, and include choices for jumping to these areas.

Not only does the program find the location automatically for you, but the worksheet titles can be set so that the screen is properly adjusted for easy viewing. If you have dozens of distant ranges that need to be reached, it's all the more reason to have many view choices on one or more menus.

WRITE FOR CLARITY

Macros may need to be modified, and you must therefore ensure that they are readable and understandable, especially when they serve as worksheet documentation. Several techniques are available to keep your macros easy to read or revise.

First, your macros should all be in the same general area of the worksheet. Ideally, they should be diagonally opposite your data area, allowing you to insert or delete rows and columns in the data without affecting the macros, and vice versa.

Each macro should end with a terminating macro command, such as {quit}, {return}, {branch}, or {menubranch}. You should also separate macros with a blank row. This not only makes them more readable, but in the event of a missing {quit} command, it prevents 1-2-3 from reading down a macro and continuing with the one below.

> CAUTION ◆ *Watch out for stray characters in the cells between macros. A careless tap of the Space bar can create the link that will run one macro into the next, causing havoc when the macro executes.*

Use ALL CAPS for range names, and small letters for everything else. In this way, the locations that are referenced will stand out from the Lotus commands, macro keywords, and @ functions that are used:

```
{goto}START ~ {down}{left 2}
/cOTHER_CELL ~ ~ /rff2 ~ ~ {branch \NEXT_MACRO}
```

Some people do the opposite, and leave everything in capital letters except the range names. Too many capitals can make a macro hard to read, but try both methods and then stick with one of them. A consistent method is better than none at all.

Don't make a macro too long; whenever possible, 50 or 60 characters should be the maximum. No matter how simple the macro is, if you have to scroll the screen to the right in order to read it, you will have a harder time understanding it.

A macro should not be too short, either. It can be difficult to read down a long column of macro code when each cell has only a few characters.

With the length of the macro line a consideration, each line should ideally be a logical whole that completes one phase of the routine. The following print macro demonstrates a reasonable way to divide one macro among the cells in a column:

```
/ppcarDATA ˜ oml8 ˜ mr132 ˜ s\027\064\015 ˜
h ¦ My Report, as of @ ˜ f ¦ Pg. # ˜
brBORDER_ROWS ˜ q
agpq{return}
```

Does this macro need any explanation? Probably not, because each line begins with a new operation and is clear in its function.

> ★ **TRICK** ◆ *You can use empty braces, {}, in a cell to serve as a filler within a macro. Especially useful during the development stage, the braces can reserve a cell for future code or temporarily take the place of code that you do not want executed during testing procedures:*

```
{menucall \MENU3}
{\DO_PRINT1}
{}
{}
{\DO_CONTINUE}
```

If you give all your macros, including the ones that are not keyboard-invocable, a name that begins with a backslash, they will all be grouped together at the end of the range names list. This is because the backslash comes after the alphabetic characters in the sorted range name list.

Not only are all the macros grouped together, but you can instantly tell whether a formula or macro refers to a data cell or to a macro cell:

```
{if @sum(SUMMARY) > = BALANCE}{branch \DO_SUMMARY}
```

Descriptions for each line of the macro may be useful for code that is hard to interpret, but don't get carried away and define each line. Code like the following may be helpful for instructional purposes, but you will quickly get tired of the clutter:

Start print routine, clear all settings	/ppca
Specify DATA as the print range	rDATA ˜
Set left margin to 10, right to 132	oml10 ˜ mr132 ˜

PLACE A CALL WITH MACRO SUBROUTINES

A macro routine might require many lines to complete its task, but keep separate routines as separate entities. It is easier to write and test your macros if they are broken down into unique operations. Moreover, the main macro that calls the subroutines will be short and easy to decipher:

```
{\NEW_DATE}
{\COMPILE}
{\SORT_DATA}
{\PRINT_DATA1}
{\PRINT_DATA2}
{\SAVE}
{quit}
```

If a macro is used frequently in your application, there is all the more reason to make it a separate subroutine that can be called when necessary. This offers the double advantage of saving room in your macro code and making it easier to revise the subroutine by just editing it in one location.

For example, here is a macro that resets the screen to a home screen area. You could call it after running any routine that takes the cell pointer to distant parts of the worksheet:

```
/wtc/wwc{goto}HOME_SCREEN~{down 18}/wwh
{window}{branch \M}
```

Written as a subroutine, the macro could be called just by enclosing its name in braces in another macro:

```
{\GO_HOME}
```

TAKE ADVANTAGE OF LOOPING MACROS

Before making the transition from keystroke macros to Command Language macros, a user may neglect the basic tools of a programming language. One of the most important of these tools is the ability to *loop*—that is, to repeat the same code a given number of times. Lotus provides several methods of using macros in loops. By utilizing one of these methods, you can condense an otherwise long macro to just a few lines.

Suppose you want to copy one row at a time from a range named LIST to a range named COPY_AREA. Then, COPY_AREA is printed with the new row of data by a macro named \DO_PRINT. The macro needs to repeat for

each row in LIST. Figure 1.4 shows a looping macro based on the {for} statement. It executes the macro \DO_COPY (and therefore \DO_PRINT) the
number of times that there are rows in LIST.

If you were to use individual routines for each copy, you would need one for each
row in LIST. If there were just six rows, the macro would have to look like this:

```
{goto}LIST ~
/c{esc}.{end}{right} ~ PRINT_AREA ~
/ppagpq{down}
/c{esc}.{end}{right} ~ PRINT_AREA ~
/ppagpq{down}
/c{esc}.{end}{right} ~ PRINT_AREA ~
/ppagpq{down}
/c{esc}.{end}{right} ~ PRINT_AREA ~
/ppagpq{down}
/c{esc}.{end}{right} ~ PRINT_AREA ~
/ppagpq{down}
/c{esc}.{end}{right} ~ PRINT_AREA ~
/ppagpq
```

Although using individual macros for each step certainly works, it has several
major shortcomings. First, it takes up much more room than the looping macro.
Second, there must be exactly the right number of repetitions to handle the range
LIST. Third, if you want to change one part of the copy routine, you would have

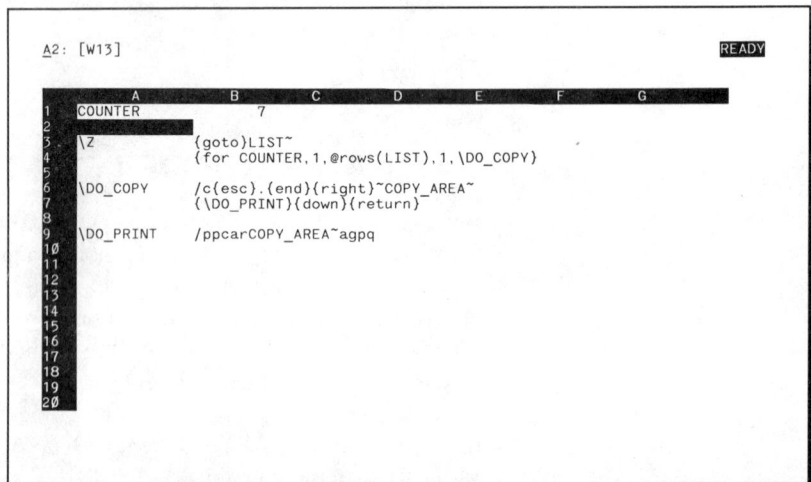

Figure 1.4 ◆ *A looping macro*

to change it in all the lines of the macro. The looping macro would only have to be revised in one line. Fourth, and most important, the number of rows in LIST cannot be changed without revising the macro manually.

BE CONCISE AND SPECIFY ALL LOTUS MENU SETTINGS

Whenever you save a Lotus worksheet, all the settings within the Lotus menus are also saved. Retained are the print ranges and options, the current graph settings, database input, criteria, and output ranges, and so on. The fact that you can retrieve a file and immediately print the range that had been printed last is on the one hand a convenience, and on the other a potential disaster. There is no way to be sure that those settings have not been altered by you or another user.

If you plan to use a print, graph, database, or any other Lotus menu command regularly, put the routine into a macro and always write the macro so that it resets the Lotus command options. Then you will never have to check the current settings before running it. The macro will handle it all in exactly the same manner each time it is run.

For instance, a print macro should begin with Print Printer Clear All, a graph macro with Graph Reset Graph, and so on. If you do not reset the options to their default values, you will have no control over the options that you do not address in the macro.

Any macro routine that sets one of the Lotus menu commands should start with the appropriate clear statement, as shown in this list:

Print Printer Clear All	*/ppca*
Graph Reset Graph	*/grg*
Data Query Reset	*/dqr*
Data Sort Reset	*/dsr*
Data Table Reset (& repeat)	*/dtr/dt*
Data Regression Reset	*/drr*
Data Parse Reset	*/dpr*

Note that when you choose Reset from the Data Table menu prior to creating a data table, you are immediately returned to the READY mode, which forces you to repeat the Data Table command to proceed with the operation.

A print macro, then, might look like this:

/ppcarDATA ˜ oml7 ˜ mr75 ˜ qagpq

Most Lotus users never change their Global Default Print settings, so they all have the same default print options. However, those options can be modified, and a copy of Lotus on another system can have its own default settings.

If you have a worksheet application that will be shared on different computers with which you are not familiar, safe practice requires that the application first set the global print settings. The \0 macro is the perfect place to take care of this:

/wgdpl4 ˜ r76 ˜ t2 ˜ b2 ˜ p66 ˜ wnsX{esc} ˜ q

This macro changes all the global printer settings to the Lotus default settings. Of course, you could also use other values depending on your needs, but the important factor is that you now know exactly how they are set.

> **TIP** ◆ *Note that when the macro shown above specifies the setup string, it first types an* X: sX{esc} ˜ . *This ensures that the routine will work whether or not there is already a string specified. If there is an existing setup string, the* X *is simply appended to it, and the* {esc} *erases the entire string. If there is no string, the* X *is entered and then erased by the* {esc}. *Try it and see how it works.*

◆ TESTING AND DEBUGGING MACROS

Lotus macros are always consistent and fast. Their results, however, may not be as you intended. By the time you reach the Ctrl-Break key, a misguided macro may have already decimated your worksheet. This section covers several valuable techniques and good habits that will aid you in refining your macros.

CATCHING THE MOST COMMON MACRO PROBLEMS

The most frequent bug in a macro is not a logic or command error, but simply that the macro text was entered incorrectly. When executed, instead of being read as Lotus menu commands, a cell formula, or other specific action, the macro is interpreted only as text to be written into the worksheet. Upon reaching the first tilde or cell pointer directional key, the program enters the text into the current cell at the cell pointer, obliterating whatever happens to be there. Here is a typical example. Can you tell what's wrong with it?

{goto}MESSAGE ~ \ppcarDATA ~ oml10 ~ mr132 ~ qagq

The macro is almost correct; the only problem is the use of the backslash instead of the forward slash key to call the Lotus menu. When the macro executes, the cell pointer jumps to the range named MESSAGE, but then the backslash is typed. This is nothing but a label prefix, and everything that follows will be typed into the edit window as the rest of the label, just as though you had typed it from the keyboard.

When the first tilde is reached, the text is entered into the current cell of the worksheet. The rest of the command, starting with oml, will also be entered into the worksheet in the same cell—any hopes of executing the Print command are long gone.

Using the STEP mode during testing (discussed shortly) is a perfect way to prevent this common problem. As you work the macro step by step, you can watch the results go by on the screen. If you see what should be a print macro start typing characters into the edit window, you will know that something is wrong, and you can stop to fix it.

The second most common problem with macros occurs when hard cell addresses are referenced within the code, a problem that was described earlier. When cells have been moved about the worksheet, the macro still executes as written, but all the cells that it references are no longer the correct ones. Range names completely eliminate this problem (see Chapter 2 for a discussion of range names). They also give the added benefit of making a macro more readable with their descriptive, 15-character names.

Calling a macro menu can be another stumbling point if you forget to use a proper menu command, either {menubranch}, {menucall}, or /xm, and instead use the {branch} command. If {branch} were used to call a menu named \MENU1, Lotus would go to the range \MENU1 and execute it as though it were just another cell of macro text, rather than a menu (as you intended). The results could be disastrous.

REINING IN MACROS WITH THE STEP MODE

Lotus provides a simple, built-in macro debugging tool, the macro STEP mode. It regulates an invoked macro by allowing it to execute only one step at a time. You can toggle it on or off by pressing Alt-F2 (Alt-F1 in Lotus 1A).

When on, a STEP indicator will appear at the bottom of the screen.

Using the STEP mode changes nothing but the speed of execution. You can watch the macro go through its tasks, one step at a time, as you press a key (any key will do) to allow each character of the macro text to execute.

Any commands in braces will be executed as one step, so that {right 4} will move the cell pointer four cells to the right in one step of the macro.

> ⊗ **CAUTION** ◆ *Lotus Command Language keywords, such as {branch}, {if}, or {for}, are not displayed as they execute— they operate internally. If you have many such commands in a macro, the STEP mode will reveal little about the executing macro. You will, however, still have the benefit of controlling its speed of execution. Splitting the screen will help you to debug this type of macro.*

2.2 ◆ ———

The Step mode is enhanced in Release 2.2, so that the current line of the macro being executed is shown at the bottom of the screen, and the current command in that line is highlighted. This can be of great assistance, and may obviate the need for some of the other macro debugging techniques discussed in this chapter.

SPLITTING THE SCREEN TO VIEW THE DATA AND THE MACRO

With the Worksheet Windows command, you can split your worksheet into two windows. This is an ideal tool for testing macros, whether the STEP mode is on or off. Split the screen horizontally and set the windows to Unsynchronized:

/wwh/wwu

Have the macro that you are testing displayed in the upper screen, and the active cell pointer in the lower one. When you run the macro, the upper screen will remain stable while the cell pointer does its assigned tasks in the lower one.

You can also use the split screen to display two separate areas of the worksheet that are directly affected by the action of the macro. For a Data Query Extract command, for example, have one part of the screen at the extract area. If there are formulas that reference the extract area, have those displayed in the other window. By setting up the screen before invoking the macro, you will be able to follow its progress and confirm the results.

PREPARING FOR TESTING

New macro programmers are often impatient with excitement, while old pros may simply overlook the basic safety rules. Before you hit the invoke key, there are several steps you should take to protect your valuable investment (the worksheet) from the genie you are about to unleash (the macro).

First, make sure that you have saved the worksheet recently. That's disaster planning. With a recent copy of your work on disk, a bug-ridden macro can wreak havoc on your worksheet without causing permanent damage—simply retrieve the worksheet from disk. You do not need to save every time you test a macro; just be sure that the worksheet on disk is reasonably current.

Whenever you are about to test a macro, move the cell pointer to a blank cell. Then, if you should run into the common problem of miscoded macros that was described above, the macro will not overwrite anything of value. You can erase the garbled text in the cell, fix the macro, and try again.

Finally, if you are feeling uncertain about the chances of your new macro running successfully, just run it in step mode for complete security.

INSERTING BREAKPOINTS INTO A MACRO

During the testing of a macro in Release 2.01, it can sometimes be hard to determine just where in the macro you are at any particular point. This is especially true when there are Command Language keywords in the macro, which do not display as they execute. Although Lotus has no built-in macro tool for calling out different spots in a macro, you can insert your own debugging telltales, commonly known as *breakpoints*.

All of the following methods rely on your inserting extra code into your macro that will then let you know when that point in the code has been executed.

> **TIP** ◆ *If you need to use many breakpoints to keep yourself informed, you may want to create a backup of the macro by copying it to a different location. If you should damage the macro while inserting or deleting the breakpoints, the other copy will allow you to fix the damaged portion.*

You can have Lotus alert you with a sound by inserting the {beep} command at key points in the macro. This is a relatively harmless addition to a macro, as it does not affect its operation or output. This keyword can produce four different tones: {beep}, {beep 2}, {beep 3}, and {beep 4}, so you can vary the tone at different points in the macro.

When the pause keyword, {?}, is inserted into a macro, the macro will halt until you press the Enter key. You will know that the point in the macro has been reached, and you will even have time to make notes or catch a breath before hitting Enter to continue. Moreover, while the macro is paused you are free to move the cell pointer to any other location. This can be a great help when you want to check the status of other cells. Just be sure the cell pointer is in an acceptable location when you allow the macro to resume.

The pause command forces a halt and allows you to move the cell pointer, but if you have several pauses in a macro, it does not tell you which pause you have reached. If you do not need to move about the worksheet during a pause in execution, you can use the {getlabel} command. This one allows you to include a prompt as a parameter, so that the macro will pause and display a prompt. You can include whatever relevant message you need to let you know where the macro is.

This command requires that a cell be specified to receive the user input. It is frequently advantageous to have one variable cell with a catchall name such as CHOICE for just such a purpose. A macro might then look like this:

```
{\DO_STARTUP}
{getlabel Returned from \Startup macro,CHOICE}
{getlabel Be sure that the disk is in B:,CHOICE}
{\COMBINE_FILES}
{getlabel All files brought in,CHOICE}
```

Remember that if your macro uses Command Language keywords, inserting breakpoints may be the only method of tracking the course of the macro.

The macro keyword {indicate} changes the Lotus control panel indicator in the upper right corner of the screen. Using this technique may be convenient for macro routines that take a long time to execute. You can include up to five characters in the command, such as {indicate "DATA"} or {indicate "FILES"}. The last line of the macro can include the command without a parameter, {indicate}, which restores the indicator to its default mode.

2.2 ◆ ———

⊗ CAUTION ◆ *The {indicate} command was enhanced in Release 2.2 so that it could display up to 240 characters in the mode indicator (if your screen can show that many), instead of the five characters allowed under Release 2.01.*

However, along with this benefit comes one small incompatibility. Under Release 2.01, any parameter you used for the {indicate} command was assumed to be text, so that {indicate 1-2-3} simply displayed the text 1-2-3 in the mode indicator.

Under Release 2.2, however, the enhanced command can take either text, a string formula, a cell address, or a range name as a parameter. For example, {indicate CELLNAME} displays in the mode indicator whatever is in the cell named CELLNAME, as long as it evaluates to a string. If you tried to use {indicate 1-2-3}, the macro would fail because 1-2-3 is a numeric formula.

In order for this macro to work under Release 2.2, you would have to enclose the parameter in quotes as follows:

{indicate "1-2-3"}

The quotes would be ignored under Release 2.01, but would ensure that the macro works under both releases of 1-2-3.

To include longer, more informative messages during lengthy macro routines, you can use the {let} statement. Give one cell a range name, such as MESSAGE. Then split the screen with the Worksheet Windows command, set the windows to Unsynchronized, and position one window on the cell named MESSAGE. You can then insert commands within the macro to pass messages to that cell, such as:

{let MESSAGE, "Running extract routine for totals"}

AVOIDING MACRO PITFALLS

During the development stage, you can avoid many macro problems by writing and testing your macros in small pieces. Trying to debug a long, complex macro can be difficult and nerve-wracking. Moreover, if you develop the routines in small chunks, your code will tend to be structured in a more efficient, more readable format.

The {windowsoff} and {paneloff} commands can speed up the execution of a macro and eliminate the frantic screen activity so typical of a running macro. Unfortunately, these commands make debugging almost impossible, and you should therefore not use them until the macro is finished and working.

Some macros have results that may not be desirable during the testing phase: multipaged printing, file combine operations, sorting, or data tables that have long calculation times. In those instances, write and debug the macro so that it does not initiate the final command.

If it is a print macro, leave out the g (Go) command. For data extraction, don't include the e for Extract. If you have a routine that retrieves another file, be especially sure to protect yourself from accidentally invoking it and losing your current worksheet from memory.

◆ RECORDING KEYSTROKES FOR MACROS

The usual method for writing a macro is to perform the desired routine manually first, at the same time taking notes on the keystrokes you are typing. When you are finished, you type the keystrokes into the macro in the worksheet. The process is therefore one of performing the task and taking notes, writing the macro code, and then repeating these steps for the next phase of the macro.

An obvious improvement to this method would be to have Lotus record your keystrokes directly into a macro as you manually perform the commands. And that's exactly what happens when you use the Learn add-in program for Release 2.01 and the Worksheet Learn command in Release 2.2.

The Learn add-in program will be covered first in the discussion that follows, after which the few differences between Learn and the Worksheet Learn command for Release 2.2 will be discussed.

THE LEARN ADD-IN FOR RELEASE 2.01

The Learn add-in program is included with more recent copies of 1-2-3 Release 2.01, and is attached to Lotus in the same way as any other add-in (see Appendix A for information on using add-ins). It requires only about 5K of memory and is simple to use. When activated, all the keystrokes you type are entered into a range of cells in a column as strings of text. Symphony users will recognize all of the features of this add-in, as it performs just like the Learn command in that program.

The Learn menu has only a few choices. The first, Range, allows you to designate the range of cells in a column that will hold the recorded keystrokes. These cells can be erased at any time, so that a new macro can be recorded by choosing the command Erase from the Learn menu. The range can be canceled by using the appropriately named command Cancel. Finally, the choices No and Yes toggle the keystroke recording function off and on. You can also use the key combination Alt-F5 as a quick on/off toggle for the LEARN mode. When Learn is recording your keystrokes, an indicator light at the bottom of the screen will show that you are in the LEARN mode.

Figure 1.5 shows the Learn menu at the top of the screen and the LEARN mode indicator at the bottom. The keystrokes recorded in the Learn range (column B) are for a print routine. It is at this point that you could turn off Learn and copy the recorded output to its permanent location in the worksheet, and then give it a macro name.

```
B1: '{GOTO}DATA~
Range  Erase  Cancel  No  Yes  Quit                              MENU
Specify range to store keystrokes
           A        B        C        D        E        F        G        H
 1                {GOTO}DATA~
 2                {RIGHT}
 3                {RIGHT}
 4                {DOWN}
 5                {DOWN}
 6                {DOWN}
 7                @now~
 8                /rfd1~
 9                /ppcar.{END}{RIGHT}{END}{DOWN}~oml10~mr1
10                32~s\015~hThis is a header!!@~
11                fAnad{BACKSPACE}{BACKSPACE}d a footer he
12                re!Pg. #~qagpq
13
14
15
16
17
18
19
20
                              LEARN
```

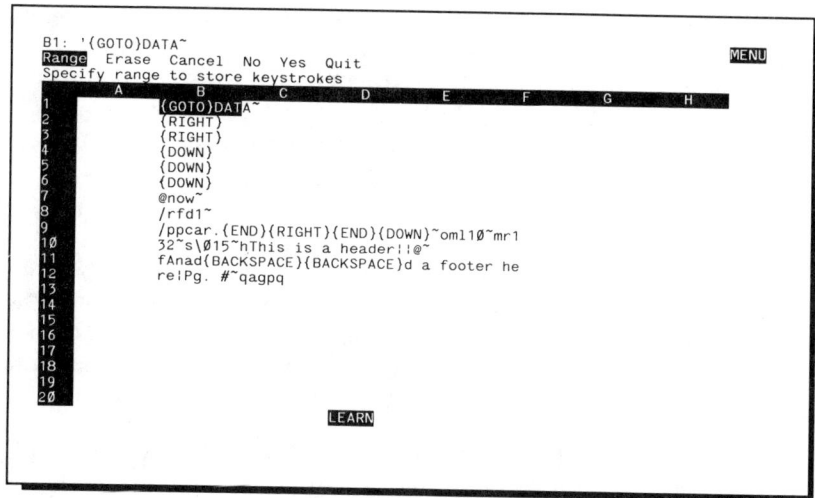

Figure 1.5 ◆ *Using the Learn add-in to record keystrokes*

As you read the recorded keystrokes in Figure 1.5, you may realize that you will need to edit the new macro for clarity and simplicity.

When recording, Learn does not combine cell pointer movements into one command. Instead of {right 4}, you will see {right}{right}{right}{right}. All nontypeable keystrokes are capitalized, which conflicts with the macro style used in this book, and is not as readable. Learn will put a maximum of 40 characters in a cell before moving down to the next one. Whatever the number, though, the breaks between cells may not be at appropriate points in the macro. These matters of style will not affect a recorded macro's accuracy, but the macro may be difficult to decipher.

The cells that you specify for the Learn range need only be in one column. Including cells in an adjoining column does not affect the width of the output from the recorded keystrokes. When defining the Learn range, you should include plenty of extra cells down the column. If the range fills up, Learn will have to cancel the recording process. Note that you can append keystrokes to a recorded macro by increasing the size of the Learn range (if necessary), turning on the LEARN mode, and continuing with your keystrokes from the point at which you left off.

A further note of caution when you are working in a large worksheet: If you have Recalculation set to Automatic, you may encounter delays when using Learn. Each time the add-in enters your keystrokes into a cell in the Learn range, the worksheet is forced into a recalculation, just as though you had made a cell entry. Setting Recalculation to Manual solves the problem.

You may find the Learn add-in most helpful if you are not already skilled at writing macros. It will help you get started with the macro-writing process while also boosting your speed and ensuring accuracy. Since it can only create keystroke macros, though, you must add Command Language keywords and routines separately, in the normal editing fashion.

The Learn program is particularly helpful when writing "on the fly" macros for jobs such as editing a column of formulas. A macro to do the job might look like this:

{edit}{home}{right 6} + @pi{right 4}{del 3}{down}

With the Learn add-in, you would simply start recording, edit and repair one of the formulas, move the cell pointer down to the next formula, and turn off the LEARN mode. Then give the macro a name (or use the Run key in Release 2.2) and let it go to work on the remaining formulas in the column.

THE WORKSHEET LEARN COMMAND IN RELEASE 2.2

2.2 ◆ ――――

The features of the Learn add-in were included within the Release 2.2 program so that you can record keystrokes for macros at any time. The differences between the add-in and the command are few.

First, of course, there is no need to attach an add-in because the command is always available. The Worksheet Learn command's menu is identical to the add-in's, except for the absence of the No and Yes choices. The Learn key (Alt-F5) has replaced them as the means of toggling the LEARN mode off and on.

As with the add-in, you should specify a Learn range that is bigger than you think you will need in order to avoid the "Learn range is full" error message while recording keystrokes. Once you have defined the range, press Alt-F5 at any time to start recording keystrokes to the range.

One difference between the add-in and the command is that the command uses the abbreviated style {r} for {right}, {l} for {left}, and so on. Line lengths are again limited to 40 characters, and unfortunately it still does not combine multiple directional commands into one command, such as {r 5}. You will still want to edit the macro and clean it up after it is recorded.

◆ ENHANCING YOUR MACROS WITH SELF-MODIFYING CODE ――――――――――

One of the most powerful macro programming features is one that is not even built into the macro language. This is the ability that macros have to modify themselves. There are three basic methods available to macros that allow them to change their code: substitution, string formulas, and renaming.

A macro consists of two components: the text of the macro code, and the cell or cells that serve as the macro's location. By changing the text within the location, or by redefining the location of a macro name, you can change the macro.

Using text substitution, you can modify the macro either by directly editing the cell or by copying or otherwise substituting the text from a different cell into the macro cell.

String formulas allow a macro to be modified by changing conditions in the worksheet, without physically changing its internal text. The outward display of the macro changes, but the inner formula remains the same.

Invoking a macro causes Lotus to go to the macro's named location and execute the text that it finds there. If the macro name is redefined to a new location, then invoking the macro causes a new one to be executed.

Whether through text modification, string formulas, or renaming, the methods of changing a macro can all be performed by macros themselves. This ability allows macros to react to conditions in the worksheet and to create code that is tailored for a specific application, such as the following:

- Include worksheet data in macro commands
- Access worksheet cells by implanting a range name into the macro
- Include hard cell addresses in a macro
- Vary the choices on a macro menu
- Make unique file names for all files associated with an application

ACCESSING DIFFERENT MENUS WITH ONE MACRO

You can enhance the generally accepted convention of having a macro named \M invoke a main menu by changing the contents of the menu that is called by \M. Thus, users are presented with choices that are appropriate to the current status of the worksheet or to their location in it. Figure 1.6 shows an example of an abbreviated application that has two menus, either one of which can be called by \M.

Look at the \0 macro in row 1. Every time the worksheet is retrieved, this macro performs two functions. First, it uses the macro {let} statement to replace the contents of cell \M with the contents of cell \GET_MENU1. These cells are in rows 3 and 5. Then, the main menu is called by the {branch \M} statement. At this point, \M always calls the menu named \MENU1.

On \MENU1, there is a choice for Data_Entry, which branches to a macro routine named \DATA_ENTRY. Before it branches, though, it uses the {let} statement to replace the contents of \M with the text in cell \GET_MENU2 (cell B6). Then, the \DATA_ENTRY macro jumps the cell pointer to the data area and calls \M. This time, the new menu for data entry, \MENU2, appears, as seen in Figure 1.7.

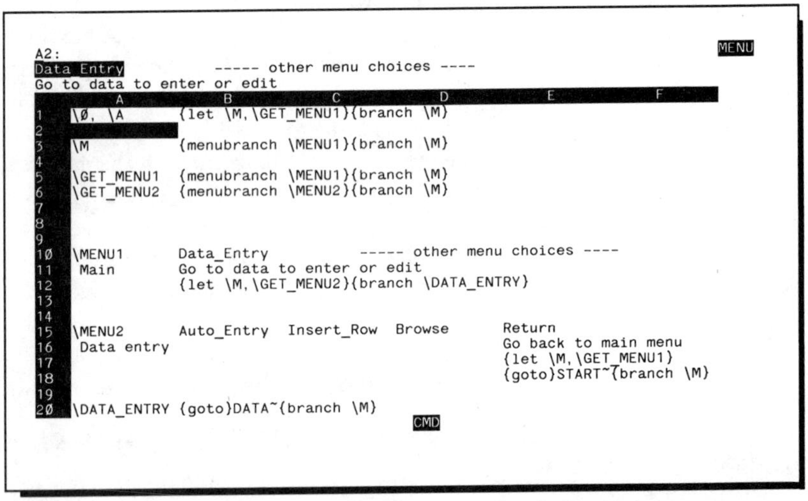

```
A2:                                                        MENU
Data Entry              ----- other menu choices ----
Go to data to enter or edit
         A          B          C          D          E          F
 1   \Ø, \A      {let \M,\GET_MENU1}{branch \M}
 2
 3   \M          {menubranch \MENU1}{branch \M}
 4
 5   \GET_MENU1  {menubranch \MENU1}{branch \M}
 6   \GET_MENU2  {menubranch \MENU2}{branch \M}
 7
 8
 9
10   \MENU1      Data_Entry        ----- other menu choices ----
11   Main        Go to data to enter or edit
12               {let \M,\GET_MENU2}{branch \DATA_ENTRY}
13
14
15   \MENU2      Auto_Entry  Insert_Row  Browse    Return
16   Data entry                                    Go back to main menu
17                                                 {let \M,\GET_MENU1}
18                                                 {goto}START~{branch \M}
19
20   \DATA_ENTRY {goto}DATA~{branch \M}       CMD
```

Figure 1.6 ◆ *Two different menus that are each called by \M*

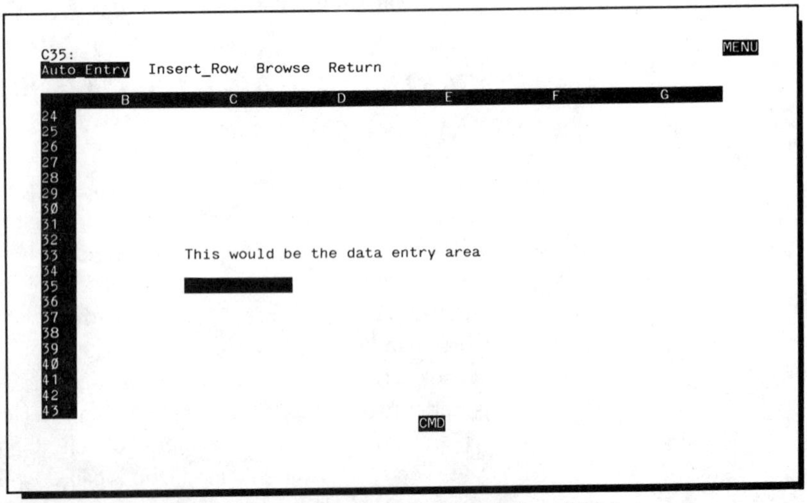

```
C35:                                                       MENU
Auto Entry  Insert_Row  Browse  Return

         B          C          D          E          F          G
24
25
26
27
28
29
30
31
32
33               This would be the data entry area
34
35
36
37
38
39
40
41
42
43                                        CMD
```

Figure 1.7 ◆ *A secondary menu that is also called with \M*

This menu, \MENU2, has choices that are relevant to data entry. While in that area entering or editing data, \M always invokes this menu. The user need only remember that Alt-M is the menu key, no matter what the current status of the worksheet.

Notice that the data entry menu has a choice named Return, which fulfills two purposes. It moves the cell pointer back from the data area to its original location, and it also changes \M so that it will call \MENU1. (Refer again to the macro code in Figure 1.6.)

Note that this method can be used in Lotus 1A if the Copy command is substituted for the {let} statement. The renaming method of changing a macro also achieves the same results, and it works in Lotus 1A and Lotus 2. Either one of the two {menubranch} statements could be renamed as \M, so that the command to change from \MENU1 to \MENU2 would be executed in this manner:

```
/rnd\M ˜ /rnc\M ˜ \GET_MENU2 ˜
```

The name \M is first deleted and then renamed to the new location. The macro could also flag the new menu by entering the text \M next to the proper cell. In this way, the active menu is always shown—a great help during the debugging phase.

CREATING MENUS THAT ADAPT

Sometimes a menu is needed in which the choices themselves will adapt to the needs of the worksheet. The following example is an excellent way of speeding up and exemplifying tedious data entry routines. It provides a menu of standard dates that are all based on the current date.

The menu shown in Figure 1.8 displays four dates: the current date and three others, each one week later than the next. The choices are built upon the @now function, returning a value that is then formatted as a date, as the figure shows.

> ★ **TRICK** ◆ *It is illegal to use values for menu choices with the {menubranch} command of Lotus 2. The technique works only with the /xm macro command that was originally found in Lotus 1A. This is one case where the older-style menus can be used to great advantage in Lotus 2.*

When the menu is called, the dates are displayed, and you can easily select one from the menu. The selection causes that date to be entered into the current cell, as the macro code in row 11 shows. That cell is then formatted for dates by the macro in row 12. By using this method, the person doing the data entry need never know that such things as date functions and formats exist.

```
B9: (D2) @NOW                                                    MENU
24-Nov  Ø1-Dec  Ø8-Dec  15-Dec
Choose date to enter
        A         B            C           D           E
1      \Z        /xm\MENU1~
2
3
4
5                 @NOW        @NOW+7      @NOW+14     @NOW+21
6                 ¦           ¦           ¦           ¦
7                 ¦           ¦           ¦           ¦
8
9      \MENU1     24-Nov      Ø1-Dec      Ø8-Dec      15-Dec
1Ø                Choose date to enter
11                @now{calc}~  @now+7{calc}~ @now+14{calc}~@now+14{calc}~
12                /rfd1~       /rfd1~        /rfd1~        /rfd1~
13
14
15
16
17
18
19
2Ø
                                          CMD
```

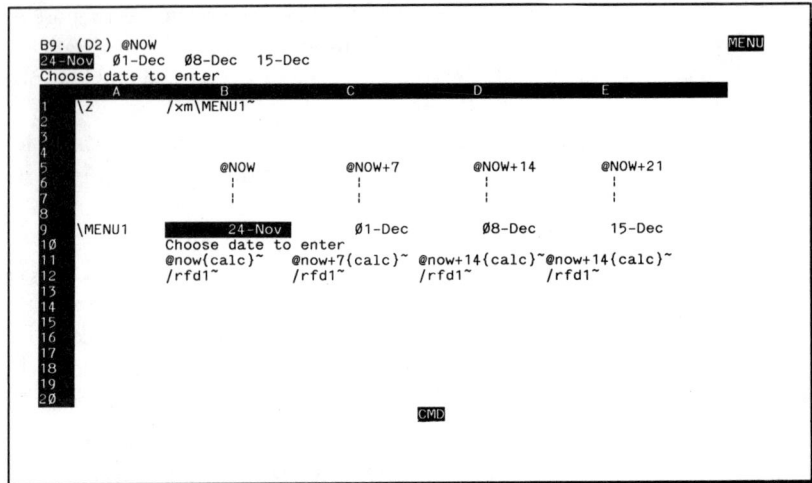

Figure 1.8 ◆ *Displaying dates on a menu*

USING FILE NAMES THAT ADAPT
TO THE WORKSHEET

A valuable technique when writing worksheet applications is to give auxiliary files a name that is relevant to the application. For instance, a monthly worksheet can be saved under a new name at the beginning of each month. In January the name would be FILEJAN, in February FILEFEB, and so forth.

Including a Month Name in the File Name

The short macro in cell B2 of Figure 1.9 shows how this is done. A large part of the underlying string formula can be seen in the control panel.

Here is the complete formula, but with only four months of the year shown. It is broken into three parts at the ampersands (&) that concatenate one part to another:

```
+"/fsFILE"
&@choose(@month(@now)--1,"JAN","FEB","MAR","APR")
&"~r{esc}"
```

The first section of the macro string formula begins with the File Save command. It prefaces the file name with four characters, FILE. Next, an @choose function pulls out the name of the month from a list of three-character month names. It bases the selection on the current month number, **@month(@now)**,

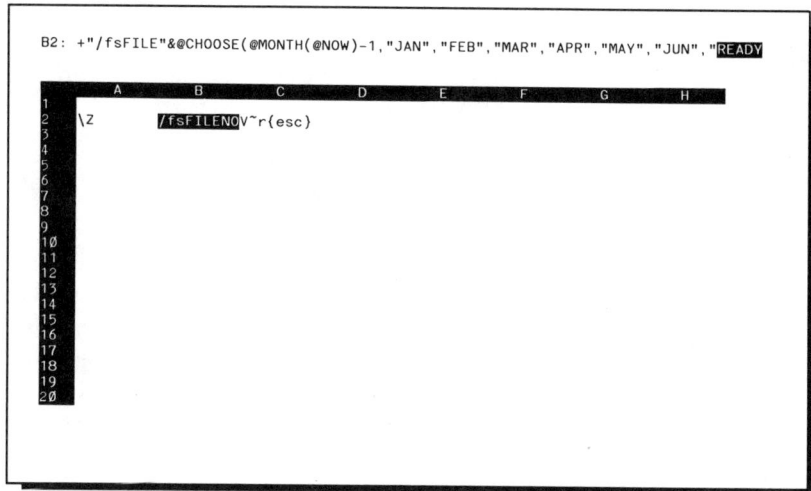

Figure 1.9 ◆ *A macro that saves a worksheet as the current month name*

less 1 because the @choose function references its first choice as zero. In the worksheets shown, the current month is November, which produces the result NOV. Of course, the month will be correct only if you set the computer's system date before entering Lotus.

The formula is completed in the third section above with the Enter and Replace commands.

> **TIP** ◆ *The final {esc} command is needed so that the macro will succeed whether or not it must replace a file of the same name on disk. If a file does not already exist, the r will serve to give the Replace command, and the {esc} will execute without effect. If the file does not already exist, the r is not needed, as the Save command will already have been completed. The r will instead be typed into the edit window as ordinary text. That is when the {esc} is needed, as it will simply erase the character and allow the macro to continue.*

Whatever the current month, the macro will save the worksheet with the proper file name. In October, for example, the macro formula would look like this:

/fsFILEOCT˜r {esc}

Including the Date in a Name

Here is another short macro based on a string formula that appends the current month and day to a file name so that a file would be saved as FIL10-14 on

October 14. Since file names must be eight characters or less, only three characters are available for the body of the file name when this style is used. Figure 1.10 shows the macro; notice the string formula in the control panel. It is very similar to the previous example, as its three components show:

```
+"/fsFIL"
&@string(@month(@now),0)&"-"&@string(@day(@now),0)
&"~r{esc}"
```

The first part begins the File Save command as before. The next section returns the month number of the current date; since the month is November, an 11 is returned. It is evaluated as a string with no decimals in order to be used in a string formula. A hyphen is then placed in the formula, which is followed by the calculation of the current day, 1, again as a string.

The formula is finished in the third line with the Enter and Replace for the Save command.

Assuming your computer's system date was set correctly, on March 29 the formula would return this:

```
/fsFIL3-29~r{esc}
```

Macro Substitution with Variable Cells

String formulas in your macros will add to the overall recalculation time of the worksheet, and can be difficult to decipher when long or complex. Macro

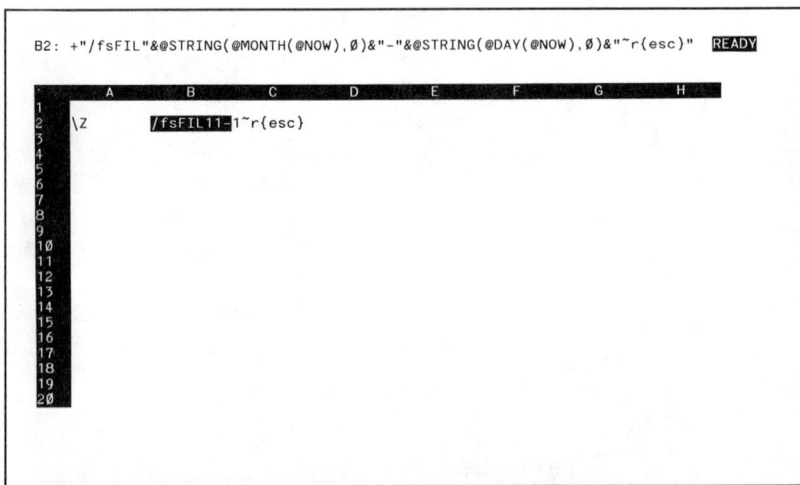

Figure 1.10 ◆ *A macro that saves a worksheet as the current date*

modification through either direct or indirect substitution avoids some of these drawbacks.

Figure 1.11 presents two macros that save the worksheet under the current month and day, just as the string formula macro did in Figure 1.10. Both macros are the same except in the way the substitution of the day and month numbers occur.

The macro in the top half of the screen uses the direct method of substitution to create the file name that contains the month and day numbers. The substitution takes place in cell B5, named NAME1, which contains the text 11-1. The macro \X starts in B3, where it uses the {let} statement to create the month and day numbers in NAME1. The formula it uses is the same one used in the string formula of Figure 1.10. The macro continues in B4 with the File Save command and the first three letters of the file name, FIL. In B5 it picks up the month and day component of the name, and in B6 the Enter key is pressed to complete the command.

This process of "laying the track in front of the train" is a tremendously effective technique. Bear in mind that the modifying cell must have a text entry—it cannot be blank or numeric. If there are times when you want to skip the cell completely, just have the macro fill it with the double braces, {}, which will cause the macro to continue past it to the next cell. In this case, the file will be saved under the name FIL.

In the lower window of Figure 1.11, the macro \Z (cell B20) uses the indirect method of substitution. This time, the modifying cell, here called NAME2, is

```
B5: U '11-1                                                              READY

         A        B        C        D        E        F        G        H
1
2
3   \X        (let NAME1,@string(@month(@now),0)&"-"&@string(@day(@now),0))
4             /fsFIL
5   NAME1     11-1
6             ~r(esc)
7
8
9

         A        B        C        D        E        F        G        H
14
15
16  NAME2     11-1
17             {return}
18
19
20  \Z        (let NAME2,@string(@month(@now),0)&"-"&@string(@day(@now),0))
21             /fsFIL(NAME2)~r(esc)
22
23
```

Figure 1.11 ◆ *Using a variable cell to modify a macro*

outside of the macro at B16. Note the {return} statement in B17 below NAME2. The macro starts with the same command that started \X in the upper window, and enters the month and day numbers into NAME2. In B21, the macro continues with the File Save command, and here is where the two techniques differ.

This time, after the FIL of the file name a subroutine call, {NAME2}, is made to the range NAME2. The macro continues execution in NAME2, which happens to contain the characters needed for the rest of the file name. The macro reads those characters into the File Save command, and when it reaches the last one it continues in the cell below where it finds the {return} command, causing control to return to B21. There, the File Save command is finished with the tilde (Enter key), and the macro is done.

With this method, you must ensure that the variable cell has either a blank cell below it or, preferably, a {return} command to ensure that the macro does not wantonly continue reading instructions down that column. The advantages of indirect substitution are that the variable cell can be used by other macros, and the macro code that addresses the cell need not be split into three lines of code, as was the macro in the upper window of Figure 1.11.

With either method, the variable cell should be unprotected with the Range Unprotect command so that it can be used even when protection is enabled.

PRINTING FROM A VARIABLE LIST OF RANGES

Self-modifying macros graciously adapt to the current data in the worksheet, so that one macro can handle many different situations. Figure 1.12 shows a print routine that prints each range whose name appears in the table named LIST.

This routine is based on a {for} loop that uses the number of rows in LIST to set the maximum number of loops. The macro's first command, in cell B1, must set the cell named COUNTER to 1, its starting value (more on this below). The print routine is then initialized by specifying all the relevant settings except the range. The {for} loop kicks in while the print menu is still active, and instructs the macro to continue executing at \DO_PRINT, the macro that does the actual printing. The {for} loop will invoke \DO_PRINT seven times, the number of rows in LIST.

You can see the routine \DO_PRINT in the control panel. It is shown here divided into convenient segments:

```
+"{recalc \DO_PRINT}r"
&@INDEX($LIST,0,$COUNTER – 1)
&"~a{beep 3}"
```

```
B8:  +"{recalc \DO_PRINT}r"&@INDEX($LIST,Ø,$COUNTER-1)&"~a{beep 3}"          READY

          A              B          C          D          E          F          G
1     \Z             {let COUNTER,1}~
2                    /ppcaoml1Ø~mr132~s\Ø15~q
3                    {for COUNTER,1,@rows(LIST),1,\DO_PRINT}
4                    q{quit}
5
6     COUNTER               1
7
8     \DO_PRINT      {recalc \DO_PRINT}rReport_North~a{beep 3}
9                                             |
1Ø                                            |
11    LIST           Report_North       {beep} command replaces Go
12                   Report_South       and Page for testing purposes
13                   Report_East
14                   Report_West
15                   Range_1
16                   Data_List
17                   Summary
18
19
2Ø
```

Figure 1.12 ◆ *A print macro that prints all ranges shown in a table*

The string formula begins by using the {recalc} command to update itself—it must evaluate to pick up the new value of COUNTER, and thereby display the next name in LIST.

> ⊗ **CAUTION** ◆ *When using a string formula macro, be sure that it will be properly evaluated when first invoked. The {for} command, for example, always finishes by leaving the counter cell showing one step more than the maximum for the loop cycle. This would cause the @index function used here to attempt to access a row outside the rows in LIST, a condition that forces it to show ERR. If COUNTER were not set to a valid number before the first loop, \DO_PRINT would show ERR and the macro would fail.*

After the formula is recalculated, an *r* chooses Range from the print menu, which then accepts the name that is displayed by the second section of the formula shown previously.

This is an @index function that displays a name from LIST for each iteration of the {for} macro. It uses zero as a column offset parameter, since it is looking at the only column in LIST. The row offset in the function is set to COUNTER−1, so that when COUNTER is 1, @index will evaluate row 0 of LIST. That is the first row, and it contains Report_North.

The third line of the macro above provides an Enter to accept the print range, and then an Align command. A Go command would normally be issued at this point, followed by a Page command if each range was supposed to start on a new page.

> ☑ **TIP** ◆ *The \DO_PRINT macro in Figure 1.12 demonstrates how a macro can be revised for testing purposes. In this case, the command {beep 3} is used instead of the Go and Page commands. A beep sounds to signify that the range would normally be printed at that point.*

When the last range has been printed, the macro continues in the next cell below the {for} statement, B4. It issues a final q to quit the Print menu, and then a macro {quit} to end the macro. By combining a looping macro with a self-modifying string function macro, the routine is kept relatively short. Moreover, it can be used with a long or short list of names and can easily be revised to include headers, footers, borders, and the like.

Of course, you may prefer to use substitution instead of a string formula. A variable cell with a {return} command below it is needed; let's call it PRINT_RANGE. The macro \Z can then be rewritten to look like this:

```
/ppcaoml10~mr132~s\015~q
{for COUNTER,1,@rows(LIST),1,\DO_PRINT}
q{quit}
```

and \DO_PRINT like this:

```
{let PRINT_RANGE,@index(LIST,0,COUNTER-1)}
r{PRINT_RANGE}~a{beep 3}
```

REFERENCING CELL ADDRESSES WITHIN A MACRO

The cardinal rule against including hard cell addresses within a macro does have an exception, which occurs when a macro is no longer just a macro. When is that?

A macro is not simply a macro when it is also a formula. With the string formulas and functions in 1-2-3, you can write a macro that dynamically adapts to cell movements in the worksheet, just as a numeric formula does. Here is the macro that was shown earlier in this chapter, and it appears to break the primary rule of cell referencing:

```
/re$B$16~
```

But look at Figure 1.13, where this macro is written as ordinary text in \X, and also as a string formula in \Z. Both macros perform the same job of erasing cell B16, which is flagged in the display and contains the word *Four*. Although both macros appear the same on the screen, notice the differing cell contents, as shown to the right of each macro, and also in the control panel where \Z is displayed. Each will react differently to changes in the worksheet.

In Figure 1.14, a row has been inserted at row 14. If macro \X were invoked, it would still erase B16. Unfortunately, that cell no longer contains the target cell, which is now at B17. \X is blind to any movements in the worksheet.

The @cell function in \Z, however, has allowed the macro to dynamically adjust to the movement of the cell it addresses. It will still erase its target cell, now B17. Including the @cell function in a string formula allows this macro to be just as flexible as one that uses range names for cell references. Remember that the string formula may need to be evaluated before executing to ensure that its result is accurate.

String formulas are not a replacement for the proper use of range names within macros. If an area of the worksheet is important enough to be addressed in a macro, then that location just may deserve a range name to declare its identity. String formulas, unlike range names, do not aid in the interpretation and documentation of the worksheet. In this case, consider them as an adjunct to the normal use of range names, and an exception to the requirement of using only names within a macro.

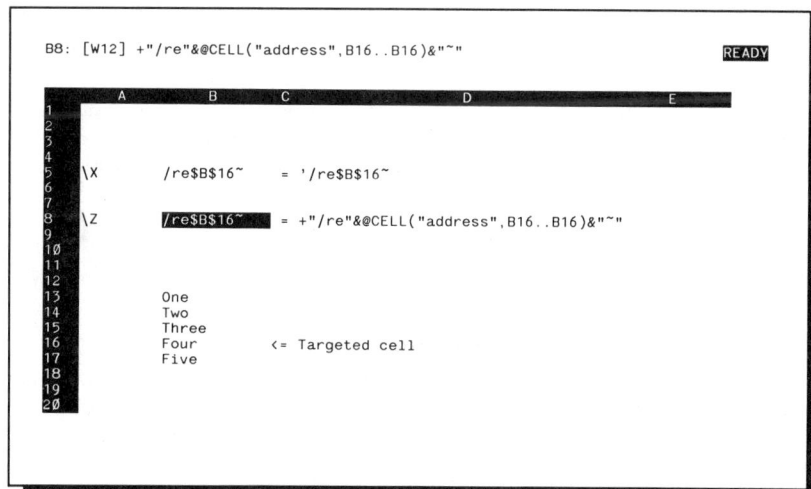

```
B8: [W12] +"/re"&@CELL("address",B16..B16)&"~"                    READY

         A         B          C                  D                   E
1
2
3
4
5   \X        /re$B$16~   = '/re$B$16~
6
7
8   \Z        /re$B$16~   = +"/re"&@CELL("address",B16..B16)&"~"
9
10
11
12
13            One
14            Two
15            Three
16            Four        <= Targeted cell
17            Five
18
19
20
```

Figure 1.13 ◆ *String formulas allow macros to use cell addresses*

```
B8:  [W12] +"/re"&@CELL("address",B17..B17)&"~"                            READY

         A        B          C             D                    E
  1
  2
  3
  4
  5   \X        /re$B$16~     =  '/re$B$16~
  6
  7
  8   \Z        /re$B$17~     =  +"/re"&@CELL("address",B17..B17)&"~"
  9
 10
 11
 12
 13            One
 14   - - - - - - - - - -  row inserted here
 15            Two
 16            Three
 17            Four            <= Targeted cell
 18            Five
 19
 20
```

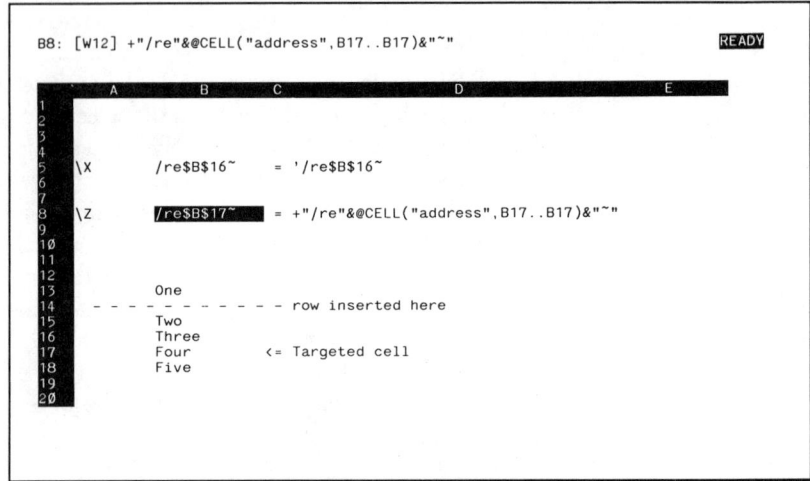

Figure 1.14 ◆ *Plain text macros cannot adjust to cell movements*

◆ THE MACRO LIBRARY MANAGER IN RELEASE 2.2

2.2 ◆ ——— Macros have many virtues, but because they are part of the worksheet they also have some inherent weaknesses. It was in response to these weaknesses that the Lotus Development Corporation created the Macro Library Manager, a small add-in program that comes with 1-2-3 Release 2.2. Although the add-in does not work with any other releases of 1-2-3, an identical add-in has long been a part of Lotus's Symphony.

WEAKNESSES OF MACROS

The Macro Library Manager does much to alleviate the following drawbacks of macros:

- ◆ Macros are vulnerable to damage if you inadvertently delete a row or erase a range that contains macro code, or unknowingly insert a row that splits a macro, causing it to stop when it reaches that blank row.

◆ Taking macros from one worksheet to use in another is somewhat inconvenient. You must use the File Combine command to bring all the relevant rows of code into the other worksheet, and then give a range name to each macro. If you want to transfer macros from several worksheets into one, you must repeat the transfer process for each of them. If you ever change a macro in one worksheet that is used in another, you must either change it as well in the other, or perform the transfer process yet again.

◆ Macros, like data, can be difficult to transport among multiple worksheets. And if the macros are only needed occasionally, the space they require in each worksheet may make you think about buying a larger hard disk.

◆ Since macros are worksheet-specific, it is no small task to create a macro-driven solution to pass control among several different worksheets. For example, a consolidation routine might require that one worksheet retrieve another and pass it data, and then that worksheet would process the data and pass it to another worksheet, or perhaps back to the original one.

THE NATURE OF A MACRO LIBRARY

The name *macro library* is somewhat misleading because a macro library can contain almost any text, numbers, formulas, or range names. In fact, a macro library is really like having another worksheet in memory that is "invisible" to you, but which is nonetheless accessible, although not to the extent of a normal worksheet.

Like a normal worksheet, a macro library exists on disk (with an MLB file extension) as well as in memory. You define a library within the active worksheet, and then save the library to disk. You can load as many as ten existing libraries from disk into memory at the same time.

★ *TRICK* ◆ *A library can contain any worksheet data, and you need not limit its use to macros. Its independence from the worksheet allows it to solve common problems in novel ways. For example, a linking formula refers only to a single cell, and is unable to perform a lookup on a table of data in another worksheet. But you can perform such a function with a table of data in a macro library and a macro to perform the lookup. If the data has the range name TABLE, the following macro could be used to pull out a value and place it in the cell named TARGET in the worksheet:*

{let TARGET,@index(TABLE,[col],[row])}

Once a library is in memory, you have access to it only through macros. This is why it is best called a macro library. You may run macros that reside in both the worksheet and the library, and those macros can affect ranges in either.

The importance of using range names within a macro library is even more critical than within the worksheet. You won't be able to access a specific cell address in a macro library because a library has no rows and columns. Instead, you refer to a range name, just as you do in the worksheet.

Although the Copy command will not copy data between the worksheet and the library, the macro {let} command, for example, allows you to do so. Also, you cannot access cells between the library and the worksheet with formulas, but you can use formulas within a macro. For example, if LIB_RANGE is in a library and WKS_TOTAL is within the worksheet, the following one-line macro is valid:

{if @sum(LIB_RANGE)>10}
{let WKS_TOTAL = @sum(LIB_RANGE)}

You may use formulas within the library, but they should refer only to other cells therein. If you save a range as a library that contains formulas referring to cells outside of the library, they will evaluate to zero. (This is similar to using the File Xtract command on a range that contains formulas but does not include the target cells of the formulas; in the extracted file that is created, the formulas will refer to blank cells.) This means you are not allowed to save as a library a range that contains a linking formula.

You might think macro libraries will occupy too much of your computer's memory to be useful to you. After all, the add-in program requires about 14K of memory in which to run. Plus, each cell that you save to the library takes up just as much RAM in the library as it does in the worksheet. On top of that, any blank cells in the saved range will each require memory in the library, so that the library could actually take up more memory than the worksheet. However, it is possible to save memory if you use your libraries efficiently. Since a library can be removed from memory, create several small ones instead of one large one, and bring them in and out of memory as needed.

Convenience and flexibility are what give macro libraries their real power. Don't let the simplicity of this add-in's commands fool you. You will find that the Macro Library Manager can be applied to a tremendous variety of spreadsheets, and is a powerful adjunct to 1-2-3.

USING THE MACRO LIBRARY MANAGER

After you attach the program to 1-2-3 (see Appendix A for more information on using add-ins), its command menu appears whenever you invoke the add-in. The menu has six choices: Save, Edit, Load, Remove, Name-List, and Quit. The following discussion of these commands will provide an overview of how to use the add-in, starting with the Save command.

Save

Before you create a macro library, you must first create your macros within the worksheet in the usual way. When your macros are finished, tested, and debugged, bring up the Macro Library Manager and issue the Save command. You will be asked for the name of the library to which you want to save the macros. The library is much like a worksheet in that it is kept as a file on disk as well as copied to memory when you use the Manager's Load or Save command.

Specify either an existing library (which will be replaced by the macros you are saving) or a new one, and then specify the range of the worksheet that you want to save. Be sure to include all the cells of your macros, and as few empty cells as possible. You can even attach a password to the library, just as you would with a worksheet file, if you want protection for sensitive data or macros. The cell contents and range names that you specify will be removed from the worksheet and placed in the macro library in RAM. Once you have created a library, you do not have to retain the worksheet from which it came.

> **TIP** ♦ *You will benefit by saving the source worksheet because you can include comments in it that describe the macros or data that were sent to the library. Storing extraneous data in the worksheet but not in the library will keep your macro libraries lean.*

Edit

Once saved, the contents of a macro library are outside of the worksheet and cannot be changed (except by macros), which is why the macros are safe from accidental deletion. When you want to modify the macros, you must first bring them back into the worksheet with the Edit command, and then make your modifications in the usual fashion. When done, you again use the Save command to replace the contents of the library with the newly revised macros (or create a new library).

The Edit command brings in both the cell contents and range names, and duplicates the exact structure in the worksheet that you first created before using the Save command. Because the range names are brought back into the worksheet, this add-in is a more complete data-transfer device than the File Combine command.

The incoming range names could create a conflict if there are any identical range names already in the worksheet. Therefore, you are given the choice of ignoring any duplicate range names, so that the incoming name and data will not be imported in conflict with an existing name, or overwriting the existing name with the incoming one. In the latter case, the existing range name will be redefined to the location of the incoming range name.

Note that although an existing range name is redefined, any formulas that referred to that name will continue to refer to its original cell, not the new one. This process is therefore akin to first deleting the name, and then redefining it at the new location.

> **TIP** ◆ *If you have retained a macro library's source worksheet because it has comments or notations, just edit the code in it and then save the macros back to the library. If you want to edit the code in the library itself, be sure to bring it back into its source worksheet at the same location from which it was saved so that the comments will match up with the library data.*

Load

The Load command allows you to bring a macro library disk file into memory. The process is somewhat like loading a worksheet from disk, but you can have up to ten libraries in memory at the same time. Of course, the libraries in memory are completely independent of the worksheet.

When loading multiple libraries, there is always the chance that a range name in one will also exist in another or in the worksheet. This is not a problem until later, when the range name is addressed in a macro. In the case of duplicate names, 1-2-3 uses the first one it finds, and the names are always searched in the same sequence.

The worksheet is checked first. If the name is not found there, the macro library that was most recently loaded is searched. If it is not there, the second most recent one is searched, and so on. You can see the order in which the libraries were loaded by invoking the Manager's Edit, Remove, or Name-List commands, each of which lists all the current libraries. They are shown in the chronological order of loading.

Remove

You remove a macro library from memory with the Remove command. You do this either to free up the RAM that the library was using, or to make room for another library when you already have ten loaded. Removing a library does not, however, erase the library file from disk. To do so, you would use 1-2-3's File Erase Other command.

Name-List and Quit

The Name-List command is similar to the worksheet command, Range Name Table, in that it simply creates a list of all the range names contained in a macro library. Since macro libraries have no cell addresses, the list contains only names and no addresses. Use this command to remind you of the names in a library, or to get the exact spelling of the names.

Invoking the Manager's Quit command, like pressing Escape, simply returns you to the worksheet and the Ready mode.

SELF-MODIFYING MACROS IN A LIBRARY

Because a macro library is so much like a worksheet, self-modifying macros work with great success in a library, so long as any formulas in the macro library refer to locations therein.

Suppose you create the following string formula macro to be placed in a library:

```
+"/ppcar"&PRINT_RANGE&"~agq"
```

The formula evaluates depending on the cell PRINT_RANGE, which must also be within the library. The macro that uses this print routine would therefore have to set the value of PRINT_RANGE; you could not enter that value manually from the worksheet.

However, if you use an indirect substitution in the macro, then no formulas are involved and the library macro could make a subroutine call to a cell variable either in the worksheet or the library. In this case, the cell PRINT_RANGE could reside within the worksheet, and the macro above would be written like this:

```
/ppcar{PRINT_RANGE}~agq
```

With macro libraries, you may not need to worry about recalculating your string formula macros before they are executed. This is because the library automatically refreshes itself whenever any of its cells are changed. For instance, when the value of PRINT_RANGE is set in the first example above, the string formula would automatically evaluate to the new contents of that cell without having to first invoke a {recalc} command.

On the other hand, although formulas in a library cannot refer to the worksheet, formulas in a macro can. So if a macro refers to a worksheet cell, you should make sure that the worksheet is up to date.

The Macro Library Manager is an excellent tool for storing and running your macros. You can load and remove libraries as you need them so that, for example, you have a library of worksheet-building macros for use during the construction phase of your worksheet that will not clutter the worksheet itself.

Using the Manager for data storage opens up new opportunities in problem solving. It is almost like having as many as ten other worksheets available at the same time, except that you must access the data through macros.

◆ SUMMARY

Although macros are never required, they can enhance the operation of any worksheet. Their virtues are so significant that they top the list of features for adding control and performance to worksheet applications.

In this chapter, you learned how macros can strengthen many aspects of the worksheet. In particular, this chapter has presented the basics of writing macros and demonstrated the difference between keystroke and command language macros. You also learned about several interesting tricks with the \0 macro. Macro etiquette is important; good habits help in developing good macros. Macros must always be tested, and tips were offered on debugging and testing macro routines. The Lotus add-in, Learn, and the Worksheet Learn command in Release 2.2, are tools that can help in the macro writing process.

Macros can modify themselves "in flight," and this fact greatly expands their power and flexibility. Using self-modifying techniques can make your macros compact, easy to revise, and adaptable to the needs of the worksheet.

Finally, if you are using Release 2.2, the Macro Library Manager offers flexibility and memory savings to your macros.

The next chapter gives you a closer look at range names, one of the most valuable Lotus tools. Every worksheet can benefit from their use, and without them macro-driven applications are virtually impossible to create. Range names simplify and speed up the repetitive task of entering range addresses into formulas, worksheet commands, and macros, while decreasing the chance of addressing errors. They can be used throughout the worksheet, and so play a major part in worksheet documentation.

TWO:

*Using Range Names
for Clarity, Speed, and
Accuracy*

2

◆ ◆ ◆

LOTUS HAS MANY SPREADSHEET, DATABASE, AND GRAPHICS capabilities that work in concert to make it a versatile, well-integrated package. It also has tools that work behind the scenes to increase the overall productivity of the spreadsheet. Macros head this list, but range names follow close behind. They can be used in all three of the worksheet features that reference ranges: formulas, worksheet commands, and macros.

Unfortunately, because range names are seldom a requirement they are often ignored or underused. This chapter looks at the ways in which range names can put you in control of the worksheet by enhancing your 1-2-3 applications in three vital ways:

- ◆ Speeding up and simplifying worksheet routines

- ◆ Decreasing errors

- ◆ Serving as the first line of defense in debugging and documenting worksheets

◆ THE MECHANICS OF RANGE NAMES

The Range Name Create command provides a simple and convenient means of addressing ranges in the worksheet, whether for one cell or a block of contiguous cells. The name of a range can be used whenever 1-2-3 requires that a range be specified, whether in formulas, as shown here:

`@sum(FIRST_QTR)`

or in worksheet commands like this one:

`Enter Print range: FIRST_QTR`

or, finally, in macros:

`/ppcarFIRST_QTR ~`

WHAT'S IN A NAME

A range name can be as long as 15 characters, which allows for a reasonably descriptive name. A name can contain any of the letters, numbers, spaces, and LICS (Lotus International Character Set) characters that are available within 1-2-3. Actually, any character you can get into a worksheet cell can then be used in a name by way of the Range Name Labels command.

You can run into trouble, though, if you are not judicious with your choice of characters. For instance, you can give a cell a name that may be concise and describe the cell's use, but also describes a 1-2-3 cell address: A1, AM800, GO99, IQ100, EZ1, or GW1990. When executing a command, 1-2-3 always ignores the name and defers to the cell address itself. Try to print a range that is named IQ100; Lotus will print the cell with the address IQ100.

Avoid the use of braces, {}. Within macros braces are reserved for macro commands and keywords, so a range name that contained braces would invariably cause trouble.

It is also best to avoid characters that imply a number or formula, such as the following: +, −, (, ., @, #, and $. A formula that uses these names: −SUM−, $TOTAL, TOTAL+, $/GAL, or SEP(TOTAL) would be almost unreadable.

+$$TOTAL/$$/GAL − −SUM − +@SUM(SEP(TOTAL))

Avoid spaces so that one name does not appear to be two individual names. You can use the underline character to create a name having two words: FIRST_QUARTER or SEP_TOTAL.

> ⊗ **CAUTION** ◆ *As you fly through the 1-2-3 command menus, be wary of the Range Name Reset command; it is one of the unforgiving ones in Lotus. As soon as your finger hits the R of Reset, every range name in the worksheet will be gone; there is no last chance, No/Yes menu for this one. A recently saved worksheet or a range name table is the only defense against this disaster.*

APPROPRIATE AREAS TO NAME

A general rule for the use of range names is to name any area that is regularly used for any purpose, such as cell variables that are referenced by many formulas, print ranges, data entry areas, and databases. You should also name any area that receives critical use, including data that gets sorted, ranges that get overwritten with data from another range or worksheet file, all macros, and any ranges referenced by a macro.

Don't worry if that sounds like practically every cell in your worksheet. As you use range names more and more, you will begin to see patterns in the ways they are used, just as you find patterns among the routines and layouts of your worksheets. Here are some areas that typically receive range names, with examples of common range names for each area.

Variables	MONTH, TIME, SALARY, INTEREST, TAX_RATE, BOILING_TEMP, LENGTH, WIDTH, FACTOR, COUNTER
Print ranges	REPORT1, REPORT2, REPORT2_TOTALS, BORDER_ROWS
Work areas	DATA_ENTRY, DATA_SUMMARY, DATA_TOTALS, USER_INPUT, MENU_SCREEN
Tables for @vlookup or @index functions	TABLE_RATES, TABLE_ID, TABLE_MARKUP, TABLE_MOLEC_WT
Macros	\0 and \M, \MENU1, \MENU2, \PRINT_REPORT1, \QUERY_DATA1, \SAVE_TOTALS, \LOOP1
Databases	INPUT1, CRIT1, OUTPUT1, CRIT1_A, CRIT1_B
Sort ranges	SORT_RANGE1, SORTKEY1_A, SORTKEY1_B, SORT_RANGE2

WHAT'S IN A RANGE

Ranges will expand and contract as rows or columns are inserted or deleted, and formulas or commands that refer to a range are automatically updated for the new coordinates.

The dimensions of a range name also follow the range of cells as it changes in size or location. The bonus is that the name itself never changes, even though the coordinates of its range have shifted.

The Name Stays the Same

In Figure 2.1, the range B7..G17 has been filled with 1s and given the name TEST_RANGE. The formula in B3 sums this range, as you can see in the control panel, returning the sum of 66. To use this range in a worksheet command,

```
B3:  @SUM(TEST_RANGE)                                              READY

         A         B         C         D         E         F         G         H
 1
 2
 3              66    =    @SUM(B7..G17)
 4
 5
 6
 7              1         1         1         1         1         1
 8              1         1         1         1         1         1
 9              1         1         1         1         1         1
10              1         1         1         1         1         1
11              1         1         1         1         1         1
12              1         1         1         1         1         1
13              1         1         1         1         1         1
14              1         1         1         1         1         1
15              1         1         1         1         1         1
16              1         1         1         1         1         1
17              1         1         1         1         1         1
18
19
20
```

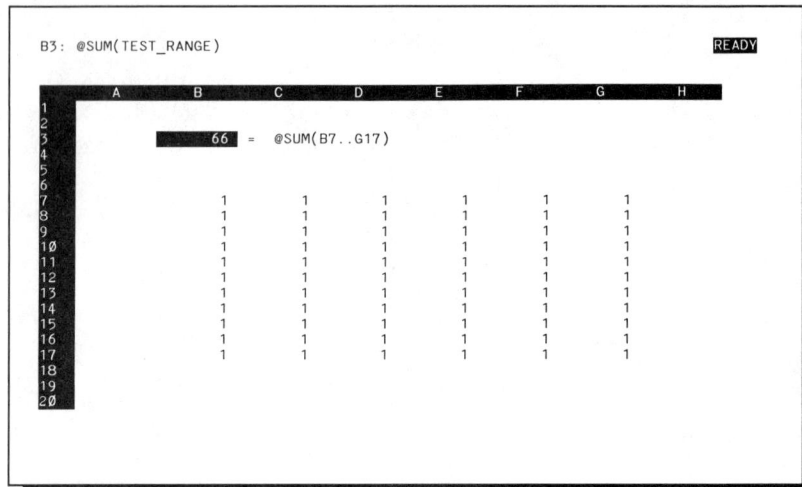

Figure 2.1 ◆ *The range TEST_RANGE*

such as Print, you could enter the name TEST_RANGE at the prompt for the print range.

Deleting several rows and columns from within the range and also from the space above and to the left of it gives the result shown in Figure 2.2. The coordinates of the range are now A5..C9, but the formula is still referencing TEST_RANGE, as you can see in the control panel. Its result is 15, the number of cells left in the range.

Need to print what's left? Just specify the same name, TEST_RANGE, and all 15 cells will be printed. If you were to use the coordinates of the range instead, you would have to carefully note the addresses of two diagonal corners, such as A5..C9, and type those into the print range prompt. Checking those coordinates is a tedious process that would have to be repeated each time you printed, in case those coordinates had changed.

"Popping" Range Names

The cornerstone cells of any range are vulnerable to deletion or as the target of a Move command. If either of these two cells is lost, the range effectively suffers a "blowout," and any formulas that referred to it will now show references to ERR. The *cornerstones* can be either of the diagonal pairs of cells in a range, depending on which pair was used when writing the formula that references the range.

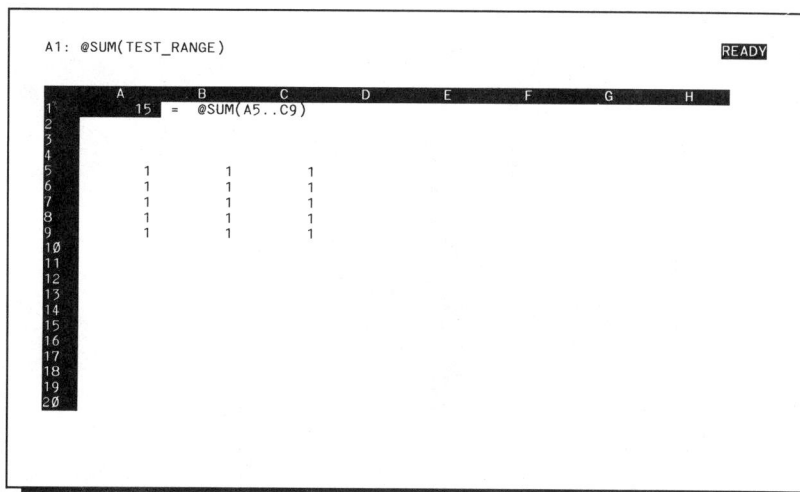

Figure 2.2 ◆ *Revised TEST_RANGE after worksheet changes*

Range names are vulnerable in the same way, but use only the upper left and lower right corners for their definition, even if you create the name using the other pair of corners. The next example demonstrates this.

Figure 2.3 should look familiar: this time the @sum formula has been duplicated, but uses the other pair of corners to define the sum range: @sum(B17..G7). To the left of each formula is the actual cell display as seen in the control panel. Both refer to TEST_RANGE because both are defining the same rectangle of cells.

In Figure 2.4, a blank cell has been moved to G7, destroying the range B17..G7. The second formula now shows ERR, because it referenced the range using those same coordinates, as still shown in text to its right. In cell A4, it appears that the name TEST_RANGE has also gone to ERR, but don't let that mislead you. This is one of the technicalities of range names and ranges that can be confusing.

The name was displayed in this formula because the range of cells was, indeed, TEST_RANGE. But the coordinates that were destroyed were not those that defined that name. When the formula's reference was destroyed, the coordinates changed to ERR and the name could obviously no longer be displayed.

The first formula is still intact, and to its left you can see the range name. Both this formula and the range name use the upper left and lower right cells for their definitions: B7..G17. They were therefore able to survive the destruction of the range that was defined by the opposite pair of cells, B17..G7.

```
B3:  @SUM(TEST_RANGE)                                              READY

            A           B       C       D       E       F       G
1
2
3   @SUM(TEST_RANGE)    66  =  @SUM(B7..G17)
4   @SUM(TEST_RANGE)    66  =  @SUM(B17..G7)
5
6
7                        1       1       1       1       1       1
8                        1       1       1       1       1       1
9                        1       1       1       1       1       1
10                       1       1       1       1       1       1
11                       1       1       1       1       1       1
12                       1       1       1       1       1       1
13                       1       1       1       1       1       1
14                       1       1       1       1       1       1
15                       1       1       1       1       1       1
16                       1       1       1       1       1       1
17                       1       1       1       1       1       1
18
19
20
```

Figure 2.3 ◆ *Two @sum formulas using opposite corners of TEST_RANGE*

```
B3:  @SUM(TEST_RANGE)                                              READY

            A           B       C       D       E       F       G
1
2
3   @SUM(TEST_RANGE)    65  =  @SUM(B7..G17)
4   @SUM(ERR)           ERR =  @SUM(B17..G7)
5
6
7                        1       1       1       1       1
8                        1       1       1       1       1       1
9                        1       1       1       1       1       1
10                       1       1       1       1       1       1
11                       1       1       1       1       1       1
12                       1       1       1       1       1       1
13                       1       1       1       1       1       1
14                       1       1       1       1       1       1
15                       1       1       1       1       1       1
16                       1       1       1       1       1       1
17                       1       1       1       1       1       1
18
19
20
```

Figure 2.4 ◆ *Destroying a cornerstone cell destroys a range*

The range B7..G17 can be destroyed by popping the upper left cell, which kills the remaining formula as well as the range name. Where did the name TEST_RANGE go? Using the Range Name Table command to place the list of range names into the worksheet would show that the coordinates of TEST_RANGE are ERR—it, too, is lost forever and must be redefined.

RANGE NAMES HAVE PRIORITY OVER CELL ADDRESSES

Here is a fact about range names that illustrates their power: when referenced in formulas, range names always take precedence over the cell addresses that they name. If a formula references a range that is named, the name will appear within the formula, replacing the cell coordinates (except when editing the formula).

You can redefine the address of a named range by using the Range Name Create command. When asked to enter the range for the existing name, press the Backspace key, and the name will be "unglued" from the cells it defines. Then define the name's new worksheet range.

Although this gives range names some real control, it can also be dangerous. In this section, you will see two examples: the first illustrates one of the worst kinds of spreadsheet bugs, and the second is a great trick for revising many formulas with just one small routine.

Figure 2.5 shows a worksheet with cell entries in C4, C6, and C8. In column D are formulas that refer to each number in C, as reflected in column F, where each formula is shown formatted as text. Notice the formula in D6; it refers to cell C6, which has the range name MY_CELL. Sum formulas in C10 and D10 total each column.

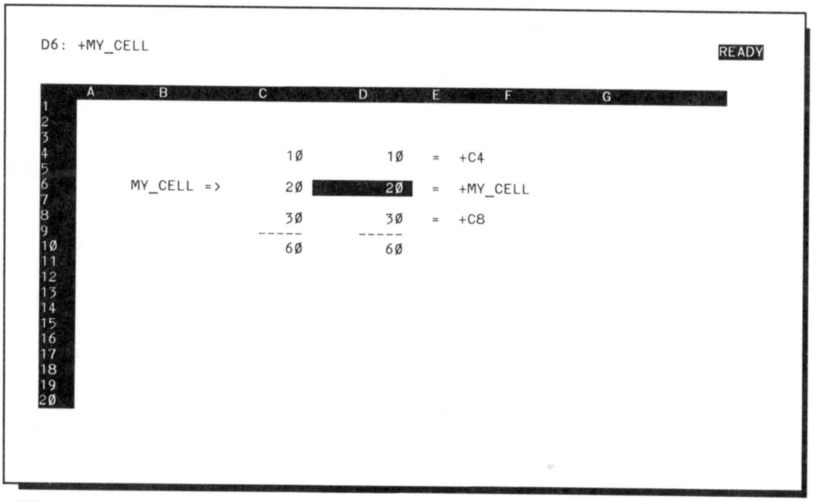

Figure 2.5 ◆ *Range name MY_CELL*

Suppose you decide to change the name MY_CELL from C6 to C8. You could use these commands to redefine the name:

/rncMY_CELL ˜ {bs}C8 ˜

If you did, you would get the results shown in Figure 2.6. C8 is now named MY_CELL, and the formula in D8 refers to it. Unfortunately, D6 still refers to MY_CELL, and the duplication is reflected in the sum formulas—the two columns are no longer equal.

Range names take priority over the cell addresses, and what happened is consistent with that: any formula that refers to a range name will address the new location when the name is redefined, as though the Move command had been used to move the cells. If you do not want that to happen, which is usually the case, follow this simple rule: delete before you redefine a name's address.

By deleting the range name first, all references to it will revert back to the underlying cell addresses, where they will safely remain when you define the name in a new location. The commands to replace those shown above would be as follows:

/rndMY_CELL ˜ /rncMY_CELL ˜ C8 ˜

Here is a trick that takes advantage of the danger illustrated above, and will let you quickly redefine the range coordinates in multiple formulas.

Figure 2.7 shows four formulas that reference a simple table. They all refer to the Amount column, range C4..C10, as shown to the right of each formula. The column labeled Extras is not included in any of the formulas.

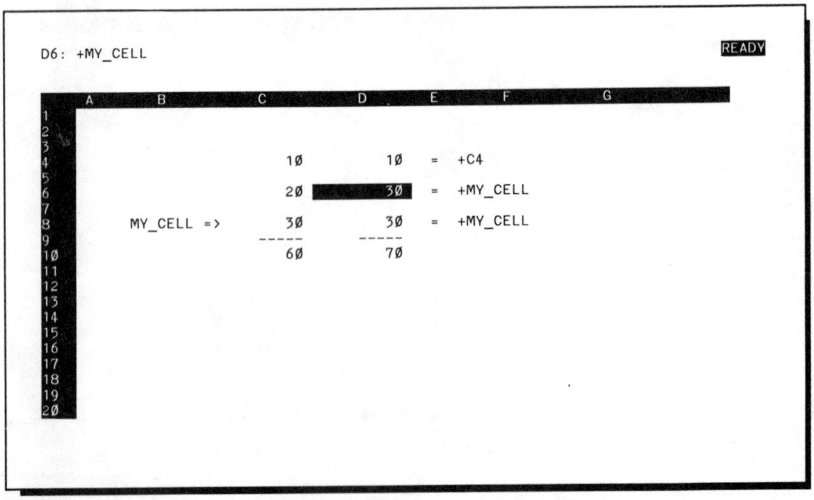

Figure 2.6 ◆ *Redefining a name can cause unexpected results*

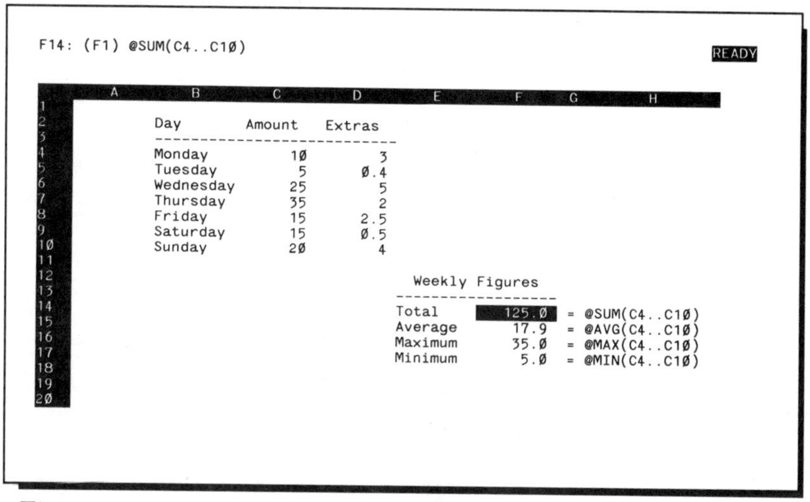

```
F14: (F1) @SUM(C4..C1Ø)                                              READY

         A          B         C         D        E        F     G        H
 1
 2       Day        Amount    Extras
 3       ------------------------------
 4       Monday          1Ø        3
 5       Tuesday          5      Ø.4
 6       Wednesday       25        5
 7       Thursday        35        2
 8       Friday          15      2.5
 9       Saturday        15      Ø.5
1Ø       Sunday          2Ø        4
11
12                            Weekly Figures
13                            ------------------
14       Total          125.Ø   = @SUM(C4..C1Ø)
15       Average         17.9   = @AVG(C4..C1Ø)
16       Maximum         35.Ø   = @MAX(C4..C1Ø)
17       Minimum          5.Ø   = @MIN(C4..C1Ø)
18
19
2Ø
```

Figure 2.7 ♦ *Formulas referencing a range*

What if you decided to include column D, Extras, in the @sum and other formulas? You could simply go to each formula and edit its contents, changing the reference from C4..C10 to C4..D10. This would be an adequate solution for 4 formulas, but what if you had 40, and they were scattered over a large worksheet? Here is a method that uses a range name to revise the formula references; it is fast and reliable.

This solution is based on the fact that formulas always follow a range's name as the name is expanded, contracted, moved, or redefined. Looking again at Figure 2.7, first assign a temporary range name, called TEMP, to the column that the formulas reference:

    /rncTEMP ˜ C4..C10 ˜

In Figure 2.8, each formula now refers to the named range TEMP. Notice that the display gives no indication of what the coordinates of that range are; the name TEMP has primary control.

The trick at this point is to redefine the range name while leaving the cells untouched. Simply expand the name TEMP one column to the right:

    /rncTEMP ˜ {right} ˜

The task is done, and since the name TEMP is no longer needed, it can be deleted.

    /rndTEMP ˜

```
F14: (F1) @SUM(TEMP)                                          READY

        A        B        C        D        E        F      G      H
 1
 2          Day       Amount    Extras
 3          ------------------------------
 4          Monday      10         3
 5          Tuesday      5        0.4
 6          Wednesday   25         5
 7          Thursday    35         2
 8          Friday      15        2.5
 9          Saturday    15        0.5
10          Sunday      20         4
11
12                             Weekly Figures
13                             -----------------
14                    Total      125.0    = @SUM(TEMP)
15                    Average     17.9    = @AVG(TEMP)
16                    Maximum     35.0    = @MAX(TEMP)
17                    Minimum      5.0    = @MIN(TEMP)
18
19
20
```

Figure 2.8 ◆ *Creating the range name TEMP*

Figure 2.9 shows the finished worksheet. The Amount and Extras column have not been changed, but the formulas now reference both, as the results show. Looking to the right of each formula, you will see that the TEMP name is gone, but the coordinates it had defined have been left in its place.

Note that if you really did have 40 formulas referring to the range C4..C10, then you should absolutely give the range a name of its own. The solution to the problem would have been more obvious.

> **TIP** ◆ *You may want to rename a range name while leaving its range address intact. For example, change the name of the range A1..L20 from ALL_YEAR to JAN_DEC. You don't have to delete the first name when you create the second. Instead, follow the keystrokes*
>
> **/rncALL_YEAR ˜ {edit}**
>
> *and you will be in Edit mode and able to change the name. When you are done, press Enter and A1..L20 will now have the new name JAN_DEC. Any formulas that referred to the old name will refer to the new one.*

◆ *FUNCTION KEY F3:* {*name*} _____

Instead of typing a range name in response to a Lotus command prompt, you can press the F3 {name} key to display a menu of all available range names.

```
F14: (F1) @SUM(C4..D1Ø)                                              READY

          A      B          C           D        E       F       G        H
1
2           Day          Amount     Extras
3          -------------------------------
4           Monday          1Ø          3
5           Tuesday          5         Ø.4
6           Wednesday       25          5
7           Thursday        35          2
8           Friday          15         2.5
9           Saturday        15         Ø.5
1Ø          Sunday          2Ø          4
11
12                              Weekly Figures
13                              ---------------
14                         Total      142.4    = @SUM(C4..D1Ø)
15                         Average     1Ø.2    = @AVG(C4..D1Ø)
16                         Maximum     35.Ø    = @MAX(C4..D1Ø)
17                         Minimum      Ø.4    = @MIN(C4..D1Ø)
18
19
2Ø
```

Figure 2.9 ♦ _Formulas now reference the redefined range_

The pointer can then be used to choose a name, which will be accepted by the command. Choosing in this way alleviates the pressure of having to spell a name exactly, especially when there can be names that look like these:

```
TTL_SALES_COMM
MG_PER_LITER
SWT_PRTY_LGST
```

Just as in file operations where file names are displayed, you can display a full screen of range names by pressing the {name} key a second time. This can be helpful when you are searching for a particular name.

In Release 2.01, you cannot use the {name} key to enter a range name into a formula. This restriction was removed in Release 2.2 to allow you to employ F3 while editing a cell to place a range name into a formula. However, note that F3 cannot place a range name into a non-formula cell, such as a text cell found in a macro.

The {name} key works in all Lotus commands that require a range to be specified, including the function key F5 {goto}. Here are several examples of commands that accept range names as input, and can therefore use the {name} key.

- ♦ Copy and Move, both From and To ranges

- ♦ All Range commands—Format, Label, Erase, and so on

- ♦ File Xtract (range)

2.2 ♦ —————

- Print Printer Range

- Data Query Input, Criterion, and Output

- Data Sort Data-Range and Sort Key Columns

- Graph A-range, B-range, C-range, and so on

- Graph Options Data-Labels A, B, C, and so on

If you frequently refer to the list of names and their coordinates while writing formulas or macros, try the following short macro. It will let you move through and view the list, and when you press Enter you will escape back to the worksheet:

```
/rnc{name}{?}{esc 5}
```

If you only want to use this routine while editing, start the macro with an Enter, to leave the edit mode, and finish it with an {edit} command to return to editing the cell:

```
~/rnc{name}{?}{esc 5}{edit}
```

◆ USING RANGE NAMES IN FORMULAS

Writing formulas is a frequent chore in a worksheet, and formulas are frequent sources of errors. Their inner workings are hidden from view, and long formulas can be difficult to decipher or debug. Range names can help on all of these points.

REFERENCING RANGES

When a formula refers to a named cell or range, the name appears in the formula in place of the cell coordinates. The advantages of this are twofold. First, the name makes the formula readable by replacing a meaningless cell address with a descriptive name. Second, a formula that should refer to a named cell will be quite obviously in error when the name does not appear in the formula.

It is important to keep each worksheet variable in its own cell (see Chapter 3). A *variable cell* is an important item in the worksheet that will be referenced frequently, and whose contents might be changed as the worksheet develops or what-if tests are made. If each variable has a range name, then referencing the variable in a formula is greatly simplified, the formula becomes readable, and any mistakes will be immediately visible.

For example, the following formula means nothing in itself, and there is no way of telling if it is correctly written:

+$B$16*(1+$H$29)

With range names, the formula comes to life and displays its meaning even to the first-time user:

+$RETAIL*(1+$SALES_TAX)

Figure 2.10 shows a more complex example. The formula in cell AE124 is displayed in text in row 127, and can also be seen in the control panel. Row 130 shows the formula again as text, but this time without range names, as it would appear in the edit window. As you can see, range names make the formula much more readable. You can read the formula in row 127 as follows: "If ITEM number is greater than 50, include sales tax from TABLE_CODES, based on the STATE_CODE number, otherwise just show cell RETAIL."

RANGE NAMES IN LINKED FORMULAS

2.2 ◆ ———

In Release 2.2, range names follow all of these rules except in the case of formulas that link to another worksheet. Although not dangerously different, you should be aware of how to use names in linking formulas.

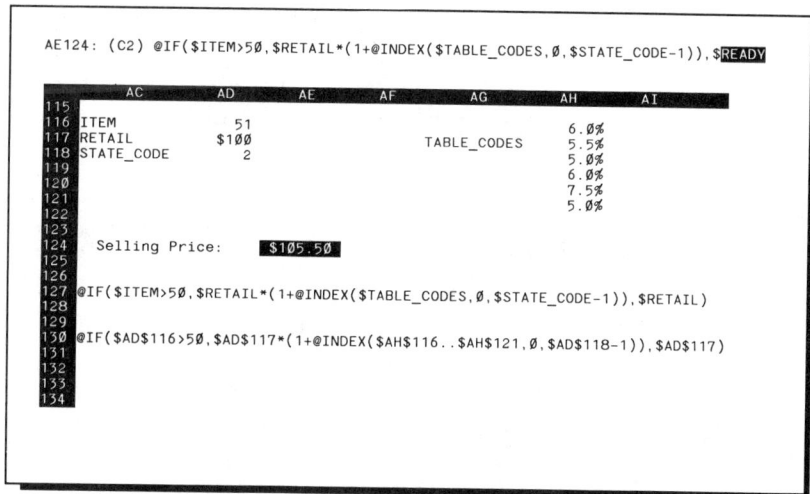

```
AE124:  (C2) @IF($ITEM>5Ø,$RETAIL*(1+@INDEX($TABLE_CODES,Ø,$STATE_CODE-1)),$    READY

            AC          AD        AE        AF        AG        AH        AI
115
116  ITEM            51                                        6.Ø%
117  RETAIL        $1ØØ                      TABLE_CODES       5.5%
118  STATE_CODE       2                                        5.Ø%
119                                                            6.Ø%
120                                                            7.5%
121                                                            5.Ø%
122
123
124     Selling Price:        $1Ø5.5Ø
125
126
127  @IF($ITEM>5Ø,$RETAIL*(1+@INDEX($TABLE_CODES,Ø,$STATE_CODE-1)),$RETAIL)
128
129
130  @IF($AD$116>5Ø,$AD$117*(1+@INDEX($AH$116..$AH$121,Ø,$AD$118-1)),$AD$117)
131
132
133
134
```

Figure 2.10 ◆ *Range names add clarity to formulas*

When you use a range name in a linking formula, the name appears in the formula as it normally does if it is a valid name in the source spreadsheet. For example:

+ <<MYFILE>>MYCELLNAME

But unlike a worksheet formula, the range name's underlying cell addresses are not brought in from the source file. Therefore, when you edit the linking formula, the range name remains and does not turn into its cell address. In the same vein, if you write a linking formula that refers to a cell address that happens to have a range name, the cell address and not the name will appear in the formula.

Deleting a name in the source worksheet will cause a linking formula that refers to it to result in ERR. The formula will not revert back to the name's actual address as a normal formula would.

Even though the address of the name is not used, you can still copy a linking formula that has a range name and it will adjust relative to its new position, just as it does in formulas within the worksheet. Suppose the name MYCELLNAME in the example above referred to cell J21. If you copied the linking formula one cell to the right and one row down, the resulting formula would look like this:

+ <<MYFILE>>K22

As you can see, copying the formula to an adjoining cell gives you a convenient way to determine the exact cell address of the range name—something you can't find out by simply editing the formula.

Remember that a linking formula only refers to a single-cell range. If you enter the range C1..E9, 1-2-3 simply truncates it to C1. If you refer to a multicelled range name, don't be misled by the name appearing in the formula; while the name is accepted in the formula, only the value in the upper left corner of the range is used.

DEBUGGING AND DOCUMENTATION

Formulas not only become more readable with range names, but any errors in range addressing can be clearly seen, since the range name does not appear within the finished formula.

Often a formula that contains a reference to a worksheet variable is copied to a series of cells, where each performs a calculation on the adjacent cell. The variable is given an absolute reference so that it will not adjust as the formula is copied. If a cell named TSP_PER_LB is the variable, using it in a formula produces this series:

```
+D4*$TSP_PER_LB
+D5*$TSP_PER_LB
+D6*$TSP_PER_LB
+D7*$TSP_PER_LB
+D8*$TSP_PER_LB
```

If one of those formulas were to be accidentally changed or be overwritten, you might get lucky and later see an unreasonable result displayed. If you were not that lucky, you would still notice a problem when you compare the formulas in the column and see references such as these:

```
+D4*$TSP_PER_LB
+D5*$TSP_PER_LB
+D6*C4
+D7*$TSP_PER_LB
+D8*$TSP_PER_LB
```

One way to quickly scan a column of formulas for addressing accuracy is to format the column as text, and expand the column so that the entire formula is visible. Instead of seeing the results of each formula on the screen, you instead see the actual cell contents, just as it appears in the control panel when the pointer is on the formula's cell.

Here is a fast way to scan a long column of formulas for correct cell references when the preceding technique (formatting as text and expanding the column) cannot be fully exploited because the formulas are wider than 72 characters, the width of the 1-2-3 display. It utilizes the print option for Cell-Formulas, and prints the formulas to a disk file. In this format, the range names are shown in each formula, just as though you were viewing it in the control panel of the display, except the entire formula is displayed. Use these print settings:

- ◆ Print to File, enter a file name
- ◆ Range is the range of formulas
- ◆ Options Margin Left to 0
- ◆ Options Margin Right to 240
- ◆ Options Other Unformatted
- ◆ Options Other Cell-Formulas
- ◆ Go

You can then use the System command to go to DOS where the file can be viewed, or use the File Import command to bring the text file back into the worksheet for viewing. In the example shown above, the print file would look like this:

```
E4:     (F2) +D4*$TSP_PER_LB
E5:     (F2) +D5*$TSP_PER_LB
E6:     (F2) +D6*C4
E7:     (F2) +D7*$TSP_PER_LB
E8:     (F2) +D8*$TSP_PER_LB
```

Even when you print the formulas you may not be able to view them in their entirety if you use many range names in them. The maximum right margin when printing is 240, the same as the maximum length of a cell entry, and a formula with range names could conceivably be longer than this.

You might wonder how Lotus could allow the formula in the first place if it were over 240 characters. Even though Lotus displays the range names in the control panel, it uses the actual cell addresses for internal housekeeping within the program. When printing to disk, though, the range names are used, and the resulting output could have lines of text that exceed 240 characters.

◆ WORKSHEET COMMANDS

You can use range names instead of coordinates (or pointing to coordinates) in every worksheet command that requires a range to be specified. Since coordinates can change as you use worksheets, each time you go to sort, print, or graph a range you must first make a note of the addresses of a pair of the range's diagonal corner cells. The name of a range, on the other hand, is always the same no matter how the coordinates have expanded, contracted, or moved.

Although range names are actually displayed within the text of a formula, this is not so in worksheet commands. Once a name is used as the input range in a command, it is replaced by the ranges's coordinates. Try this with a named range in your worksheet:

```
/ppcarMY_RANGE ˜ r
```

You will see that Lotus highlights MY_RANGE as the range to be printed, but the cell coordinates, not the name, are displayed in the control panel. There is no way of telling if those coordinates are the correct ones without comparing them against those of MY_RANGE.

When in doubt of the accuracy of an existing range setting in a command, clear the setting and again specify the range using the range name.

PREVENTING DISASTER

Consistently using range names for frequent, critical operations can save the life of your worksheet. One of the worst disasters is to sort a range of data without including all of the relevant columns within the sort range. Unless you have a recent copy saved to disk, you might not be able to untangle the scrambled records.

If you regularly sort several ranges in a worksheet, you should give each one a name, such as SORT_RANGE1 and SORT_RANGE2. As always, the coordinates of those ranges continually change as you insert rows or columns, or move data to a new location, but only the name of the data range is needed whenever you sort. Not only does this give you more control, but it can save you time and possibly save the life of your data.

⊗ **CAUTION** ◆ *You can still court disaster if you want to include an adjacent column within the range to be sorted, but forget to revise the name to include that column. Remember that the ultimate device for control is a recently saved copy of the worksheet— always save the worksheet before performing potentially dangerous commands.*

FILE OPERATIONS

During a File Combine command when bringing in a Named or Specified Range from another worksheet, you are prompted to enter the name or coordinates of the range. In Lotus 2, you can use either a range name or the range coordinates, but note that in Lotus 1A you were required to use a range name. Other than for keyboard-invocable macros, this is the only time that range names have been a requirement in Lotus.

If you are going to perform the File Combine operation only once, you could use the coordinates of the range had you previously made a note of them. Throughout the life of a worksheet, though, the range coordinates change many times. If you will be combining a specific range from a worksheet regularly, then that range should definitely have a name.

When consolidating several worksheets into one, there is all the more reason to use a range name in each of them, and it can be the same name for all files. Even though the range may fall in different locations in each worksheet, the name will catch them all.

For example, if three worksheets each have a similar summary area showing worksheet totals, you could name that range YEARLY_TOTAL. Consolidating all three into one grand total would be done with this simple, easy-to-read macro:

```
/fcanYEARLY_TOTAL ˜ FILE_1 ˜
/fcanYEARLY_TOTAL ˜ FILE_2 ˜
/fcanYEARLY_TOTAL ˜ FILE_3 ˜
```

The File Xtract command saves a specified range in the current worksheet to a separate file. As usual, you can save much time, and prevent addressing errors, by having a range name already prepared. If you perform the Xtract command regularly, having a name for the range makes the procedure almost effortless.

EMBEDDED RANGES

The Graph Options Titles and Graph Options Legend commands take text entries as their input; you won't be able to point to or type in a range as you do, for example, with the Print Range command. However, as will be explained in Chapter 11, you can also refer to a cell in the worksheet that contains the text for the title or legend by proceeding the address or range name of that cell with a backslash.

In Release 2.2, this same method will also allow you to define a print header or footer. In all of these commands, it is essential that you refer only to range names, never to cell addresses.

This is important because, as with macros, your entries are just text and their range references will not adjust as changes are made in the worksheet. If you enter the reference \B5 to one of these commands and later insert a row at B3, your reference will no longer be to the correct cell. Unless you specifically plan not to move any of the referenced cells, it is critical that you use range names. Instead of \B5, you could use a range name such as \GRAPH_TITLE1 or \PRN_HEADER1.

2.2 ◆ ────

◆ MACROS ─────────────────────────────

All the benefits of range names that have so far been discussed in relation to formulas and commands also apply to macros. Range names add convenience and speed when writing macros, reduce errors when referencing cell addresses, and provide an excellent documentation and debugging tool. But there is one characteristic of macros that is not true of formulas or worksheet commands: they are text that cannot respond to changes in the worksheet. This makes the use of range names an absolute necessity.

(MACROS) – (RANGE NAMES) = ERR

Here is a primary rule for writing macros that will be repeated again and again: *In macros, never use cell coordinates to reference a location in the worksheet.* For example, don't write a macro like this:

```
{let B16,M29}{goto}R31 ~
```

Instead, write this:

```
{let YTD,DEC_TOTAL}{goto}MONTHLY ~
```

This rule is based on the simple fact that macros are nothing more than static text in the worksheet. They do not adjust to worksheet cell movements, as do formulas, nor do they have the benefit of an all-knowing user who can take the time to note the current coordinates of a range before executing a worksheet command. Skirting this rule by including hard cell coordinates within a macro is the most common cause of macros that destroy worksheets.

Now that this rule has been eternally etched in granite, don't forget the exception to it discussed in Chapter 1. When macros are written as string formulas, they will adjust to changes in the worksheet just like any other formula. You can safely include cell addresses in these macros; they will always reference the correct range, even when that range is moved.

MACROS THAT TELL A STORY

Macros, like formulas, can be agonizing to decipher when only hard cell addresses are used:

```
{if J13 = M44}{branch AA109}
```

With range names, they become not only readable, but descriptive:

```
{if DEPT_TOTAL = DEPT_GOAL}{branch \REACHED_GOAL}
```

A worksheet can use macros to carry out all the normal routines and duties. When macros use range names, and each line of code is one logical step of the routine, the need for detailed macro descriptions almost disappears. The reader can quickly scan the macro to get a clear picture of what is happening, and the macros become an excellent, built-in form of documentation.

The debugging process for macros that do not use range names can be a nightmare. Trying to trace the course of each step involves many excursions around the worksheet to track down the cell references. Each one must be checked to verify what is in that location, and if that address is still relevant to the macro. When range names have been used, then the intent of the macro is clear, and you are assured that the macro still addresses the cells that the names define.

◆ THE RANGE NAME TABLE COMMAND

The Range Name Table command produces an alphabetical listing of all range names and their addresses in the worksheet. It requires two columns, and the names and addresses in the table will overwrite anything in those columns.

Although it may be used infrequently, a table of range names and addresses can be a convenient tool for dealing with worksheet documentation and maintenance. It is a feature that was missing from Lotus 1A, where a list of range names could only be kept by hand.

DOCUMENTING THE WORKSHEET

A complete list of range names and addresses aids in determining the general flow of worksheet routines. Assuming that the names were not created at random, it can serve as a sort of guidebook to the important locations in the worksheet.

As a part of the worksheet's permanent documentation, the range name table becomes a record of all range names and their addresses within the worksheet. As the developer of the worksheet, you can add a short description next to each name. This can be a first-rate tool when modifications are necessary.

BROWSING THE TABLE

You can track down destroyed (popped) range names by looking through the addresses for ERR, and mistakes in naming style can also be found in this way. Here is a range name list showing a macro that was named with a forward slash instead of a backslash, and a name that now references ERR:

```
/PRINT_DATA        B41
BALANCE            Q159..AA169
```

INTEREST_RATE	B26
MONTHLY_INPUT	M100..P125
TOTALS	ERR
\M	B33
\MENU1	B36

Names can be checked for spelling errors that would cause future problems when using them, and a series of names that cover similar and adjacent ranges can be verified for accuracy. Notice the misspelling of QTR_2, and the range address of QTR_3 in this list:

QRR_2	O100..R200
QTR_1	K100..N200
QTR_3	S98..V198
QTR_4	W100..Z200

SORTING THE TABLE

You can find duplicate range names (which name the same cell or range) by sorting the list with the address column as the primary sort key. In this order, all ranges that begin in the same "neighborhood" are grouped together.

By writing a string formula to pull out the last part of each address, you can sort them on the second address coordinate, such as the G8 in F6..G8. This sorting technique is described in detail in Chapter 13. To extract the second half of the address from the cell at B17, the following string formula would be used (it will work on any range address):

@right(B17,@length(B17) – @find(".",B17,0) – 2)

USING THE TABLE AS A DATABASE

Here is another trick that uses the range name table as the input for a Data Query Find command. The @find function is used as the criterion to search on all characters in each record. This string function serves as a powerful ally of the Data Query command; their combined use is covered more thoroughly in Chapter 10.

Figure 2.11 shows the layout for this interesting combination of Lotus features. The Range Name Table command has been invoked with the cell pointer in cell A13. The column of addresses serves as the data input range, and it is given a column title, Address, in cell B12.

```
D16: @FIND("F",B13,0)+1                                          READY

        A           B          C          D         E       F       G
11
12  Name        Address
13  A           B2
14  B           B3..C3
15  C         * F3                         Address         <=
16  D           B5                            ERR          <= Criterion
17  E         * F6..G8
18  F           B7
19  G           B8
20  H           D2
21  I           E4
22  J           D6
23  K         * E10..F12
24  L           H14
25
26
27
28
29
30
```

Figure 2.11 ◆ *Data Query on the range name table*

The criterion used in this case, D15..D16, will find all range names that use column F as either of their borders. Cell D16 holds the string function @find, as shown here and also in the control panel at the top of the screen:

> @find("F",B13,0) + 1

Using this formula ensures that all occurrences of the letter *F* in the table will be found. This includes any *internal occurrences*—that is, any characters to the right of the first character of the address. The addition of 1 to the result of the @find allows the criteria to select addresses that have an *F* as the first character and do not have another *F*. The addresses that will be found in the table are noted with an asterisk (*).

Don't be stymied by the ERR displayed by the formula in D16. Because the address in B13, which it references, does not contain an F, the formula returns an ERR, as it always will when the character being sought is not found. The displayed result will not affect the search.

2.2 ◆ ———

Use the Range Search command in Release 2.2 to find specified cell addresses within the range name table. When looking for a specific row, column, or address, you can limit the range of the search to the address column. Using this command is easier than setting up a data query command, but because it only searches for text, its capabilities are very limited.

For example, with the data query routine you could search for all addresses in the range name table that are beyond column Z by using this criterion, where B10 is the first record in the address column of the table:

> @code(@mid(B10,1,1)) > = 65

So use the Range Search command for quick or straightforward searches, but don't hesitate to structure a database (a relatively simple task) to perform more complex searches.

In a large worksheet with dozens of names, these techniques can save time and prevent errors by letting you easily check for names that cover specific rows or columns or individual addresses.

◆ SUMMARY

Without range names, the 1-2-3 worksheet would be an inflexible and difficult working environment. In this chapter, you have seen how range names can enhance worksheet formulas, commands, and macros. Range names simplify the job of entering cell references, while also ensuring accuracy. By using them for all the major functions of the worksheet, you create a primary source of worksheet documentation.

In the next chapter, you will learn how to build worksheets that reflect your design intentions and perform reliably. As in any construction process, even minor attention to worksheet planning and layout will bring major rewards as a job continues.

THREE:

Building Worksheets That Work

3

◆ ◆ ◆

THE WORKSHEET ENVIRONMENT'S POWER AND FLEXIBILITY
allow projects to be created in practically any manner that suits your needs.
There is no ideal way to construct a worksheet, but whatever method is applied
should follow a consistent design framework. The results will be predictable,
and the worksheet will be easy to navigate.

In this chapter, the building process is described in terms of the components
that make up a worksheet: the types of data and where the data can be placed
for efficient use of the worksheet. The need for separating worksheet variables
from formulas is discussed, with emphasis on the importance of giving those
variables range names.

By relating to other cells in the worksheet, formulas serve as a web that binds
the cells together. This chapter discusses techniques for writing formulas, and
how that job can be facilitated through the use of several important formula
tools, including variables, range names, intermediate formula step cells, and
absolute cell references, which allow formulas to be copied anywhere in the
worksheet without losing track of the cells to which they refer.

If you are being overwhelmed by the size of your worksheets, the last part of
this chapter will be of help. It deals with controlling worksheet memory
requirements by eliminating excess data, avoiding sinister "blank but not
empty" cells, entering numbers instead of formulas, and structuring databases
for efficiency.

◆ WORKSHEET LAYOUT: DATA, VARIABLES, AND MACROS

A worksheet with thousands of active cells has a tremendous number of
unique components. If they are not logically structured, the quantity and
diversity of these parts can undermine the performance and reliability of the
worksheet.

Although you may be faced with a seemingly countless number of cells, they will fall into several broad categories:

◆ Cells or ranges that give the user visual control of the normal worksheet routines

◆ Variable cells or tables

◆ Macros

◆ Input Data

◆ Process Data

◆ Output Data

By keeping these categories in mind while building the application, you will automatically establish a framework that will help you to control activities within the worksheet.

VISUAL CONTROL OF ROUTINE PROCESSES

No cells or ranges are more important than those that give the user visual control, even though their function is purely extraneous in that it is in no way required by the mechanical processes of a worksheet. The purpose of these ranges is similar in all worksheet applications: to assist the user with the normal operating chores of the worksheet.

Provide a Safe Harbor with the Home Screen

During the construction phase, just about every cell in a worksheet application is somehow addressed. The cell pointer is constantly jumping about as various parts are slowly put together. When the job is done, though, the normal worksheet routines usually require that only a few areas actually be reached by the cell pointer.

Organize the movement of the cell pointer to these areas by providing the user with a home screen. This is a one-screen range of cells that is used as the "home base" for all movement within the worksheet. Whenever the cell pointer jumps to a range to perform a task, such as entering data or viewing formula results, it is always returned to the home screen, from which other tasks can then be performed.

The usefulness of the home screen depends upon two considerations. First, assume that the cell pointer will be moved about among different ranges during the normal operation of the worksheet. Of course, there are instances, although not typical, when only one section of a worksheet will be used. A loan amortization worksheet might include just one range, as opposed to a worksheet containing multiple financial tools in several different locations.

Second, the home screen is most effective when it is used in concert with macros. By choosing a location from a View menu, as discussed in Chapter 1, you can make the cell pointer jump to a different range while under macro control and then return to the home screen via another macro. The user does not need to know its location or range name. Figure 3.1 shows a home screen that could be used in almost any situation. In this case, the screen is windowed. The lower one has only one row, while the home screen occupies the upper 18 rows.

★ **TRICK** ◆ *Using a windowed display is a throwback to Lotus 1A, when the {windowsoff} macro command was not available. Macros execute more quickly when the display does not have to be constantly refreshed, which is why the {windowsoff} command in Lotus 2 is so effective. Running macros in a small display, such as the one-row window shown in Figure 3.1, has the same effect on their performance because it eliminates 19 rows of screen rewriting. Besides allowing macros to run faster, the split screen also provides a stable display and a convenient place for the macro to pass messages to the user, benefits that are valuable even beyond Lotus 1A.*

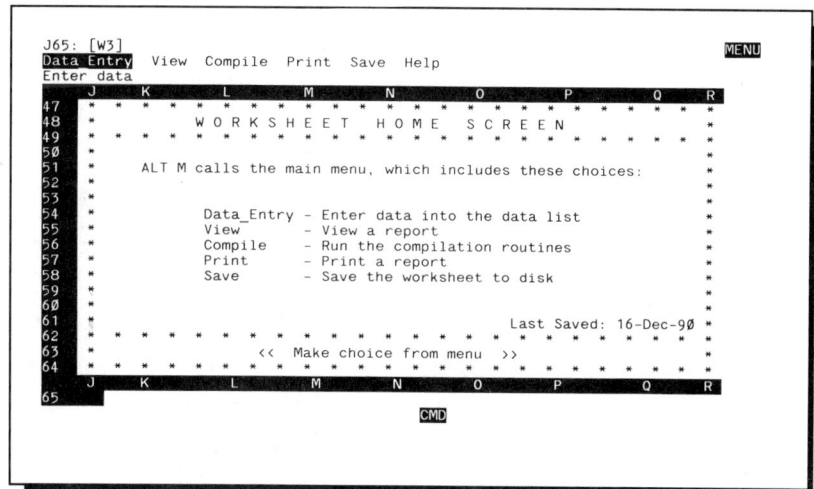

```
J65: [W3]                                                    MENU
Data Entry  View  Compile  Print  Save  Help
Enter data
   J    K     L      M      N      O      P      Q      R
47 *  *   *    *   *    *   *    *   *    *   *    *   *    *   *
48 *           W O R K S H E E T   H O M E   S C R E E N       *
49 *  *   *    *   *    *   *    *   *    *   *    *   *    *   *
50 *                                                           *
51 *      ALT M calls the main menu, which includes these choices:  *
52 *                                                           *
53 *                                                           *
54 *           Data_Entry - Enter data into the data list      *
55 *           View       - View a report                      *
56 *           Compile    - Run the compilation routines       *
57 *           Print      - Print a report                     *
58 *           Save       - Save the worksheet to disk         *
59 *                                                           *
60 *                                                           *
61 *                              Last Saved: 16-Dec-90 *
62 *  *   *    *   *    *   *    *   *    *   *    *   *    *   *
63 *              << Make choice from menu >>                   *
64 *  *   *    *   *    *   *    *   *    *   *    *   *    *   *
   J    K     L      M      N      O      P      Q      R
65
                              CMD
```

Figure 3.1 ◆ *A home screen for a worksheet application*

It can be disconcerting to be left with a completely static screen as a result of the {windowsoff} command. By splitting the screen in this manner, the cell pointer can do its mad dance in the lower window, indicating macro activity to the user, while the upper one remains stable and continues to display messages.

In many instances, a split screen can be an advantage during macro routines. For instance, while the cell pointer is active in the lower window, column widths can be adjusted before printing a range. Since the changes were made in the lower window, they are not permanent and will be gone when that window is cleared.

To automate the jump back to the home screen, a macro subroutine is needed. Here is one that is built on the macro that was shown in Chapter 1; its name could be \GO_HOME:

```
/wtc/wwc{goto}HOME_SCREEN~{down 18}/wwh/wwu
{let MESSAGE_PAD,MESSAGE1}
{window}{branch \M}
```

This one routine refreshes the display to the home screen, no matter where the cell pointer is located when the routine is called.

First, any worksheet titles are cleared, as is the worksheet window. The cell pointer jumps to the home screen (here named HOME_SCREEN), moves down 18 rows, and splits the screen horizontally. The two windows are unsynchronized, so that cell pointer movement in one will not scroll the other.

The macro {let} statement then copies one of the messages, MESSAGE1, to the MESSAGE_PAD cell. At that point, the cell pointer is hopped to the lower window. Finally, the main menu is called, leaving the user in the home position, as shown in Figure 3.1.

This home screen is surrounded by a border, just generic asterisks here, with a title area at the top. This is followed by a brief reminder about using Alt-M to call the main menu, and below this is a list of the choices on the main menu.

Lower down and to the right is a cell that contains the date on which the worksheet was last saved. The worksheet file is dated by DOS when it is saved, and having that information in the worksheet can be helpful. Of course, this dating system is only reliable when the computer's system date has been set correctly on startup, and when a macro is used to enter the date saved:

```
{let DATE_SAVED,@now}/fsFILENAME~r{esc}
```

Below the date last saved is one row that serves as a message area. During the macro routines that drive the worksheet, appropriate status messages can be displayed in this row. The left-hand cell of this row can be named MESSAGE-_PAD or STATUS_REPORT; if you want more than one row for messages, use two cells for that name. Before branching to a macro routine that involves some waiting, the macro can display a message:

```
{let MESSAGE_PAD,MESSAGE3}
{\DO_PRINT1}
{let MESSAGE_PAD,MESSAGE1}
{branch \M}
```

In this example, there are several message cells that can be copied by the {let} statement to the home screen message area, as explained in the next section. In Figure 3.1 the message being displayed is the default, MESSAGE1, which simply reminds the user that a menu is active and that a choice needs to be made.

Status Messages during Macro Routines

The home screen need only be as large as one screen, but quite a few prompts may be displayed in the message row of that screen. A separate area for these messages makes it easy to add to or revise them. You should create messages for any routine that takes more than a few seconds to execute. They can also show progress reports at different stages of a routine, a technique which was used for debugging macros in Chapter 1. Here are some typical one-line messages:

```
<<   Make choice from menu   >>
<<   Printing, please wait   >>
<<   Saving worksheet to disk   >>
<<   Combining in FILE1   >>
<<   Combining in FILE2   >>
<<   Combining in FILE3   >>
<<   Calculating totals   >>
```

You can use several macro methods for choosing a message to be displayed, one of which uses the {let} statement as demonstrated in the previous section. First, though, give each message a range name. For example, the first two messages above would be named MESSAGE1 and MESSAGE2. Then, the message that is shown while printing can be displayed simply by copying MESSAGE2 to the message pad.

The Copy command could also be used in place of the macro {let} statement if the message were more than one line:

```
/cMESSAGE1 ˜ MESSAGE_PAD ˜
```

Another method involves using a string formula within the message pad which evaluates to a new message as a number in a flag cell is changed. The formula looks like this:

```
@index($MESSAGE_NAMES,0,$MESSAGE_CHOICE – 1)
```

The range MESSAGE_NAMES is the list of messages down one column, and MESSAGE_CHOICE is a cell containing the number of the message to be displayed. The @index function always refers to the first item on the list as item 0, so for convenience 1 is subtracted from the function's row reference (the value in MESSAGE_CHOICE). Therefore, when the cell MESSAGE_CHOICE is set to 1, the first message on the list is shown. The macro to set the message pad to the second message on the list looks like this:

```
{let MESSAGE_CHOICE,2}{recalc MESSAGE_PAD} ˜
```

The {recalc} command ensures that the formula in the message pad cell is evaluated to display the new message.

You may have noticed that the range names were made absolute in the formula ($MESSAGE_NAMES) but were not in the macro. This allows the formula to refer to the same cells no matter where it is copied. Macros, though, are just text that cannot change, so absolute or relative references are not an issue—the text in the macro will always refer to the named cell. Absolute references will be discussed in detail later in this chapter.

Help Screens

When building worksheet applications that will be used by others, including help screens can be good insurance against future problems. Help screens are larger and more informative than the one-line message pad, and can include brief directions for operating procedures, descriptions of worksheet data, or what to do in the event of a problem. They will not eliminate the need for more detailed instructions, but when they are coupled with macro-driven routines they can supply a valuable dose of information and confidence to the user.

For a complete system, every macro menu could have individual help choices that would display the appropriate message. For a simpler system of accessing help only while at the home screen, the main menu can have one choice labeled Help. This calls up a submenu of help items, from which a help screen is displayed.

One screen of the worksheet (18 rows if using the split-screen method) is named HELP_SCREEN, where one of the help messages is displayed. Figure 3.2 shows the macro structure to implement help in an application.

Choosing Help from the main menu calls the Help menu, \MENU4, with this menu subroutine call:

```
{menucall \MENU4}
{\HELP}{branch \M}
```

The Help menu has several choices, including one called More, that calls a second Help menu if more choices are needed (that menu is not shown here).

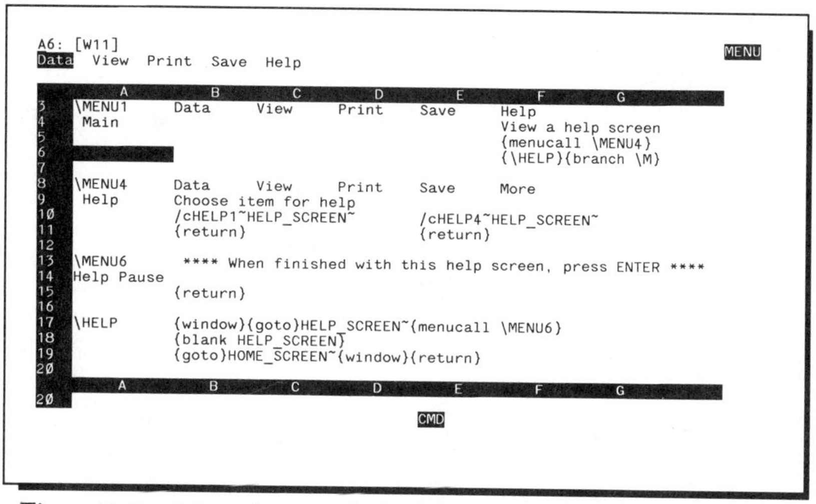

```
A6:  [W11]                                                              MENU
Data  View  Print  Save  Help

     A          B          C          D          E          F          G
3  \MENU1     Data       View       Print      Save       Help
4   Main                                                   View a help screen
5                                                          {menucall \MENU4}
6                                                          (\HELP){branch \M}
7
8  \MENU4     Data       View       Print      Save       More
9   Help      Choose item for help
10            /cHELP1~HELP_SCREEN~             /cHELP4~HELP_SCREEN~
11            {return}                         {return}
12
13 \MENU6     **** When finished with this help screen, press ENTER ****
14 Help Pause
15            {return}
16
17 \HELP      {window}{goto}HELP_SCREEN~(menucall \MENU6}
18            {blank HELP_SCREEN}
19            {goto}HOME_SCREEN~{window}{return}
20
     A          B          C          D          E          F          G
20
                                      CMD
```

Figure 3.2 ◆ *Menu choices to display help screens*

When a selection is made, the appropriate help screen is copied to the help display area, HELP_SCREEN. In this example, menu choice Data copies the range HELP1. The Save choice copies HELP_4:

        /cHELP4 ˜ HELP_SCREEN ˜
        {return}

Each help message consists of 18 cells of text down a column. Even a short help message should still be kept within an 18-cell range. That way, all the help message ranges will be the same size, and a short one can be expanded easily if necessary.

   Note that the Copy command is used instead of the macro {let} statement since {let} can only reference a single cell. Once the data is copied, control is returned to the calling macro in the main menu.

   That macro then calls the help subroutine, \HELP, which handles the viewing of the help screen:

        {window}{goto}HELP_SCREEN ˜ {menucall \MENU6}
        {blank HELP_SCREEN}
        {goto}HOME_SCREEN ˜ {window}{return}

The cell pointer jumps to the upper window, and then to the help area, HELP_SCREEN. A subroutine {menucall} is made to \MENU6. Look at \MENU6 in Figure 3.2 and you will see that it only has one choice. With this menu active, the cell pointer is immovable in the help area and the user sees the one menu prompt on the screen:

   **** When finished with this help screen, press ENTER ****.

The only choice that can be made is the one that returns control to \HELP. That macro erases the help area to conserve the few hundred bytes of memory and disk space that the now unneeded message would occupy. It resets the display to the home screen, sends the cell pointer to the lower window, and returns control to the main menu. Note that pressing Escape from the help screen gives the same result as pressing Enter—the macro continues in the next step after the menu call.

> **TIP** ◆ *To save space within the worksheet, you can build another worksheet just for help messages. Every 18 lines (or 20 for a full-screen message) of that worksheet would contain one help screen, each with its own range name, such as MESSAGE1, MESSAGE2, and so on. After getting the number of the desired help message, the macro would perform the File Combine Named/Specified-Range command and bring in one of the help ranges from the help file. In the following example, the variable cell HELP_CHOICE holds the number (as text in this case) of the selected screen, and the help file is named MESSAGES:*

```
{window}{blank HELP_SCREEN}
{goto}HELP_SCREEN ˜
/fccnMESSAGE{HELP_CHOICE} ˜ MESSAGES ˜
{menucall \MENU6}
```

If you copy a blank cell to an occupied cell, the occupied cell will become blank. When performing a File Combine operation, though, an incoming blank cell will not erase an occupied cell. Since the incoming help message may not be a full 18 rows, the HELP_SCREEN range must first be erased for this technique to be successful.

Responding to a Call for Help in Release 2.2

2.2 ◆ ———

Offering help from a macro menu may not always be the best approach. In Release 2.2, the macro keyword {help} gives you another method for providing the spreadsheet user with help. Where the keyword {edit} performs the same task as pressing F2, {help} brings up the Lotus help screens just as pressing F1 does. You will probably never need Lotus help screens in your macro driven applications, but you can use the keyword to see if another user has pressed F1, and then bring up your own help screens.

For a quick demonstration of this, write the following macro named \Z:

```
{get TYPED}
{if TYPED = "{HELP}"} {\HELP} ˜ {branch \Z}
{TYPED}
{branch \Z}
```

Name a cell TYPED for a variable cell, and another cell \HELP, which will be the help macro. Just enter the command

```
{beep 2} {return}
```

into \HELP for now. Invoke \Z and type a few keystrokes other than F1. The macro checks each keystroke you type, looking to see if you have pressed F1. If you have not, it simply executes your keystroke and then branches to \Z and checks your next one. Now press F1 and see what happens: you will hear the tone from the {beep 2} command in \HELP. The macro will return and then branch to \Z. Although the tilde after the call to \HELP is not needed, it refreshes the screen so that you can see the word {HELP} in the cell named TYPED. Notice, however, that the 1-2-3 help screens were not invoked; the macro had control of the keyboard and provided its own processing for the F1 keystroke.

Of course, instead of the beep command in \HELP, you can call the associated help routines shown in Figure 3.2. For example, a macro that automates data entry will have control of the keyboard, and therefore provides help when needed, by checking each keystroke and responding with help when F1 is pressed. With a few minor additions, you can make the help context sensitive based on, for example, the column in which the cursor resides. To do so, change the macro invoked when F1 is pressed, as shown in the following one-line macro:

```
{if TYPED = "{HELP}"}
{let CHOICE,@string(@cellpointer("col"),0)} {\HELP} ˜ {branch \Z}
```

Next, write the help macro so that it brings the appropriate help screen from the help file into the help display area:

```
/fccnMESSAGE{CHOICE} ˜ MESSAGES ˜
```

Worksheet Information

Another area of the worksheet that can serve as one part of the documentation is a general information area. The information in this range could be placed in the home screen, but generally it is needed only occasionally for reference purposes. Moreover, by keeping it in its own area you will not feel that you must limit its size to only one screen.

In this range you would put any facts relevant to the "life" of the worksheet:

- The author(s)

- Date of last revision (not during its normal use, but when changes were made in its operating procedures)

- Who is responsible for its upkeep

- The names of other worksheet files necessary to its proper functioning

- The type of printer that is addressed by the print macros

- Restrictions on the validity of its use—will it work for anyone in the shop, or just for certain departments?

- Major assumptions built into the worksheet

If you want this information to be available to all users, simply write it in the form of one or more help screens, and include an Info choice on a help menu.

ALLOWING FOR CHANGE WITH VARIABLES

Just about every worksheet contains some information that is subject to revision. Formulas may be written just once, but the data on which they depend may be changed frequently as the worksheet is put through its what-if paces. Any cell that is referenced in a formula can be thought of as a *variable*. More specifically, a formula variable is a critical cell in the analysis being made, the contents of which can be changed to produce new results throughout the model. A number that is used within a formula is best described as a *constant*.

In the 1-2-3 worksheet, a variable can also take the form of a *table variable*, a range of cells that is referenced as one table. Formulas such as @index and @vlookup always look to a range as their source. Sometimes these ranges might just be some rows and columns of worksheet data. At other times, the range is a table that is maintained specifically for one of the list selection formulas, and in that sense the table becomes another worksheet variable.

There is another type of variable that may not be referenced by formulas. This is a *range variable*, a range of cells that determines the flow of commands during worksheet routines. For instance, the criterion used in a database query is a variable in that it can be revised as needed to change the outcome of the query. A macro {if} statement might reference a cell that holds a date to determine how the macro should branch. Or, a column of cells might contain range names that a macro would access to print those ranges.

Whatever form they take—formula, table, or range—worksheet variables deserve attention when you build an application.

Formula Variables

Following a structured plan as you build an application becomes even more important when worksheet variables are considered. These are the cells that determine the numeric results of the worksheet, and as such, they must be identified early and kept in a known location in the worksheet.

> ⊗ **CAUTION** ◆ *If any formulas in your worksheet contain numbers, be careful! Those formulas are hard-coded and cannot be changed without revising each one in the worksheet. If you see the need for a number in a formula, think about creating a variable cell to contain that number, and referencing the cell within the formula.*

Suppose you keep track of your checking account in a worksheet. You have a beginning balance of $1,200 from the year before, on which all the totals are based. If checks written are entered in column C, and deposits in D, then the balance could be calculated in column E and would look like this:

    1200 – C3 + D3

You could copy this formula down column E and get a running balance as you enter checks and deposits. What would happen if your first bank statement of the new year included an overdraft fee of $20? Your formulas should actually be using $1,180, not $1,200, and you would have to rewrite the first one and copy it down the column. Not a problem, but imagine a worksheet where those formulas were scattered throughout many locations, and you have not kept track of just where they were. That's trouble. The formula should have been written in this manner, where cell D1 contains the beginning balance amount:

    $D$1 – C3 + D3

As you can see from the previous example, variable cells are valuable for several reasons:

- ◆ *Convenience and ease of revision* By pulling out the beginning balance to one separate cell, that number can be changed at any time. Every formula that references that cell will be automatically updated.

- ◆ *Accuracy* Every reference to a variable cell will be to exactly the same number. There is no chance of one formula referring to a previous value or being typed improperly.

◆ *Documentation* Having one cell labeled Beginning Balance makes the nature of that number and the formulas that depend on it clear. This is one way to convey the assumptions of the builder to the users.

★ **TRICK** ◆ *This is not a trick so much as a reminder of good, sound practice. If you give each variable cell a range name, that name will appear in any formula that references the variable. The formula will be easy to write, easy to read, and will obviously be in error if the name does not appear within it. Thus, for the previous example, you could name the variable cell (D1) so that the formula would look like this:*

$BEGIN_BALANCE – C3 + D3

The need for variable cells depends on the nature of the worksheet and the data it contains. The value contained in a variable may represent almost any category of data, such as inflation rate, start date, capacity, or interest rate.

Remember to enter a {return} command in the cell below a variable cell if you plan to use the variable as a subroutine to a macro, as described in Chapter 1.

Note that the contents of the cell can be a number, a function, or a formula that summarizes other data in the worksheet. A number can be entered ahead of time by the developer, input by the user, or brought in from another file.

★ **TRICK** ◆ *Variable cells can also contain text. A worksheet template that will be used by many different branch locations could have one cell named BRANCH_NAME. The first time it is retrieved at a new location, that cell is filled in with the location name. Any title areas in the worksheet simply need a formula that addresses BRANCH_NAME to label the worksheet appropriately:*

+"Summary Report for "&$BRANCH_NAME

Table Variables

A variable might consist of many cells when those cells are referenced by one of the lookup formulas: @vlookup, @hlookup, @index, or @choose. When these formulas address a table that is specifically for their own use, that table can then be considered a variable.

Suppose that a macro retrieves a certain file based on the total in one cell in the worksheet, named TOTAL_CELL. If that total is greater than 40,000 but less than 50,000, then FILE_A is retrieved; from 50,000 to 60,000, FILE_B; and so on. A series of macro {if} commands could do this:

```
{if TOTAL_CELL>40000#and#TOTAL_CELL<50000}/frFILE_A ~
{if TOTAL_CELL>50000#and#TOTAL_CELL<60000}/frFILE_B ~
```

There is a shorter solution that is also much easier to revise if the need should arise. It requires an @vlookup function written into a string formula in the macro, with an accompanying table. Figure 3.3 shows this solution.

The macro in \Z, shown below and in the control panel, consists of a string formula with the @vlookup function:

```
+"/fr"&@vlookup($TOTAL_CELL,$TABLE_FILES,1)&"~"
```

The function returns the file name from TABLE_FILES depending on the value of TOTAL_CELL. In this example, the total of 63,000 means that the third name in the table will be selected: FILE_C.

To revise the file names, you would simply go to TABLE_FILES and revise the names in column C. The same is true for the values in column B in that table. Or, those values could just as easily rely on another worksheet variable cell. In that case, the first value in the table could be 10,000 greater than that cell, and each succeeding value would be 10,000 greater than the one above.

This ease and flexibility demonstrates the importance of separating variables from the other data in the worksheet.

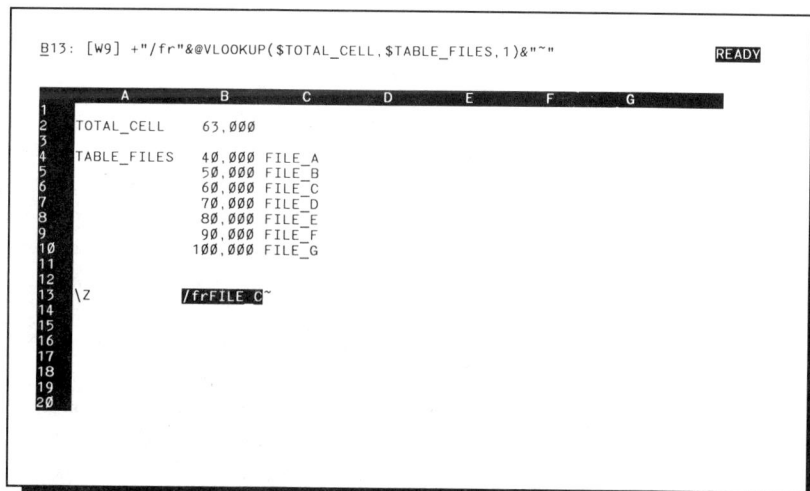

Figure 3.3 ♦ *A table that serves as a variable*

Range Variables

A formula can return a value based on the contents of a variable cell or table. Worksheet commands and macros can also rely on the contents of cells to determine the direction they take, and these cells must therefore be considered as variables. The database criterion that was mentioned earlier is a perfect example of this.

When the Data Query command prompts for the database criterion, it is not asking for a value, but for a range of cells in the worksheet. The content of these cells is immaterial—it is the range itself that is referenced by the command.

If the value in the criterion cells is later revised, then the results of the Data Query command will change accordingly. This is exactly like a formula that evaluates to a new result in response to a change in a variable cell.

INCLUDING MACROS IN YOUR WORKSHEETS

Macros are a unique component of the worksheet, and you should pay attention to their layout. Since almost every worksheet contains macros (or should), you can include the following macro range structure in each new project that you create:

- ◆ Autoexec macro, \0

- ◆ Main menu macro call, \M

- ◆ Menus

- ◆ Subroutines

Whether or not you end up needing a \0 macro, understanding the structure of the macro layout allows you to expand your macros as the need arises. A \M macro prompts you to create a main menu, which in turn leads to submenus and subroutines.

> **TIP** ◆ *When writing macros, you may want to enter comments that document the code. If you try to put the comments to the right of the macros, you may run into alignment problems because the macro menus can be as wide as eight columns. Use the column directly to the left of the macro to enter its name: \Z, \M, \DO_PRINT, and so on. Then enter any comments in the column to*

*the left of the name column. Set the comment column's width to 72,
and you will be able to quickly pop back and forth between the macro
code and the comments.*

IDENTIFYING AND PLACING WORKSHEET DATA

A worksheet always contains data, and it can contain text, numbers, formulas, functions, or any combination of these. Although all the components discussed so far are also data, they are being considered separately because they are unique in their use. Worksheet data can be grouped into three categories: input data, process data, and output data.

The dividing line between these types may often be cloudy, as the nature of the spreadsheet is such that a cell that receives input may be next to a formula cell (process), and both get printed (output). But if you keep these three categories in mind during the construction process, your control over the development phase will be stronger, and the results more reliable.

Input Data

Input data is any information that is entered or revised by the user. The location of input cells must therefore be known (or accessible) by the user. A good example of input data is an address list. The user enters information directly into the cells of the list, and there is no processing of any sort.

> ★ **TRICK** ◆ *Since input cells must be available to the user,
> any range that falls into this category should be listed on the
> View menu. Their location need not be known by the user if a macro
> handles the jump.*

Cells can also receive user input through macro input commands, such as {getlabel} and {getnumber}. The cell pointer does not need to be moved for this method, and the user need not know where the data was sent. These cells are rarely used for heavy data entry or record keeping. For these reasons, they are not purely input cells, and are better described as variable or data process cells.

Process Data

There are many different types of process cells or ranges in a worksheet, and they can contain any type of data. In general, if a cell does not receive user input and is not printed or otherwise viewed, then it falls under the category of *process data*. This type of cell or range usually performs intermediate steps—using input values to produce results that can then be output. There are many styles of process cells:

◆ Formulas

◆ Work areas for temporary storage

◆ Data that is kept for graphing analysis

◆ All output ranges associated with the Data commands, including Extract, Table, Distribution, and Regression

◆ Ranges that receive file input for intermediate processing

Note once again that although a formula is a process cell, it can also be formatted for printing or viewing purposes and can therefore fall under the category of output cell.

Output Data

Any cell that has a specific format, column width, or spacing between it and other cells may very well be an *output cell*. These factors imply that someone will be looking at it, whether on paper or within the worksheet, and the appearance carries much importance.

> ⊗ **CAUTION** ◆ *The fluid nature of the spreadsheet can often create confusion when process cells are mistakenly treated as output cells. Much time can be wasted trying to format several ranges so that they look nice when printed. It is frequently much safer, and produces better results, to create a range that is strictly an output area.*

Just because a cell can be printed doesn't mean it should be. Go ahead and create a separate print area in a distant part of the worksheet. Use formulas to pick up the cells that you want to display, and then arrange that area for easy printing. Column widths can be set as needed, and formulas that total or summarize can be placed in any location that suits the final printout. This method requires some extra memory, but can often be an immediate solution to an otherwise long struggle.

This is especially so with data tables that are used with the Data Table command. The format of the table is too restrictive for attractive printing. There can be no blank rows or columns, and any text that is substituted into the table's input cell must be spelled exactly to find matches. Instead of trying to print a range of process cells that might look unsatisfactory, create a separate reporting area that uses those cells as the source for printing.

A small data table is shown in Figure 3.4. The table is filled with results, but as a whole is not suitable for printing.

Now look at Figure 3.5. In another part of the worksheet, a new table has been constructed. This time, enhancements have been added to make the

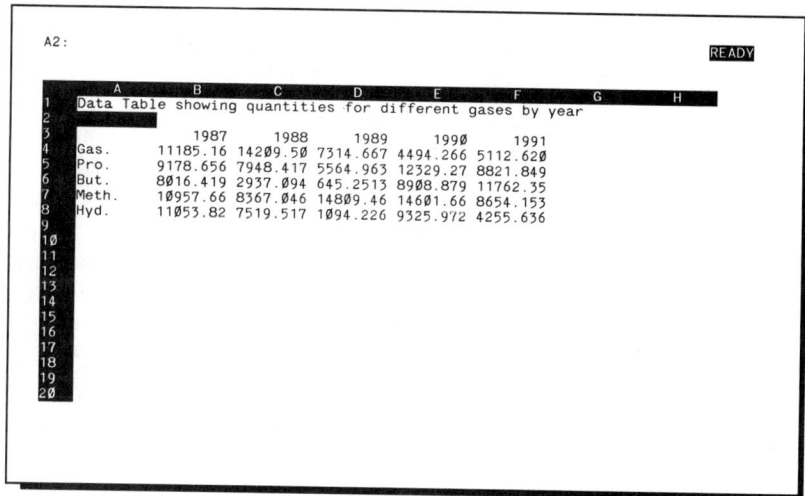

```
A2:                                                                    READY

        A         B         C         D         E         F      G       H
 1  Data Table showing quantities for different gases by year
 2
 3              1987      1988      1989      1990      1991
 4  Gas.     11185.16  14209.50  7314.667  4494.266  5112.620
 5  Pro.     9178.656  7948.417  5564.963  12329.27  8821.849
 6  But.     8016.419  2937.094  645.2513  8908.879  11762.35
 7  Meth.    10957.66  8367.046  14809.46  14601.66  8654.153
 8  Hyd.     11053.82  7519.517  1094.226  9325.972  4255.636
 9
10
11
12
13
14
15
16
17
18
19
20
```

Figure 3.4 ◆ *Process cells are not always suitable for printing or viewing*

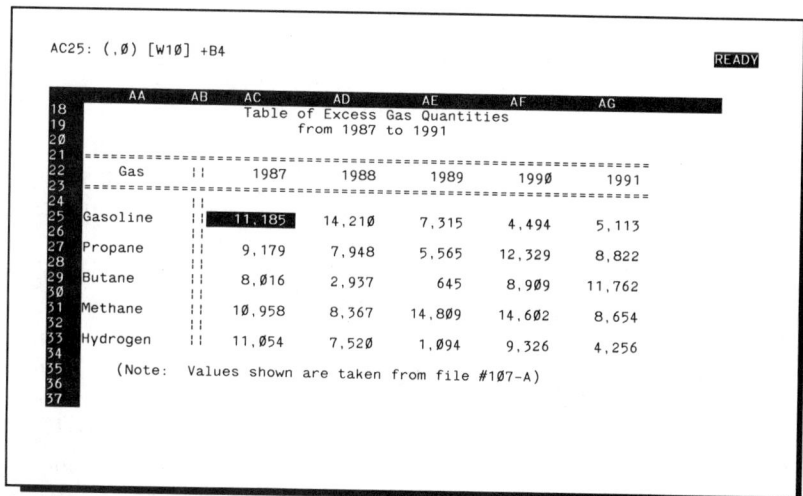

```
AC25: (,Ø) [W1Ø] +B4                                                   READY

        AA      AB      AC        AD       AE       AF       AG
18                         Table of Excess Gas Quantities
19                              from 1987 to 1991
20
21  ==================================================================
22      Gas      !!      1987     1988     1989     1990     1991
23  ==================================================================
24               !!
25  Gasoline     !!    11,185   14,210    7,315    4,494    5,113
26               !!
27  Propane      !!     9,179    7,948    5,565   12,329    8,822
28               !!
29  Butane       !!     8,016    2,937      645    8,909   11,762
30               !!
31  Methane      !!    10,958    8,367   14,809   14,602    8,654
32               !!
33  Hydrogen     !!    11,054    7,520    1,094    9,326    4,256
34
35     (Note:  Values shown are taken from file #107-A)
36
37
```

Figure 3.5 ◆ *A separate print area allows for easy formatting of the output*

table more visually attractive. This new table is purely for output. Extra rows and columns have been inserted, the labels on the left are no longer abbreviated, the columns are wider, and titles and notes have been added. Notice that the cell on which the cell pointer resides is a formula that refers to the appropriate cell in the table in Figure 3.4. Any changes in the data table will be reflected here.

ARRANGING THE LAYOUT OF THE COMPONENTS

As you have seen, the cells in a worksheet can be classified in several ways: as visual controls, variables, macros, or data. Consideration needs to be given to the location of these pieces in the worksheet. There is, of course, no perfect method, but any method is better than none. The structure outlined here is acceptable for most situations, but once again, the spreadsheet structure is fluid and there are always overlapping zones.

First, separate the active part of the worksheet from the static part. *Active* refers to the data sections, where rows and columns are inserted or deleted, and cells may be moved around frequently, even after the construction process is completed. The *static* area includes the home screen, variables, and macros. It tends to remain stable once the worksheet is finished.

TIP ◆ *The ideal way to separate the active and static sections of a worksheet is by keeping each in a range that is diagonally opposed to the other. If you divide the worksheet into quadrants, then the upper left could be the static range, and the lower right the active range. Using this method, you can insert or delete rows in either section and it will not interfere with the other.*

Figure 3.6 shows the layout of a typical static section of a worksheet, the upper left quadrant. This section starts at A1 and continues all the way to Z1000, a more than generous amount in most cases. The size of this range and the location of the lower right corner obviously depend on the needs of the worksheet.

CAUTION ◆ *If you are still using Lotus 1A, separating static areas from active areas is too liberal a use of the worksheet, and will often not be acceptable. Before the sparse matrix memory management of Lotus 2, every cell in the "live" worksheet (the rectangle whose lower right corner is described by the End Home key)* *required a small amount of RAM. This memory constraint was not conducive to the wide open stretches required in this layout method.*

The active section is shown in Figure 3.7. This range starts at AA2000, and extends as far to the right and down as necessary.

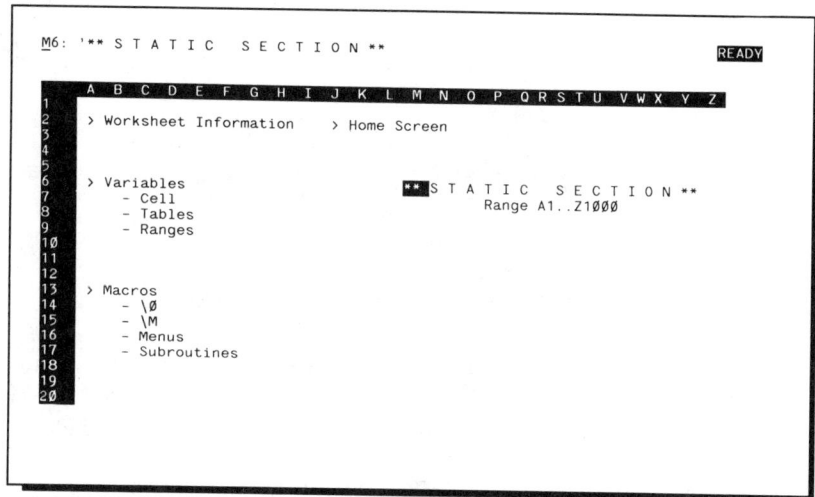

```
M6: '** S T A T I C   S E C T I O N **                          READY

        A  B  C  D  E  F  G  H  I  J  K  L  M  N  O  P  Q  R  S  T  U  V  W  X  Y  Z
1
2      > Worksheet Information      > Home Screen
3
4
5
6      > Variables
7          - Cell                         ** S T A T I C   S E C T I O N **
8          - Tables                            Range A1..Z1000
9          - Ranges
10
11
12
13     > Macros
14         - \0
15         - \M
16         - Menus
17         - Subroutines
18
19
20
```

Figure 3.6 ♦ *The static area of the worksheet in the upper left quadrant*

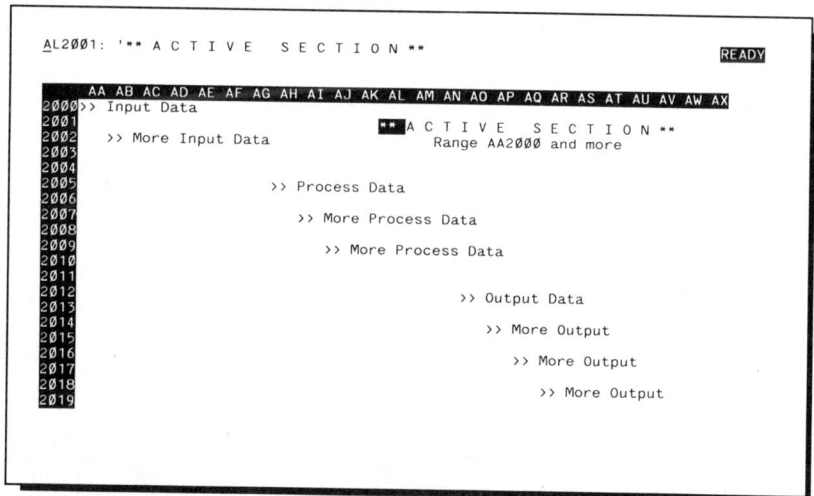

```
AL2001: '** A C T I V E   S E C T I O N **                       READY

          AA AB AC AD AE AF AG AH AI AJ AK AL AM AN AO AP AQ AR AS AT AU AV AW AX
2000 >> Input Data
2001                                    ** A C T I V E   S E C T I O N **
2002    >> More Input Data                  Range AA2000 and more
2003
2004
2005              >> Process Data
2006
2007                >> More Process Data
2008
2009                  >> More Process Data
2010
2011
2012                               >> Output Data
2013
2014                                 >> More Output
2015
2016                                   >> More Output
2017
2018                                     >> More Output
2019
```

Figure 3.7 ♦ *The active area of the worksheet in the lower right quadrant*

The benefits of separating the active and static quadrants of the worksheet also apply to the ranges within those areas. Notice how the ranges in the active area stair-step down the worksheet. By separating the ranges with blank rows and columns, you can delete a row or column or expand a column width in one range without affecting another. This is especially important with output ranges, where their look is of great importance.

Being liberal with the 8,192 rows and 256 columns of the Lotus worksheet gives you much freedom and room to stretch during the construction process. Even though there may be "miles" between occupied ranges, there are some simple ways to find those areas.

NAMING WORK AREAS

If you practice a few good habits, you will never have any problem locating ranges in the worksheet. If you blindly create the worksheet, you will find that pieces can disappear into the "Bermuda Triangle," somewhere between AC2900 and FF7000!

The main ingredient of a stable layout is range names. With names, you do not need to know the exact coordinates of every range in the worksheet. So long as the important areas are named, the ranges can be found.

> ★ **TRICK** ◆ *During the development phase, the macro View menu is an excellent tool for reaching ranges that are under construction. Instead of listing the areas that need to be viewed when the worksheet is actually finished, include the process ranges, tables, extract areas, or graphing ranges that need to be accessed during the building process. Then, jumping to a work range is simple: call the main menu with Alt-M, choose View, and then choose the area you want to reach.*

The home screen is always accessible via a macro, as is the worksheet information data, so these areas are easy to find.

Variables can be located because you always give them a range name (if you don't, go back and start over at page 1). It is easy to spot a variable within a formula that references it because the variable's range name appears in it.

Macros, too, are always named, and finding one is as simple as pressing F5 {goto} and F3 {name} twice, and then selecting a name from those that begin with the backslash (if you follow the macro naming convention used here).

Input ranges must be named, because you will have a macro that takes you to them. Whether the menu choice is named Data Entry, View, or Browse, you will have an automated method of jumping to the important areas in the worksheet.

Any range that gets printed or viewed will always be named, so it will be easy to reach. Just look at the macro that prints the range and the name will be there.

Finally, as the worksheet grows you can create a map for future documentation. It should be a rough sketch of the major areas in the worksheet. Draw a box that simulates the range, label it appropriately, and then enter its upper left and lower right coordinates. This gives a grand overview of the worksheet—but for construction and documentation purposes only. A user should never need a map to navigate through the worksheet.

◆ *BUILDING BETTER FORMULAS*

The key to the power of a spreadsheet is the interaction among thousands of individual cells. At the heart of this interaction are formulas. Anything that can be done to make formulas easier to write, interpret, or revise facilitates the workings of the entire spreadsheet.

VARIABLES

The need for separating worksheet variables from formulas has already been stressed, and it is one of the most important steps that can be taken in the construction process. When many formulas pull their data from the same cell, that one cell can be adjusted as necessary to affect the results of all the formulas. For instance, these variables

Principal	75000
Interest	12.0%
Term	30

make formulas like this one easy to manipulate:

@pmt($PRINCIPAL,$INTEREST/12,$TERM*12)

RANGE NAMES

Again, the necessity for range names has been discussed; their usefulness in building and maintaining formulas cannot be overstated. As soon as you identify a variable that one or more formulas will reference, that variable should be named.

Some formulas cannot utilize range names, such as those that are copied throughout a range and reference adjacent cells, not single-cell variables. In this case, every formula refers to different cells in the range.

> ★ **TRICK** ◆ *Even if a complex formula cannot use range names, you can still make use of them during the construction process. Name the important cells that the first formula will reference, and these names will then be available while building that one formula.*

After the accuracy of that first formula is verified and it is copied to its final locations (where the names will no longer be referenced), you can either delete the range names or leave them for future reference. For example, here is a formula that is created in cell E44 with the help of range names, and then copied down column E:

E44:	@IF(TWO>ONE,ONE/TWO,THREE)/(ONE+FOUR+FIVE)
E45:	@IF(B45>A45,A45/B45,C45)/(A45+D45+E45)
E46:	@IF(B46>A46,A46/B46,C46)/(A46+D46+E46)
E47:	@IF(B47>A47,A47/B47,C47)/(A47+D47+E47)

The first formula, cell E44, was built with the help of range names that named other cells in the same row. It is much more readable than the copies of it in E45..E47, and its accuracy is therefore easier to verify.

STEP CELLS

The term *step cells* refers to one or more cells that serve as intermediate steps in formula development. Instead of writing one long formula, you use a series of cells in which each cell contains just part of the whole. The final formula simply refers back to the other cells to build the result, and can therefore be very short. Step cells fulfill several purposes.

Each part of a formula can be written and its accuracy verified before going on to the next part. A problem formula can return an ERR, or perhaps will be rejected by Lotus because its parentheses are out of balance. It is much easier to track down the problem in one small formula than in a long formula with many parentheses and cell references.

When a formula is split among several cells, you can later inspect each step for accuracy or for purposes of revision. The meaning of the formula is much more obvious when it is broken down into logical steps, and those who must interpret it later will have a much lighter task.

Very long formulas can often be a sign of misplaced enthusiasm. But if you need to create a stupendously long formula, step formulas allow you to circumvent the 240-character maximum limit in a cell. On the other hand, any formula that even approaches 240 characters generally deserves to be split into several steps simply to make it more readable.

For an example of step cells, look now at Figure 3.8. This worksheet uses a string formula to reverse the last name-first name order of the names in column A. The final results are the formulas in column B, which are built upon the step formulas in columns C through F. The contents of the step cells for row 4 are shown here and in rows 15 through 19 of Figure 3.8.

Cell	Result	Formula
B4	*Jim Hendrix*	$+E4\&$" "$\&F4$
C4	7	@find(",",A4,0)
D4	5	@length(A4)−C4
E4	*Jim*	@right(A4,D4−2)
F4	*Hendrix*	@left(A4,C4)

By splitting the formulas among five cells, each one is kept short. Compare their length to how the formula would look if it were written as a single formula, 70 characters long, as shown in row 12.

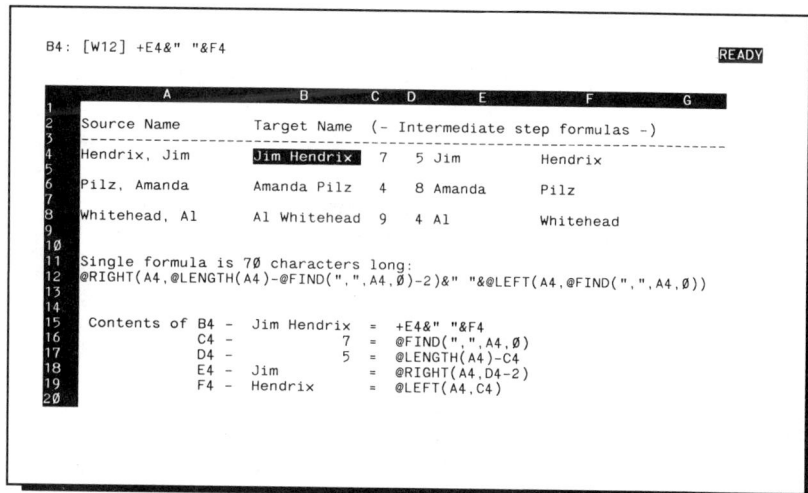

```
B4: [W12] +E4&" "&F4                                              READY

          A                B     C  D      E              F          G
1
2   Source Name       Target Name  (- Intermediate step formulas -)
3   -----------------------------------------------------------------------
4   Hendrix, Jim      Jim Hendrix  7  5 Jim            Hendrix
5
6   Pilz, Amanda      Amanda Pilz  4  8 Amanda         Pilz
7
8   Whitehead, Al     Al Whitehead 9  4 Al             Whitehead
9
10
11  Single formula is 70 characters long:
12  @RIGHT(A4,@LENGTH(A4)-@FIND(",",A4,0)-2)&" "&&LEFT(A4,@FIND(",",A4,0))
13
14
15  Contents of B4 -  Jim Hendrix  =  +E4&" "&F4
16            C4 -            7  =  @FIND(",",A4,0)
17            D4 -            5  =  @LENGTH(A4)-C4
18            E4 -  Jim          =  @RIGHT(A4,D4-2)
19            F4 -  Hendrix      =  @LEFT(A4,C4)
20
```

Figure 3.8 ♦ *Intermediate step cells facilitate formula writing*

This example is not an extreme case, and the step formulas are shorter than necessary so that the example is easy to understand. In fact, once you develop this formula, you might then build a single formula to do the job and eliminate the steps. The steps would serve only to aid in development.

ABSOLUTE CELL REFERENCES

When formulas are copied, the references they make to other cells are adjusted according to the address of the new destination. This allows you, for example, to copy one formula down a column and have it address the appropriate cells in each row.

> **TIP** ◆ *Cell addresses within a formula are not real addresses, but more accurately are references to cells that are "this far left (or right) and this far up (or down)." A formula in B4 that refers to cell A1 is actually referring to the cell that is "one cell left and three cells up."*

When a formula is copied, the directional reference remains the same, only now the cell to which it refers has a different address. If the formula in B4 that refers to A1 is copied to D24, the new formula will now refer to C21, the cell that is one left and three up. This is known as *relative* cell addressing, and it greatly simplifies the job of building a worksheet.

Relative and absolute cell references apply equally to file linking formulas in Release 2.2. When copied, relative addresses in linking formulas adjust to cells in the linked spreadsheet exactly as they would in the active one. If you want to lock in an absolute row, column, or both, precede the column or row reference with a dollar sign. As in prior releases, an absolute range name reference, such as $TOTAL, implies that both column and row are absolute.

There are many times when you will not want a cell reference to adjust when a formula is copied, such as when formulas rely on worksheet variables. The nature of a variable cell insists that if a formula is copied, the new formula must still reference the variable. In those cases, you must use *absolute* cell references. In Lotus, you form absolute references by prefacing the column or row address with a dollar sign.

> **TIP** ◆ *The F4 {abs} key enters the dollar signs into a formula's cell reference for you. You can use it while writing,*

pointing, or editing a formula. Each press of the key cycles the address through the four different referencing options, as shown here:

```
+ $C$4
+ C$4
+ $C4
+ C4
```

You can take advantage of the fact that either the column, the row, or both can be made absolute. Figure 3.9 is a worksheet that utilizes all three means of absolute referencing. This table calculates the volume of a gas at a given temperature (row 9) and atmospheric pressure (column A).

The formula requires that the cells N_MOLES and R_FACTOR be multiplied by T (Temperature), and the result divided by P (Pressure), or V = NRT/P. To create the formula in cell C11 (shown in the control panel) and copy it to the entire table, each cell reference must be made absolute in its own way:

$R_FACTOR	$C$5	*absolute column and row*
$N_MOLES	$C$6	*absolute column and row*
C$9		*Temperature in row 9 of the current column*
$A11		*Pressure in column A of the current row*

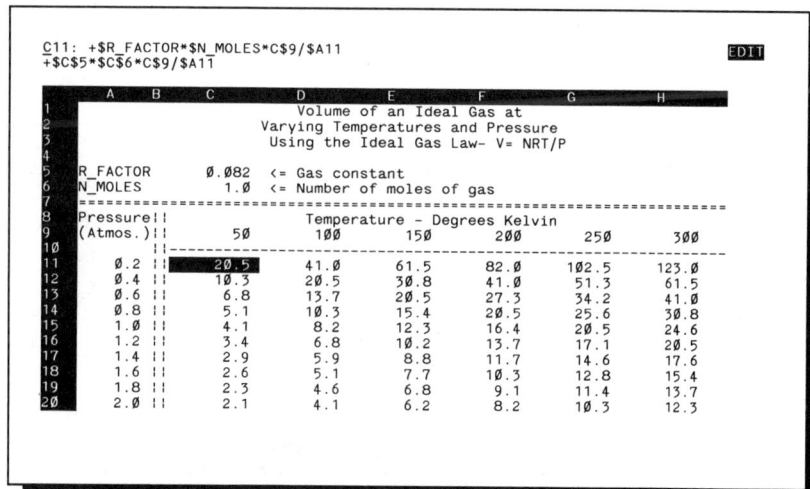

```
C11: +$R_FACTOR*$N_MOLES*C9/$A11                              EDIT
+$C$5*$C$6*C9/$A11

        A    B      C           D         E         F         G         H
1                         Volume of an Ideal Gas at
2                         Varying Temperatures and Pressure
3                         Using the Ideal Gas Law- V= NRT/P
4
5    R_FACTOR      0.082   <= Gas constant
6    N_MOLES        1.0    <= Number of moles of gas
7    ========================================================================
8    Pressure!!                Temperature - Degrees Kelvin
9    (Atmos.)!!     50       100       150       200       250       300
10            !!------------------------------------------------------------
11      0.2  !!    20.5      41.0      61.5      82.0     102.5     123.0
12      0.4  !!    10.3      20.5      30.8      41.0      51.3      61.5
13      0.6  !!     6.8      13.7      20.5      27.3      34.2      41.0
14      0.8  !!     5.1      10.3      15.4      20.5      25.6      30.8
15      1.0  !!     4.1       8.2      12.3      16.4      20.5      24.6
16      1.2  !!     3.4       6.8      10.2      13.7      17.1      20.5
17      1.4  !!     2.9       5.9       8.8      11.7      14.6      17.6
18      1.6  !!     2.6       5.1       7.7      10.3      12.8      15.4
19      1.8  !!     2.3       4.6       6.8       9.1      11.4      13.7
20      2.0  !!     2.1       4.1       6.2       8.2      10.3      12.3
```

Figure 3.9 ◆ *Absolute cell references allow one formula to be copied throughout a table*

When the formula in C11 is copied down the columns and across the rows, it adjusts to each new location. Remember that row 9 is the temperatures, and column A the pressures. Here are representative samples of the resulting formula:

```
C11:        +$R_FACTOR*$N_MOLES*C$9/$A11
D11:        +$R_FACTOR*$N_MOLES*D$9/$A11
E11:        +$R_FACTOR*$N_MOLES*E$9/$A11

C12:        +$R_FACTOR*$N_MOLES*C$9/$A12
D12:        +$R_FACTOR*$N_MOLES*D$9/$A12
E12:        +$R_FACTOR*$N_MOLES*E$9/$A12

C13:        +$R_FACTOR*$N_MOLES*C$9/$A13
D13:        +$R_FACTOR*$N_MOLES*D$9/$A13
E13:        +$R_FACTOR*$N_MOLES*E$9/$A13
```

You can verify the validity of the formulas by checking that in any column or row, the volume of the gas doubles as the temperature is doubled, and halves as the pressure is doubled. Absolute cell references can also help out in what may seem an unlikely situation.

The @count function returns the count of any occupied cells in the range it references. A slightly nasty glitch in Lotus appears when the formula addresses only one cell, such as @count(C4): the result is always 1, whether or not the cell is occupied. If you reference several individual cells, the result will always total 1 for each cell, so that @count(C4,F9,H32) always returns 3.

You can fool Lotus into thinking that an individual cell is a range by referring to the cell as a range. To do this, you must attach an absolute reference to one end of the range. Confusing? Here are the two examples from above, written so that the function will count only the cells that are actually occupied:

```
@count(C4..$C4)
@count($C$4..C4,F9..F$9,H$32..$H$32)
```

The trick requires that each corner of a range have a form of reference that is different from the other corner. You can see that it does not matter whether a row, a column, or both are made absolute, as long as both corners are different. Lotus will think of each cell reference as a unique range, and will then count the cell correctly—1 if it is occupied and 0 if it is empty.

◆ OPTIMIZING SPREADSHEET SIZE

When Lotus 2 was released in 1985, it had two major enhancements that eased its memory requirements. The first was sparse matrix memory management, which allowed any cell in the worksheet to be used, including IV8192, without its having to set aside memory for all unoccupied cells in the live area of the worksheet.

The second was the ability to access expanded memory for worksheet data. Suddenly, megabytes of memory were available, and many of the memory constraints of Lotus 1A were gone forever.

But having money in the bank doesn't mean you should squander it, and although memory is not the issue it once was, neither are worksheets as small as they used to be! Planning for the efficient use of memory not only means that a larger worksheet can be built, but also that it will be retrieved and saved faster, recalculations may be shorter, and the data it contains may be in a more usable format.

FORMULAS VERSUS NUMBERS

A number that you see displayed on the screen can come from either a formula or a number in the underlying cell, and it makes no difference to someone viewing the number on a printed page. When building a worksheet, you must consider whether a cell that displays a value needs to be a formula, or whether it can do its job just as well as an actual ("hard") number.

Considering Resources

If you are not conservative in their use, formulas can sap the resources of your computer in several ways. The most obvious drawback is slow recalculation times. Every new formula in a worksheet forces a longer recalculation.

Formulas can also require much more RAM than plain numbers do. Imagine replacing 1,000 cells that contain this formula with just the number that represents each formula's result:

```
@round((@sin(A4)) + (B4*1.5/C4),2)
```

All those extra characters add up to about 50 bytes per formula that could be saved by replacing it with a hard number. The more space they occupy in memory, the more space they will occupy on disk, meaning that the worksheet will take longer to load and save, and disks will fill up more quickly.

Formulas must also be guarded against inadvertent errors. The rows or columns that contain cells to which the formulas refer cannot be deleted, nor can any other cell be moved on top of the referenced cells. If you want to use the value of the formula in another location, you must be careful not to copy it there, as that would cause it to reference a whole new set of cells. Bringing in a worksheet with the File Combine command also causes formulas in the incoming worksheet to address new cells in a relative manner.

All these considerations add up to the fact that you should not use formulas unless they are absolutely needed.

Making the Appropriate Choice

The point of using a formula instead of a number is twofold: to bring together in one location a variety of numbers, text, @ functions, or other cells, and to automatically evaluate as changes are made to the cells it references.

Only the second aspect, that of automatically updating to meet changes in the worksheet, truly represents the need for formulas. Although it may be a convenience to write a formula to produce a total, if that total is never going to change then it should be entered as a value.

A typically overused formula is the @date function. Dates entered with this function can be used in date arithmetic, so it certainly serves an important purpose. But frequently there is no need to leave the dates in the form of a function, since they are never going to be changed. Instead, they should be turned into values.

Turning Formulas into Numbers

There are two instances when formulas can be evaluated into hard numbers. The first is after they are already entered into the worksheet, and the other is while they are being written, but before they are entered.

The Range Value command is the quickest way to translate a range of formulas into the values they produce. If you still use Lotus 1A, then you will have to extract the range of formulas with the command File Xtract Values, and then issue the command File Combine Copy Entire to bring the file back in on top of the range. Either method achieves the same result: numbers instead of formulas.

To turn formulas into numbers more efficiently, you can do the job as a formula is entered into the worksheet so that only a hard number is entered. There is just one way to accomplish this, and it works because the F9 {calc} key does not recalculate the entire worksheet in EDIT mode; it merely evaluates any formula that is being edited in the current cell. The routine, then, is to write the formula, press F9, and then press Enter.

★ **TRICK** ◆ *With the help of a data entry macro, converting formulas to numbers during data entry can not only be automated, but can also be completely invisible to the user.*

Figure 3.10 demonstrates a macro that facilitates the entry of dates as values. Since date functions can be time-consuming to enter without a macro, it serves both purposes.

```
D19: (D1) [W1Ø]                                                    READY
Enter YEAR- 19

          A             B              C            D        E      F
 1  YEAR            74
 2  MONTH            2
 3  DAY             25
 4
 5  \Z            {getnumber Enter YEAR- 19,YEAR}
 6               {getnumber Enter MONTH- ,MONTH}
 7               {getnumber Enter DAY- ,DAY}
 8               @date(YEAR,MONTH,DAY){calc}~/rfd1~
 9
10
11
12                     ---------------------------
13             Name                    Birth Date
14                     ---------------------------
15             Jim                     1Ø-Jan-5Ø
16             Madeline                12-Oct-3Ø
17             Frinesse                28-Sep-46
18             Josh                    Ø2-Sep-51
19             Carl                    Ø1-Sep-74
20             Irma

                                      CMD
```

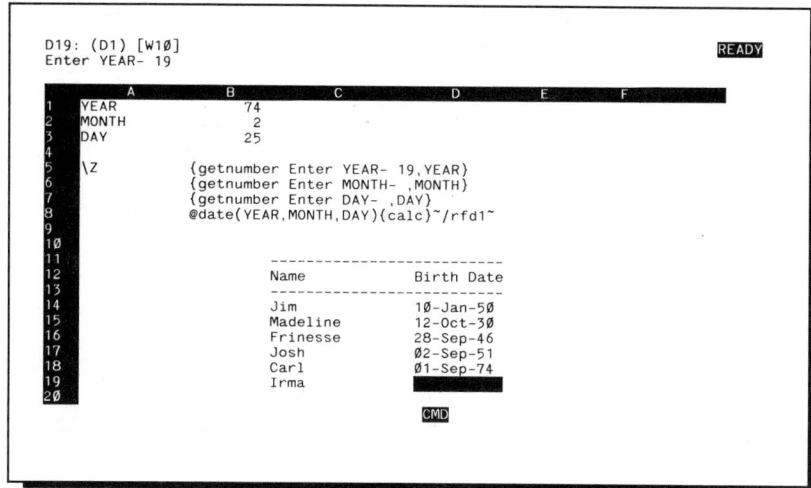

Figure 3.10 ◆ *A macro to facilitate the entry of formulas as values*

Macro \Z would be called when the cell pointer was on the cell in which the date would be entered. It consists of three {getnumber} statements that each place the user's input into one of the three variable cells YEAR, MONTH, and DAY.

```
{getnumber Enter YEAR- 19,YEAR}
{getnumber Enter MONTH- ,MONTH}
{getnumber Enter DAY- ,DAY}
@date(YEAR,MONTH,DAY){calc} ~ /rfd1 ~
```

It is only the last line of the code that actually enters the date. That line simply writes the @date function using the variable cells for the function's parameters. No absolute references are required because the formula is not going to be copied. Before the Enter key is pressed, the {calc} command is given, which turns the function into a hard number. Then the value is entered into the worksheet and the cell is given a date format.

This method can also be used for formulas that will refer in a relative fashion to other cells. Here is a macro that writes an @sum function that totals the entries to the left in the current row, and is then entered as a hard number:

```
@sum({left}.{end}{left}){calc} ~
```

Don't get too carried away with eliminating formulas. Remember that the method shown here assumes (and requires) that any future changes to the data will always be done with the macro.

ELIMINATING UNNEEDED CELLS

Your worksheets can become overburdened with data, but sometimes there is a certain amount of excess that can be eliminated. There are several practices you can follow to conserve room in the worksheet and on disk.

Blank Cells Can Occupy Space

A truly blank cell is never a problem in the worksheet, but there are cells that can appear blank and yet still take up RAM.

> ⊗ **CAUTION** ◆ *Never use the spacebar to "erase" a cell. There are dozens of reasons why you should not, but in the context of this chapter, a space occupies "space." If you continually hit the spacebar to wipe out a cell, your worksheet will be sprinkled with RAM-eating space characters.*
>
> *Another reason is that a space in a cell can defeat the efficient use of the End key when you are moving about the worksheet, which is important during the construction phase. If you want to return a cell to a blank state, use the Range Erase command.*

When a cell is formatted, 4 bytes of RAM are required to hold the setting, whether or not the cell contains data. Even when a formatted cell is empty, it occupies both RAM and disk space.

> ☑ **TIP** ◆ *A blank cell does not occupy disk space, because Lotus has nothing to remember about it. When a cell has a format, though, it needs to be so noted in the disk file so it can be brought in the next time the worksheet is loaded. Therefore, it will take up space on disk, and not just 4 bytes. The cell's address must also be saved on disk, and a total of 9 bytes of disk space is used for every empty but formatted cell.*

If you are building a worksheet that will someday have hundreds or thousands of rows of data, do not set aside those extra rows. If you do so and format one column for dates, another for percentage, and a third for currency, your worksheet will grow large even before you enter any data.

Instead of creating the rows ahead of time, insert rows as needed, perhaps ten at a time, and format them accordingly.

Cleaning Up before Saving

Sometimes quite a bit of data can be eliminated from a large worksheet to reduce its size before it is saved to disk. This will not only save disk space, but will also speed the saving and retrieving process.

For example, the cells in a Data Query Output range may not be needed once they have been used, and can be erased before issuing the Save command.

> **CAUTION** ◆ *Don't forget that the extracted cells have the same format as the source cells in the Input range. If you really want to clean up the Output range, delete the rows, if possible, or erase them and then give the Range Format Reset command to get rid of any cell formatting.*

Temporary work areas that contain regression analysis output, data distribution tables, or that receive file input from other worksheets can often be treated as a scratch pad, and left blank until the next session.

A range that is filled with formulas may be a prime candidate for erasure before saving. Don't panic, because the formulas from just one row may be all that is needed to rebuild the entire range.

> **TIP** ◆ *Macros come to the rescue again. If you have several areas that are big enough to be worth erasing before saving, write a macro to do the whole job. Here is a macro that erases several work areas before saving the worksheet:*

```
/reWORK_AREA1 ˜ /reOUTPUT1 ˜ /rfrOUTPUT1 ˜
{goto}OUTPUT2 ˜ {down}/wdr{end down} ˜
/fsFILENAME ˜ r{esc}
```

Rebuilding after Retrieving

After all this erasing, the worksheet may not be in great shape when it is retrieved the next time. Some areas will remain blank until needed again, but others will have to be rebuilt. This is an excellent occasion for the \0 macro. If a range of formulas has been erased before saving, then a short \0 macro can put it back together again:

```
/cFORMULAS ˜ FORMULA_RANGE ˜
```

ORGANIZING WORKSHEET DATA

When you are building a worksheet that will analyze large amounts of data, you should think carefully about the categories into which the data will fall. If data is not organized efficiently, it will be difficult to access and may waste a lot of space. The most critical area of worksheet database control is data redundancy. There are two ways to deal with that problem: turning many columns into one and substituting codes for repetitious data.

Turning Many Columns into One

In this case, the topic of data redundancy is not about entire records (rows) being mistakenly duplicated throughout the database. Instead, the subject is data that is wastefully structured, even though it is accurate and unique. For example, a separate column is frequently assigned to each category of data in a worksheet database, with columns labeled January to December (or Arizona to Wyoming, or Mercury to Pluto).

You may not need a column for each category or field if you label just one column Month (or State, or Planet), and enter the appropriate information in that column.

You wouldn't take up a column for each Social Security number in an employee list, because the data would be virtually unusable in that format. Instead, you have one column titled SS#, and enter each employee's number in that column.

Doing the same with the categories mentioned above will produce some immediate benefits, most obviously the now smaller worksheet—one column is doing the job of many. The smaller worksheet makes it easier to enter data and saves much room when printing.

Let's see how you can combine multiple columns. Figure 3.11 shows an inventory tracking worksheet for a chemistry stockroom. Column A holds the date, and each column to the right holds the quantity of each element used. Some dates have multiple quantities entered. There could be over 100 columns to this worksheet if every element were represented.

Keeping data in multiple columns can produce an attractive format in some situations, and you may sometimes want to maintain individual columns so that whoever is viewing the data can quickly scan the various categories to pick out relevant data. As shown in this example, totals can be placed at the top of each column. This is simply a matter of using data both for input and output. However, when the amount of data or the number of categories grows large, having multiple columns becomes more and more of a hindrance.

Look now at Figure 3.12, which is a single-column database that exactly matches the data in Figure 3.11. This time, column A still holds the date, but all the element columns are rolled into just one named Element, column C. Column D is titled Amount, where the amount used for each element is entered.

```
A8: (D1) [W11] 33163                                              READY
```

	A	B	C	D	E	F	G	H
1								
2			Quantities Distributed from Inventory					
3	--------		-------	------	-------	------	---------	---------
4	Date	¦¦	Arsenic	Barium	Calcium	Iodine	Magnesium	Manganese
5								
6	8.4	¦¦	2.2	0.3	1.9	1.0	1.5	1.5
7	--------		-------	------	-------	------	---------	---------
8	17-Oct-90	¦¦	1.2			0.3	0.5	
9	27-Oct-90	¦¦		0.1			0.7	
10	27-Oct-90	¦¦				0.4		
11	31-Oct-90	¦¦	1.0					
12	31-Oct-90	¦¦			0.8			
13	04-Nov-90	¦¦			1.1			
14	13-Nov-90	¦¦				0.3		0.9
15	15-Nov-90	¦¦		0.2			0.3	
16	15-Nov-90	¦¦						0.6
17								
18								
19								
20								

Figure 3.11 ♦ *Database with multiple columns for categories*

```
A57: (D1) [W11] 33163                                            READY
```

	A	B	C	D
52	Quantities Distributed			
53	from Inventory			
54	---------		-------	------
55	Date	¦¦	Element	Amount
56	---------		-------	------
57	17-Oct-90	¦¦	As	1.2
58	17-Oct-90	¦¦	I	0.3
59	17-Oct-90	¦¦	Mg	0.5
60	27-Oct-90	¦¦	Ba	0.1
61	27-Oct-90	¦¦	Mg	0.7
62	27-Oct-90	¦¦	I	0.4
63	31-Oct-90	¦¦	As	1.0
64	31-Oct-90	¦¦	Ca	0.8
65	04-Nov-90	¦¦	Ca	1.1
66	13-Nov-90	¦¦	I	0.3
67	13-Nov-90	¦¦	Mn	0.9
68	15-Nov-90	¦¦	Ba	0.2
69	15-Nov-90	¦¦	Mg	0.3
70	15-Nov-90	¦¦	Mn	0.6
71				

Figure 3.12 ♦ *Database with single column for ID codes*

A potentially mile-wide worksheet is now contained in just three columns. Where before one record may have held several quantities, now each record represents just one entry. The list will print in the width of one page, and could easily be sorted by Date, Element, or Amount. Of course, there is no direct means of totaling the quantities used of each element, but with a little effort some effective database reporting can be created using the @D data functions. This will be covered in Chapter 10.

Substituting Codes for Repetitious Data

When a single column is used to identify a record, problems can arise if variations are entered into the spelling or syntax of entries in that field. If different people are entering data into the worksheet, the problem can be compounded. Having magnesium spelled as mag., mangesium, and mg. will make it impossible to get an accurate total or count for each element. If the list is sorted, the results will be unpredictable.

The solution is to set up a table of standard codes, one of which is always suitable to describe that field for any record. In the examples in Figures 3.11 and 3.12, the chemical elements already have standardized abbreviations, so those are employed. Short codes are fast and easy to enter and are less likely to be misspelled. Codes can be used for many different types of data:

Months	*1–12*
Years	*85, 86, 87, 88*
Jobs Classifications	*A–N*
Regional Office	*01–99*
Employee	*EDM, IRW, RR, CNR*
Cloud Variety	*CUM, NIM, CIR*

TIP ◆ *Entering data quickly and correctly are top priorities, and macros take care of both. Set up data entry macros and use menus for selecting the identifier code. The user will not have to remember spellings, the entry will always be accurate, and the process will move quickly.*

WHEN A SPREADSHEET IS NOT A SPREADSHEET

The 1-2-3 spreadsheet is such a dynamic environment that it can often be overused to the point of abuse. Knowing a tool's capabilities allows it to be put to appropriate use. If you find yourself reaching into the toolbox and pulling out a hammer, a saw, and a straightedge to fix a leaking faucet, you may get the job done but you would be better off using another toolbox.

Text can be entered into the worksheet and later revised, but Lotus is not a word processor. If you frequently need to work with text, you may get the job done more efficiently in a word processor, and later import the text into Lotus if necessary. Or, you can treat yourself to an add-in word processor and have the best of both worlds.

Lotus can handle data quite well, but its abilities can sometimes lead you astray. If you find that the worksheet is being used mainly for data operations, such as entering, revising, sorting, and printing, you may want to consider moving the data to a database program, or consider using a database add-in program. When you have no more memory left for your worksheet, or the worksheet takes five minutes to load, the question may already be decided.

Lotus can make attractive graphs quickly, but if you are continually using tricks to sneak text into the body of the graph, or spending an inordinate amount of time trying to make graphs look pretty, that is the time to investigate one of the many presentation graphics program, whether add-in or stand-alone. You can then use Lotus for data analysis, its primary function, and produce the graphs you want with the help of another package.

◆ SUMMARY

This chapter has brought together many factors that need consideration when constructing a worksheet application. The different types of data you can enter into a worksheet are ancillary visual control data, variables, macros, and input, process, and output data. A plan for the layout of the data, based on the worksheet being split into quadrants, makes the worksheet easier to use. Range names should be used liberally in the design and construction of a worksheet.

You can improve the process of building formulas by the use of worksheet variables, range names, and formula step cells. By integrating absolute cell references into a formula, that one formula can be easily copied throughout a table or worksheet.

Finally, many factors affect the ultimate size of a worksheet: substituting numbers for formulas is important, as are strategies for reducing the size of a worksheet. Last, there are several points to consider when building a worksheet database that can greatly reduce its size and improve its performance.

The next chapter deals with the flip side of spreadsheet construction—not destruction, but debugging. You will learn where problems can arise and how to deal with them when they do.

FOUR:

Debugging the
Spreadsheet

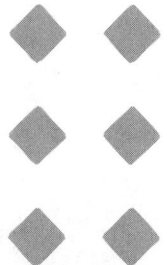

4
♦ ♦ ♦

PRACTICING GOOD WORK HABITS DURING THE DEVELOPMENT
of your worksheet is the best way to keep a worksheet bug-free. The learning
process itself provides you with the tools necessary to build a worksheet that
will not only perform successfully, but will also be easy to revise. This chapter
looks at some of the tools and techniques that are available to avoid problems
and to solve them when they arise. The subject of troubleshooting is, unfortunately, infinitely large, so this chapter concentrates on solutions to some
common, garden-variety bugs.

Worksheet documentation can consist of almost any pertinent information,
but there are several built-in worksheet tools and techniques that can help to
document the worksheet. These will be covered in the first part of this chapter.

The process of debugging formulas will then be covered—a critical topic, since
formulas are so important to the functioning of the worksheet. Following this will
be a discussion of circular references. Although not always a bug, the CIRC indicator is usually a sign that something is wrong. The last part of the chapter deals with
some common hidden dangers that can lurk in any worksheet.

⊗ *CAUTION* ♦ *Whenever you suspect that there is a serious
problem with a worksheet, you should immediately save it
under a new name, leaving the original file untouched on disk. The
debugging process can often be destructive, so it is best to work on a
copy, saving it to disk as necessary. When you have determined the
source of the problem, you can retrieve the original worksheet and
make your corrections there.*

♦ BUILT-IN DOCUMENTATION TECHNIQUES

There are many ways to document both the contents and the correct or normal
usage of a worksheet. The most popular is undoubtedly the "It's so obvious, what is
there to say?" type. On the other hand, a 200-page manuscript would be more

than most people could tolerate. The target of any documentation is to provide a practical description of the worksheet that is understandable to those who will need to interpret it, including yourself at a later date.

Many stand-alone programs are available that can help to document or troubleshoot a 1-2-3 worksheet. Although their use is beyond the scope of this book, your work routines may be such that a worksheet analyzer can help considerably. For example, if you are responsible for the maintenance of many worksheets that are created by others, you may need the extensive debugging features. Or, if you distribute worksheets to others, they may appreciate having a standardized set of documentation that these programs can produce.

The first line of defense in documenting a worksheet can be provided by several features that are found right within the Lotus worksheet. Several of these have been mentioned already as documentation aids: range names and macros. Other techniques include providing a worksheet map, using the Text format, printing row and column labels, and printing cell formulas.

RANGE NAMES

The liberal use of range names can do more to document a worksheet than any other method you can employ. They are easy to use, and they automatically keep track of the cells they name. Range names can be modified as necessary, and they also provide many benefits to the construction and use of a worksheet.

> **TIP** ◆ *The list of range names provided by the Range Name Table command can provide a simple but valuable piece of permanent documentation. Next to each name and address, enter a brief description of the name, including any pertinent remarks. You can keep this either within the worksheet, or in a separate documentation file.*

MACROS

Every worksheet can benefit from the inclusion of macro routines. After range names, macros are number two on the list of built-in features that serve as worksheet documentation. Where range names document the relationships among the cells, macros describe the necessary working routines that the worksheet normally follows. If every routine is written into a macro, then each one will be available for inspection or revision.

Build your macros around a hierarchical series of menus, write them in a structured manner, and anyone will be able to read their story and determine the normal working routines.

WORKSHEET MAP

If you lay out your worksheet in an orderly fashion, then a brief map of its structure can reveal the major ranges at a glance. This is particularly helpful if a worksheet has large tracts of processing cells that are never printed or viewed. Their existence will stand out on the map for all to see.

> **TIP** ◆ *Every range shown on the map should also show up in the range name table. This means that the table is a good way to verify the items on the map, and can serve as an index to them.*

FORMAT AS TEXT

The format style called Text is rarely called into action except for documentation purposes. When a formula cell is given a Text format, it displays its contents, not the result. Where a formula normally returns the result 4, when formatted as Text it displays its internal contents, such as 2+2 or @int(@pi+1).

Printing a worksheet that has been formatted using the Text style can provide yet another means of documenting its contents.

> **CAUTION** ◆ *Although formatted in Text style, the cell is still a formula, and it will therefore display only as much as the column width will allow. You may have to adjust the width of the column to view the entire formula. The maximum number of characters that can be viewed on the screen at one time is 72.*

INCLUDE ROW NUMBERS AND COLUMN LETTERS IN PRINTOUTS

This documentation technique is not built into Lotus: no print option allows you to print with the row numbers showing down the left-hand side of the page, and the column letters across the top. During the construction process, and later for reference purposes, having the rows and columns identified can be helpful. Fortunately, a little work can provide you with just such a printout.

Figure 4.1 shows a worksheet that can print the row and column labels for any range. Each cell in row 1 has the appropriate column letter, and each cell down column A has the appropriate row number. To include these row and column labels in a printout, set the print option Borders Rows to row 1 (range A1), and set Borders Columns to column A (again range A1).

Macro \Z, which starts in D6, performs the steps that are necessary to build the column labels from A to Z in row 1, and the row numbers 1 to 100 down column A:

```
/dfA2..A100 ˜ 2 ˜ 1 ˜ 9999 ˜
{home}/wcs4 ˜
@mid(@cell("address",{down}),1,
@find("$",@cell("address",{down}),1) – 1) ˜
/c ˜ B1..Z1 ˜
/rv{end}{right} ˜ ˜
/rlc{end}{right} ˜
```

In general, any worksheet can be printed using row 1 and column A for the labels—just extend them to the right and down as far as necessary. Depending on the needs of the worksheet in which the \Z macro is used, the number and location of the cells that are filled can be changed by editing the macro.

This macro is particularly helpful because entering the column letters manually would be a difficult task. The macro breezes through it by using the long

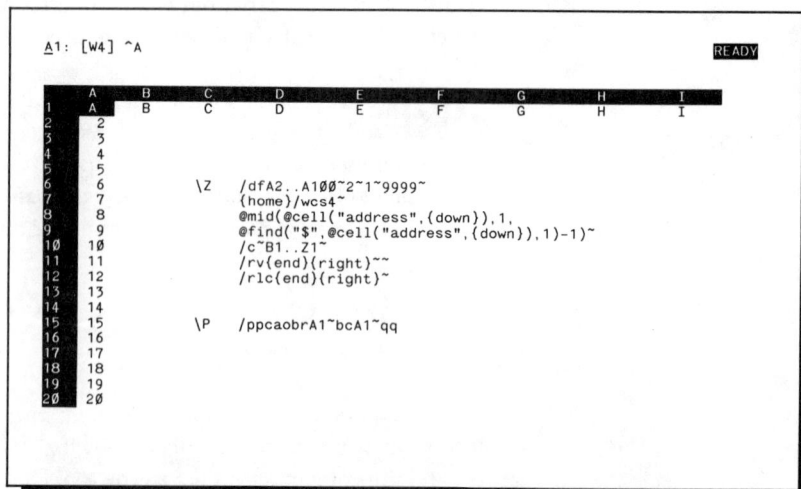

Figure 4.1 ◆ *A worksheet that prints with row and column labels*

@mid formula in the third and fourth lines shown above. The formula returns the column letter for any column in the worksheet, including columns with double letters, such as AA, CF, or GV.

The formula is shown here (split into two lines for clarity) as it appears in A1 before the Range Value command turns it into the actual letter A:

```
@mid(@cell("address",A2..A2),1,
@find("$",@cell("address",A2..A2),1) – 1)
```

Try typing this formula into A1 and copying it across that row. Remember not to include any spaces.

The macro \P in cell D15 of Figure 4.1 simply sets the printing borders to the correct row and column and then quits:

```
/ppcaobrA1 ˜ bcA1 ˜ qq
```

After invoking \P, you can specify the other print settings for the range that you want to print. If the macro text in the range C6..H15 in Figure 4.1 were printed with the row and column labels set as print borders by \P, the output would look like this:

A	C	D	E	F	G	H
6	\Z	/dfA2..A100 ˜ 2 ˜ 1 ˜ 9999 ˜				
7		{home}/wcs4 ˜				
8		@mid(@cell("address",{down}),1,				
9		@find("$",@cell("address",{down}),1) – 1) ˜				
10		/c ˜ B1.. Z1 ˜				
11		/rv{end}{right} ˜ ˜				
12		/rlc{end}{right} ˜				
13						
14						
15	\P	/ppcaobrA1 ˜ bcA1 ˜ qq				

If you build the row and column labels in an otherwise empty worksheet, you can save that worksheet and later bring it into another worksheet for printing. If the labeled worksheet were named ROW_COL, you could bring it into an active worksheet by placing the cell pointer in A1 and issuing the command

```
fcceROW_COL ˜
```

PRINTING CELL FORMULAS

Always available on the Print menu is the Options Other Cell-Formulas command. This prints the contents of each cell in the print range in one long list. Each row in the printout contains four separate pieces of information about the cell:

◆ Address

◆ Format

◆ Protection status

◆ Contents

Don't abuse this feature by using it to print every worksheet you create, cell by cell. You, too, will feel abused when trying to file away the mountain of paper that is produced. Printing the cell contents should generally be reserved for just a few instances.

When a problem arises in the worksheet, it can be helpful to have a full list of all its cells. While viewing one formula on the screen, you can quickly look at the cells it references by scanning the printed list.

You can document long or convoluted formulas by printing them out with the Cell-Formulas option. You can then annotate the printout with a thorough discussion of what the formulas are doing.

2.2 ◆ ————

⭐ **TRICK** ◆ *A useful and paper-saving solution is to print the cell contents of all or part of the worksheet, but send the output to a file, not to the printer. Then, if you have Release 2.2, use the File Import Text command to bring the print file back into a blank worksheet. In this form, the entire worksheet is in one long column of text. Now you can use the Range Search command to search through the list for any of the cell attributes or contents. These include references to a specific cell address, values (including ERR), @ functions, formulas, text, cell formats, or column widths.*

If you are using Release 2.01, you might want to use your word processor to browse and search through the printout of your worksheet's cells. But there are still plenty of tricks available in both Releases 2.01 and 2.2 to make it worthwhile to import the file back into 1-2-3.

The list of cells is printed in a row-by-row format so that cell B4, D4, and W4 come before A5. In 1-2-3, it is easy to sort the list of cells so that all cells from each column are grouped together. Plus, by addressing the list as a database and using the @find function in the criterion, even in Release 2.01 you can find any characters in the list, no matter where they fall within a line. Chapter 2 demonstrated this technique as a tool for searching a range name list, and Chapter 10 further explains the use of @find for this type of search.

◆ CATCHING FORMULA ERRORS

Formulas are at the core of the worksheet, and their integrity is therefore critical. The fact that they are built of many components that are hidden within a cell makes them the most common source of errors in the worksheet. You can take steps to ensure the validity of worksheet formulas, and later take actions to correct a bugged or suspect formula.

NUMBERS THAT REPLACE FORMULAS

The most common worksheet error (and perhaps the most embarrassing one) is mistakenly replacing a formula with a hard number. While the other formulas are being recalculated, that one cell remains stagnant and unchanging. Consider yourself lucky if the number is grossly out of range when compared to the values displayed by other nearby formulas. It will then stand out from the rest and, if your luck still holds, you will notice it. If you don't find it, be assured that whoever looks at the printout will undoubtedly find it immediately.

If you suspect that a range of formulas has a problem, you can format that range using the Text format, and then quickly scan the cells for one that contains only a number. You will probably not need to expand the column width to display the entire length of the formulas, because the difference between the formulas and a number will be quite obvious, as shown in the following example:

```
@if(@sum
@if(@sum
   1482
@if(@sum
@if(@sum
```

If the range of formulas is too large to scan without losing patience, try printing the range to disk with the Cell-Formulas option. Import the list back into a worksheet, and perform a Data Query Find with criteria that will spot the offending cell. Several possible search criteria are available. The following two examples assume the formulas in the input range start at A10.

Each formula will probably contain either an @ function or a plus sign. The search criteria can therefore look for all rows that do *not* have at least one of the characters (the other operators could also be included) by using the @find function to search for the @ or +. The result is included as the source for an @iserr function so that only characters that do not match will be found. The search formula is shown here divided into lines. Note the #and# operator, which combines the two pieces into one statement for the criterion:

@iserr(@find("@",A10,0) + 1)#and#
@iserr(@find(" + ",A10,0) + 1)

If the formulas are too varied to base the selection on specific characters, you can search for all rows that have just a few characters. Formulas are generally much longer than a plain number:

@length(A10)<15

DIVIDING BY ZERO

One of the most common formula problems that results in an error is that of dividing by zero. This is not a bug; dividing by zero is simply not a valid operation. The resulting ERR, however, can cause other formulas to also result in ERR, which—although accurate—is usually undesirable. Seeing many cells on a printout that display ERR can be disconcerting.

The formula should be written to take appropriate action if a cell that is used as a divisor has a value of zero (whether a number or a text entry). The @if function provides the solution:

@if(DIVISOR = 0,0,DIVIDEND/DIVISOR)

In this case, if DIVISOR equals zero, then no division is performed, and only zero is displayed. To calculate the percentage that each item on a list of expenses is of the total expenses, the @if statement would look like this:

@if(EXPENSES = 0,0,POSTAGE/EXPENSES)

With string arithmetic, you can have a blank cell displayed when the divisor equals zero:

@if(EXPENSES = 0," ",POSTAGE/EXPENSES)

Or, you can have a text value displayed that indicates something more than just a blank cell, but has no numeric value:

@if(EXPENSES = 0,"-",POSTAGE/EXPENSES)

SPACES ARE COUNTED, TOO

The @count function returns the number of occupied cells in a range, whether text or numbers. There are other @ functions that utilize this counting capability to do their job, including @avg, @std, and @var. The @avg function, for example, returns the same result as would (@sum/@count). A deadly error can occur when these functions address a range that contains a text cell. The worst-case example is when the text cell contains only a space character that was entered either by accident or to "erase" the contents of the cell.

Figure 4.2 shows a range in each of four columns. Three functions below them—@avg, @count, and @sum—reference each range, rows 2 through 5.

The range in column B contains a blank cell and three others with numbers, as reflected in the @count function. The average is 2, as expected.

In column C, the first cell in the range is 0. This does not change the sum, but does change the average because the count is now 4.

Column D has text in the first cell, which is counted by the two functions just as the zero is counted in column C. They return the appropriate results.

The range in E presents a dilemma. It looks just like the first range in B, but returns the same results as C and D. The problem resides in the first cell, which appears to be blank, but in fact contains a space. Its label prefix can be seen in the control panel. It is counted just as any other text cell would be. The extreme danger lies in the fact that you cannot see the space character.

> ⊗ **CAUTION** ◆ *It is normally a good habit to include at least one extra cell at each end of a range that is referenced by an @ function. This allows the formula to adjust its cell referencing if extra rows or columns are inserted within that range. Watch out, though, if the function is performing a count on the range.*

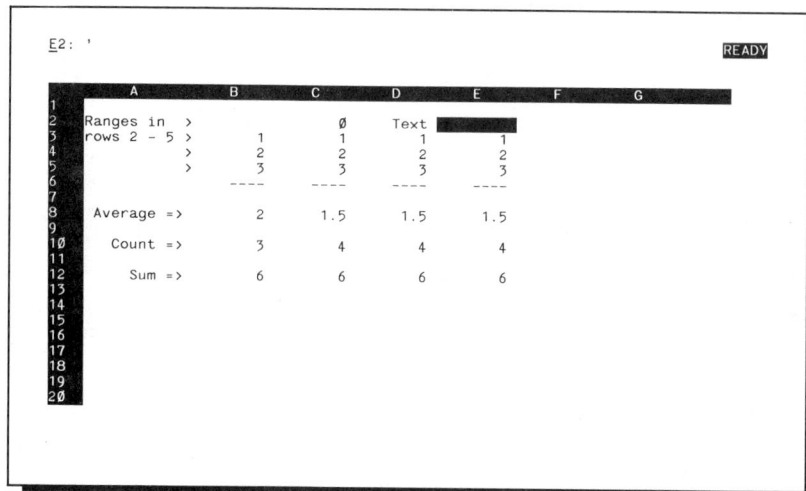

E2: '   READY

	A	B	C	D	E	F	G
1							
2	Ranges in >		0	Text			
3	rows 2 - 5 >	1	1	1	1		
4	>	2	2	2	2		
5	>	3	3	3	3		
6		----	----	----	----		
7							
8	Average =>	2	1.5	1.5	1.5		
9							
10	Count =>	3	4	4	4		
11							
12	Sum =>	6	6	6	6		

Figure 4.2 ◆ *Functions that count do so for all occupied cells*

In Figure 4.2, the dividing-line cells in row 6 would normally be included in an @ function's range. But when the function is a counting one, including the dividing line cell would produce an incorrect (or undesirable) result. In this case, the range should be precisely defined.

INCORRECT CELL REFERENCES

A formula that addresses even one wrong cell is as incorrect as though all its references were wrong. The formula may have been written incorrectly in the first place, or something may have happened to alter its cell references from the intended ones. You can employ several techniques when writing formulas that will improve the chances of their addressing the correct cells: use range names, point to cells, verify before copying, include extra cells in the range, and look out for migrating cell references.

Range Names

As always, range names are a fantastic aid to any cell referencing in the worksheet, whether in formulas, commands, or macros. If many formulas refer to the same range, that range can be named. If one of the formulas no longer refers to that name, you will know something is wrong. When writing a complex formula, naming key cells that it references can serve to verify that the formula was written correctly.

Pointing

Instead of typing the cell coordinates into a formula, use the cell pointer to indicate the cells to be referenced. Not only is this easier than trying to remember the exact address of each reference, but it also gives you visual assurance that the correct cell is being chosen.

Referencing Hidden Columns or Cells

You can hide columns and format cells as Hidden. Unfortunately, if information can be hidden, it can also be mistakenly included in a formula. Be sure to check for hidden data if formulas do not seem to be returning the correct results.

Verify before Copying

Before you copy one formula to many locations, you should double-check and triple-check its accuracy. This will save you from compounding an error and having to find each occurrence of it in the worksheet.

Include Extra Cells in the Range

A formula automatically adjusts its references to a range when rows or columns are inserted or deleted into that range. By including an extra cell, row, or column at both ends of the range, you can later increase the size of the range while expanding the reference in the formula. Note the previous caution when functions that count are being used.

Migrating Cell References

There is one cause of invalid cell references in formulas that occurs regularly but may give no evidence of having happened. This is when the Move command accidentally pulls a formula's reference cells to a new location, thereby changing the formula. Figure 4.3 shows how this can happen.

This is a simple table that has formulas in row 11 that sum the numbers entered in each column. It has totals in column H that sum the items in each row. The formula in B11 that sums column B can be seen in the control panel. In the lower right are two formulas: one sums column H, the TOTAL column, and the other sums row 11, the totals for each month. They are both displaying the same result, as expected.

Now look at Figure 4.4. Someone has decided that the entry for Paper in January actually belongs under Pens in April. Because the number needed to be moved to the new spot, the Move command was naturally used to make the change—a fatal decision.

Figure 4.3 ◆ *Functions referencing ranges*

```
B11: @SUM(B5..E7)                                              READY

          A        B      C       D       E       F      G      H
1
2                 Jan.   Feb.   March   April    May   June   TOTAL
3       ----------------------------------------------------------
4
5       Pencils     1      2       3       4       5      6      21
6       Erasers     1      2       3       4       5      6      21
7       Pens        1      2       3      1Ø       5      6      27
8       Paper clips 1      2       3       4       5      6      21
9       Paper              2       3       4       5      6      51
1Ø              -----  -----   -----   -----   -----  -----  -----
11               36     1Ø      15      26      25     3Ø  Wrong!
12
13                                            Sum Col. H =>    141
14                                            Sum Row 11 =>    142
15
16
17
18      Cell H11 =>  @IF(@SUM(H5..H9)<>@SUM(B11..G11),"Wrong!",@SUM(H5..H9))
19
2Ø
```

Figure 4.4 ◆ *The Move command has altered the cell references in a function*

As you can see in the control panel, when cell B9 was moved to E7 it pulled the sum function's cell references right along with it. Fortunately, the error in the cell reference stands out and can be corrected. In a long formula, a change such as this may not be as obvious and may go unnoticed. Use the Move command with caution.

There are also other indications that something is amiss in this example. The bizarre result being displayed for the sum in B11 indicates that something is grossly wrong. Moreover, the totals for column H and row 11 no longer match. Finally, the formula in H11 is displaying an error message, indicating that the two totals do not agree. This is a *cross-footing* formula that is written to catch just this kind of problem. The formula is shown in row 18. More on cross-footing later in this chapter.

Note that if the @sum functions had been written to include the dividing-line cells in row 10, the Move command would not have harmed the formulas. Only the corner cells of a range, not the internal cells, affect the reference of that range in a formula.

FUNCTION REFERENCES BASED ON OFFSETS

Some functions in 1-2-3 select a result from a list of many based on a given value. Some choose one cell from a range of cells, such as @index. Others select characters from a text cell, such as @mid. Another function, @choose, selects from an internal set of choices.

All of these functions have one thing in common: the items they reference are all named according to how far they are offset from the first one. The first item has no offset, and is therefore referred to as item zero; the next as item one; and so on. If you forget this and assume that the first must be item one, you will get results that are incorrect or ERR.

The functions that select a cell from a range of cells always refer to the first column or row in the range as zero. These functions include @vlookup, @hlookup, @index, and all of the @d data functions. For example, an @index function that selects the item in the second column (offset of 1) in the third row (offset of 2) from the range J11..K20 would return the value from the cell in K13:

@index(J11..K20,1,2)

The string functions @find, @mid, and @replace make their selection based on a starting point within the string being referenced. The first character in the string has an offset of zero. Using the @mid function, if you select three characters from the string Inconsequential starting at the character with an offset of 5, the result will be *seq*:

@mid("Inconsequential",5,3)

The @choose function makes its choice from a set of items written into the formula, based on a choose value. The first item has an offset of zero. Choosing the item with an offset of two returns the third item in the list, so that this example would return 30:

@choose(2,10,20,30,40,50)

If any of these functions return unexpected results or display ERR, be sure to check the reference they make to the list of choices.

INVALID ROUNDING DUE TO CELL FORMAT

One of the first and most difficult hurdles to overcome within the 1-2-3 worksheet is the concept of cell contents versus cell display. It is easy to get fooled by what you see on the screen, and make an incorrect assumption about what is in a cell.

A typical example of this occurs when a cell's format causes a value to be displayed that is not the same as the actual value within the cell. Figure 4.5 shows a sum function that sums six cells, each displaying 7, in the range B1..B6. By any manner of thinking, the sum should not be the 39 as shown, but 42. The

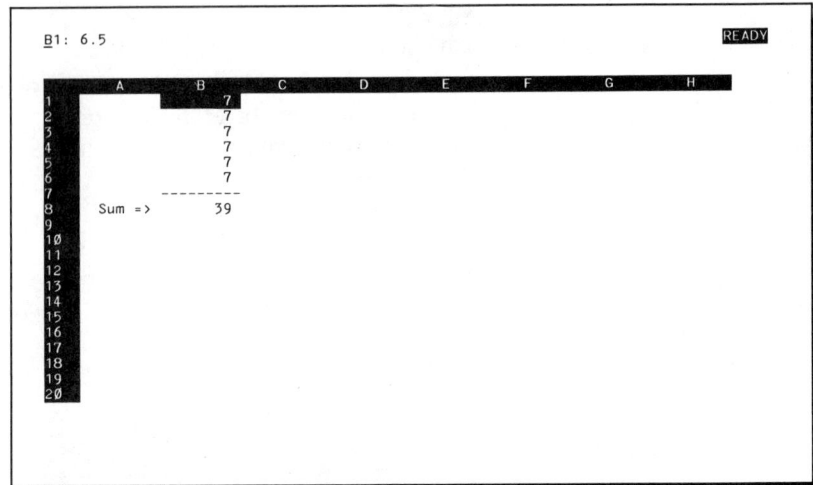

Figure 4.5 ◆ *Cell format can distort the displayed results*

reason for this erroneous sum can be seen in the control panel, where the content of the first cell is not 7, but 6.5. As it turns out, all of the cell values are actually 6.5, with a format of Fixed with zero decimals: (F0). The cell format is not indicated in the control panel because it has been set globally.

This extreme example points out the danger of leaving the contents of a cell unchanged while relying on the format of the cell (display) to remove significant information. This is the opposite of the more subtle problem that everyone encountered when moving from slide rules to calculators.

With calculators, you could suddenly supply answers with 12 or more digits, seeming to indicate extreme accuracy. Unfortunately, in real-life situations those extra digits are rarely significant digits, and should generally be disposed of. When you put 14.7 gallons of gas into your car after having driven 415.5 miles, then the miles per gallon will only be accurate to three digits, the minimum accuracy obtained in the calculation. The correct mileage is 28.3, not 28.265306122448984 as calculated.

There are two methods of solving the problem in Figure 4.5. Either the numbers themselves can be altered, or the way they are displayed can be changed. Figure 4.6 shows both.

The first method assumes that the exact value in each cell is not critical. Each number is altered so that it conforms with the desired display format, as shown in column D (the cell contents are shown in column F). Here the @round function is employed to round each value to a whole number (no digits to the right of the decimal). Each cell rounds up to 7, and the sum of the

```
B1: 6.5                                                              READY

        A         B         C         D      E        F           G        H
1                      7                      7     =  @ROUND(B1,Ø)
2                      7                      7     =  @ROUND(B2,Ø)
3                      7                      7     =  @ROUND(B3,Ø)
4                      7                      7     =  @ROUND(B4,Ø)
5                      7                      7     =  @ROUND(B5,Ø)
6                      7                      7     =  @ROUND(B6,Ø)
7                 ---------             ---------      ---------------
8      Sum =>         39                     42     =  @SUM(F1..F6)
9
1Ø
11                                         6.5
12                                         6.5
13                                         6.5      <= Format as Fixed-1
14                                         6.5
15                                         6.5
16                                         6.5
17                                     ---------
18                                        39.Ø
19
2Ø
```

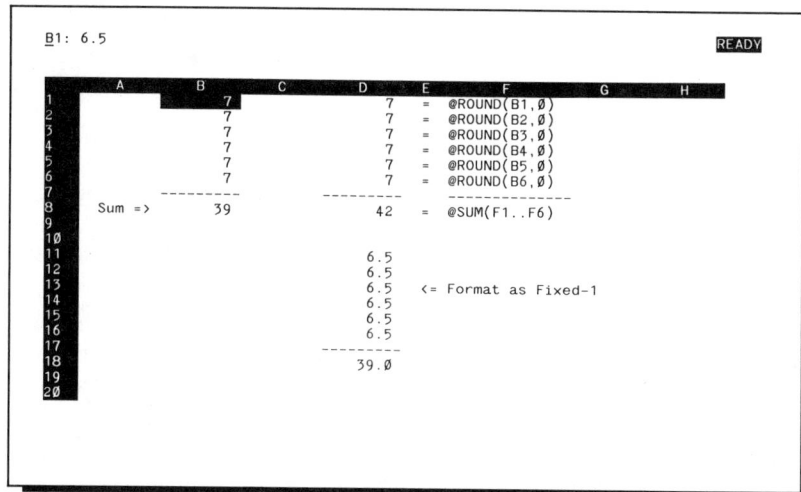

Figure 4.6 ◆ *Resolving the contents versus display dispute*

rounded numbers is then 42. With this technique, the numbers could just as easily be entered as integers in the first place, since their decimal value is of no importance.

Using the second method implies that the actual values are more important than the way they will look on the screen. In the range starting at D11, the numbers are left untouched, having instead been given a format that reflects the true contents, fixed with one decimal: (F1). The sum shows 39, which makes sense for the values that are displayed.

Either method can be used, depending on which has priority—the values being entered or the way they look when displayed.

VERIFYING FORMULAS

Once formulas are entered, there are two techniques for ensuring that they are correct and that they remain that way: using simple test data and including cross-footing formulas.

Using Simple Test Data

The first thing to do when checking the accuracy of a formula is to supply it with simple data that will return predictable results. All of the examples in this book are kept simple and brief for the same reason, since complex data would only obscure the point being demonstrated.

By filling a formula's data range with nothing but 1s, any invalid formulas will be likely to stand out clearly. Similarly, any cell that is supposed to be a formula but is actually a hard number will also be obvious.

Include Cross-Footing Formulas

Many problems can be averted by using extra formulas to double-check the intended results. Not only does a secondary formula validate the primary formula, but in the process of creating it you are approaching the data from a new direction, giving you a second and confirming perspective of the data.

Earlier in this chapter, the use of cross-footing formulas was mentioned as a check against formulas that reference their data incorrectly. In Figure 4.4, the cross-foot formula in H11 served as a validation check by comparing the total of the sum formulas in row 11 to that of those in column H. If the totals were not the same, it issued an error message. This is a simple way to include a permanent check in a critical formula.

> ⊗ CAUTION ◆ *When the range being checked contains calculations that involve unresolved or repeating decimals, the cross-foot formula may find an imbalance that you do not want flagged. This is due to internal rounding errors that cause the two sets of totals to differ slightly.*
>
> *The solution is to round the formulas in each component of the cross-foot formula. Here, split into three lines for clarity, is the cross-foot formula from Figure 4.4 that incorporates the @round function:*
>
> ```
> @if(@round(@sum(H5..H9),2)< >
> @round(@sum(B11..G11),2),
> "Wrong!",@sum(H5..H9))
> ```

Another use for validation formulas is to sum a range of percentages, expecting a result of 1. This would be the case when a list of items is totaled, and then each item is divided by the total to return its percent value. All of the percents should add up to 1, the whole.

To verify the integrity of a range of cell that includes subtotal cells that roll up into a grand total, you can often simply sum up the entire range and divide by 2. The result should be the same as the grand total.

◆ CIRCULAR REFERENCES

A circular reference is caused by a formula that includes its own cell among those it references. A sum formula in B12 that references the range (A1..G29) would cause a circular reference. This condition can be caused either by the formula directly referencing itself, or because a cell that it references refers back to it (an indirect circular reference).

There are situations where you can ignore the CIRC indicator at the bottom of the screen, but those times will always be the result of your intending to build a circular reference into the worksheet. Any other time indicates an error condition, or at least a condition that needs attention.

The most common source of circular references is when a formula's cell is included in the range that it addresses, as described above. When pointing to a range to be referenced in a formula, it is often a common mistake to pull the range all the way back to the formula's cell, creating a circular reference.

Sometimes the problem arises because the formula cell is moved to a more convenient location, and that location happens to be inside of the range it addresses.

A more confusing and far more "circular" situation occurs when a formula refers back to itself indirectly. The link that creates the circular reference may go through many cells before referring back to the formula cell.

Once the CIRC indicator appears on your screen, the immediate task is to find the offending cell. This is as simple as invoking the Worksheet Status screen, and checking the Circular Reference spot. Even if the reference is indirect, the cell that is causing the problem will be shown, and you can return to the worksheet to edit the formula and correct the circular condition.

◆ OTHER HIDDEN DANGERS _____

There are certain problems that can sneak up on an unsuspecting user at the most unexpected times. Here are a few of the more common ones.

COMMAND SETTINGS THAT MYSTERIOUSLY CHANGE

When the worksheet is saved, all the command settings are saved with it. These include the options for printing, graphing, and all of the data commands. When the worksheet is later retrieved, every command that was executed before can again be executed just by giving the Go command (or View or Extract). Unfortunately, a user often assumes that those settings are the same as they were, when in fact they have been changed.

The only safe way to handle this "thin ice" is to clear all the options for a command, and then specify each one as necessary. Although this is tedious, in a worksheet of anything but the smallest size this is the only way to guarantee that a command will perform as anticipated. This is why the speed and convenience of macros are necessary to the full use of the worksheet.

As discussed in Chapter 1, one reason for writing macros is that they can execute worksheet commands consistently. This means that the macro must be in control of the command, and the only way to have total control is to specify every necessary setting, just as though you were doing it by hand:

/ppcarDATA ˜ oml10 ˜ mr132 ˜ s\015 ˜ qagpq

With macros, it is easy to set every option each time a command is invoked. The command will perform exactly as you expect it to.

FINDING HIDDEN CELLS

Cells that are formatted as Hidden can be difficult to find once they are "lost." If you suspect that there are some cells hiding in the worksheet, there are two courses of action you can take, which you will recognize from previous examples.

The first is to set up a database for the range in question and perform a search for all cells with a Hidden format. Note that the Range Search command of Release 2.2 won't do the job in this situation, as it can only search through a cell's contents, not its format. If the data starts in A10 and includes column B and C, then entering these functions in the criterion range would do the job:

```
@cell("format",A10..A10) = "H"
@cell("format",B10..B10) = "H"
@cell("format",C10..C10) = "H"
```

If the worksheet is too large or to fragmented to use the database method, print the whole worksheet to disk using the Cell-Formulas option. Then, use the File Import Text command to send the print file back into a worksheet (preferably a new empty one). In Release 2.2, use the Range Search command to search for occurrences of the characters (H), which is how the Hidden format is represented in the printout. If you have Release 2.01, set up a database on the list of cells. The criterion would specify (H), so that if the list of cells started in A10, then the criterion would look like this:

```
@find("(H)",A10,0)
```

Any hidden cells would be found, and their addresses could be noted before returning to the original worksheet.

NUMBERS MISTAKENLY ENTERED AS TEXT

It is deadly when a formula is mistakenly overwritten by a number, but an equally disastrous problem is created when a number is mistakenly entered as text. Sometimes a novice user tries to align a number in the cell by inserting spaces in front of it. But even an experienced user can accidentally tap the Space bar while entering a number, turning it into text that—although it looks like a number—has no numeric value.

If you suspect that a stray cell was mistakenly entered as text, you can check a range by setting up a quick database and performing a search. (Remember, the Range Search command in Release 2.2 won't be of any help here.) The criteria would find any cells containing text. If the data under the column titles starts in A10, then the criteria would use this logical function:

```
@isstring(A10)
```

If a new user has entered a whole range of numbers as text, it is an easy matter to correct. Just write a formula that changes the text back into an actual number, copy the formula for the entire range, and use the Range Value command to copy the formulas back onto the original cells as values:

```
@value(A10)
```

Chapter 7 goes into more detail on methods of fixing numbers that were erroneously entered as text.

INVALID DATA

Whenever you use data, you may face the inherent problem of having bad information to begin with. With computers, this problem is compounded by the immense quantity of data that they can collect, and by the fact that the data is, of necessity, generally hidden from sight.

Database programs usually have some means of validating data before it can be entered into a record. Unfortunately, there is no way to format a cell in 1-2-3 so that it will, for example, only accept numeric entries greater than zero, or only text entries of exactly three characters.

The only way to control the data that is entered into a worksheet is through the use of macros. Figure 4.7 shows a data entry macro that not only automates and speeds up data entry, but also validates the data before it is accepted into the worksheet. The macro starts by jumping to the range DATA, which begins at C17. The user is prompted to enter the first item, a three-character ID, which is stored in the variable cell CHOICE:

```
{goto}DATA ~
{getlabel "Enter 3 character ID- ",CHOICE}
```

```
D18: [W12]                                                              READY
Enter 3 digit Shelf Number- S/

     A          B          C          D          E          F          G
1  CHOICE     abc
2
3  \Z                    {goto}DATA~
4  \GET_ID               {getlabel Enter 3 character ID- ,CHOICE}
5                        {if @length(CHOICE)<>3}{beep 2}{branch \GET_ID}
6                        @upper(CHOICE){calc}~{right}
7  \GET_SHELF            {getnumber Enter 3 digit Shelf Number- S/,CHOICE}
8                        {if @iserr(CHOICE)}{beep 2}{branch \GET_SHELF}
9                        {if CHOICE<100#or#CHOICE>999}{beep 2}{branch \GET_SHELF}
10                       +"S/"&@string(CHOICE,0){calc}~
11                       {down}{left}{branch \GET_ID}
12
13
14
15                       ID         Storage Unit
16                       -------------------------
17            DATA =>     ZYX        S/789
18                       ABC
19
20
                                    CMD
```

Figure 4.7 ◆ *Data entry and validation macro*

A macro {if} statement then checks the entry in CHOICE. If its string length is not the required three characters, the macro beeps and branches back to \GET_ID, which repeats the prompt, and the user must again enter information:

{if @length(CHOICE)<>3}{beep 2}{branch \GET_ID}

If the information is correct, the macro in row 6 enters CHOICE into the cell pointer's current cell. By using the @upper function, whatever was entered into CHOICE will be automatically capitalized when it is put into the range DATA. The {calc} command simply turns the @upper function into a hard value. The cell pointer moves right to the next cell in the current row of DATA:

@upper(CHOICE){calc} ~ {right}

Note that two methods could restrict the choices for the ID even further. If there are only a small number of valid ID codes, they could be supplied in one or more menus. The user would simply select one from the menu, guaranteeing that the ID is valid. If there were too many valid codes to conveniently put into menus, a lookup table could be used.

The table would be one long list containing every valid code. The user would be prompted to enter a code, and the entry would be validated against the table, named TABLE_ID in this example, with this macro:

{if @iserr(@vlookup(@upper(CHOICE),
    TABLE_ID,0))}{branch \GET_ID}

The degree of validation depends only on the requirements of the worksheet.

The macro in Figure 4.7 continues with the routine \GET_SHELF in row 7, which prompts the user for a three-digit Shelf Number. It prefaces the input with a two-character prefix, S/, to remind the user of how the data will look when it is finally entered. You can see the prompt in the control panel, and here is the macro:

```
{getnumber "Enter 3 digit Shelf Number- S/",CHOICE}
```

Then the macro checks CHOICE to make sure that only a number was entered and that CHOICE is not displaying ERR. If CHOICE is a valid number, a second validation makes sure that it falls between 100 and 999, no more or less than 3 digits. If not, the macro will branch back to \GET_SHELF to repeat the Shelf Number input:

```
{if @iserr(CHOICE)}{beep 2}{branch \GET_SHELF}
{if CHOICE<100#or#CHOICE>999}{beep 2}{branch
\GET_SHELF}
```

If CHOICE is OK, the macro continues in row 10. A string formula is created that attaches the Shelf Number preface, S/, to the three-digit number that was just entered in CHOICE. The formula is evaluated and entered into the current cell:

```
+"S\"&@string(CHOICE,0){calc}~
```

The last line of the macro moves the cell pointer down and left to a new cell in the ID column, and the macro repeats at \GET_ID:

```
{down}{left}{branch \GET_ID}
```

The importance of using macros for data entry cannot be overstated. The time saved and the accuracy achieved are far too beneficial to ignore.

WORKSHEET TEMPLATES THAT GROW THEIR OWN DATA

A worksheet *template* is a worksheet that normally has no data in it, only the shell that is ready to accept data. Sometimes, however, a blank template can suddenly become filled with data. The mystery can almost always be tracked to a user who forgot to save the template under a new name, and just repeated the save keystrokes by rote: SLASH FILE SAVE ENTER REPLACE.

To circumvent this possibility, you can include a \0 macro that immediately prompts the user for a file name, and then saves the worksheet under that name:

```
\0              {getlabel "Please enter new file name- ",NAME}
                /fs
NAME            Newname
                ~
```

◆ SUMMARY

This chapter has discussed many common bugs that can occur in a worksheet, and how they can be controlled. There are built-in techniques for documenting a worksheet that will also enhance its overall capabilities. You have also learned the many ways that formulas can become bugged, and methods for determining the source of the error.

Circular references are rarely intended, but are quite simple to correct once the problem is noticed. Finally, some important hidden dangers can trip up even an expert Lotus user. By keeping a watchful eye during worksheet development and having some debugging tools at the ready, you can produce worksheets that run smoothly and reliably.

The next chapter deals with the marriage of Lotus and your hard disk. You will be introduced to several timesaving techniques, and you will learn how to build an automated menu system that will take you into Lotus and then to the subdirectory of your choice.

FIVE:

Integrating 1-2-3 with Your Hard Disk

5

◆ ◆ ◆

FILE OPERATIONS ARE AN ESSENTIAL PART OF ALL WORKSHEET
routines. A solid footing for control can be built on a well-organized file system
that allows fast access to the 1-2-3 program and its worksheet files. This chapter
shows you how to merge 1-2-3 and your hard disk into a solid working partnership.

First, you learn the benefits of using a hard disk with 1-2-3, which lays the
foundation for the topics covered later in the chapter, and will perhaps help to
convert those of you who still use floppies exclusively.

Then, the organization of files on the hard disk is considered, along with the
basic DOS commands needed to control subdirectories. This chapter presents
a simple but effective DOS menu system that can automate your entry into
1-2-3. If you dabble with DOS, parts of this system will be familiar—file paths,
the Path statement, and batch files.

Lotus is well-equipped to handle files on a hard disk. In this chapter, you will
learn about the File Directory command, the Global Default subdirectory, the
123.CNF file, the AUTO123 worksheet, and the \0 macro. All of these features are then combined to create the Lotus Gateway application, which takes
you from the DOS prompt into 1-2-3, and then to the worksheet subdirectory
of your choice.

Every topic discussed here is an important part of using the Lotus worksheet,
and is as relevant on a floppy-disk system as it is on a hard disk. With floppies,
however, the advantages described will not be as apparent, and the techniques
demonstrated will often be unnecessary. Even if you do not have a hard disk
yet, you should start to master the features shown here, and build a model of
the Gateway on your floppy system to appreciate its unique benefits.

◆ A HARD DISK OFFERS CAPACITY, SPEED, AND CONVENIENCE _____

A hard disk will enhance every program you use, especially 1-2-3. The
spreadsheet is a working environment, and a hard disk serves to expand that
workplace in many ways.

CAPACITY

A 20-megabyte hard disk has the capacity of approximately 60 standard floppy disks. (Don't forget to factor that in when determining the cost of a hard disk; you will be replacing at least that many floppies.) This huge capacity allows you to avoid file duplication because all your files can be stored in one place. Startup configuration files, DOS files, and your favorite utilities need not be copied to different disks.

A drive with megabytes of storage can keep every program you own at the ready. Memory-resident programs can be loaded at any time, and all of their ancillary files will always be available. For Lotus, all of its associated programs and configuration files can be stored in one subdirectory, and only one copy of the Lotus drive set, 123.SET, is needed.

A large-capacity disk allows worksheets larger than the standard 360K floppy disk to be saved. With expanded memory opening up megabytes of RAM, large disks become even more important. With the increase in disk capacity comes the equally important increase in performance.

SPEED

The first thing you will notice when using 1-2-3 on a hard disk is that it loads many times faster than it does from a floppy disk. Where it may take 16 seconds to load from a floppy, it takes only 4 or 5 seconds on a moderately fast hard disk—a 300 to 400 percent increase in speed. The speed difference when loading worksheet files is just as significant, as is the time saved by not having to switch floppy disks for different worksheet files, or even trying to find the right disk.

What do you do with all this savings in time?

- Develop safer work habits by saving your worksheets more frequently.

- Easily retrieve files from which to extract information for another worksheet.

- Share data more readily with other programs.

- Experiment with two or three different versions of a worksheet.

- Leave work early.

In general, your control of the environment is greatly improved with the added speed of a hard disk.

TIP ◆ *Many users consistently load the program by typing LOTUS at the DOS prompt. This calls the Lotus Access System, from which you can run 1-2-3, PrintGraph, Translate, or Install. But 99 percent of the time you use 1-2-3, and you can jump directly into the worksheet from DOS by typing 123. Not only does this save time, it also saves you about 7K of RAM. You can access the other programs directly from DOS by typing PGRAPH, TRANS, or INSTALL.*

CONVENIENCE

Now that Lotus Development Corporation has removed copy protection from 1-2-3, you no longer need the Copyon or Copyhard program to run it directly from your hard disk. With megabytes of room, your 1-2-3 subdirectory can hold multiple driver set files, *.SET, for running different configurations of the spreadsheet. You can also have more than one version of the 123.CNF file to use with different global default settings.

Your worksheet template files and macro libraries are all just a few keystrokes away, making them all the more valuable. Since all your programs are instantly available, you will tend to make more use of them, which in itself gives you more control over the working environment.

When previously time-consuming worksheet routines become almost effortless with a hard disk, you will realize what a valuable addition it is to your system.

CAUTION ◆ *The size and convenience of a hard disk can lull the unwary user into complacency. Remember that you must keep backup copies of all your files on other disks. You can either save a worksheet directly to a floppy disk when you are done working with it, or use the DOS command BACKUP or XCOPY to back up all your data files at one time. Hard disks are reliable, but the surest way to cause a problem is by not having the insurance of a recent backup.*

A CLASSIC DEMONSTRATION OF CONTROL WITH A HARD DISK

If you do not use a hard disk, or if you have one but have not yet integrated it into your normal working routines, here's a simple example of its use with 1-2-3 that should open your eyes to its convenience, as well as show you a valuable technique that is often neglected.

You cannot print a graph from within the worksheet, and this fact has often been lamented. Typically, to print a graph on a floppy disk system, you have to go through these steps:

1. Save graph to *.PIC file.

2. Save current worksheet to disk.

3. Quit 1-2-3.

4. Replace drive A disk with PrintGraph disk.

5. Run PrintGraph, print your graph, and quit to DOS.

6. Replace drive A disk with Lotus System disk.

7. Load 1-2-3.

8. Retrieve worksheet and continue.

This can be agonizingly slow with floppy disks—slow enough that users do not readily print just one graph. With a hard disk, the program disks do not need to be swapped, which eliminates steps 4 and 6. Moreover, the speed at which the files are saved and the programs are run makes this entire routine almost, but not quite, painless. Here's how to make it completely painless:

1. Save graph to *.PIC file.

2. Use the System command to go to DOS.

3. Run PrintGraph, print your graph, and quit to DOS.

4. Type *EXIT* to return to 1-2-3 and your worksheet.

That is all there is to it. Since the 1-2-3 program subdirectory will be the current directory at DOS, PrintGraph is immediately ready to call. Note that if you have a very large worksheet in memory, or less than 640K of RAM to begin with, there may not be enough memory available to use the system command to run PrintGraph or another program. Floppy disk users: Don't forget that the System command is available to you, too, as long as the DOS file, COMMAND.COM, is on your A drive disk. You will still have to switch to your PrintGraph disk, but the time saved by using this technique will be even greater than for hard disk users.

With the ease of this routine, you can now call PrintGraph from within the worksheet, with almost no waiting, and with just 12 keystrokes:

```
/s
PGRAPH
EXIT
```

♦ ORGANIZING YOUR FILES

Because a hard disk can hold so much more than a floppy, keeping your files in order is critical. There are two basic rules to file organization: each program should reside in its own subdirectory, and data files that have a similar purpose should be kept together in a subdirectory of their own.

KEEP APPLES WITH APPLES, AND ORANGES WITH ORANGES

All 1-2-3 program files (from the Lotus program disks) should be kept together in one subdirectory; give it an obvious name such as *Lotus* or *123*. In another subdirectory for data files, you might keep tax-related worksheets from Lotus, as well as files from your word processor, financial-planning program, and so on. This subdirectory could have the name Taxes. All of the files in it would be related in some way to your taxes. Where on your disk you create these subdirectories is a matter of choice.

> ⊗ **CAUTION** ♦ *Some people prefer to keep all Lotus worksheet files together as a child of the Lotus program subdirectory, such as C:\123\Wksht. You will quickly outgrow this system due to its organizational weakness—it would lead you to keep separate subdirectories for word processor documents, database files, and so on. Trying to find all files related to your taxes would then require you to search through half a dozen subdirectories. Treat your hard disk as you would your file cabinet, and create subdirectories (folders) for items that are related by topic.*

Although it is important to keep related files together, a subdirectory should not contain so many files that it cannot be scanned easily for a given name. If a subdirectory becomes unwieldy, then it's time to create a secondary subdirectory and split the files between the two, using logical criteria to determine the split.

MAKING BACKUPS OF WORKSHEET FILES

Consider the necessity of making backups both a tip and a caution, because having a backup copy of a file serves two purposes. First, it is insurance against disk problems that could destroy the original. Second, the backup also serves as a protected copy of a previous version of a file. If you unknowingly delete or otherwise damage a portion of the active worksheet and then save it to disk, you can retrieve the backup and your losses will be mitigated.

There are two simple ways to back up your worksheet files, and both are valid for hard-disk or floppy-disk systems. The first, and perhaps most reliable, is to always save the worksheet to a backup floppy disk when you are done with the file for the day. This gives immediate insurance and also keeps the backup worksheet current.

The second method is perhaps an easier routine to follow, and that is to follow a normal hard disk backup procedure on a regular basis. You can make backup copies of all files on the hard disk daily or weekly using the DOS BACKUP command. The problem with this method is that you may end up having a backup copy that is a week old when an important worksheet is accidentally destroyed.

> **TIP** ♦ *If you do not want to follow a daily backup routine, this technique can protect worksheets during their development, although not against total hard disk failure. Maintain a subdirectory named TEMP that holds files temporarily. While building a worksheet, you can occasionally save the file to TEMP instead of to the normal directory for the worksheet. The extra file serves as a temporary backup copy. Empty the TEMP subdirectory of all files on a regular basis.*

> **TIP** ♦ *Another way to prevent short-term losses is to archive your worksheet under different names. While building a worksheet, give the file a name of less than eight characters and tag a version number to the end. You could call the first draft FILE1, the second FILE2, and so on. This technique can save many hours of work when a worksheet that has already been saved back to disk is discovered to have been damaged by an ill-behaved macro.*

♦ DOS DUTIES: FILE PATHS, TREE, AND BATCH FILES

If you already know and use DOS commands, and you are familiar with DOS file names in Lotus, you may want to skim this section. If you are not fluent with the language of DOS, take the time to read about the essential commands for dealing with files on a hard disk. Then you can refer to your DOS manual or other reference books for more detailed information.

THE PATH TO A FILE

A file name in DOS can include an extra segment called the *path*. The file's path is the chain of subdirectories that must be followed to find that file. In this way, you can have two files with the same name on the same disk, but with different paths:

A:\Data\Taxes\CHECKS.WK1

and

A:\Data\Budget\CHECKS.WK1

Lotus conforms to the DOS path rule, in that it allows you to specify the file name with its complete path when saving or retrieving the file. For example, you can specify B:\Budget\1990\FILENAME.XYZ.

You can even use different file extensions for worksheets, graphs, and print files besides *.WK1, *.PIC, and *.PRN. This is not a common practice, though, because only the files with the default extensions will be displayed by 1-2-3 in file operation menus. Here are examples of the four parts that define a file's name.

Drive	Path	Name	Extension
A	\Budget\Taxes\	CHECKS	.WK1
C	\Nadine\	FILELIST	.PRN
C	\1990\March\Expenses\	CALCTOTL	.MAR
D	\	GRAPH_1	.PIC

TIP ♦ *Using numbers in subdirectory or file names is legitimate, but 1-2-3 Release 2.01 is less flexible when you use a number as the first character of a subdirectory name. If you try to change to a directory such as 1990, 1-2-3 will beep when you type the first character, the number 1, into the File Directory command, and will not accept the name. Solution: When prompted for the subdirectory name, type a letter first, then backspace over it and type in the numbers.*

VIEWING THE DIRECTORY TREE

If you use or have seen demonstrated one of the many hard-disk management programs on the market, you may have appreciated its graphic representation of the hard disk's subdirectory organization. The TREE command in DOS will display your hard-disk structure, but, unfortunately, not in a particularly attractive or useful way (depending on your version of DOS). Nonetheless, type *TREE C:* at the prompt and you will see the subdirectory listing of your hard disk scroll by on the screen. Remember that this is an external DOS command, so the file TREE.EXE or TREE.COM must be in the current subdirectory, or in one that is on the current path. This command will be used again later in the construction of the Lotus Gateway.

BATCH FILES

A batch file is nothing more than a text file, with the file name extension .BAT, that is made up of lines of text that issue DOS commands, one after another in a "batch." Batch files are therefore similar to Lotus keystroke macros. DOS also has a small but effective batch programming language that will interest the curious user. Within narrower limits, it extends the batch language just as the Lotus Command Language extends the power of macros.

Creating a Batch File

You can use your word processor to create a batch file, as long as you save or export the document to ASCII format—pure text, with no word processor formatting codes included. You can also use the DOS-supplied program, EDLIN, which is fast for these short writing tasks but not particularly fun to use. Better still, you can use 1-2-3 to create and save any type of text file. The method of printing to a disk file is explained further in Chapter 12.

A Batch File to Start Lotus

Here is a batch file named 123.BAT that will take you into the Lotus worksheet and, when you quit Lotus, return you to the root directory of the disk:

```
C:
cd \123
123
cd \
```

All the lines contain normal DOS commands that can be typed from the keyboard in the usual manner. Here is a description of those commands:

C:	*Change drives to C (ensures that C is the current drive)*
cd \123	*Change to the 123 subdirectory (named 123 for this example)*
123	*Call the Lotus program*
cd \	*When back at DOS, change to C:\, the root directory*

If you frequently use the Lotus System command, you may want to add one more line to 123.BAT: the EXIT statement. You should enter EXIT before the 123 command, and preferably before C:. This will prevent you from loading a second copy of Lotus if you have used the System command to leave a 1-2-3 session that is already in memory. Be careful though, because you may want to go to DOS temporarily from another program, and then run Lotus. With the EXIT statement in 123.BAT, you would simply pop back into the first program, and never reach Lotus!

Of course, you can create a batch file to start any other program just by revising the subdirectory and file names.

A Menu System for Batch Files

With a little thought, you can create a simple menu system that will allow you to access Lotus and all the other programs on your hard disk. By automating the routine task of going in and out of your programs, you will eliminate many Change Directory commands as well as the time-consuming precision that is required to spell each subdirectory.

> **TIP** ◆ *You should make it a point to complete your hard-disk organization by establishing your batch files in a DOS menuing system that is activated with a batch file called MENU. In this way, whenever you quit a program that was called by a batch file, you will be returned to the menu system, from which another program can be called.*

◆ *LOTUS FILE COMMANDS AND FEATURES* _____

If you have planned your hard-disk organization well, your Lotus worksheets are logically organized into subdirectories that may also include data files from other programs. The tools supplied with 1-2-3 make the process of navigating the hard disk and accessing those worksheets relatively simple, and will serve to complete the Gateway application described later in this chapter.

You can use the File Directory command to change to a new default subdirectory during a 1-2-3 session. You can set the Global Default Directory so all sessions of Lotus begin in the same subdirectory, as long as you have used the Update command to save the current default settings to the 123.CNF file. When a worksheet uses the name AUTO123 and resides in the default subdirectory, it will be automatically retrieved when 1-2-3 is first loaded. Finally, the auto-invoking macro, named \0, will serve as the final link in the automated Lotus Gateway.

FILE DIRECTORY

You can use the File Directory command to change the current directory at any time. If you change to C:\Budget, whenever you execute a file command the files listed in the 1-2-3 menu will be those in \Budget.

> **TIP** ◆ *The current directory on a drive remains active until you change it, even when you change to a different drive. If you use the File Directory command to change to D:\, drive C will still be set to its current directory, \Budget. To return to \Budget, you need only specify the drive, C, in the File Directory command. This saves many keystrokes when you are returning to a path that is long and complex.*

Figure 5.1 shows a disk's root directory during the File Retrieve command. The Name key, F3, was pressed to display a full screen listing, although there are no worksheet files to be shown, only subdirectories. To choose one of the displayed subdirectories, highlight it and press Enter; the worksheet files or subdirectories beneath it will then be offered.

> **CAUTION** ◆ *When you retrieve a worksheet from a displayed subdirectory, you are not changing the default directory. If you plan to use several files from one subdirectory, use the File Directory command to set that subdirectory as the default.*

If you save a new, as yet unnamed, worksheet by specifying only a file name, it is saved to the default drive and subdirectory. For example, if the current default directory is C:\TAXES, saving the worksheet using this command

/fsFILENAME ˜

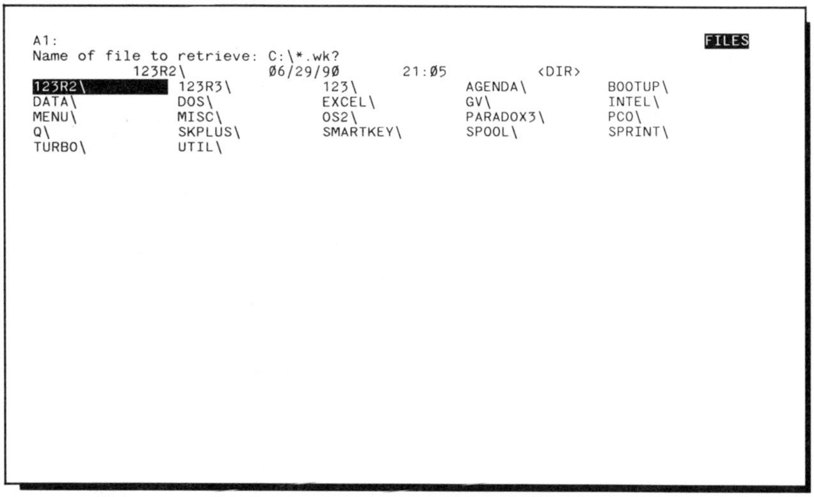

```
A1:                                                                    FILES
Name of file to retrieve: C:\*.wk?
           123R2\           06/29/90         21:05         <DIR>
123R2\           123R3\          123\            AGENDA\        BOOTUP\
DATA\            DOS\            EXCEL\          GV\            INTEL\
MENU\            MISC\           OS2\            PARADOX3\      PCO\
Q\               SKPLUS\         SMARTKEY\       SPOOL\         SPRINT\
TURBO\           UTIL\
```

Figure 5.1 ◆ *Screen during File Retrieve command*

simply saves it within C:\TAXES. Once saved, the file's drive and path become integral parts of its name. The file retrieved from the C:\Taxes sub-directory, for example, is by default saved back to C:\Taxes, since that path is part of the file name. Even if you change to a new subdirectory with the File Directory command, the worksheet will still be saved to C:\Taxes if you do not specify otherwise. This fact is completely consistent with DOS, but can cause problems when you are not specific about where you want to save your worksheet.

There are two methods you can use to save your worksheet to a different drive or subdirectory, depending on whether you want the default directory to change. If you do not want to change the default directory, then you must spec-ify the file's new path when prompted for a file name by the File Save com-mand. You will need to press the Escape key three times to clear the default file name, path, and the drive before you enter the new ones:

/fs{esc 3}C:\Budget\FILENAME ~

If you want to change to a new subdirectory and save the worksheet there, you should first specify the new path with the File Directory command:

/fdC:\Budget ~

Then, when you invoke the File Save command and its prompt offers you the file name and its previous path, simply press Escape once to clear the name and its original path. The new default drive and subdirectory will be offered, at which point you can just type in the file name:

/fs{esc}FILENAME ~

The file will be saved to the current directory, C:\Budget.

> **TIP** ◆ *Instead of writing the path and file name all over again, you may choose to edit the existing ones. When the file name prompt appears, press the spacebar once. This inserts a space after the file name and puts you into an edit mode. Delete the extra space, and then edit the path and name to your liking. Use the Insert key to get into Overwrite mode if you like, and when you are done, press Enter as usual.*

When performing 1-2-3 file operations, you can edit the *.wk? in the edit window to display only the files you want, just as in the DOS DIR command. For example, if you want to retrieve one of a group of files that are called TOTLJAN, TOTLFEB, TOTLMAR, and so on, at the File Retrieve prompt edit the file name from C:\Budget*.wk? to C:\Budget\TOTL*.wk?.

CHANGING GLOBAL SETTINGS

The File Directory command changes the default subdirectory for the current 1-2-3 work session. The next time the program is loaded, the default directory will be the one that had been set by the Worksheet Global Default Directory command.

The Update command on the Default menu saves the settings on that menu to the Lotus program file called 123.CNF, which Lotus reads each time the program is run.

If you want to use \Misc as the startup subdirectory on your C drive, enter that drive and path as follows:

/wgdd{esc}C:\Misc ~ uq

The {esc} erases the previous setting from the prompt line, and the *u* at the end updates the current settings to the 123.CNF file. The next time you load 1-2-3, C:\Misc will be the default directory.

To view the current Global Default settings, use the command Worksheet Global Default Status. Figure 5.2 shows the status screen after the directory change.

```
A1:                                                              STAT
Press any key to continue...
                        ──── Default Settings ────
  Printer:                              Directory: D:\TIPS&TRX
    Interface       Parallel 1
    Auto linefeed   No                  Autoexecute macros: Yes
    Margins
      Left 4    Right 76   Top 2  Bottom 2  International:
    Page length     60                    Punctuation       A
    Wait            No                      Decimal         Period
    Setup string                            Argument        Comma
    Name            HP 2686 LaserJet Se...  Thousands       Comma
                                            Currency        Prefix: $
  Add-In:                               Date format (D4)  A (MM/DD/YY)
    1                                   Time format (D8)  A (HH:MM:SS)
    2                                     Negative        Parentheses
    3
    4                                   Help access method: Instant
    5                                   Clock display:      None
    6                                   Undo:               Disabled
    7                                   Beep:               No
    8
```

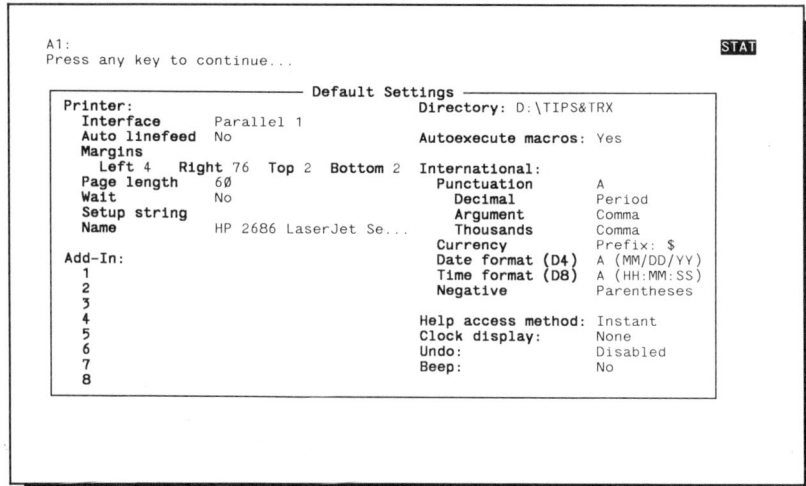

Figure 5.2 ◆ *The Worksheet Global Default Status screen in Release 2.2*

THE AUTO123 WORKSHEET: A BRIDGE FROM DOS TO EXPANDED APPLICATIONS

Once 1-2-3 is loaded into memory, it checks the default subdirectory, as specified in 123.CNF, for a worksheet file named AUTO123. This is the Lotus equivalent of the AUTOEXEC.BAT file, and if it exists, it is automatically loaded. There is nothing more to this feature, and at first it seems rather straightforward; it certainly is not emphasized in the Lotus manual. It is, however, a powerful link between DOS and the expanded use of the program.

A small enhancement to Release 2.2 gives you another way to load a file automatically when 1-2-3 is loaded into memory. When entering the command to run 1-2-3 from the DOS prompt, you can use the parameter -w, followed by a worksheet name that you want to load. For example, to load the worksheet called FILENAME that resides in the DATA subdirectory on drive C, you would enter this command:

123 -wC:\DATA\FILENAME

This feature gives you the flexibility of automating your entry into 1-2-3 without being dependent on the uniquely named AUTO123 worksheet. Note, however, that the parameter -w will not work if you are loading 1-2-3 from a batch file.

By itself, the AUTO123 worksheet is perhaps just a convenience for loading a regularly used worksheet, but when it is combined with the next feature, it becomes a powerful tool for controlling your entrance into 1-2-3.

THE \0 MACRO: GATEKEEPER TO LOTUS APPLICATIONS

Every worksheet can have one macro with the name \0 (backslash zero), which is the auto-invoke macro. Just as Lotus automatically loads the AUTO123 worksheet, the \0 macro is automatically invoked each time the worksheet that contains it is retrieved. You cannot invoke it by pressing Alt-0, but you can give it a second macro name, such as \A.

With this last tool, the Lotus worksheet can be completely automated, from DOS until you quit Lotus.

The uses for the \0 macro are as varied as your needs and your imagination, but its essential purpose is to serve as the gatekeeper to all of your Lotus applications. For example, the quickest route to a daily log worksheet named TIME_ON is to include this macro, named \0, in your AUTO123 worksheet, where it will retrieve TIME_ON every time you run Lotus:

```
/frTIME_ON ~
```

Perhaps you have set your computer to download data from an on-line information service each night during the off-peak hours, and store it in a text file named NEW_DATA, in a subdirectory called OVERWIRE. If you want to view that data the first thing each morning, use this simple \0 macro in your AUTO123 worksheet:

```
/fdOVERWIRE ~
{goto}START ~
/fitNEW_DATA ~
/fsNEW_DATA ~ r{esc}
{quit}
```

In this macro, the file is immediately saved under a new name, which in this case is a good practice that avoids overwriting the AUTO123 worksheet.

> **TIP** ◆ *There may be times when the \0 macro is more of a hindrance than a help. For example, you might find it inconvenient to have the autoexec macro flash into action each time you retrieve a worksheet that is under construction. Or you might be examining someone else's worksheets and prefer that they not take off on their own. You have several options: You can press Alt-F2 to put the worksheet into STEP mode before retrieving the file, and once the*

\0 macro starts you can cancel it by pressing Ctrl-Break. Or, you can press Ctrl-Break while the worksheet is loading, which will cancel the \0 macro as soon as it begins. Finally, if you have Release 2.2, use the Worksheet Global Default Autoexec command to disable the action of the \0 macro.

You have seen how Lotus can be automatically loaded from DOS through the use of batch files, and how Lotus can be automated with its AUTO123 worksheet and \0 macro. Now the entire Gateway process will be described, culminating in an automated worksheet that allows the user to select a working subdirectory from a list.

◆ THE LOTUS GATEWAY

You and anyone else who uses your computer will benefit from the Lotus Gateway. The biggest winner will be you, the one who planned and constructed it. Once it is in place, you will have an orderly system for dealing with the daily routines of the computer, including the use of all your other programs.

Even though you may be thoroughly familiar with the organization of your hard disk, a menu system that automates the normal routines relieves you of the repetitive typing (and spelling) that you do to move from program to program throughout the day. Novices on your computer will appreciate the ease with which they can enter Lotus, and the security of knowing their worksheets are being saved to the proper subdirectory. If you develop a DOS menu system, when you (or another user) quit Lotus, a menu screen can pop up to serve as a system-wide home base.

More knowledgeable users are not necessarily familiar with your hard disk's organization, and will not have to explore it if the normal routines are put in front of them in the form of the menu and batch file system. By combining all of the parts of the Gateway system, you will gain speed, accuracy, and consistency—in a word, control.

BUILDING THE LOTUS GATEWAY

As you build the Lotus Gateway, you will incorporate the features and commands already discussed in this chapter. There are five steps to complete. The first two are DOS activities, and the last three belong to Lotus:

1. Organize your files within subdirectories.

2. Create a 123.BAT file.

3. Set the Lotus global default file directory.

4. Build an AUTO123 worksheet in the default directory.

5. Place a \0 macro in the AUTO123 worksheet.

In the following sections, the role that each of these steps has in building the Lotus Gateway is briefly described. Then, a variety of worksheet applications that capitalize on this automated system is presented. These include worksheets with menus that allow the user to choose a working subdirectory, drive, or Lotus application.

File Subdirectories

You have already arranged your programs in their own subdirectories, such as C:\123 and C:\WP. You have categorized your worksheets and other data files according to activity or purpose, in subdirectories such as C:\Budget, C:\Personal, or C:\Misc.

The 123.BAT Batch File

To get into 1-2-3, you have written the batch file 123.BAT. If you have completed a batch file menu system, this and other batch files reside in a subdirectory named Menu or Batch. The last command in 123.BAT will then be MENU (or whatever calls your menu batch file):

```
C:
cd \123
123
MENU
```

The Global Default Directory

As 123 is loaded into RAM, it reads the configuration file 123.CNF. In this file Lotus stores its global default settings. The default directory used for this example is C:\Misc, which 123 makes its current directory.

The AUTO123 Worksheet

In the subdirectory C:\Misc is a worksheet file named AUTO123. This worksheet is automatically retrieved by 123.

The \0 Macro

Within the AUTO123 worksheet is the macro named \0, which is auto-invoked when the worksheet is retrieved. This macro has countless uses as the starting gun for Lotus applications. In this example it is used to call another macro that expands the application into an easy-to-use menu-driven worksheet, the final destination of the Lotus Gateway.

CREATING A MENU OF SUBDIRECTORIES

The easy-to-build and -operate AUTO123 worksheet consists of a \0 macro that branches to a Lotus macro menu. The menu contains choices for the various worksheet subdirectories on the disk. When one is selected, the macro changes to that directory, erases the AUTO123 worksheet from memory, and leaves the user ready to retrieve worksheet files.

Here is the \0 auto-invoke macro:

```
{home}{menubranch \MENU1}{branch \Z}
```

It first sends the cell pointer to Home, where an introductory screen is displayed, as you can see in Figure 5.3. This screen gives the user helpful information, and ensures that the worksheet looks the same each time it is used. After the Home screen is displayed, the menu \MENU1, which displays the subdirectory choices, is called. Notice in Figure 5.3 that the menu items do not describe the exact path, but are simply English descriptions of each subdirectory. The path itself is contained in the macro code that actually changes the subdirectory for each menu choice. The macro layout is shown in Figure 5.4. Although it is not completely visible in that worksheet, the code for the first item on the menu, Expenses, changes to the \Expenses subdirectory:

```
/fdC:\Expenses ~
/wey
```

The fourth choice on the menu changes to a subdirectory for a user named Sarah:

```
/fdC:\User\Sarah ~
/wey
```

After the directory is changed, the worksheet is erased, leaving the user ready to retrieve another.

Expanding the Menu

To expand or modify the choices, simply edit the menu macro. Remember that you will have to press Ctrl-Break to get out of the menu when you retrieve

```
A1:                                                              MENU
Expenses  Budget  Chris  Sarah  Misc
Monthly expenses
       A           B            C          D          E          F
1
2
3
4           ============================================
5                 CHOOSE A SUBDIRECTORY FROM THE MENU
6           ============================================
7
8           This is the home quadrant of the screen.  It
9           can be used for helpful information or as an
10          introduction to the process of choosing a
11          subdirectory.
12
13          ============================================
14
15
16          ============================================
17
18
19
20                              CMD
```

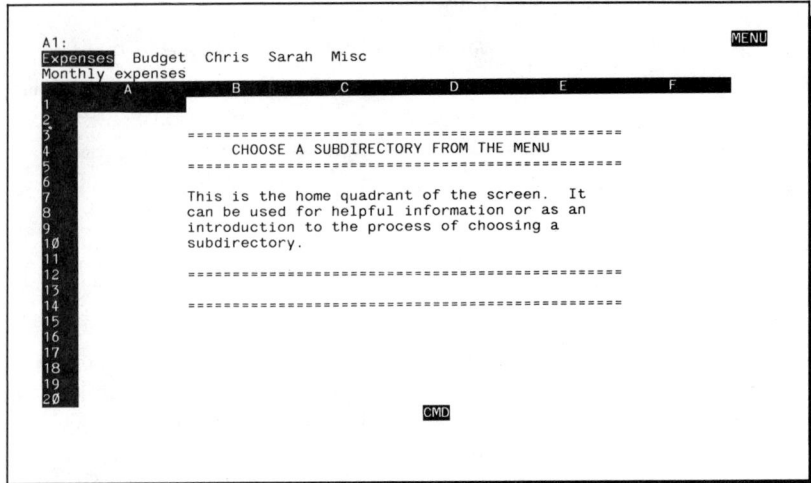

Figure 5.3 ◆ *The home screen for the AUTO123 worksheet*

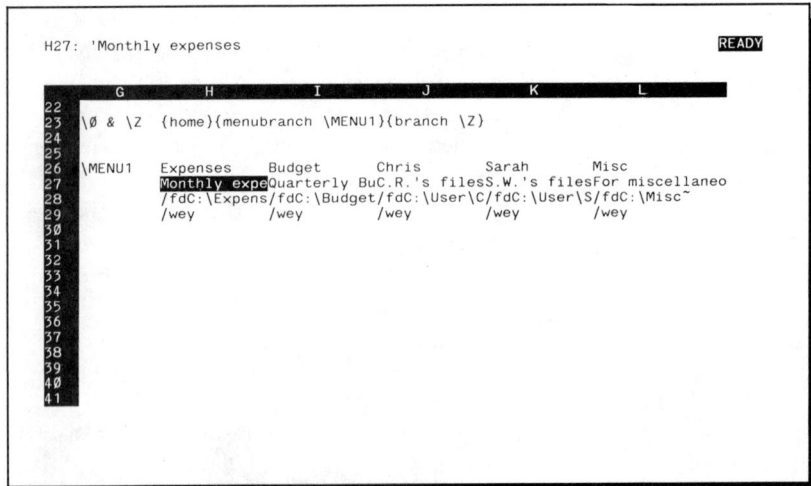

```
H27:  'Monthly expenses                                        READY

       G          H            I          J          K          L
22
23  \Ø & \Z   {home}{menubranch \MENU1}{branch \Z}
24
25
26  \MENU1    Expenses    Budget      Chris       Sarah      Misc
27            Monthly expeQuarterly BuC.R.'s filesS.W.'s filesFor miscellaneo
28            /fdC:\Expens/fdC:\Budget/fdC:\User\C/fdC:\User\S/fdC:\Misc~
29            /wey        /wey        /wey        /wey        /wey
30
31
32
33
34
35
36
37
38
39
40
41
```

Figure 5.4 ◆ *The AUTO123 menu for changing subdirectories*

the AUTO123 worksheet. When changing a menu item, be sure to change not
only the description that the user sees in the first and second lines of the menu,
but also, and especially, the macro code that changes the directory in the third
line. The spelling of the subdirectory in the third line must be exact; a quick
test run should prove its accuracy.

A Lotus macro menu can have up to eight choices, which may be more than enough. There are several features you may want to add to expand this system, which will require branching to other menus.

Adding Drive Choices

If you want to be able to access your floppy disk drives from an AUTO123 menu, or if you have more than one hard disk, you can add a separate menu for drive choices that is called by the \0 macro. Such a menu might look like this:

A:	B:	C:	D:
Drive A:	Drive B:	Hard disk C:	Hard disk D:
/fdA:\ ˜	/fdB:\ ˜	/fdC:\ ˜	/fdD:\ ˜
/wey	/wey	{menubranch \MENU1}	{menubranch \MENU2}

If drive A or B is chosen, the macro changes the default directory to that drive, and then, since floppy disks do not normally have subdirectories, erases the worksheet and quits. If drive C or D, both of which are hard disks, is chosen, the macro changes to the drive selected and then branches to a secondary menu that displays the subdirectories appropriate to the chosen drive. In this way, a hierarchy of menus is established. Each one is specific to one drive and has up to eight choices for that drive.

One Menu per User or Function

Building a top-down structure of menus can also improve the usefulness of this system by supplying a separate menu for each worksheet function and for each user. For instance, if users each have several subdirectories of their own, the top menu could list the users by name, and then branch to a separate menu of subdirectory choices for each user. Or the top menu might list different tasks that are performed in Lotus, where each one has several subtasks associated with it. At the top would be listed subjects such as Taxes, Budget, Clients, and Misc. Each of these items would have its own menu that further expands the choices, perhaps through more than one submenu. The final choice changes to the appropriate subdirectory and erases the worksheet.

A Menu of Specific Lotus Applications

Sometimes the Lotus user is not going to access a worksheet directly, but will instead use a "canned" application or template. There may be no need for the user to select a drive or subdirectory, since those choices are irrelevant to the task that needs to be performed.

The items on this menu would be descriptive of worksheet applications, and when chosen, would not only change to the right subdirectory, but would also retrieve the proper worksheet.

FULL-SCREEN MENU DISPLAY

If your hard disk has quite a few subdirectories, you may wish to use the AUTO123 worksheet shown in Figure 5.5. It displays a full screen of subdirectory choices. This worksheet consists of a screen of subdirectory names and a macro that is called by the \0 macro. The user is prompted to pick the letter of the subdirectory that is wanted. When Enter is pressed, the macro changes to the listed subdirectory, erases the current worksheet, and leaves the user ready for work.

For a Better View, Use the Tree

To help fill in the text of a potentially large list of subdirectories, you can use the DOS command TREE to bring in a complete list of all subdirectories on disk. Although the format of the imported list will not be appropriate for the intended purpose, it will serve as a current, complete list of all subdirectories. Writing the menu screen of subdirectories with this list as a guide will ensure

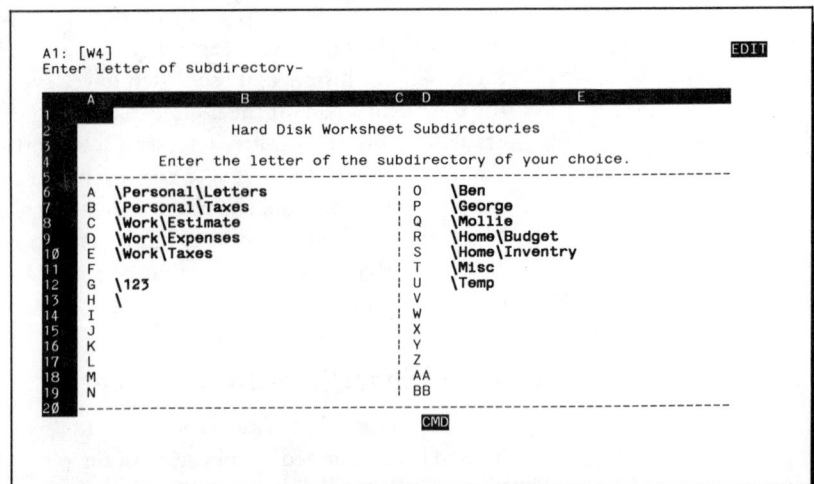

```
A1: [W4]                                                              EDIT
Enter letter of subdirectory-
         A              B              C   D              E
 1
 2                      Hard Disk Worksheet Subdirectories
 3
 4              Enter the letter of the subdirectory of your choice.
 5    -----------------------------------------------------------------
 6    A  \Personal\Letters          !  O   \Ben
 7    B  \Personal\Taxes            !  P   \George
 8    C  \Work\Estimate             !  Q   \Mollie
 9    D  \Work\Expenses             !  R   \Home\Budget
10    E  \Work\Taxes                !  S   \Home\Inventry
11    F                             !  T   \Misc
12    G  \123                       !  U   \Temp
13    H  \                          !  V
14    I                             !  W
15    J                             !  X
16    K                             !  Y
17    L                             !  Z
18    M                             !  AA
19    N                             !  BB
20    -----------------------------------------------------------------
                                   CMD
```

Figure 5.5 ◆ *Full-screen menu in the Gateway worksheet*

accuracy and prevent spelling errors. There are only two steps required when using this method, and the technique is a valuable one to master.

First, use the System command to temporarily leave Lotus and go to DOS. Then, to get the listing of all subdirectories on drive C, enter this command at the DOS prompt:

TREE C: > C:\Misc\TREEFILE.PRN

The greater-than symbol (>) redirects the output of the TREE command from the screen to the file TREEFILE.PRN, in the subdirectory C:\Misc. Remember from earlier in this chapter that the TREE command is an external DOS command. Also, you would substitute an actual subdirectory name in the command if you are not using one named \Misc. The output file is a text file that you can view from DOS, your word processor, or Lotus. This same technique will create output files from any DOS command that produces output, such as DIR or CHKDSK. The file is put into \Misc since that is the catchall subdirectory, but any other location would serve as well.

Return to Lotus by typing *EXIT*, and move the cell pointer to any out-of-the-way location, such as cell A100 in the example worksheet. Then import the text file that was just created, using this command:

/fit{esc}C:\Misc\TREEFILE.PRN ~

The imported list is shown in Figure 5.6. You now have a complete list of subdirectories from which to work. When typing the subdirectory paths into

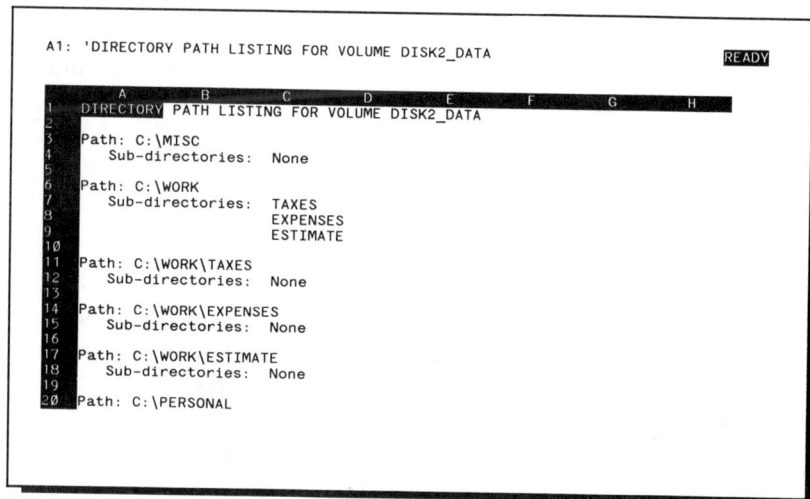

```
A1:  'DIRECTORY PATH LISTING FOR VOLUME DISK2_DATA                    READY

          A       B         C         D        E        F        G       H
 1   DIRECTORY PATH LISTING FOR VOLUME DISK2_DATA
 2
 3   Path: C:\MISC
 4        Sub-directories:   None
 5
 6   Path: C:\WORK
 7        Sub-directories:   TAXES
 8                           EXPENSES
 9                           ESTIMATE
10
11   Path: C:\WORK\TAXES
12        Sub-directories:   None
13
14   Path: C:\WORK\EXPENSES
15        Sub-directories:   None
16
17   Path: C:\WORK\ESTIMATE
18        Sub-directories:   None
19
20   Path: C:\PERSONAL
```

Figure 5.6 ◆ *The imported text from the TREE listing*

the AUTO123 worksheet full-screen menu, remember that a backslash is the repeating label prefix, so you must preface your entries with an apostrophe to make them normal text that is left justified. If a subdirectory name and path is particularly long or complex, you can copy it to the menu and edit it there.

When you are finished with the list, erase the imported text from the worksheet. You can erase the file TREEFILE.PRN either from within Lotus by using the File Erase command, or from DOS when you quit Lotus.

The Menu of Subdirectories

In Figure 5.5, you saw the main screen with its list of subdirectories, which the user sees on entrance into the worksheet. You are responsible for ensuring that this list contains subdirectories that are on the disk and that are relevant to your needs and the needs of other users. They must be spelled correctly, and notice that the backslashes are included in the names to make a complete path listing. The imported TREE output will be of much assistance when creating this screen.

Each choice has a letter to its left that is used for the Range Name Label Right command to give each subdirectory cell the corresponding name. Cell B6, for example, is named A, cell B7 is B, cell B8 is C, and so on. The user will choose these letters to change to a subdirectory.

The screen is split into two columns of choices in this worksheet. If some of your paths are long, you might want to have just one wide screen. Or, you could list the paths at the left with a short description of the path on the right. If you have too many choices for one screen, you can modify the macro to allow scrolling with the PgUp or PgDn key.

You can list the subdirectories in any order that makes sense to you. You could first create one long list from the TREE input, and then sort that list and copy it to the display portion of the screen. Or you might want to group the subdirectories by user, or perhaps by project.

Full-Screen Gateway Macro

This compact macro makes use of a self-modifying string formula macro, which in turn relies on the mysterious @ function, @@. Together these form a powerful team. The complete macro is shown in Figure 5.7.

When the worksheet is retrieved, the \0 macro at I29 is automatically invoked:

```
{goto}HOME_SCREEN ˜ {beep 2}
```

```
I31: +"/fdC:"&@@(CHOICE)&"~"                                    READY

         H              I           J        K        L        M        N
26
27  CHOICE             G
28
29  \Ø and \Z          {goto}HOME_SCREEN~{beep 2}
30                     {getlabel Enter letter of subdirectory-  ,CHOICE)
31                     /fdC:\123~
32                     /wey
33
34
35
36
37
38
39
40
41
42
43
44
45
```

Figure 5.7 ◆ *Macro for the Gateway worksheet*

The macro first sets up the screen for the user by jumping the cell pointer to the range HOME_SCREEN, which, in this case, resides in the upper left corner of the worksheet. Moving the cell pointer here ensures that the screen will look the same every time the worksheet is used. A beep is then sounded to get the user's attention, which can be helpful for users who are unfamiliar with the system.

Next, a data input command prompts the user for a letter of a subdirectory:

    {getlabel "Enter letter of subdirectory- ",CHOICE}

The response is recorded in the cell named CHOICE, I27 in Figure 5.7. As you can see, the user has entered a G, choosing the \123 subdirectory from the menu in Figure 5.5.

The third line of the macro appears to be a simple text macro. It issues the File Directory command to change to the \123 subdirectory:

    /fdC:\123 ˜

But look in the control panel and you will see that it is actually a string formula:

    +"/fdC:"&@@(CHOICE)&"˜"

The first part of the formula begins the command; it is just text that does not change—+"/fdC:". Concatenated to that is the @ function @@, which refers to CHOICE. But the function does not result in the letter G that is in the cell

CHOICE. Instead, the @@ function makes an *indirect reference* to the cell that is named by the range name G and returns its contents—\123. This powerful but infrequently used function is tailor-made for this application. It provides an instant link to the directory named in the menu.

The final segment of the string formula is just a tilde (˜) to complete the File Directory command. The last line of the macro erases the worksheet, leaving the user ready to retrieve or create another worksheet.

Changing Drives and Menu Choices

The Gateway macro has been kept as short and concise as possible, and it will do the job quite well in its present form. However, you can add enhancements to expand its capabilities, adapt it to your particular system, improve its reliability, or just make it more interesting to use.

As in the macro menu described earlier, you may want to prompt the user for a disk drive first, and then display a list of subdirectories on the menu screen for that particular drive. Several alterations are required for this routine, as shown in Figure 5.8.

When first retrieved, the list of subdirectories on the menu screen (shown in Figure 5.5) should be blank, as the drive to display has not yet been determined. Although you should initially save this template worksheet with a blank menu display, the \0 macro also erases that area to ensure a fresh menu:

```
{goto}HOME_SCREEN ˜ {beep 2}
{blank LISTA}{blank LISTB}
```

```
I41: [W11] +"/fd"&@@(CHOICE)&"˜"                                    READY

           H         I          J            K              L
26
27   \Ø and \Z      {goto}HOME_SCREEN˜{beep 2}
28                   {blank LISTA}{blank LISTB}
29                   {menubranch \MENU1}
30
31   \MENU1          A:         B:           C:             D:
32                   Drive A:   Drive B:     Hard disk C:   Hard disk D:
33                   /fdA:\˜    /fdB:\˜       /fdC:\˜        /fdD:\˜
34                   /wey       /wey         /cLIST1A˜LISTA˜ /cLIST2A˜LISTA˜
35                                           /cLIST1B˜LISTB˜ /cLIST2B˜LISTB˜
36                                           {branch \CHOOSE} {branch \CHOOSE}
37
38   CHOICE          G
39
40   \CHOOSE         {getlabel Enter letter of subdirectory- ,CHOICE}
41                   /fd\123˜
42                   /wey
43
44
45
```

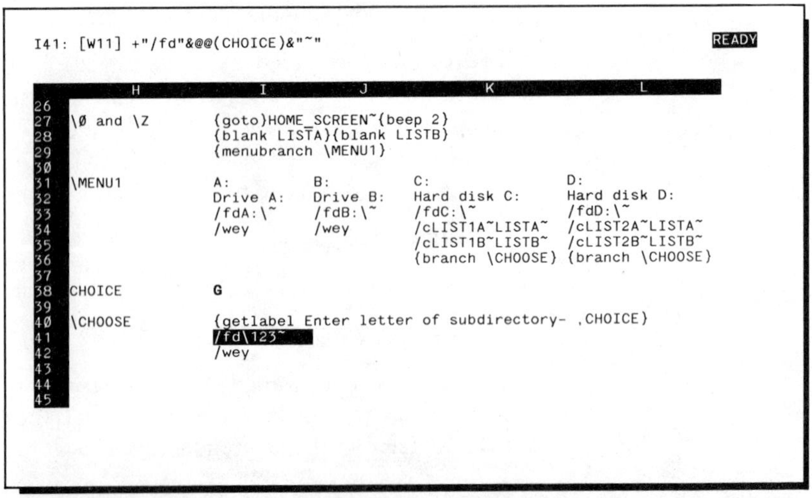

Figure 5.8 ♦ *Revised Gateway macro for variable menu display*

The two halves of the menu screen have been given range names: the left is LISTA and the right is LISTB. Using two separate areas allows you to erase either one without affecting the divider column or the columns of selection letters.

Once the screen is blank, the \0 macro calls the macro menu, \MENU1. This menu fulfills the same purpose as the menu described earlier in the section named Adding Drive Choices. It allows the user to make one of the disk drives the current drive.

If a floppy drive is chosen, the Lotus directory is changed and the AUTO123 worksheet is erased. If hard disk C is chosen, several steps are taken to adapt the menu screen to the subdirectories that are available on that drive:

```
/fdC:\ ~
/cLIST1A ~ LISTA ~
/cLIST1B ~ LISTB ~
{branch \CHOOSE}
```

The macro first issues the File Directory command to change to drive C. Then, a screen of subdirectories specific to drive C is copied onto each half of the menu screen. The two ranges, LIST1A and LIST1B, are specifically for drive C. They are contained elsewhere in the worksheet and duplicate the width and number of rows on the menu screen. The macro \CHOOSE is then called, from which the user can choose a subdirectory as usual.

The choice for drive D invokes a similar routine, only this time the macro changes to drive D and two different lists of subdirectories are copied to the menu screen:

```
/fdD:\ ~
/cLIST2A ~ LISTA ~
/cLIST2B ~ LISTB ~
{branch \CHOOSE}
```

Again, the macro branches to \CHOOSE, which is similar to the macro shown in Figure 5.7. This time, though, it does not have to jump to the menu screen, and no drive designation is included in the File Directory command— the drive has already been selected:

```
{getlabel "Enter letter of subdirectory- ",CHOICE}
/fd\123 ~
/wey
```

The string formula in \CHOOSE will also look familiar:

```
+"/fd"&@@(CHOICE)&" ~ "
```

The subdirectory chosen by the user is made the current one, the AUTO123 worksheet is erased, and the user is ready to retrieve or create a new worksheet.

RETURNING TO THE AUTO123 WORKSHEET

For users who are unfamiliar with negotiating a hard disk, the following technique is quite helpful. It is also convenient for experienced but infrequent users. When you are finished with a task in one subdirectory on the hard disk, a worksheet named MENU can be retrieved that automatically calls up the AUTO123 menu worksheet.

Into each subdirectory that is used for Lotus files, copy a worksheet named MENU, which is simply a "springboard" worksheet. It contains only a \0 macro that performs two tasks: it changes back to the global default subdirectory (in this case \Misc) and it retrieves the AUTO123 worksheet:

```
/wgdd ˜ q
/frAUTO123 ˜
```

When a user is ready to work in another subdirectory, all that is needed is to retrieve the worksheet named MENU. It immediately changes to the global default subdirectory and then retrieves the AUTO123 worksheet, from which another subdirectory or application can be chosen. Note that invoking the Worksheet Global Default Directory command makes that directory the current one, as though you had used the File Directory command. Although this system requires the extra MENU worksheet in many subdirectories, the convenience it offers users cannot be overestimated.

If an automated worksheet application is being used, its main menu can have a Quit choice that either retrieves the MENU worksheet or executes the commands found in MENU.

◆ *SUMMARY*

This chapter has given you the tools to take full advantage of Lotus on your hard disk. You have seen how to organize your disk into logical subdirectories. You have also seen how to construct a Lotus Gateway that automates the entire process of entering Lotus, changing to a subdirectory of your choice, and returning to DOS when you quit Lotus.

The next chapter discusses the many factors that affect the Lotus environment, including your computer and related hardware, expanded memory, and the Lotus add-in, Speedup. The System command is included in the discussion as an essential link to the DOS environment in which Lotus resides. Finally, a technique is introduced that automates the transfer of worksheet data and program control to another program.

SIX:

Living in the Lotus Environment

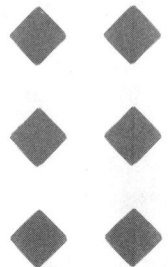

6

◆ ◆ ◆

THE LOTUS WORKSHEET ENVIRONMENT CAN BE HEAVILY influenced by the larger environment in which it exists—that of the entire computer system. As distasteful (or complex) as this system may be to some, by manipulating its components you can make some noticeable improvements to the speed and operator control of the 1-2-3 program.

The computer's hardware is discussed first in this chapter, as that is the most visible dimension of the computer system. The items that directly affect the performance of 1-2-3 include the hard disk, expanded memory, the computer's CPU, the math coprocessor, and the printer. These parts can always be improved by the outlay of money, but some of them can do more to enhance 1-2-3 than others costing more.

Next come several topics that can increase the performance of 1-2-3, including two uses for expanded RAM, virtual disks and print spoolers, and the Lotus supplied add-in Speedup for Release 2.01.

Once safely inside the Lotus worksheet, there are many reasons not to ignore the "world outside,"—the DOS environment. The last part of this chapter covers the System command, and how its easy access to DOS allows you to take care of many tasks that would otherwise be difficult to perform. Finally, an automated method for passing control from Lotus to another program and back again is demonstrated.

◆ HARDWARE: DEFINING THE LIMITS OF THE ENVIRONMENT

Your computer system consists of hardware and software, and its performance can be affected by either of these.

This section looks at the different hardware components of the typical PC system that, with upgrading, can show worthwhile improvements in the performance of 1-2-3. The items singled out include hard disks, expanded memory, the CPU, math coprocessors, the video display, and the printer.

If you are about to purchase a computer or are ready to upgrade your present system, the topics covered here will be of help in your decision. Remember, faster hardware is the most obvious way to speed up your system, but it is not the cheapest and not necessarily the most effective for your needs.

> **TIP** ◆ *Before spending any serious money on your computer's hardware, be sure that you first check its WPM. If that is not up to par, new hardware will have little impact on the overall speed of the system. You can upgrade your WPM at little or no cost, but you will need to make a small commitment in time and patience. To check the WPM in your system, try one of the typing tests in a typing course text book or computer program to determine your typing speed in WPM (words per minute)!*

HARD DISK STORAGE: MAXIMIZING FILE HANDLING

Whatever type of computer you are using, adding a hard disk to the system will give an immediate increase in performance and user satisfaction. Hard disks have become so common that their price has fallen to levels that almost make them competitive with floppy disks. Refer back to Chapter 5, where the major advantages of a hard disk are discussed: capacity, speed, and convenience.

Any improvement in performance is always the most obvious benefit when new hardware is installed. You can test the speed of a hard disk compared to a floppy disk when loading a worksheet by using the simple macro shown in Figure 6.1.

The macro code in B4 is the routine that will be tested, in this case it is a File Combine command that brings in a worksheet named FILENAME. The incoming file should be large enough to provide a good test of more than just a few seconds. Run the macro in an otherwise blank worksheet so the results will be consistent.

As usual, the capitalized text in column A describes the necessary range names in column B. The macro starts by setting Recalculation to Manual, a simple precaution to prevent a possibly long recalculation from occurring when the other file is brought in. Then, the cell pointer is moved to a cell below the macro where FILENAME will be brought into the worksheet:

```
/wgrm{goto}ELAPSED~{left}{down 3}
```

The second line of the macro sets the cell named START to the current value of @now, and then the file operation is performed in the next line, cell B4.

```
B9: (D6) [W13] 32271.57235                                          READY

              A            B           C              D               E
1
2     \Z              /wgrm(goto)ELAPSED~(left){down 3}
3                     {let START,@now}
4                     /fcceFILENAME~
5                     {let FINISH,@now)
6                     (recalc ELAPSED)~
7
8
9     START            Ø1:44:11 PM
1Ø    FINISH           Ø1:44:42 PM
11
12    ELAPSED        >  12:ØØ:31 AM   =  (FINISH-START)
13                   >  31.ØØØØØØØØ17 =  (FINISH-START)/(1/24/6Ø/6Ø)
14
15
16
17
18
19
2Ø
```

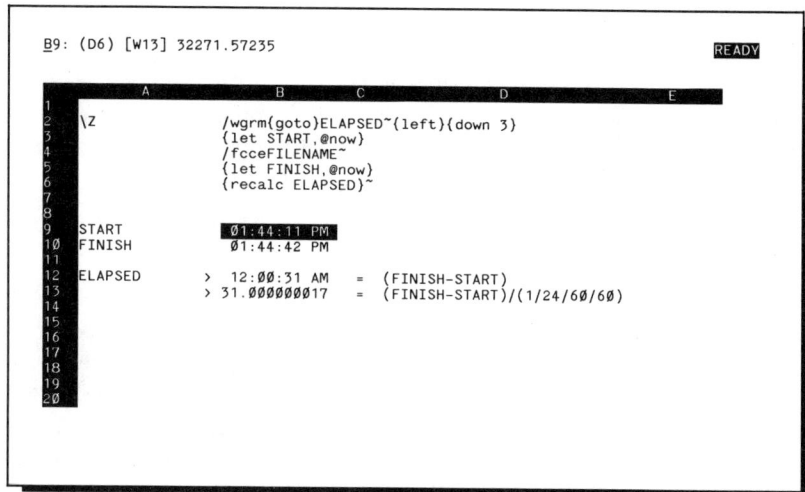

Figure 6.1 ◆ *Testing the file-loading speed of a disk system*

Once the file is in the worksheet, the cell named FINISH is also set to the value of @now:

```
{let START,@now}
/fcceFILENAME ~
{let FINISH,@now}
```

Finally, since Recalculation has been set to Manual, the two formulas in ELAPSED, cells B9 and B10, are recalculated. They will then display the elapsed time of the file operation, which is simply the difference between FINISH and START:

```
{recalc ELAPSED} ~
```

★ **TRICK** ◆ *Note that the formula in cell B13 of Figure 6.1 provides the time in seconds only; it uses the General format, not the Time format. Dividing a value by (1/24/60/60), yields the time in seconds. To display the time in minutes and fractions of a minute, divide by (1/24/60).*

This timer macro can test the speed of any routine; just replace the code in B4 with the one you wish to test. To test the recalculation time of the entire worksheet, simply put a {calc} command in B4. To time the speed of the computer's display response, insert {pgdn 10} into the test cell. To test the difference in speed of a macro routine both with and without the {windowsoff} command, just call the other macro from cell B4. Run the timer routine, and then test it again with a {windowsoff} statement:

```
{let START,@now}
{windowsoff}{\DO_SUBROUTINE}
{let FINISH,@now}
{recalc ELAPSED} ~
```

The hard disk may surprise you with its performance, and the convenience of a hard disk is a daily pleasure. The benefits are obvious when you can use the System command to jump to DOS and then immediately into your word processor or the PrintGraph program, all in a split second. No matter what your work routines may be, if you need more performance from your system, consider the hard disk at the top of the list.

EMS MEMORY: EXPANDING THE ENVIRONMENT

The Expanded Memory Specification (EMS) was established in 1985 to provide more memory than the conventional 640K available in DOS. Designed through a joint effort among Lotus, Intel, and Microsoft, the LIM standard consists of an EMS memory board and special configuration software. Application programs must be written specifically to address this expanded RAM.

Do not confuse *expanded* memory with the *extended* memory that can be used on 80286, 80386, and 80486 machines. Both types of memory serve as RAM beyond the normal DOS 640K, but *expanded* RAM is the type that can be used by 1-2-3 Release 2.01 and 2.2, as well as many other DOS-based programs. To run 1-2-3 Release 3, your computer must have at least 384K of *extended* RAM (more if you want 1-2-3 to run faster), although it can use all three types of RAM for data storage. Therefore, Release 3 runs only on 80286 and newer machines.

EMS memory was introduced with Release 2.0 of 1-2-3, and it cannot be used by earlier versions of the spreadsheet. You can add up to 32 megabytes of expanded memory to your system, although Lotus can access only 4 megabytes. When the extra RAM capability and sparse matrix memory were combined in Release 2.0, the limits of the Lotus spreadsheet were greatly expanded.

Lotus does not use the storage space in expanded RAM as it does conventional RAM; it is more of a supplement to it. Only three components of a worksheet are stored there:

- ◆ Labels

- ◆ Real numbers

- ◆ Formulas

Everything else must remain in conventional memory.

Depending on the type of information in your worksheet, Lotus may store more or less of it in expanded memory. The typical worksheet might split its storage about 50/50 between conventional and expanded RAM, such as 45K each for a total of 90K storage. Often, a worksheet tends to have more for expanded memory, and the percentages may be closer to 40/60. But the allocations can swing widely either way. For example, in a mailing list worksheet that is virtually all text cells, the percentage may reach 25 percent conventional and 75 percent expanded. In a sheet that is packed with nothing but integers, however, there will be nothing stored in expanded memory.

In actual use, then, even a megabyte of expanded RAM may be more than enough for worksheets, and 2 megabytes would provide extra room for other applications, discussed later.

There are two factors that will push the need for expanded memory in your system: data or programs. If you build large worksheets (data), your available RAM may dwindle quickly. If you use memory-resident or add-in programs along with Lotus (programs), you may be left with little RAM before you even start to build a spreadsheet.

2.2 ◆ ——— You will find that Release 2.2 uses about 25K more RAM than Release 2.01. There may be times when you begrudge the loss of even this modest amount of memory, but when you consider the extras you get in Release 2.2, it may seem like a bargain.

You can check the memory capacity of your system from within Lotus by using the Worksheet Status command. Shown here are the first two lines of the Status screen that indicate the memory that Lotus recognizes in your system. Each reference to memory shows how much is available for worksheets, and how much of that is already in use:

```
Available Memory:
Conventional..... 226871 of 226871 Bytes (100%)
Expanded......... 671416 of 671416 Bytes (100%)
```

The numbers you see for your own system will be different from those shown here, depending on the memory installed and the software being used. Your conventional RAM might be higher than this example, as a memory-resident program was being used that took about 100K of RAM.

2.2 ◆ ———

⊠   *TIP ◆ Expanded RAM plays an even more important role in Release 2.2, because without it the Undo feature can be quite ineffectual. Unfortunately, in order to store a second copy of a worksheet in memory, the Undo feature must have at least half of all the available RAM as a buffer. Once your worksheet grows to moderate size, if you don't have expanded RAM to serve as the Undo buffer, your conventional RAM will be over-taxed, and you will most likely want to use the Worksheet Global Default Other Undo command to disable Undo.*

You may be intimidated by the thought of megabytes of expanded memory on top of 640K of conventional RAM. Be assured that a "loaded" system runs no differently than a lighter one, and requires only an investment of money on your part—and not necessarily a large amount.

Later, you will read about print buffers and RAM disks. These handy tools require many kilobytes of RAM to perform their jobs effectively. The expanded memory boards generally come with software to install these features within the expanded memory, leaving the conventional RAM free for applications that must be run there.

There are other programs besides Lotus that can take advantage of EMS memory for data storage. If you use Allways or other Lotus add-in programs—such as a word processor, cell annotator, or graphics add-in—then you have a double need for expanded memory. First, the add-in program itself must reside in the limited conventional RAM, thereby lowering the amount available for worksheets and increasing the need for EMS for worksheet storage. Second, most add-ins are designed to keep their data in expanded RAM, when available, which means that once loaded, the add-in will no longer stress the normal RAM capabilities.

If you decide to add expanded memory to your computer, you will be surprised how valuable even a megabyte can be, and that may be a good number with which to start. Since most boards on the market hold twice that much, you can add more memory later as the need arises (or as the price of memory chips fall). For those who dabble in large worksheets or multiple programs, EMS memory may provide the relief valve needed.

THE COMPUTER: INCREASING OVERALL PERFORMANCE

The most obvious method of increasing the performance of Lotus and all your software is by using the biggest and fastest microcomputer available. It may also be the most expensive method. If you are planning to buy a new computer, then the speed at which it runs is the primary category for comparison, assuming that quality, warranty, compatibility, and price are equivalent. The decision to upgrade to a new, faster computer, though, is not an easy one and should be given due consideration.

The most important point to remember when budgeting your computer dollar is that the computer itself is just one part of the system cost. Consider this list of components that might be purchased for a computer of any size or speed:

- Monitor
- Display adapter card
- Second floppy disk
- Hard disk
- Memory card (expanded/extended)
- Printer
- Modem
- Miscellaneous supplies, such as cables, floppy disks, dust covers, and paper
- Operating system
- Software

The computer is at the core of this list, but it is likely that the total cost for the items shown above will be far more than the computer itself. Depending on your work habits, upgrading just one of these items may be more cost effective. For example, unless you have unusual worksheets, a hard disk should provide you with more immediate benefits at a much lower cost than a faster computer with no hard disk.

If you want to upgrade your present computer, coprocessor boards are available that effectively add a faster CPU to your computer. The advantages are that you are saved from replacing the entire computer, while spending less money than a whole computer would cost.

Unfortunately, although the processor is fast, it is burdened by a slower system of memory, video display, and disk access of the surrounding computer. Since the card is an add-on, there can also be software compatibility problems, and some software may show only a small speed increase with the board.

In general, it may be safer to remove all the peripherals from your system and buy a new, faster computer, and then put the peripherals back into it. Again, preliminary investigation may pay the biggest dividends.

THE MATH COPROCESSOR: SPEEDING UP CALCULATION

Support for the math coprocessor was introduced with Lotus 2.0. When installed in the computer and used with software that can address it, the coprocessor is assigned all floating-point arithmetic calculations (those involving numbers with decimals). In math-intensive problems, the speed of calculations can be increased by more than ten times.

In the average worksheet, though, speed increases are rarely that dramatic, and recalculations are generally no more than two or three times faster. There is much overhead in a spreadsheet program beyond the actual math, such as maintaining the hierarchy of cells in the chain of recalculation. The coprocessor can only contribute to one part of the recalculation process.

Try the timing macro on two different computers, one with a coprocessor and the other without. Use it in a worksheet with several thousand formulas that will utilize the coprocessor, such as @log(@rand). You will then get a feel for the speed improvements to expect in worst-case situations.

If you make intensive use of Lotus, especially in the sciences, and you are not planning to buy a faster computer, then a math chip is a reasonable investment. It is easy to install and needs no upkeep. It will not, however, increase your typing speed or your skill with the spreadsheet itself.

THE VIDEO DISPLAY: CONTROLLING SCREEN RESPONSE

You may think that the display screen could not have much effect on the workings of 1-2-3, but there are factors that can make a tremendous difference in its performance.

Of course, if you want to view graphs on the screen, you will need a graphics video adapter card. These include the popular IBM CGA, EGA, and VGA standards, and the equally popular Hercules monographics. The original IBM monochrome display adapter cannot display in the graphics mode, and therefore does not allow graphing on the screen in 1-2-3.

Even though it cannot display graphs, one nice advantage to the monochrome display card is its speed in refreshing the screen. In Lotus, you can demonstrate this simply by scrolling the screen down a worksheet full of characters. The color displays cannot keep up with the monochrome when it comes to changing the characters on the screen.

The Hercules card, although a monochrome display card, also suffers from screen response that is slower than the IBM monochrome's. This is especially noticeable when it is used in "big picture" mode, the so-called 90×38 format. In this mode, the display characters are shrunk and the Lotus screen thereby "expanded" to show 82 characters across and 33 rows deep (compared to its normal size of 72 characters by 20 rows). Although this mode is particularly sluggish, even the normal Hercules 80×25 mode is slower than standard monochrome. There is, however, a way to give it a boost.

You can virtually double the screen response of a Hercules monochrome card by making a small change to your 1-2-3 driver set. All that is required is that you change the Text Display driver to IBM Monochrome, and leave the Graph Display driver as Hercules. The effect is that the normal text display will perform as fast as an IBM monochrome display, but you will be able to graph as well.

When you go through the Lotus Install program's First-Time Installation routine and choose Hercules Card for the Graph Display, you never get a chance to describe a Text Display. The Hercules driver takes care of both, but unfortunately gives the slower response in the normal text mode.

Here are the steps to go through in the Lotus Install program to make the change for your Hercules card. This assumes that your Lotus driver set file is named 123.SET, the default name. Make these selections, starting from the Install program Main Menu:

1. Advanced Options

2. Modify Current Driver Set

3. Text Display

4. IBM Monochrome Display

5. Return to Menu

6. Save Changes

If you press F10 from the main menu, you will see that your Text Display driver is now configured as an IBM monochrome, and the Graph Display as a Hercules. Your driver set will now perform like an IBM monochrome in text mode, but still produce graphs in its graphics mode.

THE PRINTER: BALANCING SPEED AND QUALITY

The printer is a peripheral device, not an integral part of the computer system. In the normal use of a computer, though, the printer has an essential role. A slow printer can have a devastating effect on your productivity, and tends to increase your impatience, discourage quick test prints, and generally bog down your work routines.

If you are in the market for a new printer, the speed option may be one of the top priorities. Also to be considered are the quality of the printed characters, the noise level, paper-handling features, and compatibility with common software such as Lotus. A combination of high speed with lower-quality output coupled with near-letter-quality but at slower speeds may be an effective combination. Large worksheets can be printed quickly, and correspondence can be printed in a higher-quality text.

Laser printers are quite fast, form a beautiful character, and are very quiet. They are expensive, though, and the many fonts they can handle are generally not needed for normal spreadsheet use. The fact that they cannot print on 14-inch-wide paper is a real detriment when working with spreadsheets.

The Print Buffer: Reducing Printing Time

One way to shorten the amount of time your computer spends printing is to use a print buffer. Print buffers that are set up in the computer's own RAM will be discussed later, but you can also purchase one as a separate piece of hardware. The external buffer is usually just a small box with RAM and a few switches and indicator lights. The printer cable is routed from the computer to the buffer input, and another from the buffer output to the printer.

This is generally more expensive and not as convenient as using the computer's own RAM for the buffer. A RAM-based buffer can be configured in expanded memory when a computer is so equipped, and the memory required will not strain the conventional 640K. Unless you are sharing a printer with other computers that could all benefit from one external buffer, the internal buffer is the way to go.

USING EXPANDED RAM FOR PRINT SPOOLERS AND VIRTUAL DISKS

Other than creating gigantic worksheets, what else can you do with a megabyte or two of expanded memory? One of the big advantages of expanded RAM is that anything stored there is conserving conventional RAM.

There are two program utilities that come with most expanded memory boards for setting up a RAM disk or print spooler within the expanded memory. A print spooler can be of much assistance to the 1-2-3 program; a RAM disk may serve only specific applications.

RAM Print Spooler

A printer never keeps up with the flow of characters from the computer, as the blinking *Wait* message in Lotus continually reminds you. A print buffer, or *spooler,* can be set up in the computer's RAM where it intercepts the data on the way from the computer to the printer. It serves as a reservoir for the print output, accepting data from the CPU at RAM speeds, while sending the normal stream of data on to the printer. The larger the buffer (kilobytes of RAM), the more pages of printout it can store, with the average page requiring about 5K of RAM.

The printer functions as usual and does not know the buffer exists. The only noticeable difference to the user is that the Wait light stays on for only a fraction of the normal time, as the computer fills up the RAM in the buffer. Then the computer is free to do other tasks, as the printer continues printing the data it receives from the buffer.

The constraints on the conventional 640K memory often limit the size and effectiveness of a print buffer. With expanded memory, you can create a sizable buffer that can store many pages without sacrificing any conventional RAM.

The software that configures the buffer should provide a convenient method of controlling the buffer, especially when it comes to "dumping" the data that will be sent to the printer. A printer that can't be silenced when necessary may be more trouble than the buffering is worth.

There are programs, such as 1-2-3 Release 3 and some word processors, that do their own spooling when printing, and therefore would not benefit from a RAM print buffer.

RAM Disk

Creating virtual disks in expanded RAM can be a worthwhile endeavor. Not only is conventional RAM spared from having to give up thousands or hundreds of thousands of kilobytes, but a disk in expanded RAM can be many times bigger. There's just no way to make a 1-megabyte RAM disk in conventional RAM.

Many programs can show tremendous increases in speed when the program code or the data they access is kept on a RAM disk. The improvements for 1-2-3, though, are not so dramatic. The entire program is already stored in RAM, and there are no overlay or secondary program files to be accessed. The same is true for worksheets. Once retrieved, Lotus never goes to the disk again until the worksheet is saved.

Since Lotus is RAM-dependent both for its program code and the worksheet, it is generally self-defeating to withhold conventional RAM for a virtual disk. Lotus is better served by having as much memory available as possible. When a RAM disk can be put "out of the way" in expanded memory, though, there are some applications and situations where a RAM disk can be a benefit to Lotus.

Most desktop computers have hard disks, but many portable computers do not. If you have a portable or laptop computer with only floppy drives but expanded memory, your work routines might warrant your keeping the 1-2-3 program on the RAM drive. This would allow you to keep another program in drive A, such as a word processor, so you could quickly move from one to another.

You could also keep the PrintGraph program and ancillary files on the RAM drive, so that you would have (almost) instant access to them. Of course, your graphs still won't print any faster, so the idea of bouncing in and out of Print-Graph may not be as attractive as it first looked.

Keeping the DOS file COMMAND.COM on a RAM disk is an effective use for a RAM drive on a floppy disk system; it will be explained later in this chapter.

Even systems with a hard disk can show improved performance when a Lotus application's secondary worksheet files are stored on a RAM disk. A large consolidation with dozens of worksheets would be a good candidate for a RAM disk. Moreover, if the secondary files are not needed once the consolidation is made, they do not need to be erased from a hard disk.

> ⊗ CAUTION ◆ *Whatever use you make of a RAM disk, do not be lulled into a false sense of security—the disk is temporary, and the slightest power glitch can remove any trace of its ever having existed. A program that locks up and forces you to reboot the computer will also condemn any files on the RAM disk. Be judicious with its use, and relegate to it only files that are either temporary or that are also safely tucked away on a "real" disk.*

◆ *SPEEDUP, THE LOTUS ADD-IN FOR RELEASE 2.01* _____

The ability to accept add-in programs was one of the major enhancements introduced with 1-2-3 Release 2.0. Speedup is an add-in program that was created by Lotus to specifically increase the performance of 1-2-3. It was released in tandem with the Learn add-in discussed in Chapter 1, and like Learn, it is free to Lotus users. Note, however, that Speedup works only with Lotus 2.01, and not with version 2.0.

When 1-2-3 Release 2.01 recalculates, every formula in the worksheet is updated. It does not change the recalculation process even if you press the F9 {calc} key a dozen times in a row. The same lengthy process would be repeated a dozen times for every formula in the worksheet.

Although a total recalculation ensures that all formulas are absolutely current at that point, it also creates intolerably long calculation times and forces the early use of manual recalculation.

The Speedup add-in provides Lotus with "intelligent recalculation"—only formulas that need to be calculated will be. It does not actually speed up the time it takes to perform a calculation, as a math coprocessor does. It simply eliminates from the chain of calculation any formulas that do not need updating, thereby decreasing the quantity of cells that must be evaluated.

Intelligent recalculation is so useful that it was built into Release 2.2, thereby eliminating the need for Speedup. Recalculation times using Release 2.01 with Speedup are quite comparable to those in Release 2.2, as a test will show later in this section.

For example, suppose you had a large worksheet with hundreds or thousands of formulas, and Recalculation was set to Automatic, but Speedup was active. You could enter a number into a cell, and if that cell were referenced by only one of the formulas, just that one formula would be recalculated. The process would take only an instant, and the worksheet would be just as current as if every formula had been recalculated.

In this way, Speedup allows you to leave Recalculation set to Automatic without your being hypnotized by the Wait light every time you enter data into a cell. Data can be entered without forcing any recalculation at all if none of that new data is referenced by any of the formula cells. In Manual Recalculation mode, the F9 {calc} key may cause only a momentary blink if no formulas need updating.

The Speedup menu consists of only three choices. The first two, Optimal and Standard, simply toggle the intelligent recalculation process on and off, although you may never need to turn it off. There may be times, however,

2.2 ◆ ———

when your worksheet has so many formulas that it takes just as long for Speedup to determine which formulas need updating as it takes for the actual recalculation.

The third menu item is called Highlight. When you are in Manual Recalculation mode, turning this choice on will cause any cell that is changed to be highlighted. The highlighted cells will remain that way until the next recalculation. The program does not highlight formulas that will need recalculating, only the cells that have had their contents changed. It serves as a good reminder that Speedup is active.

Figure 6.2 demonstrates the advantage of using Speedup in a large worksheet, by comparing its speed with both 1-2-3 Release 2.01 without Speedup and Release 2.2. The range A16..H216 is filled with formulas. Half the formulas, those in columns A through D, include a reference to another cell, KEY_CELL in B4. The other half, columns E through H, have no cell references.

The timing macro in \Z times the recalculation speed by issuing the {calc} command between the start and finish times:

```
{let START,@now}{calc}
{let FINISH,@now}{recalc ELAPSED} ~
```

A comparison can be made by running it in Release 2.2, and in Release 2.01, both with and without Speedup being active. Without Speedup, the entire worksheet is recalculated whenever F9 {calc} is pressed, whether there have been changes or not. The result is shown at F11, where the time registered at 13 seconds.

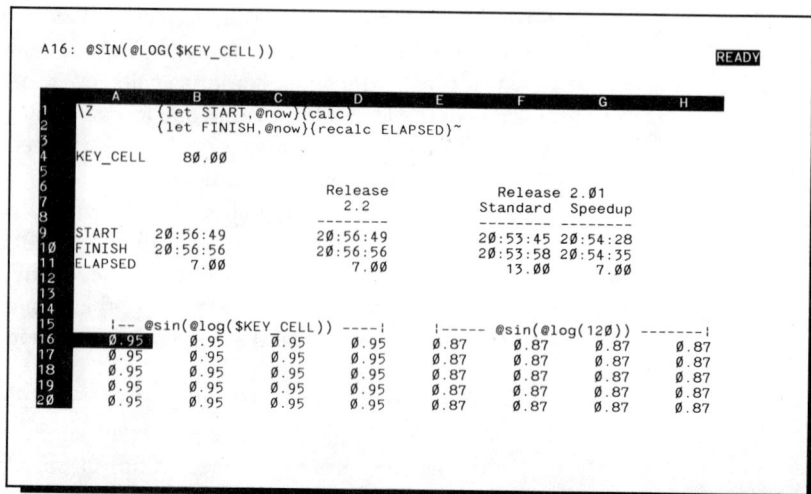

Figure 6.2 ◆ *Using the timing macro to determine recalculation speeds*

By invoking the add-in and turning on its optimal recalculation, two noticeable improvements are made. First, if no changes are made to the worksheet, the timing macro will register an elapsed time of 0—no formulas need to be evaluated. If the reference cell KEY_CELL is changed, then only the formulas in columns A through D need to be recalculated, and the resulting time will be about half as long as without the add-in, as recorded in G11. Note that the recalculation time for Release 2.2 is the same, due to its built-in capacity for intelligent recalculation (see cell D11).

Speedup takes about 6K of conventional RAM, and you can regain that memory at any time by detaching the add-in from Lotus. Before buying a faster computer, Speedup, or Release 2.2, may give you all the speed you need.

◆ *TAKING ADVANTAGE OF DOS WITH THE SYSTEM COMMAND* _____

The typical 1-2-3 work session may have no direct connection to the DOS environment that surrounds it. It can remain insulated until the final Quit command, when control is returned to DOS. But when you need to get back to the DOS environment, the DOS prompt is only one keystroke away with the System command.

> **TIP** ◆ *The first thing to do in DOS before entering Lotus is to check that the computer's system date and time are correctly set. Imagine trying to determine which worksheet file is newest when all are dated Tue 1-01-1980. Lotus displays the date and time on the screen (or the worksheet's file name in Release 2.2 if you prefer), but they will be correct only if you have set them correctly from DOS. The @now function also depends on the DOS date and time, and will only be as accurate as they are. If your computer does not have a built-in, battery-operated clock and you forget to set the computer's date and time before entering Lotus, you can easily use the System command to go to DOS and do so.*

There are unlimited possibilities once you have popped out of Lotus and back to DOS by using the System command. Here are some of the things that you can do:

- ◆ Format a floppy disk
- ◆ Run CHKDSK on a suspected disk

- View a print file

- Copy other worksheet files to your data disk or subdirectory

- Copy files to a floppy for others to use

- Print a graph with PrintGraph

- Print a word processing document

- Find a file using a hard-disk management program

- Print a disk file using the DOS command PRINT

- Receive data over the phone with a communications program

- Translate another program's file into a worksheet

- Import a Lotus print file into a word processing document

- Export a word processing document to a print file

Remember, to leave DOS and return to Lotus to resume your work, just type *EXIT.*

> ⊗ **CAUTION** ◆ *After spending some time in DOS, it is easy to forget that Lotus is already running, and you may make the mistake of typing 123 to get back into Lotus. If you have enough memory available, you will end up with two running copies of Lotus, and the active one will undoubtedly be strapped for memory. You can usually determine if you have made this mistake by issuing the Worksheet Status command and checking the amount of available memory.*

USING THE SYSTEM COMMAND

The System command is in a sense one of the most powerful commands in 1-2-3. Its only purpose is to allow a temporary exit from the worksheet without having to actually quit the program. When you are finished with any chores at the DOS level, typing *EXIT* returns control back to the worksheet, where everything is just as it was. This is essentially the same capability that the SHELL command provides in BASIC. Without this command, you would have to follow several steps before you could reach DOS. On a floppy disk system, such as employed by many laptop computers, these steps are time-consuming and may require disk swapping:

- ◆ Save worksheet to disk
- ◆ Quit Lotus
- ◆ Perform DOS chores
- ◆ Load Lotus
- ◆ Retrieve file

> **TIP** ◆ *To use the System command, the DOS file COM-MAND.COM must be available so that a secondary copy of DOS can be created for the user to enter from Lotus. On a floppy-disk system, COMMAND.COM must be on the current disk in the drive from which the computer was booted.*

You can simplify and even accelerate the process of going to DOS on a floppy disk system by using a RAM disk and the DOS command SET. If you type SET at the DOS prompt, you will see some information about your DOS environment. One of those pieces of information, which is always present, is the location where DOS can find its command processor, COMMAND-.COM. On a hard disk system, this will generally be the root level of drive C, so that SET will produce this screen output:

COMSPEC = C:\COMMAND.COM

On a floppy system that boots from drive A, the display would look like this:

COMSPEC = A:\COMMAND.COM

With the SET command, you can change the location of COMMAND-.COM to a new drive or subdirectory. On a floppy disk machine with a RAM drive labeled C, you could tell DOS to always look to that drive for its command processor. You would, of course, also have to copy the file COMMAND-.COM to that drive. Then use the SET command at the DOS prompt:

SET COMSPEC = C:\COMMAND.COM

Now, whenever you use the System command in Lotus (or the SHELL command in BASIC), DOS activates COMMAND.COM from the RAM disk, making the process much faster and eliminating the need for that file on the disk in drive A.

⊗ **CAUTION** ◆ *Note that when you go to DOS using the Lotus System command, a secondary copy of DOS is created, and changes that you make to the DOS environment may only affect that secondary environment. As soon as you type EXIT to return to Lotus, the secondary copy of DOS is destroyed. Any changes that you made (to the location of COMMAND.COM, for example) are destroyed along with it, and the primary DOS shell remains as it was originally. You must, therefore, fix the location of COMMAND-.COM before you start to work in Lotus.*

Some of the jobs that can be done at the DOS level involve running other programs. Usually the only limitation to what can be run is the amount of RAM that Lotus has not used.

⊗ **CAUTION** ◆ *Some programs may destroy the copy of Lotus and its worksheet that are being held in memory. This is especially likely to happen if you run a memory-resident program, and you should avoid such programs. Be Cautious! If you will be running another program after using the System command, or if you plan to do many tasks in DOS, always save your worksheet before leaving Lotus. This requires extra time, but it is the only way to guarantee against disaster.*

◆ TRANSFERRING PROGRAM CONTROL

It may often seem that 1-2-3 can do just about everything. To use it most effectively, though, there will be times when data needs to be transferred from the Lotus environment to another program for further processing. The data may remain in that program, or be processed and then returned to a 1-2-3 worksheet for even more processing and formatting for output.

A common example is exporting worksheet data to a file and then reading that file into a database program. There, records held within the database program can be extracted based on the Lotus data and then sent back to a worksheet. Or perhaps the worksheet data is the basis for a printed report built from records in that database. In this case, the data would not be returned to Lotus, and the transfer would be in one direction only.

Each program has its own range of strong points. The worksheet serves best as a data analyzer, and the database as a data selector and organizer.

AUTOMATING THE TRANSFER PROCESS IN RELEASE 2.2

2.2 ◆ ——————

The key to transferring program control from 1-2-3 Release 2.2 to another program is the macro command {system}. This command is new in Release 2.2, and like the \0 macro and AUTO123 worksheet, it is very simple, but powerful.

The {system} Command

On the surface, the {system} macro command appears to be just like the System command on the Lotus menu. Both commands allow you to temporarily go to the DOS prompt to conduct other business while 1-2-3 and your worksheet remain in memory. But there is one significant difference between the two methods of getting to DOS. The menu command, System, sends you to a DOS prompt and leaves you there, whereas Release 2.2's {system} macro command takes a parameter within its brackets, and that parameter is taken as a DOS command that will be executed as soon as the DOS prompt appears.

For example, the macro statement

{system "PCO" }

would temporarily exit to DOS and run a program called PCO. That program would have control of the computer and could, for example, process any data that you had saved to disk from your worksheet, perhaps as a print (text) file. But when you quit from the PCO program, you would immediately be back in 1-2-3, perhaps to import the data that had been processed by the other program.

All you have to do to apply the {system} command is supply the proper parameter. Be sure to enclose the program name in quotes, and spell it exactly as you would type it in at the DOS prompt. You can include any drive or path designation, or any of the program's command line parameters, such as:

{system "C:\PCO\PCO /q /r /i /m = 32"}

Note that you cannot use this command without a parameter; you must always specify a program to run. If you simply want a macro to return you to the DOS prompt, you can either use the menu command System:

/s

or use the {system} command with the name of the DOS command interpreter as its parameter:

{system "COMMAND"}

Like any other macro Command Language statement, the parameter can also be a range name, cell address, or formula that evaluates to a string.

Implementing the {system} Command

It's quite easy to build the {system} command into your automated worksheet routines. Suppose you have a macro-driven worksheet that has written a range of data to disk, and now the data need to be loaded into a BASIC program for further processing or reporting. Figure 6.3 shows a small macro menu named \MENU1 that does the job.

The menu for this example has two non-working choices, Data and View, that are there simply to fill out the menu and make it appear like a typical worksheet menu. The choice named Process is the one that turns over control to the BASIC program. It has only two macro statements in it:

```
{system "GWBASIC D:PROCESS"}
{branch \M}
```

The first command invokes the operating system and loads GWBASIC along with its program PROCESS, which resides on the D drive. At this point, that program has control of the computer. When PROCESS is done and returns to DOS, control is immediately returned to 1-2-3 at precisely the place where the {system} macro had finished.

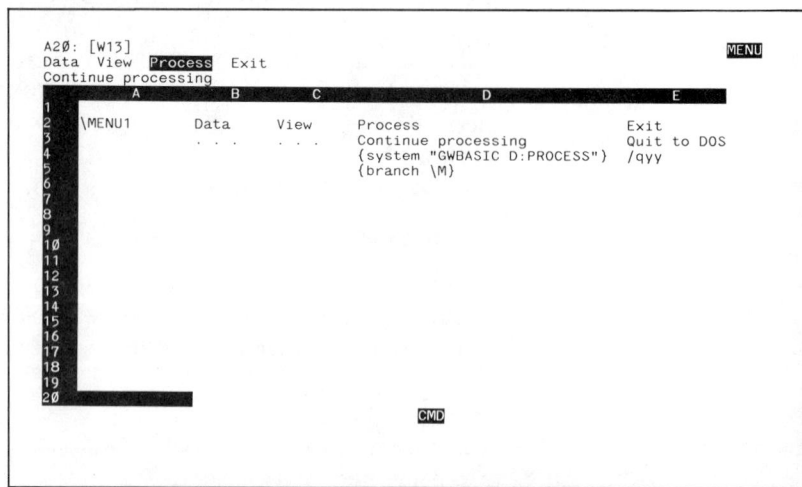

```
A2Ø: [W13]                                                      MENU
Data View  Process  Exit
Continue processing
           A        B        C           D                    E
 1
 2  \MENU1       Data      View     Process                Exit
 3               . . .     . . .    Continue processing    Quit to DOS
 4                                  {system "GWBASIC D:PROCESS"}  /qyy
 5                                  {branch \M}
 6
 7
 8
 9
10
11
12
13
14
15
16
17
18
19
2Ø
                                        CMD
```

Figure 6.3 ◆ *Automating the transfer of control with the {system} command in Release 2.2*

The command that follows simply calls \M, which in turn calls the main menu and its choices. When you want to leave the worksheet and not return, you use the Quit choice on the menu, which simply invokes the 1-2-3 Quit command.

> **TIP** ◆ *Notice that the macro to invoke the Quit command includes the extra y of confirmation that is needed when you quit from Release 2.2. This Quit macro will also work fine in Release 2.01, as you will see shortly, even though the second y is not needed. As soon as the first y is invoked, the 1-2-3 session will be over and the second y will not even be used.*

The routine of automatically turning over control to another program is very straightforward with the {system} command of Release 2.2. It will work the same no matter what kind of processing the spreadsheet or other program might do while in control of the computer. Hundreds of processing steps may occur in the worksheet before control is transferred to the other program, and hundreds more may take place in that program before control returns to Lotus.

Even though complexity does not affect the workings of this routine, memory constraints will. If you are working on a very large spreadsheet, or want to run a large program, you may not have enough memory left for DOS and the other program to load, and you will have to quit from 1-2-3 before transferring control to the other program. You must also devise another method of passing program control if you are using 1-2-3 Release 2.01, because its macro language does not have the {system} command.

The method you can use with Release 2.01, or if you are short on memory in Release 2.2, is discussed next. You will be surprised at the number of steps involved, because you must actually leave 1-2-3 with the Quit command, turn control over to the other program, and then later reload 1-2-3. But it is nonetheless a very practical method that demonstrates the use of several tools within the Lotus spreadsheet and within DOS, and is a very valuable exercise.

AUTOMATING THE TRANSFER PROCESS WITH BATCH FILES

A program called from a batch file will return control to that batch file when it is finished (when you quit Lotus, for example). The batch file regains control and will continue with any further commands. This is how the batch files explained in Chapter 5 allow a user to enter and quit Lotus gracefully. It is also the core of the system that will be built here.

The trick that makes this automated control-transfer system work is that the final command in the primary batch file, the command that will be executed after Lotus relinquishes control, simply calls another batch file. That second one, though, can be changed from within the 1-2-3 application before it is ever executed.

> ⊗ CAUTION ◆ *An automated control-transfer system only works when Lotus gives up control completely—that is, when the Quit command is used. Because the System command actually creates a new copy of DOS, and leaves the original one hidden away, a batch file that had originally called Lotus would wait endlessly for Lotus to return control to it if the System command were used to exit the program.*

Calling Lotus with a Primary Batch File

The first batch file is the one that starts the entire process. Its name would most likely be similar to the name of the Lotus application it calls. In this case, it is called RUN_APP.BAT:

```
c:
cd \123
123
DO_NEXT
```

The batch file goes to drive C and then to the 1-2-3 subdirectory, where it calls the 1-2-3 program. The worksheet application sends data at some point to one or more disk files that will later be used by the other program.

It is not until the user quits Lotus that the last command is issued, which calls the secondary batch file DO_NEXT. The contents of DO_NEXT, however, have been revised from within 1-2-3, thereby giving the worksheet application control over the events that happen outside the worksheet environment. How this is done will be explained after looking at the secondary batch file.

Transferring Control to a Secondary Batch File

At this point, Lotus has given up control, and there is data on disk that can be used by another program. The last command of the first batch file calls the second batch file DO_NEXT, which runs through these steps:

```
GWBASIC PROCESS
RUN_APP
```

In this case, control is passed to a BASIC program named PROCESS. This program can then use the data from Lotus to perform its tasks. Here, it writes new data to disk that will later be imported back into the Lotus application. When it is finished and returns control to DOS, the secondary batch file continues by calling the primary batch file RUN_APP. It in turn calls Lotus, just as it had originally.

Writing Batch Files in a Worksheet

The file DO_NEXT.BAT will be written from within the Lotus worksheet. The actual contents of the file may vary depending on the needs of the application. This example uses the same menu that was shown in Figure 6.3, although the macro for the Process choice is quite different. Figure 6.4 shows the macros needed for the routine.

In this example, the two choices on \MENU1, Process and Exit, both run the same macro routines to create the file DO_NEXT.BAT. But each macro routine produces a different version of the batch file. In effect, 1-2-3 is determining what will happen after you quit the spreadsheet. Once the batch file is created, the last macro in each issues the Quit command, and the Lotus session is ended. Here is the code under the Process choice:

```
{\PRINT PROCESS}
/qyy
```

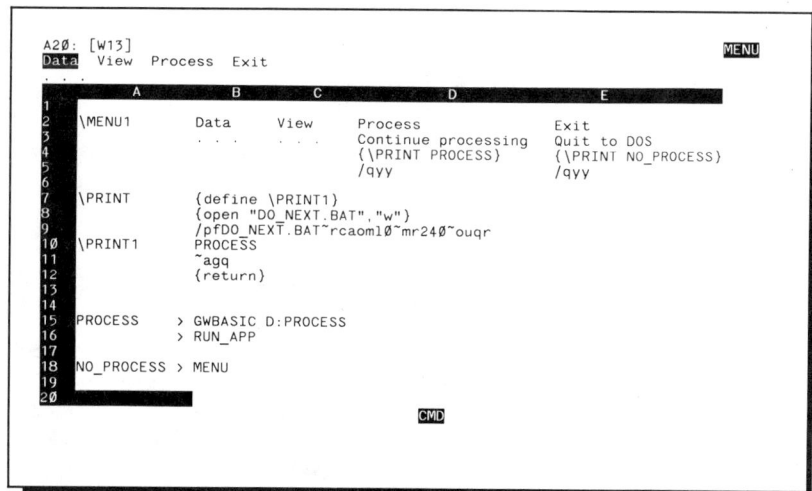

```
A2Ø: [W13]                                                            MENU
Data  View  Process  Exit

          A              B          C           D                E
1
2  \MENU1          Data       View      Process          Exit
3                  . . .      . . .     Continue processing   Quit to DOS
4                                       (\PRINT PROCESS)      (\PRINT NO_PROCESS)
5                                       /qyy                  /qyy
6
7  \PRINT          {define \PRINT1}
8                  {open "DO_NEXT.BAT","w"}
9                  /pfDO_NEXT.BAT~rcaoml0~mr240~ouqr
10 \PRINT1         PROCESS
11                 ~agq
12                 {return}
13
14
15 PROCESS    > GWBASIC D:PROCESS
16            > RUN_APP
17
18 NO_PROCESS > MENU
19
20                                      CMD
```

Figure 6.4 ◆ *Automating the transfer of control with batch files*

And here is the code under Exit:

```
{\PRINT NO_PROCESS}
/qyy
```

Both macros call the subroutine \PRINT, but each passes a different para-meter to that subroutine. Both parameters are range names, and it is one of these ranges that is printed to the file DO_NEXT.BAT by the macro \PRINT.

The first line of \PRINT, B7 in the worksheet, consists of the {define} com-mand. It specifies in which cell to place the parameter that was passed by the calling macro:

```
{define \PRINT1}
```

In this case, cell PRINT1 receives the text. It will hold the name PROCESS or the name NO_PROCESS, depending on which menu item was chosen from \MENU1. In the example, PROCESS has been chosen, as you can see in cell B10.

The next line of the print macro prepares the disk file, DO_NEXT.BAT, to receive data from the worksheet:

```
{open "DO_NEXT.BAT","w"}
```

This brings up an interesting use for the {open} statement that should be men-tioned here.

A macro can check for the existence of a file before trying to access it by using this statement. In Figure 6.4, the macro that prints to disk must be writ-ten so that it will succeed whether or not the file DO_NEXT.BAT is already on disk. The print-to-file Cancel or Replace option requires that the macro know whether or not the file already exists.

When the {open, "FILENAME", "w"} command is used to open a file for receiving data in the write mode (w), the file is immediately created if it does not already exist. Therefore, in this macro, DO_NEXT.BAT will always be on disk before the print macro starts.

⊗ **CAUTION** ◆ *Be aware that the open-for-writing statement essentially creates a new file, even when the file named in the {open} statement already exists. In that case, the file's data will be erased in anticipation of receiving new data, and it will have zero bytes of data associated with it. Since all the data in the file is lost when it is opened, you should be judicious in the use of this command. The print command works in this same manner when you are printing to a file, as you will see in Chapter 12.*

To append data to an existing file, an open-for-modification statement must be used, such as:

{open "FILENAME","m"}

If you only wish to read data from a file and not make changes, use the "r" parameter. With both the read and modify modes, the file is not overwritten when it is opened, so there is no danger of losing data.

Another aspect to consider when using the {open} statement to open a file for reading (r) or modification (m) is the order of commands used in the macro. In either case, the file by definition must already exist on disk in order to be read or appended. If the file exists, the {open} command will succeed and the macro will continue immediately in the next cell down. If the file does not already exist (or is incorrectly named in the macro), the {open} command will fail, since there is no file to read or modify. In that case, the macro continues with any code *in the same cell*, just after the {open} statement.

This provides a simple way to catch an error. You can encode the appropriate action to take (when the file doesn't exist) in the same cell as the {open} command. If the file does exist and the {open} command succeeds, then that extra code will be ignored. Bearing this in mind, the following macro is a handy way to remind the user that a macro cannot proceed because a file is not on disk:

{open "FILENAME","r"} {branch \NO_FILE}
{\USE_FILE}

If the file does not exist, the macro branches to the routine named \NO_FILE. If the file does exist, then \NO_FILE is ignored, and the macro continues in the cell below with \USE_FILE.

Getting back to the macro at hand, once the file DO_NEXT.BAT is opened, the third line of the print macro specifies that file as the destination for the output, and then sets the parameters for printing:

/pfDO_NEXT.BAT ˜ rcaoml0 ˜ mr240 ˜ ouqr

The Replace command (r) is issued since the file already exists on disk, and all print settings are cleared (ca). Then the left margin is set to 0 and the right margin to 240, and unformatted printing is chosen. These three options are the generic print-to-disk settings for creating bare text files. Note that the ranges defined by PROCESS and NO_PROCESS must each be wide enough to enclose the text they contain. Otherwise, the text will be cut off at the right margin as it is printed.

The print range is specified in \PRINT1, which was previously filled in by the {define} command at the start of \PRINT. In this case the print range is named PROCESS. That range can be seen in cells B15..B16, which contain the text that will go into DO_NEXT.BAT:

```
GWBASIC  D:PROCESS
RUN_APP
```

The printing is completed in B11, and the {return} command in B12 returns control to the calling macro—the Process choice in \MENU1. There, the Quit command is issued to leave Lotus:

```
/qyy
```

As soon as Lotus returns control to DOS, the primary batch file invokes the newly-created batch file DO_NEXT, where processing continues with the BASIC program named PROCESS.

If there were no data to be processed outside of Lotus, the user would choose Exit, which prints the range NO_PROCESS to the disk file DO_NEXT.BAT. The text for the file can be seen in B18. In this case, when the macro quits Lotus, DO_NEXT simply returns the user to the DOS menuing system. If no menuing system is being used, DO_NEXT could either be blank or contain a command to change directories back to the root level.

Note that this macro must be used when you want to quit from 1-2-3. Consider what would happen if you simply quit without first writing DO_NEXT-.BAT. The first batch file, RUN_APP, would take over as usual and call the second batch file DO_NEXT. If you had already run the Process routine, then the batch file would call GWBASIC and run the transfer routine. The only way to avoid this is by rewriting DO_NEXT for an action appropriate to quitting. Of course, when you use the {system} macro in Release 2.2, no batch files are involved and you can quit from 1-2-3 directly.

The implementation of the program transfer routine is the final link in the chain of control that connects your 1-2-3 worksheets with the "outside world" of your computing environment. This system consists only of a batch file to call 1-2-3 and a few lines of macro code that create the second batch file that transfers control. There are enough pieces, however, that you may find it confusing the first time you build it. But once you have successfully completed the task, you will see how simple it really is, and you will be able to adapt it to many situations.

◆ SUMMARY

This chapter looked at some of the factors that influence Lotus but reside outside the Lotus environment. The computer's hardware holds a dominant position in this area, but it is not just the speed of the CPU that must be considered. The other components in the system can prove just as critical to the speed of 1-2-3 and the control you have over it. These components include the hard disk, expanded memory, the math coprocessor, the display, and the printer.

Expanded memory adds a new dimension to the worksheet environment. This chapter discussed two additional uses for it outside of Lotus: print spoolers and RAM disks.

The Lotus add-in, Speedup, which can vastly increase recalculation times in Lotus 2.01, was also considered. It requires only 6K of conventional memory to run, and almost no time to master its simple, three-item menu.

The System command and the {system} macro command in Release 2.2, which allow immediate access to the DOS environment and provide many shortcuts for your daily work routines, were presented next. The last section of this chapter discussed an automated technique for passing control from Lotus to another program, and then back again.

Part 2 of this book looks at data analysis, the primary function of 1-2-3.

PART TWO:

Analysis

PART 2 COVERS SOME OF THE MORE POWERFUL FEATURES IN Lotus—those that facilitate data analysis.

The importance of maintaining the distinction between cell contents and cell display is covered in Chapter 7. You will learn how to segregate numbers from text, and how to translate numbers that have been mistakenly entered as text.

Chapter 8 covers date arithmetic, one of the most powerful and frequently misunderstood tools in Lotus. Also included in this chapter are a range of @ functions that should definitely be part of your Lotus toolbox.

String arithmetic is covered in Chapter 9. It allows you to write formulas that mix text and numeric operations, create macros that adapt to the worksheet, and combine several formulas into one. The @ functions that handle text are also covered, and you will find many interesting uses for them.

Worksheet databases are powerful analysis tools that often create problems for the user. Chapter 10 will improve your grasp of database concepts while providing a wide variety of techniques for using a Lotus database. The powerful @d data functions are also covered in this chapter.

Chapter 11 discusses the ins and outs of graphing in Lotus. It offers pointers that will help you arrange data efficiently in the worksheet, format a graph with the graphing commands, and print your work with PrintGraph.

SEVEN:

Cell Contents versus
Cell Display

7

◆ ◆ ◆

WORKSHEET DATA CAN CONSIST OF TEXT, NUMBERS, AND functions, all of which can be manipulated within a cell by formulas. The display of a numeric cell can be shown in a variety of formats, and text can be justified within a cell. This chapter emphasizes the distinction between a cell's contents (data) and its display. Some of the most common problems in the worksheet arise because this distinction is unclear.

◆ ROWS AND COLUMNS DEFINE CELLS

The Lotus worksheet consists of 256 columns, A through IV, and 8,192 rows. The intersection of each row and column forms a cell, for a total of 2,097,152 cells. There are four components to a cell:

- ◆ Contents (what has been typed into the cell)
- ◆ Display (how the contents are summarized for the screen)
- ◆ Format (the style of a cell's display)
- ◆ Protection status (protected or unprotected)

Whenever a cell is copied, moved, saved, or otherwise selected, these parts remain with it.

Each cell is unique, separate from every other cell in the worksheet. Any cell is limited to a maximum of 240 characters, but because a formula can refer to a range of cells or to other individual cells, there is really no limit to the amount of data that can be summarized in one cell. In fact, by addressing cells that reference other cells, just one cell can reference every other cell in the worksheet:

@count(A1..IV8192)

Cells can be referenced by their column and row coordinates, such as B2 or CG1929. You can also give them a range name, which you can then use instead of the actual coordinates. A formula that references a named range displays the name instead of the cell coordinates. When many names are referenced in one formula, the lengthy string of characters in the formula may seem to break the 240-character limit. In fact, formulas actually use the cell coordinates for their inner workings, and only substitute the names in the display. This is why no extra memory is needed when formulas refer to cells that have range names.

A long formula may become too long when copied to another cell, and it may be truncated by Lotus without your knowing it. This is not a common problem, but the results can be disastrous, since you may be unaware that anything has happened. When a formula is copied, any cell addresses in it will adjust to the new location. If the new references have more characters in their address, the formula will have grown in length by that many characters. The danger occurs when the number exceeds 240. Instead of producing an error, Lotus simply truncates any extra characters and returns the result for those that are left.

Figure 7.1 demonstrates this danger. The formula in B3 consists of 80 references to the value in B1, as proven by its displayed result of 80. The contents of the formula are shown in D3. The 80 repetitions of the three-character phrase +B1 produces a formula length of 240 characters.

In the lower portion of the screen, the formula has been copied to B103, and its cell references have adjusted to cell B101. There are still 80 references, as the displayed total shows, but each referenced address now consists of five

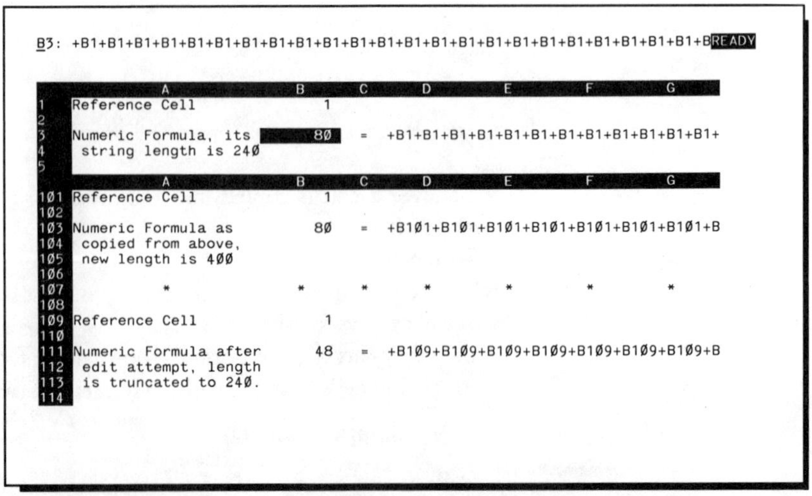

Figure 7.1 ◆ *When a long formula is copied, Lotus may truncate it*

characters, +*B101*, instead of three, +*B1*. The calculation 5*80 proves that the length of the formula is now 400, far beyond the 240 maximum! This mysterious happening is, however, short-lived.

The formula has also been copied to cell B111. Here it has been edited but no changes were made. As the Enter key was pressed, Lotus was forced to disallow the illegal extra characters. The formula result of 48 reflects the new length, as there are 48 repetitions of the five-character cell reference, +*B109*, for a total of 240.

You can generally avoid this problem by following the good practice of keeping your formulas down to a manageable length. You should be alert for this situation when performing a File Combine operation. The unseen incoming formulas will adjust to their new location in the worksheet, just as they do when copied, and a long formula could produce the error.

> **TIP** ◆ *The long formula in Figure 7.1 was not written manually. Instead, the @repeat function served as a quick tool: @repeat("+B1",80). Before entering the formula into the cell, the {calc} key was used to turn the string formula into the actual string of characters: +B1+B1+B1, and so on. This was then entered as the numeric formula shown.*

◆ CELL CONTENTS REPRESENT WORKSHEET DATA

The contents of a cell are worksheet data. They consist of text (also called *labels* or *strings*), numbers, and functions. You can mix these in any combination by using formulas. The data can be entered directly by the user, or indirectly through a formula that refers to other cells. Those cells, too, can contain either text, numbers, or formulas. Also, in Lotus 2.0 and above, you are allowed to include text directly within a formula. The addition of "text math" has proved to be one of 1-2-3's most powerful enhancements.

TEXT DATA, PLAIN AND SIMPLE

Text data can be broadly defined as any cell entry that is not numeric. Figure 7.2 shows several examples of worksheet text. The entry in C2 consists of text characters that were simply typed into the cell. All labels of this type are

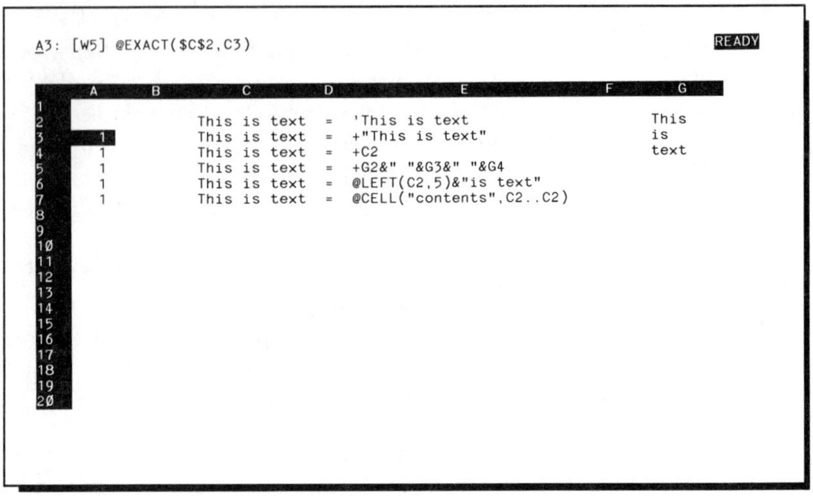

```
A3:  [W5] @EXACT($C$2,C3)                                        READY

         A       B       C           D          E              F        G
1
2                        This is text  =  'This is text                 This
3    1                   This is text  =  +"This is text"                is
4    1                   This is text  =  +C2                            text
5    1                   This is text  =  +G2&" "&G3&" "&G4
6    1                   This is text  =  @LEFT(C2,5)&"is text"
7    1                   This is text  =  @CELL("contents",C2..C2)
8
9
10
11
12
13
14
15
16
17
18
19
20
```

Figure 7.2 ◆ *Text and text values*

preceded by a label prefix, such as an apostrophe (these are discussed later in this chapter). Each of the other cells in column C displays a *text value* that is the result of a formula.

Text and text values can usually be considered synonymous. Each cell of column A in Figure 7.2 contains an @exact string function that compares the contents of the cell to its right with the text in C2. If the two are exact matches, the function returns a 1; if any differences are detected, it returns a 0. As you can see, all the text values in column C are equivalent to the actual text in C2. There are several differences, though, that should be considered when working with text data:

- ◆ Text values cannot be aligned in a cell, since they have no label prefix.

- ◆ All formulas, whether string or numeric, require recalculation time. The same conservation rules apply to both: if the data being entered is going to remain static, it should not be left as a formula.

- ◆ Text values are not "pure" text and cannot be justified using the Range Justify command.

- ◆ A formula that contains text uses about twice as much memory as the text alone would require: the text within the formula plus the text in the result of the formula.

◆ The text in the result of a string formula is stored in the limited conventional RAM, not in expanded RAM as normal text is.

> **TIP** ◆ *Fill each of 1,000 cells with 240 text characters and then check your available memory (Worksheet Status). Erase the worksheet and repeat the process, only this time make each entry a formula by enclosing it in quotes and prefacing it with a plus sign. See how much memory 1,000 string formulas require.*

Dealing with Overhanging Text

A long string of text, whether straight text or a text value, will overhang the cell in which it resides if the column width is less than the length of the text. This can be confusing to novices, as it appears that the text is actually contained in the cells that it overhangs. There are two distinct considerations when dealing with long labels:

◆ How a long label is displayed when it is interrupted by an occupied cell to its right

◆ How the label is shown when its cell is scrolled off the screen

Figure 7.3 is a worksheet that contains three long labels in column A. All three labels are the same, and long enough to extend out to column G, as in

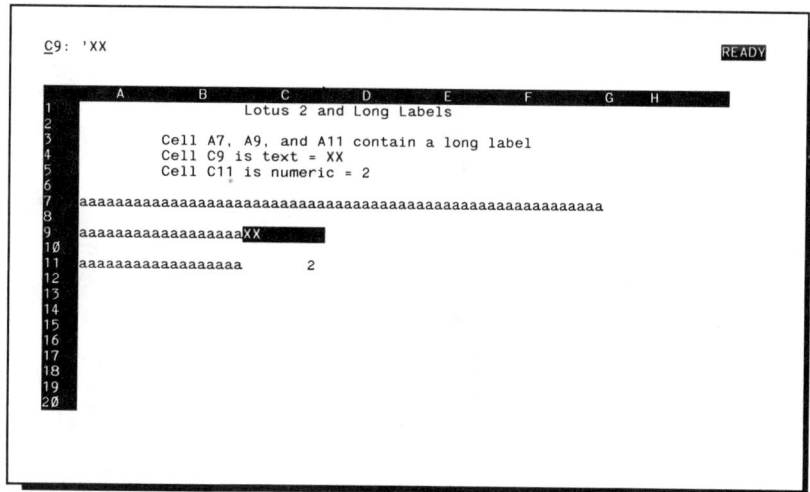

```
C9:  'XX                                                          READY

         A         B         C         D         E         F         G    H
 1                           Lotus 2 and Long Labels
 2
 3                 Cell A7, A9, and A11 contain a long label
 4                 Cell C9 is text = XX
 5                 Cell C11 is numeric = 2
 6
 7  aaaaaaaaaaaaaaaaaaaaaaaaaaaaaaaaaaaaaaaaaaaaaaaaaaaaaaaaaa
 8
 9  aaaaaaaaaaaaaaaaaaXX
10
11  aaaaaaaaaaaaaaaaaa        2
12
13
14
15
16
17
18
19
20
```

Figure 7.3 ◆ *Long labels with intervening cells*

A7. But notice how the text reacts when it is interrupted by the text entry in C9 and the numeric entry in C11. The rule is that a long label does not extend beyond an intervening occupied cell.

The second aspect of long labels can make life a lot easier when working with long text. Figure 7.4 shows the same worksheet from Figure 7.3. This time, the screen has been scrolled one column to the right. Column A is therefore off the screen, and the labels that were entered in that column can still be seen, as they extend to the right in their usual fashion.

The fact that the text remains visible even though its cell is off the screen has many advantages:

◆ A long label can be viewed in its entirety simply by scrolling the screen to the right.

◆ Multiple-row titles or headings that are made up of long labels can be viewed at either end, so that it is easy to adjust their alignment.

◆ There are several tricks with long string functions that help in determining the exact width of a print range. These will be covered in Chapter 12.

◆ An @repeat string function can be used to enter a long string of text that can be seen across an entire range of columns, saving entry time and RAM. See Chapter 9.

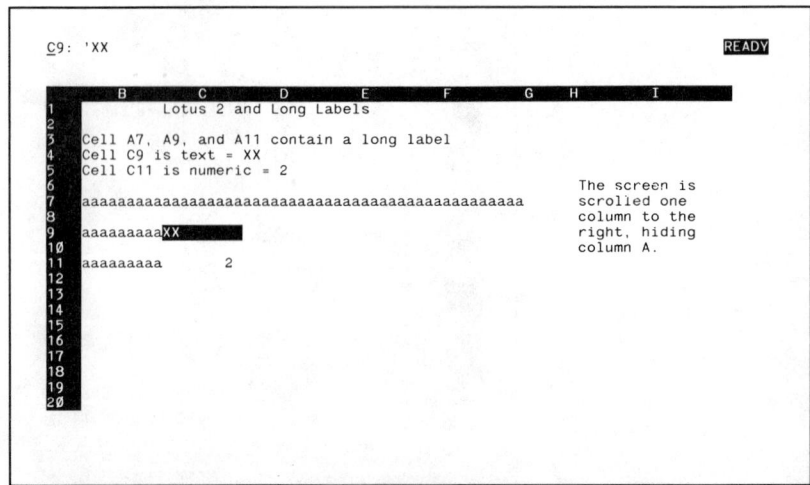

Figure 7.4 ◆ *Long labels when scrolled off-screen*

◆ Before printing, you can easily scroll to the right to see how far a long label extends, and adjust your margins or font size accordingly.

⊗ **CAUTION** ◆ *There is one caution involving long labels in 1-2-3. When specifying a print range, you must include all cells over which an overhanging label extends. In Figures 7.3 and 7.4, you would have to specify the range A7..G7 to print the long label in A7. Specifying fewer columns would cause the text in the printout to be truncated.*

The Pitfalls of Text That Must Look Like a Number

One of the biggest stumbling blocks that all new users encounter is the problem of entering text that looks like a number. You try to enter a street address but Lotus beeps at you and puts the cursor at the first letter after the numeric part of the address, waiting for you to "fix" the offending problem.

Lotus requires that an entry be either text or numeric, and it does its best to determine the nature of an entry by the first character that you type. If it decides that you are typing a number (see the next section), it will not allow you to enter an illegal one. A street address constitutes an illegal numeric entry. However, you can make any entry a text entry by prefacing it with a label prefix. When entering a Social Security number, address, or phone number, just begin the entry with a label prefix.

PUTTING A VALUE ON NUMBERS AND FORMULAS

Lotus recognizes a cell entry as being either plain text or a value. A value can be either a numeric entry or a formula that returns a number or text value. Lotus assumes that an entry is text if it is prefaced with a label prefix, and it assumes that an entry is a value if it starts with any of the numbers 0–9, or any one of these recognized characters: +, −, (, ., @, $, #. There is often little difference between a numeric entry and a formula. Both are considered to be values by Lotus, and both must follow the strict syntactical format of value entries.

The first character you type into a cell determines how Lotus will interpret the entry. The mode indicator in the upper right corner of the screen shows you whether the entry is being taken as text or value. If you start an entry with one of the valid value characters, the indicator will show *VALUE*. Use any other character, and it will display *LABEL*.

> ☑ **TIP** ◆ *When the mode indicator is displaying VALUE or LABEL, you cannot revise an entry by using the usual editing keys. Any movement with the directional keys simply moves the cell pointer and enters the characters into the current cell. If you want to edit the entry before entering it, press the F2 {edit} key and the mode will change to EDIT. You can then revise the entry in the usual way.*

When Lotus is displaying VALUE, it expects the entry to be a valid numeric or formula entry, and you must follow the rules precisely. A stray space amid the characters, unbalanced parentheses, or a misspelled @ function all warrant a beep from Lotus when you press Enter.

2.2 ◆ ─────

> ☑ **TIP** ◆ *If you find that 1-2-3's error beep is beginning to irritate your coworkers, there's a solution if you are using 1-2-3 Release 2.2. Silence the beep with the Worksheet Global Default Other Beep command. Just set it to No, and be sure to use the Update command if you want to keep the beep silent for future sessions of 1-2-3.*

When reporting an error, Lotus tries to show you the location of the error by placing the cursor at the troubled spot. Sometimes, as in the case of an illegal character, the cursor will move to exactly the right point in the entry, and the offending item can be fixed. At other times, such as when parentheses are out of balance, the cursor will only remain at the end of the line and provide no help at all. In those cases, whatever you do, don't press Escape.

> ☑ **TIP** ◆ *Lotus accepts only valid values, but it accepts any text entry. When you hear the 1-2-3 error beep upon entering a value, instead of pressing Escape and erasing your entry, just make it a label by prefacing it with a label prefix and enter it into the cell:*
>
> {home}'~
>
> *Then you can inspect and edit it as text at your leisure. When you think you have found the problem, delete the label prefix and press Enter:*
>
> {home}{del}~

Restoring Numbers That Were Entered as Text

Simple numeric values rarely become data entry problems. The most common source of error beeps when entering a number is the user's insisting on formatting the number with commas to make it look nice. Remember that the value in the cell has little to do with how it can be displayed, and that the two should never be confused. Changing the display will be discussed later in this chapter.

A more serious problem arises when the user finds out that simply including a space in front of the number allows the number to be entered in any style imaginable. This can happen when the perfectionist wants to enter a column of numbers left-justified, or containing commas, dollar signs, or percent signs. Unfortunately, the resulting text has absolutely nothing in common with a number that has that value.

Column A of Figure 7.5 has a mixture of cells that were supposed to be numbers but were mistakenly created as text. Commas and spaces have been used, and none has a numeric value, as the sum function displaying 0 in A17 shows. Fixing these is not a problem if there are only a few—just edit each cell and delete the label prefix and illegal spaces or commas. The methods used to correct these mistakes will be discussed shortly; the results are displayed in columns B and C.

> **TIP** ♦ *Figure 7.5 is a good example of why you should not try to adjust the position of numbers in the cell. None of the entries in column A is aligned on the decimal point, and the column is therefore difficult to read.*

```
A9: '$11,451.23                                                      READY

          A            B            C            D            E
1  < Column A contains the "numbers" that were entered as text >
2
3
4          Data Parse                      @value of
5      Input        Output                 Column A
6  -------------------------------------------------------------
7
8  V>>>>>>>>>>>
9  $11,451.23        11451.23                   11451.23
10    $10,470,125    10470125                    10470125
11       22.5%          0.225                       0.225
12  -125%              -1.25                       -1.25
13  1,408 3/8        1408.375                    1408.375
14  27 23/45        27.511111111                27.511111111
15       $9,079          9079                        9079
16  -------------   -------------              -------------
17               0   10492090.0911              10492090.0911
18
19
20
```

Figure 7.5 ♦ *Fixing numbers that were mistakenly entered as text*

When there are many cells to correct, a faster and more efficient means than editing must be found, and there are four ways to change text into numbers automatically:

◆ Use the @value string function

◆ Use the data parse command

◆ Use an edit macro that loops down the list

◆ Print to disk and use the File Import Numbers command

Unfortunately, in Figure 7.5, there is no consistency to the illegal characters in each cell, so the last two methods shown above will not work (but will be discussed later in this section).

Thus, your first option is to use the @value string function. This function is used to reference a string that looks like a number and return its actual numeric value. Remember that a string is just another name for a text entry, or label. As an "intelligent" function, @value can recognize certain text characters that may occur in text that looks numerical. These include commas, dollar and percent signs, and the slash symbol (/) as used in fractions.

Column D in Figure 7.5 shows the simple solution of using @value functions to refer to the data in column A. Cell D9 contains the formula @value (A9), and so on down the column. As you can see, any preceding spaces in an entry are removed, the commas are stripped out, the fractions are turned into valid decimal fractions, and the entries with a percent sign are turned into valid percents (number divided by 100). The total in cell D17 proves the validity of the numbers.

Once the formulas are copied and you are satisfied with the accuracy of the new values, you can use the Range Value command to copy the formulas back onto the bad data, and then the formulas can be erased.

Your other option is to use the Data Parse command, which is also intelligent and can handle this mixture of text entries. The format line is created in cell A8 above the first entry. It begins with the format line label prefix, which is the single vertical bar, ¦ . That character is not displayed because it is a label prefix. The V stands for value, which is followed by enough "continue the field" symbols (>) to cover the longest entry in the column.

The input column is specified (includes the format line), as well as the output column, cell B9. The Go command produces the result in column B. Note that the output is exactly the same as the results of the @value functions. Since more than one format line can be entered down the column of data, the Data Parse command allows quite a bit of flexibility when a mixture of data must be repaired. (You'll meet this command again in Chapter 13.)

Another method involves devising an edit macro that will make corrections to a range of cells. In Lotus 1A, where neither the @value nor the Data Parse methods was available, a macro was often the only automated solution. In Figure 7.5, if the numbers had been entered illegally but consistently, a macro could easily step down the column, correcting each entry. For example, if each number had just a label prefix that needed to be deleted, the macro would simply edit each cell, delete the label prefix, move down one cell, and repeat, as this macro named \Z demonstrates:

{edit}{home}{del}{down}{branch \Z}

Unfortunately, there are entries in column A of Figure 7.5 that have preceding spaces and other variations, and this macro would not fix those cells. It would leave the data in an "almost" fixed state, which is far worse than knowing all the data is wrong.

The last option, print to disk and use the File Import Numbers command, was also available in Lotus 1A, but it is also too restrictive to be used with inconsistent data. When a file is imported into Lotus as numbers, any text characters are stripped out, leaving only numbers. The only characters that are recognized as having a numeric effect are the period and percent sign. Numbers that are separated by text characters are placed into their own cell, which allows data to be neatly tucked into the worksheet columns.

With consistent data—say, with only a label prefix to be removed—the routine is to print the offending data to a disk file, and then bring the file back into a blank section of the worksheet with the File Import Numbers command, as shown in this macro:

```
/pfFILENAME ~ carBAD_DATA ~ oml0 ~ mr240 ~ ouqagq
{goto}BLANK_RANGE ~ /finFILENAME ~
```

The data is returned to the worksheet as numbers, and once you verify the quality, those numbers can be copied onto the original column of data.

Other than the period and percent sign, all other text characters serve as delimiters—numbers on either side will be placed in adjoining cells. This includes dollar signs, commas, and the slash character (/) used in Figure 7.5 above. Therefore, the data in the example would be spread across several columns as determined by the number of commas and spaces in each one. The numerator and denominator of a fraction also end up in separate cells. Because of this diversity there is no logical manner of combining the data back into the proper numbers with this method.

Turning Numbers into Text with the {contents} Macro

The previous examples showed you how to take text that looks like a formatted number and turn it back into an actual value, which could then be included in arithmetical operations and formatted as a number.

You can also take a number and turn it into text that looks like a number, but is nonetheless text, by using the @string function. This function returns an unformatted number, and will not display commas, dollar signs, or percent signs. But there are occasions when you will want to take a value and make it a string while retaining its cell formatting, and the macro command {contents} will do that for you.

Suppose you want a title area in a print range that will always shows the date and time the range was printed. The title might look like this:

Report was printed on 15-Dec at 04:35 PM

What approach should you take to construct this title? If you build part of this title into the print header by using the @ symbol in the header text, it will place the date in the header. But there is no similar function to produce the time, so the header will not do the job. You could split the text, date, and time among several cells, entering the @now function for the date and time and giving those two cells an appropriate format. Unfortunately that would require four columns in the print range whose widths would have to be set precisely. If you try to build a single string formula for the title, you could not include the date and time as shown above, because a string function such as

@string(@now,0)

produces a text result that looks like the unformatted number, such as 33222. The solution is to reserve two variable cells for the date and time, and fill them by using the {contents} macro command. Then write a string formula for the title that includes those cells.

The {contents} command copies the contents of one cell to another, but always creates a text entry in the destination cell as though you had used the following command:

{let TARGET,@string(SOURCE,0)}

The command takes four parameters, in this order:

{contents *target-cell,source-cell,width,format*}

The target cell is the cell that will be filled from the contents of the source cell. But it's the other two parameters that make the difference in this command. By specifying a width (as in column width) and format (as in cell format), the target cell will be text that looks exactly like a formatted number. The macro in Figure 7.6 shows how the {contents} macro provides the solution.

```
B4: [W13] '09:49 PM                                           READY

              A          B        C        D        E       F        G
1
2    DATE_NOW    15-Dec
3
4    TIME_NOW    09:49 PM
5
6    \Z          {let DATE_NOW,@now}
7                {let TIME_NOW,@now}
8                {contents DATE_NOW,DATE_NOW,7,115}
9                {contents TIME_NOW,TIME_NOW,9,120}~
10
11
12
13                Report was printed on 15-Dec at 09:49 PM
14                ---------------------------------------
15
16
17
18
19
20
```

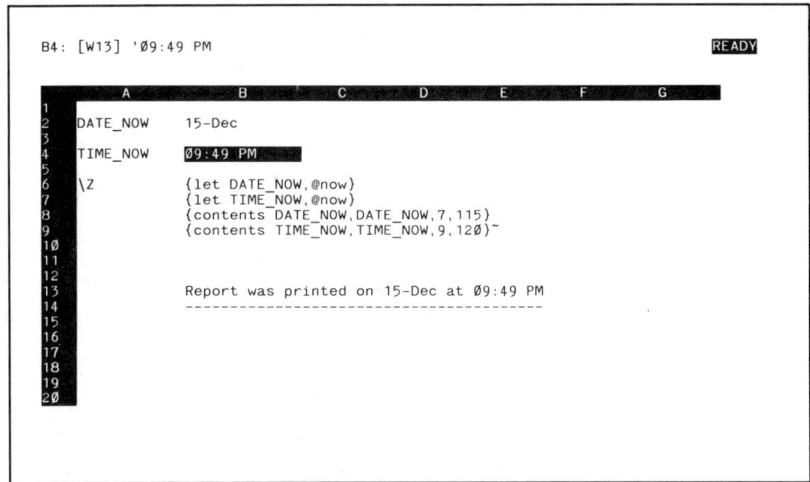

Figure 7.6 ◆ *Entering the date and time as text with the* {contents} *command*

The short macro, named \Z, uses the two cells named DATE_NOW and TIME_NOW:

```
{let DATE_NOW,@now}
{let TIME_NOW,@now}
{contents DATE_NOW,DATE_NOW,7,115}
{contents TIME_NOW,TIME_NOW,9,120} ~
```

The macro begins by setting both variable cells to the current date and time, @now. The first {contents} command uses the same source and target cell, DATE_NOW, and creates a string of seven characters that looks like a formatted number, using the format identified as 115.

The next line of the macro performs the same task on TIME_NOW, using a width of nine and a format of 120. The final tilde simply refreshes the screen so the results can be seen immediately. At this point, both variable cells have text entries that look just like the corresponding numeric entry, @now, with the appropriate format. You can see the contents of TIME_NOW in the edit window of Figure 7.6.

You may wonder why the formatting numbers 115 and 120 were used. For this macro, 1-2-3 identifies cell formats with numbers. For example, using a number from 0 to 15 specifies a Fixed format with 0 to 15 decimal places, using a number from 64 to 79 specifies the Comma format with 0 to 15 decimals, etc. (For a complete list of formats and their codes, refer to the 1-2-3 help screens for the macro commands, or look in the 1-2-3 reference manual.)

The finished title is in cell B13. Its formula can be seen in the edit window, and is repeated here:

+ "Report was printed on "&DATE_NOW&"at "&TIME_NOW

It's that simple. This routine is quite valuable because it is the only way to convert numeric data into strings with a given numeric-style format. In this case they were included in a string formula, but you could just as easily use the {contents} macro to modify a cell in a macro by direct substitution.

Combining Numbers, Text, and Addresses in Formulas

A *formula* is a combination of text, numbers, @ functions, or cell references that are summarized through *operators* (+, −, *, and so on). The result may be numeric or, in the case of string formulas, text. The precise rules of data entry must be followed by both formulas and numeric entries, or Lotus will issue its error beep and deny your request to make the entry.

Remember, if the entry is not valid but you cannot immediately see the problem, do not press Escape. Move the cursor to the start of the entry, enter a label prefix, and then press Enter. It will be entered as text and can later be repaired and tested as a formula. This is particularly important with a long formula having many parentheses, because a common problem is unbalanced parentheses. Instead of losing your work, turn it into text and get it into the cell.

There are three types of errors that can cause a formula to result in ERR:

◆ Illegal mathematical operations

◆ Illegal parameters in an @ function

◆ Destroyed cell address or range

The first two errors are easily avoided or corrected. The last error is more destructive, in that the formula has actually suffered damage. Figure 7.7 demonstrates the three error conditions. The formulas in column B are duplicated in column D, where they were given a text format. A brief explanation of the error is shown to the right of each one.

The first error displayed, cell B1, is not a problem because it is the @ function @err, which always results in ERR. The errors in the range B4..B8 are the result of illegal mathematical operations. This type of error can always be prevented or corrected by avoiding the ERR situations. For example, the formula in B6 divides by cell A1, which is blank and therefore has a value of zero. You can rewrite it to avoid the division by zero error in this way:

@if(A1 = 0,0,2/A1)

```
A1: [W5]                                                                  READY

         A        B        C            D              E          F         G
1                 ERR   =  @ERR                     @err function
2
3        Illegal operations
4                 ERR   =  +B1                       Refers to ERR cell
5                 ERR   =  2/Ø                       Division by zero
6                 ERR   =  2/A1                      Divison by zero (blank cell)
7                 ERR   =  @SQRT(-4)                 Square root, negative number
8                 ERR   =  @LOG(-1ØØ)                Log, negative number
9
1Ø       Illegal function parameters
11                ERR   =  @VALUE("test")            Invalid
12                ERR   =  @LENGTH(32)               Invalid
13                ERR   =  @INDEX(A1..A4,Ø,1ØØ)      Row number is out of range
14                ERR   =  @CHOOSE(25,1,2,3,4,5)     Choice value > 4
15                ERR   =  @DATE(87,2,31)            Invalid day (Feb. 31)
16
17       Destroyed cell address
18                ERR   =  @SUM(ERR)                 Destroyed range
19
2Ø
```

Figure 7.7 ◆ *Three causes of formulas that result in ERR*

The second set of errors, shown in B11..B15, are due to illegal parameters within an @ function. Again, you can prevent or avoid these errors by simply using care when writing the @ function, or by ensuring that the cells they reference contain data that is valid for the function.

The last formula in column B results in ERR because it references cells that have been "destroyed." The cells of the range, or even one of the range's corner cells, were either deleted or had another cell or cells moved on top of them. For example, if the formula had originally referred to the range F8..G25 and column F were deleted, the formula would then refer to a location named ERR. The original reference is gone forever, and would have to be manually written back into the formula to correct it.

The contents of a cell are of prime concern during the worksheet-building process. Once the structure is completed, though, it is the cell display that takes precedence. You should always keep in mind that the contents and appearance of a cell are separate and distinct issues, and how you make a cell look on the display is mostly independent of whatever the cell contains.

◆ CHANGING THE CELL DISPLAY

The worksheet you create is built of cells that contain data. You can change the appearance of a cell's display in two ways. If it is numeric, you can assign a format to alter its style. If it is text, you can align, or justify, the text in the cell.

THE DISPLAY SUMMARIZES CELL CONTENTS

A cell's display is the summarized result of its contents, and its appearance may often have little apparent connection to the actual contents of the cell. This is especially true on a printout, where there is no way of knowing just what is "inside" a particular cell that produces the displayed result. In the worksheet, you can move the cell pointer to a cell and inspect its contents, but looking on the back of the sheet of paper is no help!

The problem is well demonstrated in Figure 7.8. All the entries in columns A and E display the character 2. The contents of each cell are different, though, as the cells to the right in Text format show.

All the cells have a General format, and, except for the ones in the range E13..E19, all the entries have a numeric value. The only indication that the text cells are not numeric is their left alignment in the cell. Of course, this also demonstrates the tremendous power of the spreadsheet. No matter how long or short or complex the contents of a cell may be, it is simply summarized in its display to be viewed or accessed by formulas in other cells.

USING NUMERIC FORMATS TO STYLE THE DISPLAY OF VALUES

You can set the style of a numeric cell's display by giving the cell a format from the Range Format menu. A format is cell-specific and remains with the cell when it is moved, copied, or saved to file. Formatting a cell always requires 4 bytes of conventional memory, but the style of the format has no affect on the amount. Whether the format is Currency, +/−, or percent, only the same 4 bytes are required. The same is true when a worksheet is saved to disk. A cell that is formatted with 12 decimal places requires no extra disk space than one formatted with no decimals.

Different cell contents can produce the same display, as shown in Figure 7.8. But the same contents can produce different displays when cell formats come into play. Figure 7.9 shows the ten different cell formats available in Lotus. Each cell has the same contents: the @pi function.

Certainly, the cells formatted as +/− and Date (DD/MM) give no indication of having the same contents as the other cells. Of course, you can completely bypass a cell's display by giving the cell a Text format, as the entry in F12 demonstrates. This format shows the actual cell contents, just as it would be displayed in the edit window.

```
A1: [W7]                                                                    READY

        A      B        C         D        E        F        G
1               Different cell CONTENTS can produce the same DISPLAY
2                      (The Global cell Format is General)
3
4
5       2    =   The number 2                    2    =  @INT(2.25)
6
7       2    =   1+1                             2    =  @ABS(-2)
8
9       2    =   @CELL("row",D2..D2)             2    =  @DATE(Ø,1,2)
1Ø
11      2    =   +A5                             2    =  @LENGTH("To")
12
13      2    =   @LOG(1ØØ)               2       =  +"2"
14
15      2    =   @ROUND(1.8,Ø)           2       =  @CHAR(5Ø)
16
17      2    =   @VALUE(E19)             2       =  @STRING(A5,Ø)
18
19      2    =   @MAX(A5..G17)           2       =  '2 - a label
2Ø
```

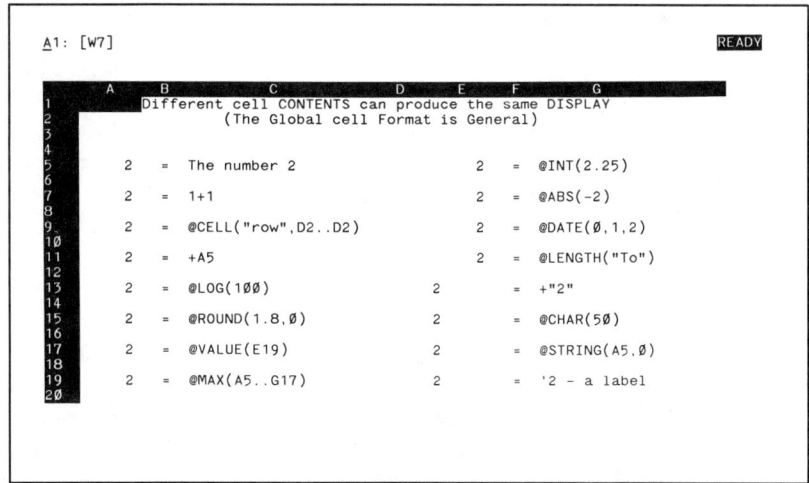

Figure 7.8 ♦ *A cell's contents cannot be determined by its display*

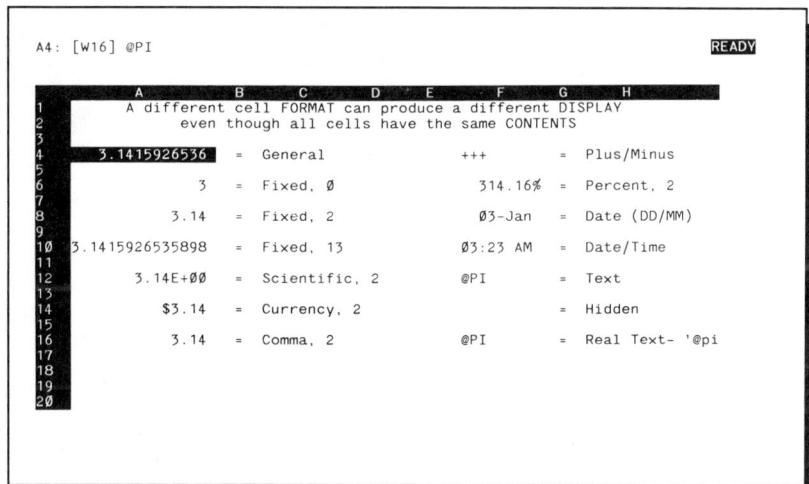

```
A4: [W16] @PI                                                               READY

        A      B      C       D      E        F      G      H
1              A different cell FORMAT can produce a different DISPLAY
2                    even though all cells have the same CONTENTS
3
4   3.1415926536   =  General               +++     =  Plus/Minus
5
6              3   =  Fixed, Ø              314.16%  =  Percent, 2
7
8           3.14   =  Fixed, 2              Ø3-Jan   =  Date (DD/MM)
9
1Ø 3.1415926535898 =  Fixed, 13            Ø3:23 AM =  Date/Time
11
12       3.14E+ØØ  =  Scientific, 2         @PI      =  Text
13
14          $3.14  =  Currency, 2                    =  Hidden
15
16           3.14  =  Comma, 2              @PI      =  Real Text- '@pi
17
18
19
2Ø
```

Figure 7.9 ♦ *Cell formats can make similar cell contents appear unrelated*

> **TIP** ♦ *The default format when you use Lotus for the first time is General. You can change the Worksheet Global Default Format so that a numeric entry will by default take on a format other than General. Text alignment, too, can be set from the default menu.*

ALIGNING TEXT WITHIN A COLUMN

Text entries cannot be given a format, but they can be justified within a cell. The alignment is determined by an entry's label prefix:

Name	Symbol	Alignment
Apostrophe	'	Left
Caret	^	Center
Double quote	''	Right
Backslash	\	Repeating

It is always faster to enter text without first typing a label prefix. No matter what the final alignment should be, just use the default alignment for data entry, and then later use the Range Label command to align an entire range of cells. When entering text that looks like a number, use the apostrophe to preface each entry, as it is the easiest to enter. Later, you can align the cells as needed.

Lotus makes all text entries left-justified by default. If you find that you often need text to be centered or right-justified, change the Label-Prefix option on the Global menu. Don't forget to choose Update if you want your new global settings to be active the next time you use Lotus.

The vertical bar, (¦), serves as another label prefix, although not to align the text within a cell. It is the special prefix used in the cell that is the format line for the Data Parse command:

```
¦L>>>>>*V>>>>>>*V>>>>>*L>>>>>
```

The vertical bar is also used as a prefix when a page break is entered into a cell, whether manually or through the Worksheet Page command:

```
¦::
```

If you want to insert a printer control code within the worksheet, the vertical bar again serves as the special label prefix, in this case followed by a second one and then the printer code:

```
¦¦\015
```

In all of these cases, you will know that the vertical bar is a true label prefix because it will not be displayed on the screen. The printer control code in the last example will display only the second vertical bar, as the first is the label prefix. For some interesting uses of this label prefix when printing, see Chapter 12.

Numbers cannot be aligned in a cell, but you often wish they could be. In fact, though, numbers always look better when right-aligned and given the same format, as they form a nice column that aligns along their decimal points. Usually, you would want numeric justification not simply to shove the numbers to the left or center of a cell, but to give them an attractive position in relation to other elements in the display.

The most common difficulty in dealing with numeric alignment is when a column is set wide enough to accommodate a long column title. The title fits nicely, but the numbers are huddled along the right-hand side of the column. There are two ways to make this display more appealing, as shown in Figure 7.10.

Column A shows the typical problem. The column is set to a width of 20, in which the titles sit comfortably but the numbers down the column are not pleasingly aligned with the titles. Column C is also set to a width of 20. Behold that this time, the numbers are indeed centered. Note also how difficult it is to scan the numbers in the column because of the misalignment of the decimal points. Besides that, the numbers aren't really numbers; they are string values that represent the numbers in column A. The formula is wonderful, though, and centers any number that appears in the adjacent cell in column A, as this formula from C6 shows:

```
@repeat(" ",(@cell("width",A6..A6)
 − @length(@string(A6,2) ) )/2)
&@string(A6,2)
```

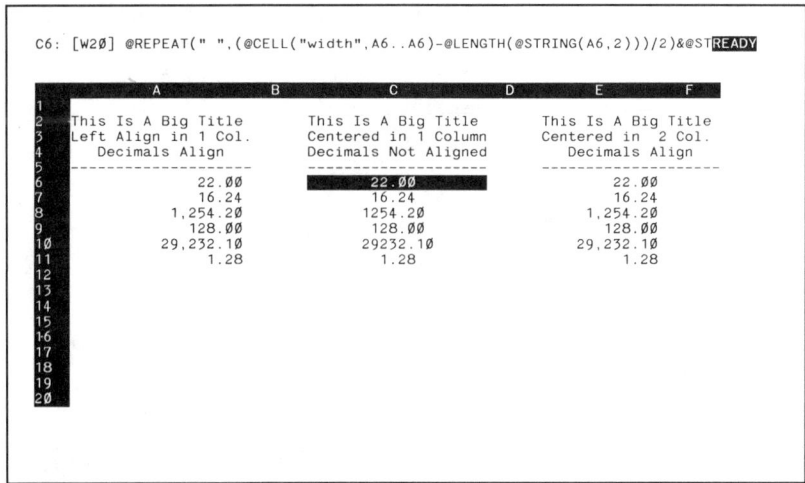

Figure 7.10 ◆ *Adjusting the display of numbers*

Of course, if you wanted to perform any mathematical operations with these numbers, you would have to turn them back into real values in another column. This is a valid routine to follow, and allows you to lay out one area for printing (output cells) while performing the calculations in another (process cells). But the work involved and the results obtained should discourage you from ever wanting numbers that are truly centered.

Column E in Figure 7.10 provides a simple and more pleasing solution. The column of numbers appears centered beneath the column title, while the decimal points are still nicely aligned. The trick is simply to use two columns instead of one.

The width of column E is 14 and column F is 6, for a total of 20. The numbers are entered as usual in column E, while column F provides the extra width for any overflow of text in the column title. You can adjust the width of both columns to make the numbers align under the titles. This method does waste one column, but that extra column requires only a tiny amount of extra RAM, and how many times have you needed all 256 columns in the worksheet?

◆ SUMMARY

In this chapter, the difference between a cell's contents and its display has been demonstrated. Cells are made up of a row and column address, can contain text or values, and return a result that is displayed on the screen. The display can be given a format if it is numeric, and aligned within the cell if it is text.

The next chapter looks at Lotus date and time arithmetic, which provide a valuable but sometimes confusing system of keeping dates. Also covered are some of the more noteworthy @ functions, as well as those that are often misused or underused.

EIGHT:

♦ ♦ ♦
♦ ♦ ♦
♦ ♦ ♦

Dealing with Dates,
and Some Notable
@ Functions

8

◆ ◆ ◆

THIS CHAPTER TOURS MANY OF THE 1-2-3 @ FUNCTIONS, WITH a special emphasis on date functions and date arithmetic. The way 1-2-3 handles dates can be confusing, and is a common source of worksheet errors. This system is not difficult to master, however, and it can provide many solutions that would otherwise not be possible.

Other functions discussed include those that are particularly powerful but often neglected, such as @cell, and those that are frequently avoided because they are difficult to understand or manipulate. The lookup functions and the @@ function fall into this category.

◆ ADDRESSING THE WORKSHEET _____

A *function* is a built-in programming shortcut that returns a result, either a numeric or a text value, from a series of internal calculations or from a stored or known value. The @ functions in Lotus help to shorten otherwise complex formulas and guarantee accuracy.

The averaging function @avg, for instance, simply takes the sum of the given range and divides it by the count of the range. The function @pi returns the value of pi to 15 places. The @now function returns the value that Lotus represents as the current date and time.

The most common functions return a numeric value. The string functions work with or return string values, and extend the power of the @ functions to include text. The next chapter discusses string arithmetic and functions.

A function usually consists of two parts. The function *name*, such as @sum, determines what operation will be performed. The function *parameters* or *arguments* are the data that the function will use. These may be a worksheet cell address or range (A5..B10), a numeric or string value, a keyword ("contents"), or another function that returns a value, cell address, and so on. A few functions consist only of the function name, such as @pi and @rand.

TIP ◆ *A function that refers to a range can refer to more than one block of cells. Although this may be common knowledge, it*

*is not common enough. To refer to more than one range, just separate
each range with a comma:*

@sum(G5..G9,A17,$B$25,C28..C35,$AA$128,D44)

The importance of range names can never be overemphasized, and their use
in @ functions can facilitate writing, reading, and revising a function. Even
though range names are never required in a worksheet, you should make them
a permanent and well-used item in your Lotus toolbox.

◆ MARKING TIME WITH DATE ARITHMETIC

Lotus' ability to perform arithmetic with dates is a feature that, in one aspect, is
similar to its ability to use range names and run macros. Worksheets can be built
and operated without ever using any of these three features. When their power is
tapped, though, the benefits gained far exceed the initial investment in learning
time (and just a touch of frustration for some). Entering dates in the Lotus style
allows you to perform many otherwise difficult or impossible tasks:

- Calculate the number of days between two dates
- Determine the day of the week for any given date
- Fill a range with the date of each day in the year
- Fill a range with the date of every Monday in the year
- Build macros that measure elapsed time
- Sort records in a database by their date
- Select records whose date meets the given criteria

PRIMER ON LOTUS INTERNAL DATES

If you enter a number as text (so that it starts with a label prefix), Lotus will
not be able to perform any numeric operations with it. It is just "dead" text.
The same is true for dates in the worksheet. If you enter dates as text, whether
as 11-23-90 or Nov. 23, 1990, Lotus will think of them only as text.

To be able to perform arithmetic, Lotus has a simple internal method of handling dates. Its system is based on three separate components:

◆ Numeric values

◆ Date formats for those values

◆ @ functions to facilitate date entry and manipulation

Just as our own calendar counts its years on the B.C.–A.D. scale, Lotus assigns a numeric *value* to each day starting from January 1, 1900, which has a value of 1. January 2, 1900, is 2; January 3, 1900, is 3; and so on. By the time you get to January 1, 1991, the value is up to 33,239.

To perform date arithmetic, you simply use the equivalent Lotus values for the dates in question. To calculate how many days there are between January 1, 1991, and March 31, 1991, you subtract 33,239 (January 1) from 33,328 (March 31). The result is 89 days.

Conversely, to determine the date 90 days after January 1, 1991, you just add 90 to 33,239. The result of 33,329 is April 1. Of course, working with dates that are numbers and seeing one displayed as 33,329 is inconvenient and not compatible with our normal use of dates (unless, like Captain Kirk, you deal in "star dates").

To display the date in a readable format, Lotus provides a *date format*. By formatting a cell as a date, any number entered into that cell takes on the appearance of a normal date. There are five different styles of date formats. Each would display the date January 11, 1991, as follows (the characters in parentheses are the format identifier that you would see in the control panel for a cell in Date format):

(D1) DD-MMM-YY	*11-Jan-91*
(D2) DD-MMM	*11-Jan*
(D3) MMM-YY	*Jan-91*
(D4) Long Intn'l	*01/11/91*
(D5) Short Intn'l	*01/11*

Note that the first style requires a column width of at least ten; otherwise, it displays the asterisks of an overloaded cell display.

So far, you have seen how Lotus keeps track of dates by working with numbers. Those numbers can be given a date format so that they are displayed in a style with which you are familiar. The final hurdle when entering Lotus dates is the translation between the date styles you are accustomed to and the internal Lotus date values. One method you can use to help in the translation is to create a table of dates with their equivalent Lotus value, and keep it next to your computer. When entering a date into the worksheet, you can refer to the table to find the correct number to use:

Date	Lotus Value
12/30/90	33,237
12/31/90	33,238
1/1/91	33,239
1/2/91	33,240
1/3/91	33,241
1/4/91	33,242

Yes, that would be ridiculous. Fortunately, Lotus is equipped to handle the translation with its built-in *date functions*. As with any @ function, they serve as shortcuts, and in this case they simplify the process of entering dates as values. They can also perform some useful date calculations, such as extracting the month or day from a given date value. By automating the date entry process, they ensure that the corresponding value is always correct.

The @date function returns the Lotus date value for the given year, month, and day of its arguments. The syntax for the function is @date(yr,mo,day). For example,

@date(91,1,11)

returns the value 33249.

Remember that the arguments for this function must be numeric—either a number, another function that returns a number, or a reference to a cell that contains a number. The months are counted from January, so December is 12. The year is counted from 1900, so that 0 represents that year, 1 for 1901, and so on. Lotus can work with dates through the year 2099, the same maximum that your PC uses. Attempting to reference a date before or after that period produces an error. An illegal date, such as September 31, also results in an error.

⊗ **CAUTION ♦** *In order for our calendar to precisely match the actual orbit of the earth around the sun, years that are divisible by 4, such as 1984, 1988, and 1992, always contain 366 days. These are known as leap years. However, this system does not quite match astronomical reality, and is in fact off by 3 days in every 400 years. Therefore, years that end in 00 (known as centesimal* *years) are not leap years, unless they are divisible by 400. So the year 1900 was not a leap year, but the year 2000 will be.*

When 1-2-3 was first written, this last fact was neglected, resulting in the inclusion of February 29, 1900, in 1-2-3's date numbering scheme, even though that day never actually existed. Lotus assigns to this date the number 60. The extra date in no way affects your arithmetic for dates on or after March 1, 1900. However, if you ever perform arithmetic with dates that fall both in that 60-day period and after it, be sure to subtract 1 from the result. So the number of days between January 1, 1991, and January 1, 1900, is calculated like this:

$$@date(91,1,1) - @date(0,1,1) - 1$$

Take note that other spreadsheets may or may not follow 1-2-3's counting order. So if your worksheet uses dates before March 1, 1900, check your date arithmetic results when moving the worksheet into another company's spreadsheet.

Lotus also has date functions for extracting the day, month, or year from a date:

@day(33249)	= 11
@month(33249)	= 1
@year(@date(91,1,11))	= 91

Using @ functions to enter dates in Lotus is therefore a three-step affair consisting of a *date function*, which returns a *value*, which is given a *date format*.

Figure 8.1 summarizes these three steps. The cell entries shown in column B

```
B8: (T) [W19] @DATE(45,6,6)                                    READY

        A          B              C              D          E
   1              Actual       Displayed
   2           Cell Entry        Value    Formatted Value
   3         ------------------------------------------
   4                      1           1     01-Jan-00
   5
   6         @PI            3.1415926536     03-Jan-00
   7
   8         @DATE(45,6,6)          16594     06-Jun-45
   9
   10        @DATE(91,1,11)         33249     11-Jan-91
   11     91
   12      1  @DATE(A11,A12,A13)    33249     11-Jan-91
   13     11
   14        @DATE(199,12,31)       73050     31-Dec-2099
   15
   16        @DATE(200,1,1)           ERR           ERR
   17
   18        @DATE(90,9,31)           ERR           ERR
   19
   20        +B10+45                33294     25-Feb-91
```

Figure 8.1 ◆ *Lotus dates are made of functions, values, and formats*

are formatted as text, and display the actual cell contents. Column C shows the value that you would see on the screen in the default General format. Each cell in column D contains the corresponding value in column C, but has been given the Date format (D1).

The first two entries, rows 4 and 6, show how any value can serve as a date value. The result of @pi can be given a date format to display the date January 3, 1900. Rows 8 and 10 show the @date function with numbers as its arguments. In row 12, the same function is using cell references as arguments, picking up the numbers to its left, rows 11 through 13.

Row 14 is the farthest into the future that Lotus can go with its dates. Row 16 shows the ERR that is produced when a date exceeds the legal limit. The date of September 31, 1990, in row 18 is also illegal. Finally, the formula in row 20 produces a value that is the result of adding 45 to the value in B10. In other words, it produces the date that is 45 days past January 11, 1991.

PRIMER ON LOTUS INTERNAL TIMES

The date capabilities described so far were virtually unchanged in the transition between Lotus 1A and Lotus 2. Several new @ functions and formats were added, but dates are still represented by integer values that can be given a date format. Lotus 2 did receive a new capability: handling times as well as dates. This was added in a surprisingly simple manner. The integer portion of a value still represents a date, but its decimal value represents a fraction of that day. Using @ functions and cell formats, that fraction can be translated into a time of day.

At midnight, the start of a day, the fractional component is 0, and increases throughout the day until it reaches 1, the beginning of the next day:

6:00 A.M.	*0.2500*
12:00 noon	*0.5000*
6:00 P.M.	*0.7500*
11:59 P.M.	*0.9993*

As Lotus has functions for tracking calendar dates, it also supplies several functions for working with times. For instance, the @time function uses the syntax @time(hr,min,sec):

@time(9,22,0) = 9:22:00 A.M.

⊗ **CAUTION** ◆ *Lotus keeps time through your computer's internal clock, which works with a 24-hour dial. To enter the time 7:30 P.M., the function must be written in 24-hour time:*

@time(19,30,0)

There are other time functions for extracting the hours, minutes, or seconds from a time:

@second(33195.72838)   = 52
@minute(@time(17,28,52))   = 28
@hour(@time(17,28,52))   = 17

@now *IS THE TIME*

The date function @now returns both the date and time as currently set on the computer's internal clock. For example, at exactly 6:00 P.M. on November 12, 1990, it produces the result 33189.75. Remember that if your computer's clock is not set to the correct time, the @now function will return the incorrect date and time. Always be sure that the clock is set correctly when you turn on your computer.

The @now function is dynamic, meaning that every time the worksheet is recalculated, any @now functions will also be updated to the current time. By entering @now into a worksheet report range and giving it a date format, the report will always have the current date displayed.

The @now function can provide the key that triggers a formula or macro:

{if @int(@now) = @date(90,4,15)}{branch \DO_TAXES}

In macro-driven applications, the @now function can be used to indicate when a procedure was run. To date- or time-stamp a worksheet, you would not want to enter the function itself, as it would change whenever the worksheet recalculated. Instead, enter only the value that the function returns. To enter the value of @now by hand, you would write the formula, press F9 {calc} to turn it into a value, and then press Enter. In a macro, the {let} command performs the job in one step:

{let DATE_STAMP,@now}

Of course, any cell that is supposed to represent a date or time must be given the proper format. If you want both the date and time, use two cells: one formatted to show the date, and the other to show the time.

The @now function of Lotus 2.0 replaced the @today function of Lotus 1A, which created a small but dangerous incompatibility when a Lotus 1A worksheet was brought into Lotus 2.0. Any formula that compared a given date with the current date (@today) would no longer work correctly. The @today function, an integer value, was changed to @now, a real number, when the worksheet was retrieved.

For example, even when the computer was telling Lotus that the date was January 1, 1991, this formula would still not return a true condition:

@date(91,1,1) = @now

The reason is that the @date function returns an integer, but @now is always a real number with its decimal fraction. So a logical test that worked in Lotus 1A never returned 1 (true) in Lotus 2.0. To correct the problem, the formula had to be rewritten without the decimal portion of the @now function:

@date(91,1,1) = @int(@now)

Then, the test would succeed on January 1. This is one of the problems that was corrected with the release of Lotus 2.01. Entering the @today function in that version automatically produces the formula

@int(@now)

So a worksheet from Lotus 1A that has the @today function will work correctly in Lotus 2.01 and 2.2.

HANDLING DATES THE EASY WAY

If you have not made extensive use of the date functions and date arithmetic, you may find the Lotus system of keeping dates a bit difficult to master. The following demonstrations may encourage you to use dates more extensively in 1-2-3.

Entering a Series of Dates

The job of creating a consecutive series of dates would be quite time-consuming if they were written manually as text. Here is a technique that performs the task in a fraction of the time that would otherwise be required.

A series of dates is commonly needed for loan amortization, scheduling, or periodic record-keeping. This first example demonstrates how to enter the date of every day in the year 1991, down one column of the worksheet.

This solution relies on the fact that Lotus dates are nothing but numbers. To create a series of dates, all you need to do is create the corresponding series of numbers. The fastest way to do that in Lotus is with the Data Fill command.

Figure 8.2 shows how this quick process is done. Although only one column needs to be filled with dates, three columns are used to show the three steps that are followed in filling the one column.

Assume that the Data Fill command has not been accessed during the Lotus session, so it is still using its default values. The cell pointer is positioned at A4, where the dates will start. The Data Fill command is called, which first asks you to enter the fill range. You can respond by marking the range A4..A8192 with these three keystrokes:

.{end}{down}

TRICK ◆ *You can specify an overly large range such as A4..A8192 because the size of the fill range will ultimately be limited by the stop value entered, not by the number of cells. Under other circumstances, you might specify an exact range to be filled and set the stop value to an overly large value, letting the size of the range determine the maximum value entered.*

The command then prompts you for a start value. In this case, you want to start with the first day of 1991, and since you don't know what the equivalent Lotus value is for that date, you use the @date function:

@date(91,1,1)

The step value for the series is 1, for each day of the year, so just press Enter to accept the command's default value of 1. The default stop value of 8192,

```
C4: (D1) 33239                                                  READY

       A          B        C          D         E          F      G
1   Data Fill          Format as           Expand width
2                      Date, 1              of column
3   -----------        ---------           ------------
4        33239         *********             Ø1-Jan-91
5        3324Ø         *********             Ø2-Jan-91
6        33241         *********             Ø3-Jan-91
7        33242         *********             Ø4-Jan-91
8        33243         *********             Ø5-Jan-91
9        33244         *********             Ø6-Jan-91
1Ø       33245         *********             Ø7-Jan-91
11       33246         *********             Ø8-Jan-91
12       33247         *********             Ø9-Jan-91
       A          B        C          D         E          F      G
362      33597         *********             25-Dec-91
363      33598         *********             26-Dec-91
364      33599         *********             27-Dec-91
365      336ØØ         *********             28-Dec-91
366      336Ø1         *********             29-Dec-91
367      336Ø2         *********             3Ø-Dec-91
368      336Ø3         *********             31-Dec-91
```

Figure 8.2 ◆ *Creating a consecutive series of dates with the Data Fill command*

however, must be changed. The stop date of the series is the last day of the year, so enter that date:

@date(91,12,31)

If you have entered the start and stop dates correctly, Lotus will fill 365 cells of column A with a series that starts at 33,239 and ends at 33,603. That range must then be given a date format; use the D1 format that displays the day, month, and year:

/rfd1{end}{down} ˜

The result of formatting the numbers in column A is shown in column C. The Date,1 format requires more spaces than the default column width of nine provides. The column must be expanded to at least ten, the result of which is shown in column E. The Data Fill command has allowed you to enter all the dates for the year in just three simple steps:

1. Fill the range from start date to end date.

2. Give the filled range a date format.

3. Expand the column to fit the style of format.

Once this process is mastered, it is just as easy to enter the dates of each Monday of the year. Using the Data Fill command, the start date would be the first Monday of the year, @date(91,1,7) in 1991. The step value would be 7 to show each succeeding Monday. The end date would again be @date(91,12,31). The formatted column would then show the date for each Monday of the year. You probably have to resort to a calendar to find the date of the first Monday of the year, but by using another Lotus @ function you can easily determine the day of the week for any date.

Determining the Day of the Week

The @day function returns the day portion of the given date. However, there is no function that returns the actual day of a date, such as *Monday* or *Tuesday*. By utilizing the @mod function, however, a formula can be written to fulfill this need. This function is simple yet powerful. It returns the remainder that results from dividing its first argument by its second, such as 23 divided by 5 leaves 3:

@mod(23,5) = 3

The trick to returning the day of the week is to divide the given date number by 7; the remainder will tell you the day of the week. Remember that 1-2-3 counts 1900 as a leap year, so for now forget about dates before March 1 of that year. The date March 1, 1900, was a Thursday, and its Lotus date number is 61. If you divide 61 by 7, you get a remainder of 5. Therefore, any date number that when divided by 7 leaves a remainder of 5 must be a Thursday. A remainder of 6 would mean a Friday, and a remainder of 0 would be a Saturday.

Earlier in this chapter, you were advised to subtract 1 from any dates prior to March 1, 1900, when performing arithmetic with dates both before and after that date. But in order to calculate the day of the week for dates before March 1, 1900, you will need to add 1 to the date number before you divide by 7, otherwise 1-2-3 will count the first day of that year as a Sunday when it was actually a Monday. By adding one to the date number, February 28, 1900, falls on a Wednesday.

Returning to the example, the result of the following formula determines the day of the first day of the year 1991:

@mod(@date(91,1,1),7) = 3

If Sunday is always 1, then the above result means the first day of 1991 is a Tuesday. It is easy to conclude that the following Monday, January 7, must be the first Monday of the year. Once you understand this technique you can write a formula that returns the day of the week for any date. This is a great way to display a date that avoids the somewhat limited styles of the date formats.

In Chapter 1, you saw a macro routine that utilized the @choose function to append the current month name to a file name. You can use the same technique to return either the day of the month or the month name. Figure 8.3 shows four different formulas that can each do the job. The first formula, cell B2, uses the @choose function to select a day name from a list of names within the function. The actual cell contents are shown to the right in column C, and also here, split into two parts for clarity:

@choose(@mod($DATE_NUM,7),"Saturday","Sunday","Monday",
"Tuesday","Wednesday","Thursday","Friday")

The function chooses the day name based on the result of the @mod function, which uses the date in B11 (named DATE_NUM) as its argument.

Entering the day names directly into the function is fine if you are not going to repeat the function many times in the worksheet. If it is going to be used frequently, the formula in B4 is better to use.

@choose(@mod($DATE_NUM,7),$D$11,$D$12,$D$13,$D$14,$D$15,
$D$16,$D$17)

This time, the choices are cell addresses that refer to cells containing the names of the days: D11..D17. If the formula is used throughout the worksheet, this method will not only save a little memory but will allow you to change the

```
B11: [W1Ø] @DATE(91,1,7)                                              READY

        A          B           C            D           E        F        G        H
1
2                Monday    @choose(@mod($DATE_NUM,7),"Saturday","Sunday","Monday"
3
4                Monday    @choose(@mod($DATE_NUM,7),$D$11,$D$12,$D$13,$D$14,$D$1
5
6                Monday    @index($TABLE_DAYS,Ø,@mod($DATE_NUM,7))
7
8                January   @index($TABLE_MONTHS,Ø,@month($DATE_NUM)-1)
9
1Ø
11  DATE_NUM      33245      T ->   Saturday        January  <- T  M
12                           A  D   Sunday          February       A  O
13                           B  A   Monday          March          B  N
14                           L  Y   Tuesday         April          L  T
15                           E  S   Wednesday       May            E  H
16                                  Thursday        June              S
17                                  Friday          July
18                                                  August
19                                                  September
2Ø                                                  October
```

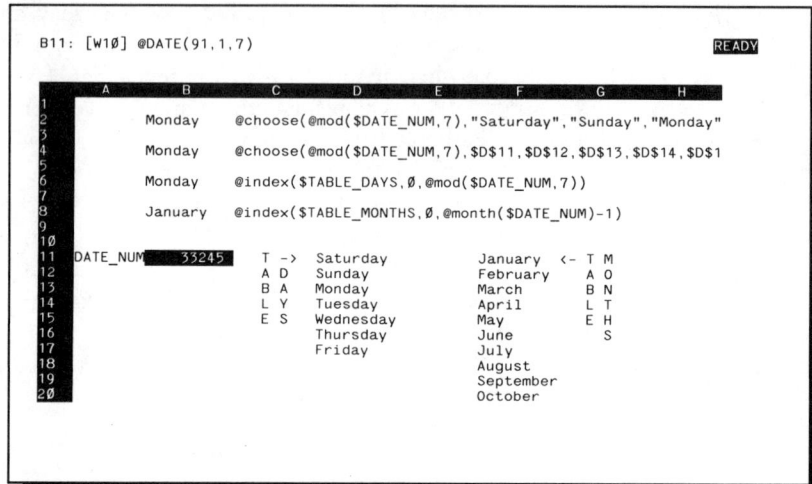

Figure 8.3 ◆ *Using @ functions to return the name of the day or month for a given date*

name styles in all the formulas by revising only the names in one location, which is one of the prime benefits of using formula variables.

The formula in B6 is easier and more efficient still:

@index($TABLE_DAYS,0,@mod($DATE_NUM,7))

This time, an @index function refers to the entire table of names at D11..D17, which is named TABLE_DAYS. The @index function uses this syntax:

@index(table_range,column#,row#)

There is just one column in that table, which the function refers to as "column 0." The row number in the function is determined by again finding the value of @mod of the date DATE_NUM. When that results in 0, the @index function returns the first item in TABLE_DAYS. That is why the first cell (D11) contains *Saturday*.

Finally, cell B8 shows a similar formula that returns the name of the month instead of the day of the month:

@index($TABLE_MONTHS,0,@month($DATE_NUM) – 1)

It selects from the list TABLE_MONTHS at F11..F22, based on the month number of DATE_NUM, less 1. It must subtract 1 so that in January it will return 0 and select the first item on the list.

In the next chapter, the discussion of string functions shows you how to combine these formulas into a standard text-style date, such as January 7, 1991.

Dealing with Dates That Are Text

A commonly occurring problem with Lotus dates is that of a date being entered as text instead of a valid Lotus date value. Typically, dates are mistakenly entered in the MM/DD/YY style: 1/7/91. This creates the same problem as that of entering numbers as text: the display looks fine, but Lotus cannot perform any calculations with the cell. Unfortunately, this lack of validity may not become apparent until the dates are needed, such as when a range is sorted using the dates as the key field, and the date 2/25/91 is sorted before 3/1/81. Trying to subtract one date from another will also prove to be a fruitless task. There are several methods of returning dates to a true Lotus value, depending on what style was used to enter them.

The easiest solution applies to dates entered in the common style mentioned above: MM/DD/YY. The function @datevalue performs similarly to the @value function that was used in Chapter 7. It takes a text entry that looks like a date and returns its actual date value:

@datevalue("1/7/91") = 33245

To correct a range of invalid dates, just enter the @datevalue function in a blank parallel cell, having it refer to the invalid date cell. Copy the formula as needed, and then use the Range Value command to copy the results over the invalid dates.

The one limitation to the @datevalue function, which can be very restrictive, is that it only works with dates that have been entered in a style Lotus recognizes as one of its own date formats:

07-Jan-91
7-Jan
Jan-91
1/7/91
01/07
1.7.91
01.07

The use of the slash and period in the last four examples would depend on the current setting of the Worksheet Global Default Other International Date format. But substituting any characters for those shown above would rule out the use of the @datevalue function. The Data Parse command has similar limitations on interpreting text dates, and would not work much better.

There is, however, a somewhat more flexible method that is a carryover from Lotus 1A: printing to disk and using the File Import Numbers command. This is yet another use for printing a worksheet range to a disk file, and it is generally quite effective for transforming dates that are text into dates that are values. It has fewer limitations on the style of the text than does the @datevalue function. Figure 8.4 shows how this technique is put to work.

Column A contains the invalid dates, all of which were entered as text. Except for the first entry in A5, their style prevents the use of the @datevalue function, even though all the numbers are in the order month, day, year. The first step in the solution is to print those cells to a disk file.

This situation is typical of those times when printing to a disk file is done to obtain "pure" data that should not be formatted for the printed page. Page breaks are eliminated, the left margin is set to 0, and the right margin is set to 240, the widest possible. This macro shows the keystrokes needed to print the bad dates to disk:

/pfFILENAME ˜ carA5..A12 ˜ oml0 ˜ mr240 ˜ ouqagq

Once the data is on disk, the cell pointer is moved to a blank column next to the dates, in this case cell B5. Here, the text file is imported back into the worksheet using the File Import Numbers command. You can see the result in columns B through D.

> **TIP** ◆ *If you are not familiar with the File Import command, try bringing in the same file using the File Import Text command. You will get the exact image of the display in the printed range, not the numbers-only result you needed. The Numbers option for this command is designed for just this kind of operation, splitting individual numbers into their own cells. (Be sure to bring the file back in as numbers.)*

```
E5: (D1) [W16] @DATE(@ABS(D5),B5,@ABS(C5))                              READY

          A              B       C        D            E              F
 1  Dates that were   Data from print file,         @date
 2  entered as text    imported as Numbers         formulas
 3                     Month    Day    Year
 4  --------------------------------------------------------------------
 5  Ø1/Ø7/91              1        7       91        Ø7-Jan-91
 6  12-31-9Ø             12      -31      -9Ø        31-Dec-9Ø
 7  1Ø//4//9Ø            1Ø        4       9Ø        Ø4-Oct-9Ø
 8  12--21--9Ø           12      -21      -9Ø        21-Dec-9Ø
 9  1Ø---3Ø-9Ø           1Ø      -3Ø      -9Ø        3Ø-Oct-9Ø
10  Ø2-Ø9-91              2       -9      -91        Ø9-Feb-91
11  12-Ø1-9Ø             12       -1      -9Ø        Ø1-Dec-9Ø
12  11-1-9Ø              11       -1      -9Ø        Ø1-Nov-9Ø
13
14
15
16
17
18
19
2Ø
```

Figure 8.4 ◆ *Correcting dates that were entered as text*

Those three columns contain the month, day, and year components of the dates in column A, neatly parsed into separate cells. Notice that the number of text characters between each item did not affect the final output. Notice, too, that the hyphens were interpreted as minus signs, and the result is many negative months and years. You can easily correct these in the next phase.

Column E contains the formulas that reconnect the three separated parts of the date. The formula for E5, which looks like this, can also be seen in the control panel at the top of the screen:

@date(@abs(D5),B5,@abs(C5))

You must be sure to reference the proper column for the year, month, day syntax of the @date function. And since some of the numbers in the day and year columns are negative, you must use the @abs function to ensure that the arguments for them are always positive. Once the formula is written, copy it down the column.

With the dates now converted to true date values, you can use the Range Value command to copy the column of formulas back on top of the erroneous dates in column A. The formulas and imported data, columns B through E, can then be erased.

◆ A POTPOURRI OF @ FUNCTIONS

Of the dozens of @ functions in Lotus, some deserve special attention. They might have a quirk or a peculiar or confusing syntax, or they might be consistently underused.

THE @count FUNCTION

The quirk in the @count function was already mentioned in Chapter 3. Whenever this function refers to just a single cell it results in 1, whether or not the cell is empty.

So remember that if you are going to reference just one cell, make one side of the single-cell range absolute:

@count(B5..$B5)

The same is true if you are using several single-cell ranges within the function's parameters; they must also be partially absolute. Of course, a range of more than one cell will be counted correctly without any absolute references:

@count(A3..A7,B5..$B5,B$14..B14,C22..H45)

THE *@rand* FUNCTION

The @rand function produces a random number between 0 and 1. You may often want to create random numbers that fall between a set range, from a low to a high. You can do this using the following formula, which produces a random integer that will be at least 25 and no greater than 100:

@round((@rand*(100 − 25) + 25),0)

For a more efficient and flexible layout, use a variable cell for the low and high values. In this example, they are named LO and HI:

@round((@rand*($HI − $LO) + $LO),0)

You can randomly select a letter of the alphabet by creating a random number between 65 and 90, and using the @char function to turn that number into a letter:

@char(@round((@rand*25) + 65,0))

One of the most exasperating situations with random numbers is when you realize you do not want them to change each time the worksheet recalculates. When random numbers are being used as test data, you may very well want to create them and then turn them back into values. Just use the Range Value command to turn the functions into numbers.

THE *@round* FUNCTION

The @round function simply rounds the value of its argument, whether it be a numeric value, expression, or cell reference. Problems with rounding usually occur not when the @round function is used, but when it is not used. Remember that you can format a cell so that it appears to be rounded, but its actual value has not changed. If you truly want rounded numbers, use this function.

By making its "number of digits" argument negative, @round will round off digits to the left of the decimal:

@round(123456, − 2) = 123500

THE *@err* FUNCTION

Who needs more errors in the worksheet? The @err function, nonetheless, has several important uses. Its result is ERR, the same as for any illegal function or formula. It does a wonderful job of uncovering cells that should contain a formula referring to a variable cell, but that have been written incorrectly or accidentally replaced with a value.

If a range of formulas are all supposed to reference a variable cell, just enter @err in that cell and recalculate the worksheet. All formulas that refer to it will display ERR. Any formulas that don't display ERR will stand out and be called to your attention.

Trying to reference a cell that displays ERR always results in ERR. If you want a formula to check a cell for the existence of an error condition, use the @iserr function. For instance, this formula will check cell A5 and return a message if A5 shows ERR:

@if(@iserr(A5),"Cell A5 is in error",A5)

On the other hand, here is a quick method of finding any cells in the worksheet that result in ERR for whatever reason. Just place the cell pointer in A1 and enter an @sum function that sums the entire worksheet. In a macro, the keystrokes would look like this:

@sum({down}.{end}{home})~

If this sum displays ERR, you will know that there is at least one cell somewhere in the worksheet that also results in ERR. You can then set out to track down the offending cell or cells. An easy way to do that is simply to enter another @sum function in the middle row of the active worksheet in column A. This checks the bottom half of the worksheet, and by repeating this operation you can continue to narrow your search.

THE @*pmt* FUNCTION

The frequently used @pmt function calculates the payment required to amortize a given loan over a given period of time. It is easy to forget that the interest rate and term must each be broken down to the same payment period, whether it be monthly, quarterly, and so on. Here the function is being used to calculate the monthly payment on a principal of $25,000, over 30 years, at 13.5 percent. The interest rate is divided by 12 to produce a monthly figure, and the term is multiplied by 12 to get the total number of months:

@pmt(25000,0.135/12,30*12) = 286.35

To calculate a quarterly payment over 30 years, the formula would look like this:

@pmt(25000,0.135/4,30*4) = 859.76

Remember that the use of the @pmt function may benefit from its parameters referring to variable cells, such as PRINCIPAL, INTEREST, and PERIOD. Then, you can easily change the values in those cells to compute a new payment.

TRANSLATING BETWEEN DEGREES AND RADIANS

The built-in trigonometric functions such as @sin and @tan take radians as their arguments, not degrees. This is apparent the first time you try to find the tangent of 45 degrees and discover that it is not 1:

@tan(45) = 1.6198

To convert between the two measurements of angle, use these formulas:

```
Degrees = Radians * (180/@pi)
Radians = Degrees * (@pi/180)
```

To calculate the tangent of 45 degrees, then, enter the formula as follows:

@tan(45*@pi/180)

If you have many functions that should return their result in degrees, create a variable cell for the conversion factor, @pi/180. Give the cell an appropriate name, such as CONVERT. You could assign a shorter name for ease of use, as long as you know what it stands for:

@tan(45*$CONVERT)

FUNCTIONS THAT SELECT FROM A LIST

Several functions in Lotus choose their result from an internal list or a table within the worksheet. In Chapter 4, these functions are discussed in light of some of the problems that commonly arise. Two of the most frequent errors arise from an invalid selection number.

Remember, in an @choose function, the first item on the selection list has an *offset* of 0, and is therefore always "item zero" on the list. This is also true for the first row or column referred to in a lookup, index, or data function.

The second problem happens when the selection number exceeds the number of choices available. If you forget that the first column in a lookup range is column 0 and write the function assuming it is column 1, it can at some point refer to a column outside the selection range. All of the following result in ERR:

```
@choose(3,A1,B1,C1)
@vlookup(1,A1..C10,3)
@index(A1..C10,1,10)
@dsum(A1..C10,3,G1..G2)
```

Another trap can occur when you copy one of these functions to another location. The reference to the selection range must be made absolute so that the cell addresses do not adjust. Likewise, if the lookup selection number is a cell address, then it, too, should be made absolute:

```
@choose($CHOICE,$A$1,$B$1,$C$1)
@vlookup(1,$A$1..$C$10,$CHOICE)
@index($A$1..$C$10,$COL,$ROW)
@dsum($DATA,$C$1,$CRIT)
```

Since some of these formulas refer to a fixed table in the worksheet, it always makes good sense to give that table a range name.

> **TIP** ◆ *The @index function can produce a result faster than the @vlookup and @hlookup function. This is because it goes directly to the cell that is identified by the column and row numbers. Lookups must search a range until a value is found that is greater than its selection value; the next lower value is then chosen.*
>
> *On the other hand, lookups are more flexible in that they do not need an exact match in the list. Use the @index function when you can pinpoint the cell to select, and use @lookup when there may only be a near match.*

THE @d DATA FUNCTIONS

The data functions in Lotus include @dsum, @davg, @dcount, @dmax, @dmin, @dstd, and @dvar. They are perhaps the most powerful and underutilized of all the functions. With these functions, you can select items from a range based on a selection criteria, and then perform the given operation on the items, such as summing them, taking their average, or counting them.

Perhaps the data functions are neglected because they are structured around a worksheet database, with a data range and criteria. This adds a layer of complexity. Moreover, they refer to a column in the data range by means of an offset number, meaning the first column is column 0. This somewhat confusing convention adds a second layer of difficulty to the functions.

Since they are so database oriented, the data functions will be covered in Chapter 10. If you feel comfortable with Lotus databases but have not used the @d functions, you should certainly bring them into your repertoire of @ functions.

THE @cell AND @cellpointer FUNCTIONS

The @cell and @cellpointer functions may seem to yield little essential information, but they can be quite handy. Each uses one of nine cell attributes (ten in Release 2.2) as its argument. The @cell function also refers to a single-cell address, or to the upper left cell when a range is used:

@cell("type",B6)

The @cellpointer function has just the one argument, as it always refers to the cell on which the cell pointer is currently sitting:

@cellpointer("address")

The attributes must be enclosed in quotes, and of course spelled correctly. Here is a list of the attributes, with a brief description of the result returned by each:

Address	*The cell address, shown in absolute form: $B$6*
Col	*The column "number," where A is 1, B is 2, and C is 3*
Contents	*The actual cell contents; the same result as simply referencing the cell in a formula: +B6*
Format	*The cell format, displayed in an abbreviated style, such as G for General, or F4 for Fixed with four decimals*
Prefix	*The label prefix for a text entry; a blank for a numeric or blank entry*
Protect	*Returns 1 if a cell is protected, 0 if unprotected; does not indicate the status of global protection*
Row	*The row number*
Type	*Returns V if the cell contains a value, L if a label, or B if it is blank. Frequently used in macros to test a cell before performing an operation on it*
Width	*The width of the cell's column*
Filename	*The name of the worksheet's file, including path*

2.2 ◆ ———

> **TIP** ◆ *You can ignore the admonition in the Lotus manual stating that you must enter a single-cell range for this formula, such as A10..A10. It recommends using the exclamation mark (!) to preface a single-cell address (!A10), which will then be turned into a range when it is entered into the worksheet. In fact, you can skip that step because Lotus automatically changes a single-cell address into a range. Just refer to the cell you want when you write the formula:*
>
> @cell("type",A10)

When you press Enter, Lotus converts the single-cell address into a range:

@cell("type",A10..A10)

This is also true for the @n and @s string functions (see Chapter 9), which also address just a single cell.

Both the @cell and @cellpointer functions can be quite useful in allowing a macro to branch, depending on the attribute of a given cell:

{if @cell("type",TEST_CELL) = "b"}{quit}
{\DO_NEXT}

You can use the @cellpointer function in a {let} statement as the value that will be entered into a cell. It is a convenient means of recording the current cell position in another cell before moving the cell pointer to a different area of the worksheet:

{let CURRENT_CELL,@cellpointer("address")}
{goto}BROWSE_RANGE ~

When you wish to return to the old position, another macro simply uses the address in that cell, as shown in this string function macro:

+"{goto}"&CURRENT_CELL&" ~ "

Although perhaps rarely used, the protection status of a cell could be checked before a macro takes action:

{if @cell("protect",ONE_CELL) = 1}{\DO_CANCEL}
{\DO_ENTRY}

THE @@ FUNCTION

The @@ function was used to good effect in the Gateway macro in Chapter 5, but it may often be neglected because its purpose is somewhat cloudy. This function needs one cell address (or a single-cell range name) for its argument. The cell that it addresses must contain text that spells out an address or range name of another cell. It is the contents of that other cell that is returned by the @@ function. It makes an *indirect reference* to the second cell.

For example, if cell B1 contains the text *C1*, and cell C1 contains the value 12, then an @@ function can pick up the value in C1 by way of B1:

@@(B1) = 12

◆ ———

When you save a Release 2.2 worksheet that contains a linking formula, 1-2-3 converts the formula into an @@ function. When the worksheet file is later retrieved back into 1-2-3, the @@ function is once again converted into a linking formula. For example, this linking formula:

>   + <<FILENAME>>B12

is converted into this formula in the worksheet file:

>   @@("<<FILENAME>>B12")

This is really a matter of minor interest, until you want to retrieve a Release 2.2 worksheet into Release 2.01 or 2.0. The @@ function is not converted in those releases, and instead simply displays ERR. But bring the worksheet back into Release 2.2, and the linking formula will once again be active.

THE @min FUNCTION

Finding the smallest value in a range is all the @min function does, so it is not difficult to use. Remember, however, that text has a value of 0 in Lotus, so if there are any text cells within the range that an @min function is referencing, the function will never return a value greater than 0. As with the @avg function, you must be sure to exclude extraneous cells from the range.

THE @if FUNCTION AND LOGICAL EXPRESSIONS

When writing a complex @if function, it is all too easy to scramble the correct syntax amidst a long string of characters, parentheses, and commas. It may be wise to create the true and false components in separate cells to test them. Then you can combine them into one function.

If the function is really complex, feel free to leave the true and false statements in their separate cells, and refer to those cells in the @if function:

>   @if(C10>D10,C10,D10)

This will not only keep the function short and concise, but it may also save memory if it keeps you from having to repeat a long formula twice—both in the logical portion and in the true or false portion. For instance, if the preceding example did not refer to other cells, it would have to reference the two formulas twice, both to compare them and to select one:

>   @if(@sum(A3..15)>@sum(B3..B15),
>   @sum(A3..A15),@sum(B3..B15))

A *logical expression* is a statement of fact that either evaluates to 1 if true, or to 0 if false:

```
5>3        = 1
5<3        = 0
@pi>3      = 1
2+2=5      = 0
3<>4       = 1
```

In a large application, you may want to save memory by eliminating the @if function altogether. You can accomplish this by substituting logical expressions for the function. For example, this @if statement returns the value of C1 if B1 is less than 100:

@if(B1<100,C1,0)

You can write it without the @if function by using a logical expression that is shorter, although a bit more difficult to interpret:

C1*(B1<100)

Depending on whether the logical expression (B1<100) is true or false, cell C1 would be multiplied by either 1 or 0. In other words, it simply paraphrases the @if statement: "if B1 is less than 100, then result in C1, otherwise result in 0."

There are logical @ functions, too, that always return either 1 or 0. These include @iserr, @isna, @isstring, and @isnumber. The function @true always returns 1, and @false always returns 0.

You can combine logical conditions with the *logical operators* #and#, #or#, and #not#. You can then form a long conditional sentence without having to nest @if statements. The resulting expression is easier to write, uses less memory, and is easier to interpret, as these two equivalent statements demonstrate:

@if(B1>B2,@if(B2>B3,B3,0),0)

@if(B1>B2#and#B2>B3,B3,0)

A logical OR statement can be formed either with a nested @if function or by using the #or# operator. Again, notice the difference in readability:

@if(B1>B2,B3,@if(B2>B3,B3,0))

@if(B1>B2#or#B2>B3,B3,0)

⊗ **CAUTION** ◆ *It can be easy to get lost in a logical brain teaser. Whenever working with logical statements, whether @if functions or combinations of expressions with logical operators, always test the expressions carefully with simple test data.*

◆ SUMMARY

You have seen how Lotus can manipulate dates by assigning a value to each day since January 1, 1900. You can enter dates into the worksheet with the help of date functions, and give the values a date format to create a suitable display. You have learned about several Lotus @ functions—their power, their quirks, and their complexities.

The next chapter continues to discuss the manipulation of data by functions, within the context of string arithmetic and the string @ functions.

NINE:

Manipulating Text
with String
Arithmetic and @
Functions

9

◆ ◆ ◆

EVERYONE KNOWS THAT THE HEIGHT OF A KITE IS A FUNCTION of the length of its string. In this chapter you'll find out how to calculate the length of a string with a Lotus function. String arithmetic and functions, added with the release of Lotus 2, give the spreadsheet the power to work with *strings*, otherwise known as text or labels. In doing so, they move Lotus a large step closer to the capabilities of a programming language.

This chapter untangles some of the complexities of working with strings by starting off with a primer on string values. A discussion of string arithmetic, the process of manipulating strings, follows, and reveals many new ways of getting a job done in the worksheet. The last part of the chapter considers the ins and outs of the string functions, and demonstrates several practical techniques, including the creation of a text-based graph within the worksheet.

◆ MANIPULATING STRINGS

Text in the worksheet can be either "straight" text that you type directly into a cell, or *text values* that result from a formula or function. Text values are also called *string values*. You may remember them from the discussion of worksheet data in Chapter 7.

A PRIMER ON STRING VALUES

The simplest way to create a string value is by starting a cell entry with a plus sign and following it with text that is enclosed in quotes, such as this example that you could enter into cell A1:

+"anything can make a string"

When a cell that contains any kind of text is referred to in another cell, that cell displays the text as a text value:

+A1 = anything can make a string

Strings cannot be manipulated with the usual arithmetical operators, but you can *concatenate* strings, or combine them into one string, by using the ampersand (&) as the operator:

```
+"One string"&" plus another" = One string plus another
+"But "&A1&"?" = But anything can make a string?
```

Lotus has many string functions that work on text in the same way that the other @ functions work on numbers. For instance, you can indeed determine the length of a string with the @length function:

```
@length("how long is this?") = 17
@length(A1) = 26
```

The string functions tend to be heavily used when working with strings. The manipulation process often involves complex tasks such as extracting only certain—precisely selected—portions of a string, comparing one string with another, or determining the width of a cell and displaying only as much of a string as will fit in it.

⊗ **CAUTION** ◆ *Even the smallest venture into string arithmetic can result in very long formulas. As with numeric formulas, you should use intermediate step cells during the creation process. Breaking the task down into smaller steps makes formulas easier to write and to interpret.*

In the normal operation of the worksheet, string values are virtually the same as straight text, and they are both displayed on the screen in the same way. One of the most exciting aspects of string values is that they are accepted by a macro just as though they were plain text. The use of string formulas as a way of creating macros that can dynamically change was discussed in Chapter 1.

There are several important differences between string values and straight text. First, like any formula, a string formula requires recalculation time. A string formula also requires more memory, both for the formula itself and for its result. You cannot use the Range Justify command with string formulas because the contents of the cell is not text but a formula that cannot simply be divided among several cells. You can, however, turn the values into straight text and then justify that. A unique report writer that uses this technique is described later in this chapter.

No matter what kind of text it is, you can never mix text and numeric values in the same formula—they are unrelated types of data. You can, however, turn a numeric value into text and then combine it with other text. Or, you can turn text that looks like a number into a numeric value and use it in a numeric expression. Several string functions can accomplish this, and they are discussed in the last part of this chapter.

CONCATENATING STRINGS

The process of combining strings—concatenation—is at the core of all string arithmetic. Earlier you were advised to use step cells when building long or involved string formulas. The process of putting those step formulas back into one formula demonstrates string concatenation.

Using String Arithmetic to Combine Text

In Chapter 8, the @choose and @index functions were combined with date functions to produce the day or month of a date in text style, as shown in Figure 8.3. By writing a string formula, the results of the formulas that produce the day (Monday) and month (January) can be concatenated with the date and year to produce a complete date listing: Monday, January 7, 1991.

Figure 9.1 shows how this is done. The formulas in the range B2..B10 do the job; the actual cell contents are shown as text to the right of each cell. The formulas in B2 and B4 should look familiar from the example in Chapter 8. Based on the date in DATE_NUM, the formula in B2 returns the day of the week:

@index($TABLE_DAYS,0,@mod($DATE_NUM,7))&", "

The formula in B4 returns the name of the month:

@index($TABLE_MONTHS,0,@month($DATE_NUM)-1)&" "

Each formula selects a result from the appropriate table, either TABLE_DAYS or TABLE_MONTHS. An ampersand has been added to the end of the first

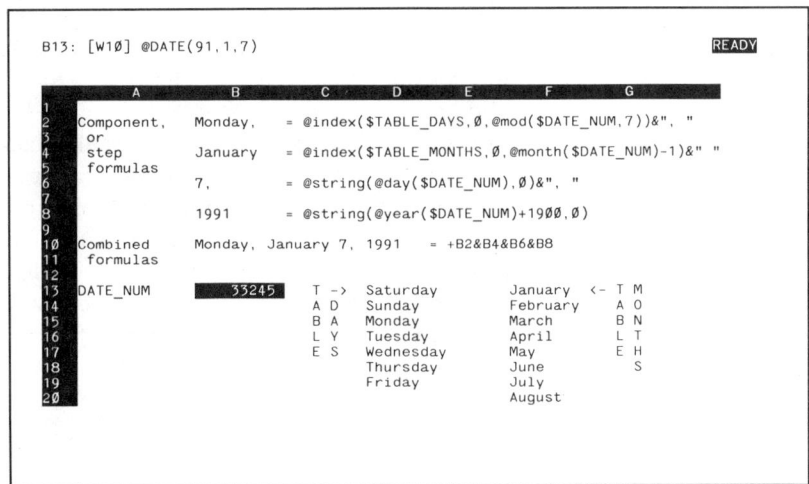

```
B13: [W1Ø] @DATE(91,1,7)                                          READY

          A          B         C      D       E       F         G
 1
 2  Component,   Monday,    = @index($TABLE_DAYS,Ø,@mod($DATE_NUM,7))&", "
 3    or
 4    step       January    = @index($TABLE_MONTHS,Ø,@month($DATE_NUM)-1)&" "
 5    formulas
 6               7,         = @string(@day($DATE_NUM),Ø)&", "
 7
 8               1991       = @string(@year($DATE_NUM)+19ØØ,Ø)
 9
1Ø  Combined     Monday, January 7, 1991    = +B2&B4&B6&B8
11    formulas
12
13  DATE_NUM       33245    T ->   Saturday      January   <- T  M
14               A  D       Sunday        February  A  O
15               B  A       Monday        March     B  N
16               L  Y       Tuesday       April     L  T
17               E  S       Wednesday     May       E  H
18                          Thursday      June         S
19                          Friday        July
2Ø                                        August
```

Figure 9.1 ◆ *String concatenation to produce a complete date*

formula, which concatenates a comma and space (enclosed in quotes) to the day name. A space is concatenated to the end of the formula in B4.

Cell B6 has a formula that returns the date for the given day, using the date function @day:

@string(@day($DATE_NUM),0)&", "

Since the final result must be text, though, the string function @string is used to turn the numeric result, 7, into a text character. The second argument of the @string function is 0, which tells it to round the result to zero decimals before displaying it. Again, a comma and a space are appended to the end. As the parts of the formula grow, you can see why step cells are such a good idea when dealing with string arithmetic.

In B8, the year has been extracted from DATE_NUM with the date function @year:

@string(@year($DATE_NUM) + 1900,0)

Since the @year function returns the number of years since 1900, 91 in this case, the value 1900 has been added to the result to produce the complete year, 1991. Again, this value has been turned into a string with the @string function.

The last formula, cell B10, combines the four component formulas into the final result:

+ B2&B4&B6&B8

It uses an ampersand between a cell reference to each one. That is how easy it is to combine string formulas when they are each contained in a separate cell. Notice that even though the result is a string value, it still overhangs the width of the cell as any text would.

String formulas can also serve as a quick way to combine step formulas back into just one formula, allowing the formula to be copied as a single unit and the step cells to be erased. Suppose that once the formula was written and proved successful in Figure 9.1, you decided to eliminate the step cells and make just one long formula. Rather than trying to type each component formula by hand, you can instead just string them together.

The first thing to do is to edit each component formula, B2 through B8, and preface it with a label prefix to turn it into straight text—text that will look like the formula, not its result. While in the edit mode, you must add an ampersand to the end of each entry, in preparation for joining it to the entry in the cell below. The last formula, B8, would also be made into text, but because it is last, it would not need an extra ampersand added.

Figure 9.2 is essentially the previous figure after a bit of cleaning up—the tables have been moved out of the way and the text to the right of each formula erased.

```
B1Ø: [W1Ø] +B2&B4&B6&B8                                          EDIT
@index($TABLE_DAYS,Ø,@mod($DATE_NUM,7))&", "&&index($TABLE_MONTHS,Ø,@month($DATE

              A          B          C       D       E       F       G
1
2     Day name     @index($TABLE_DAYS,Ø,@mod($DATE_NUM,7))&", "&
3
4     Month name   @index($TABLE_MONTHS,Ø,@month($DATE_NUM)-1)&" "&
5
6     Day date     @string(@day($DATE_NUM),Ø)&", "&
7
8     Year         @string(@year($DATE_NUM)+19ØØ,Ø)
9
1Ø    Combined     @index($TABLE_DAYS,Ø,@mod($DATE_NUM,7))&", "&&index($TABLE_
11    formulas
12
13
14    Complete     Monday, January 7, 1991
15    formula
16
17
18
19
2Ø
```

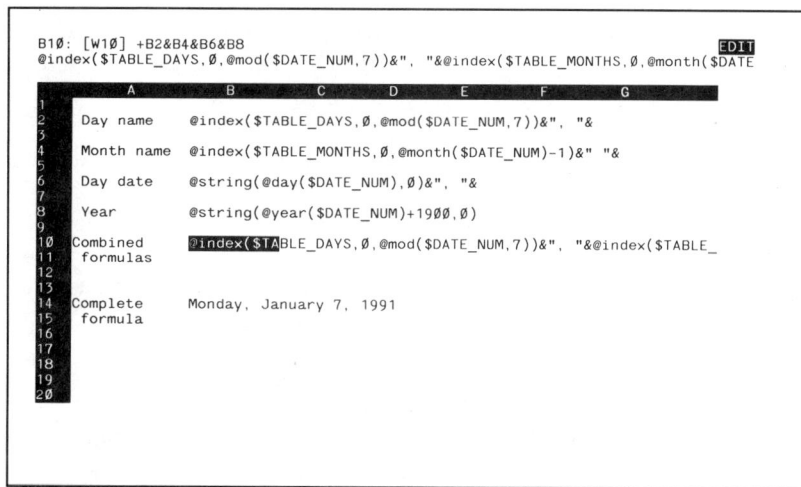

Figure 9.2 ◆ *Combining step formulas*

Cells B2 through B8 are now plain text, and they display their actual contents. But notice cell B10, which is the same formula as before, +B2&B4&B6&B8. It is still displaying the text from the four cells above, only now it displays the actual contents of those cells. What you see displayed at B10 is what the final single formula will look like. The last step will turn this formula into the single formula that displays the date.

To complete the job, you must press F2 to edit the formula in B10, and then press F9 {calc} to evaluate it. What you will get is not the date, but one long formula that consists of the text in the four step cells, B2..B8. You can see this final step in the control panel of Figure 9.2. The formula is still displayed in the top line, and the evaluated formula is shown one line down in the edit window.

When you press Enter, the new formula is entered into the cell, but not as text—it evaluates and returns the date result. This final formula has been duplicated in cell B14, and it is 137 characters long:

```
@index($TABLE_DAYS,0,@mod($DATE_NUM,7))
&", "&@index($TABLE_MONTHS,0,@month($DATE_NUM) – 1)
&" "&@string(@day($DATE_NUM),0)
&", "&@string(@year($DATE_NUM) + 1900,0)
```

Here is a summary of the procedure for combining step formulas:

1. Turn each step formula into text by prefacing it with a label prefix.

2. While editing, add an ampersand to the end of each entry except the last one.

3. If there isn't already a formula that ties them together, write one that concatenates the entries into one formula.

4. Edit and then evaluate that formula with the F9 {calc} key.

5. Press Enter, and the single formula is finished.

This method also works with numeric formulas, with one small difference. You would not include the extra ampersands of step 2, above. Instead, you would use the appropriate numeric operator, such as + or *. Remember that you cannot create a new formula that has more than 240 characters, the Lotus limit.

Using the Range Justify Command to Combine Text

The Range Justify command can justify a single column of text to a given width. The result resembles that of word processed text that fits within a specified margin. With this command, text from several cells can be combined into one, an especially useful feature. The trick to this method is to set the range wide enough so that all the text can be justified into just the first cell of the text column.

Figure 9.3 shows the process. These are the same formulas that were used in the two previous figures. First, turn each formula into text by prefacing it with a label prefix and add the ampersand, to the end, as shown. To protect these original formulas from any damage, copy the four cells to an empty range, B11 in the example. Then move those copies together into four consecutive cells down the column.

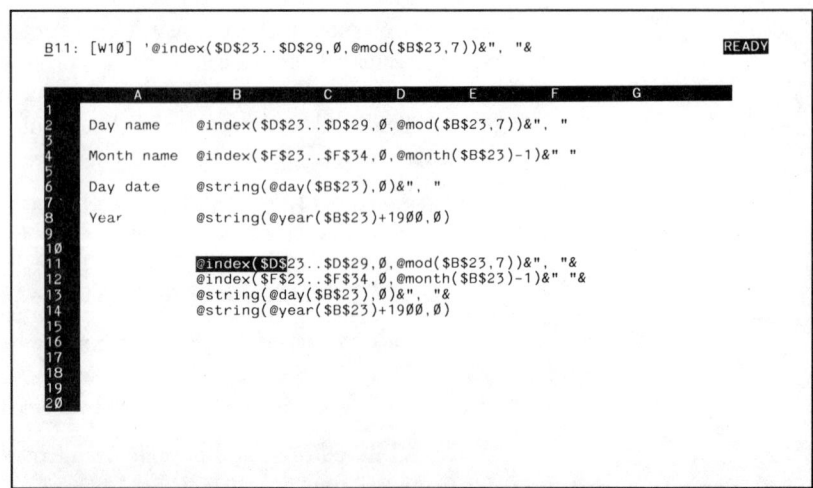

```
B11: [W10] '@index($D$23..$D$29,0,@mod($B$23,7))&", "&            READY

         A          B          C          D        E        F        G
1
2     Day name    @index($D$23..$D$29,0,@mod($B$23,7))&", "
3
4     Month name  @index($F$23..$F$34,0,@month($B$23)-1)&" "
5
6     Day date    @string(@day($B$23),0)&", "
7
8     Year        @string(@year($B$23)+1900,0)
9
10
11                @index($D$23..$D$29,0,@mod($B$23,7))&", "&
12                @index($F$23..$F$34,0,@month($B$23)-1)&" "&
13                @string(@day($B$23),0)&", "&
14                @string(@year($B$23)+1900,0)
15
16
17
18
19
20
```

Figure 9.3 ◆ *Using the Range Justify command to combine formulas*

With the cells one below the other, move the cell pointer to the first one, B11 in the example. Issue the Range Justify command and mark off the four rows, 11 through 14, but don't press Enter yet. Now expand the highlighted range four or five screens to the right—enough so that the width is greater than the 240-character maximum limit in a cell.

With the range defined (something in the neighborhood of B11..AN14 in this case), press Enter and the four cells will be combined into one at B11. The Range Justify command always includes a space between the justified cells, as that is what you would want when justifying text that will be read. In this case, though, you must edit B11 and delete the spaces.

> ⊗ **CAUTION** ◆ *You do not have to specify all the rows to be justified by the Range Justify command. If you mark only the top row, such as 11 in Figure 9.3, the command justifies all text cells below it, stopping only when a blank, numeric, or text value cell is reached. The problem is, when the cells are justified into the first cell, all cells below them in that column of the worksheet also move up the same number of rows, with disastrous results for the worksheet layout.*
>
> *By selecting just the rows that are needed, such as rows 11 through 14 in the example, you can be certain that only those cells will be affected and the cells below them will not move.*

When the spaces have been removed, delete the label prefix and press Enter. The formula now evaluates into the completed date: Monday, January 7, 1991. Here are the steps taken with the Range Justify method:

1. Turn each step formula into text by prefacing it with a label prefix.

2. While editing, add an ampersand to the end of each entry except the last one.

3. Copy the cells to a different location.

4. Move the cells next to each other, down the column.

5. Use the Range Justify command to justify the cells, specifying each row and several screens to the right.

6. Edit out the spaces between each segment.

7. Remove the label prefix and press Enter.

Whether you use string formulas or the Range Justify command, any attempt to place more than 240 characters in one cell will fail. In the case of the Range Justify command, it can fail miserably; the text you are trying to justify may actually be destroyed. This is why the precaution of copying the original formulas in Figure 9.3 to a work area was taken.

Splitting Text with the Range Justify Command

The Range Justify command can combine text, but it can just as easily break it into components. This can be useful when a long formula is causing problems. You can break a long formula into several intermediate step formulas and debug them, and later combine them back into one formula.

The first step is to turn the formula into text by adding the usual label prefix. Then you must insert a space (or spaces) between the parts that you want in separate cells. With that done, use the Range Justify command and specify several cells down the column, enough to contain the separate components of the justified text. Do not expand the width of the range into any other columns.

When you press Enter, Lotus tries to justify the text into the narrow range as best it can, and has to split the text at the spaces you inserted. You will end up with separate pieces of the formula in each cell down the column. You could then edit each one to delete any extra spaces you had inserted and any trailing operators that joined the two now separated pieces of formula. Then, remove each one's label prefix and it will be turned back into a formula, to be edited or debugged as necessary.

Formatting String Formulas with the Range Justify Command

Normally, you cannot use the Range Justify command with text values (string formulas). With the following short routine, though, you can accomplish that feat and open up new possibilities for worksheet reporting—merging worksheet data with text, and formatting it for output.

Look at Figure 9.4. In the upper window are two string formulas named TEXT_VALUES, A8..A9. Each contains text as well as cell references to the labels in A1..A4 and the named ranges in B1..B4: NORTH, SOUTH, EAST, and WEST. One formula could have been used for this example, but to avoid an overly long, complex formula, two were used instead. Part of the contents of the first formula can be seen in the control panel, and the entire formula is shown here, split into two parts for clarity:

```
+"  This month, "&$A$1&" has "&@string($NORTH,2)
&" while "&$A$2&" achieved "&@string($SOUTH,2)&". "
```

The second formula is built in a similar way:

```
+$A$3&" has taken in "&@string($EAST,2)&" and "
&$A$4&" has "&@string($WEST,2)&"."
```

```
A8: +"   This month, "&$A$1&" has "&@STRING($NORTH,2)&" while "&$A$2&" achi READY

        A         B          C          D          E          F          G
1   NORTH     123456.78
2   SOUTH      31733.29
3   EAST           2.3
4   WEST        128.28
5
6
7   <TEXT_VALUES>
8       This month, NORTH has 123456.78 while SOUTH achieved 31733.29.
9   EAST has taken in 2.30 and WEST has 128.28.
10
        I         J                    K                    L          M
29
30
31              |----------------------------------------|
32  TEXT_RANGE ->       This month, NORTH has 123456.78 while SOUTH achieved
33    K32..K35 ->      EAST has taken in 2.30 and WEST has 128.28.
34           ->
35           ->
36              |----------------------------------------|
37
```

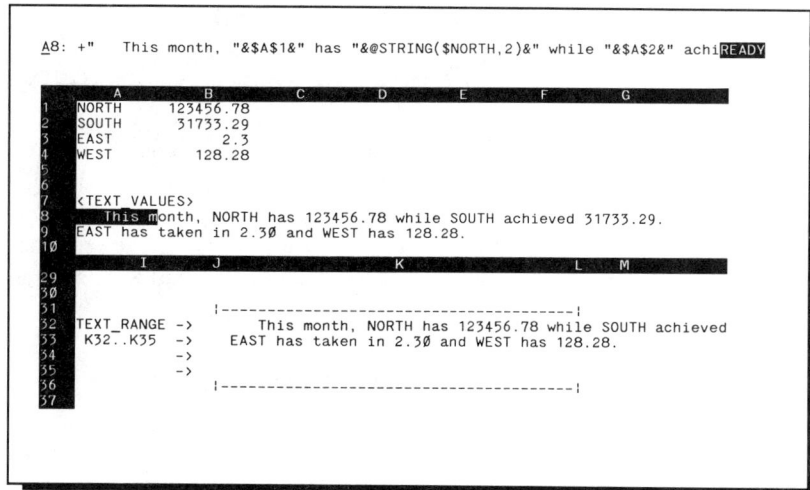

Figure 9.4 ◆ *Creating string formulas for merging and printing text with data*

Both formulas use the @string function to provide two digits to the right of the decimal for each variable. These two formulas are a small but representative example of how you can build a report from text and worksheet data.

Unfortunately, the length of each formula depends on the size of the numbers in the cells in column B and of their names in column A. Since string formulas cannot be justified, there seems to be no way to make the display attractive for a given output. Of course, you can always fiddle with the formulas by hand, but you could have done that in the first place. As usual, the idea is to automate the process, and with the combination of the string formulas, the Range Justify Command, and a macro, the idea becomes a reality.

In the lower window of Figure 9.4 is the range named TEXT_RANGE that will actually be printed; it is enclosed in the dashed lines. Note that just the one column, K, has been expanded to an appropriate width. Having a single column simplifies the definition of the output area.

The trick relies on the string formulas being turned into pure text by the Range Value command. The pure text can then be reformatted with the Range Justify command and printed.

Here is the macro that automates the process:

```
{blank TEXT_RANGE}
{calc}
/rvTEXT_VALUES~TEXT_RANGE~
/rjTEXT_RANGE~
```

It first erases the output area, TEXT_RANGE, in preparation for the new data. It then calculates the worksheet to ensure that all the formulas are current. The third line of the macro performs the Range Value command, copying the values of the two formulas to TEXT_RANGE in the lower window. You can see the copied text in that range, where the two lines extend well past the right edge of column K.

The last line of the macro justifies the text in TEXT_RANGE within that range. You can see the result in the lower window of Figure 9.5. The text fits neatly within the width of column K, and it can now be printed.

◆ A POTPOURRI OF STRING FUNCTIONS

String arithmetic usually functions in a supportive role, and therefore takes second place to numeric arithmetic. The @ functions that handle strings, therefore, are not used as frequently or intensively as the math functions. They are nonetheless powerful tools that can produce worthy results that can help you to construct and operate your worksheet, and to format it for output.

@repeat: SAY IT AGAIN

This function has a simple purpose: to repeat a label a certain number of times, up to the maximum 240 characters allowed in a cell. It can be as brief as

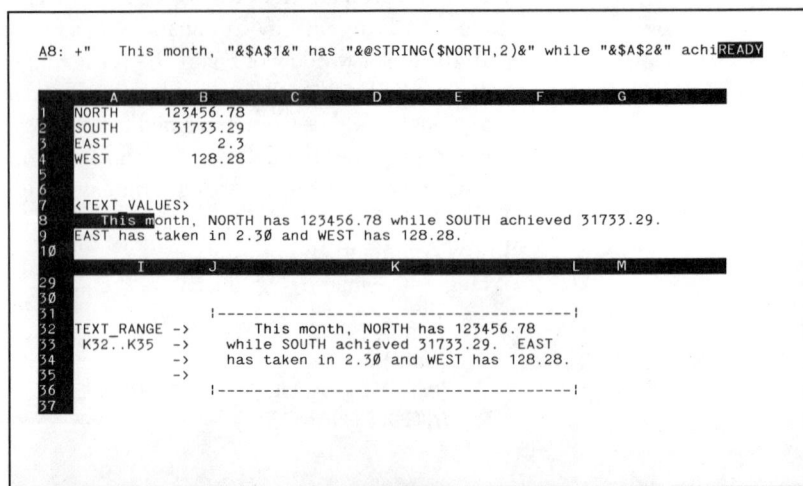

```
A8: +"   This month, "&$A$1&" has "&@STRING($NORTH,2)&" while "&$A$2&" achi READY

       A          B          C          D          E          F          G
1   NORTH    123456.78
2   SOUTH     31733.29
3   EAST          2.3
4   WEST       128.28
5
6
7   <TEXT VALUES>
8      This month, NORTH has 123456.78 while SOUTH achieved 31733.29.
9   EAST has taken in 2.30 and WEST has 128.28.
10
       I          J               K               L       M
29
30
31              !--------------------------------------!
32  TEXT_RANGE ->        This month, NORTH has 123456.78
33  K32..K35   ->        while SOUTH achieved 31733.29.   EAST
34         ->            has taken in 2.30 and WEST has 128.28.
35         ->
36              !--------------------------------------!
37
```

Figure 9.5 ◆ *The final output of the Range Justify command*

the following example, a longer version of which was used to build the long formula in Figure 7.1:

$$@repeat(''+A1'',5) = +A1+A1+A1+A1+A1$$

Even with a very short formula, however, @repeat can produce some fancy results. How fancy? Figure 9.6 shows a horizontal bar graph that performs like a normal Lotus graph but is built within the cells of the worksheet. In the control panel, you can see the contents of the first graph line in C4, which is also shown here:

$$@repeat(@char(187),@round(B4/\$SCALE,0))$$

For the repeating character, the @repeat function uses the one that has a LICS (Lotus International Character Set) code of 187, the result of the function @char(187). The value for the number of repeats is taken from the number in B4, which therefore determines the length of each bar in the graph.

Since the numbers in column B are all much larger than 240, the formula divides each by a scaling factor, the value in B19. That cell is appropriately named SCALE, and in this case SCALE is equal to 1,000. The @repeat function cannot work with "fractions of a character," but it does not round off the repeat value; it just truncates any decimal portion. This is why the @round function is used. In the formula in C4, the value 25,828 is divided by SCALE to result in 25.828, which is rounded to 26. That is the number of characters it displays in that bar of the graph.

```
C4:  @REPEAT(@CHAR(187),@ROUND(B4/$SCALE,0))                    READY

                 A        B      C    D    E    F    G    H    I    J    K    L
                          String Functions Can Build a Horizontal Bar Graph
 1
 2   ------------------------------------------------------------------------
 3
 4   January    25,828  »»»»»»»»»»»»»»»»»»»»»»»»»»
 5
 6   February   21,987  »»»»»»»»»»»»»»»»»»»»»»
 7
 8   March      14,455  »»»»»»»»»»»»»»
 9
10   April      21,553  »»»»»»»»»»»»»»»»»»»»»»
11
12   May        34,821  »»»»»»»»»»»»»»»»»»»»»»»»»»»»»»»»»»»»»
13
14   June       27,800  »»»»»»»»»»»»»»»»»»»»»»»»»»»»
15
16
17
18
19   SCALE       1,000
20
```

Figure 9.6 ◆ *Creating a horizontal bar graph with the @repeat function*

Compared to the time it takes to format a real Lotus graph, and especially to print one, this technique can give you fast visual comparisons of a range of numbers.

Here is another way to build this type of graph. The +/− cell format was designed specifically for this purpose, and produces a similar graph, although limited to just the plus or minus character. Figure 9.7 shows the same graph, this time built from the +/− cell format.

The difference between the two is that the bars in this graph are still numeric, only the format of their display looks like text. The @repeat function actually produces a text result, and can therefore stretch beyond the one screen to its full 240-character maximum. Moreover, you can easily customize the text-based graph by combining other text into or around the @repeat formula.

A more frequent use for this function has been incorporated into Figures 9.6 and 9.7. The dashed line in row 2 of each figure is not made up of repeating labels in each cell, \-. Instead, one function was entered in A2 to create the line that stretches across the screen:

@repeat("-",72)

There is a big difference between the two methods of creating a border. The repeating label prefix fills a cell with the repeated characters no matter what the width of the column is, but this can often be disrupting to the design of the border being created. The @repeat function can create borders that remain fixed in their pattern, no matter what the width of the underlying columns

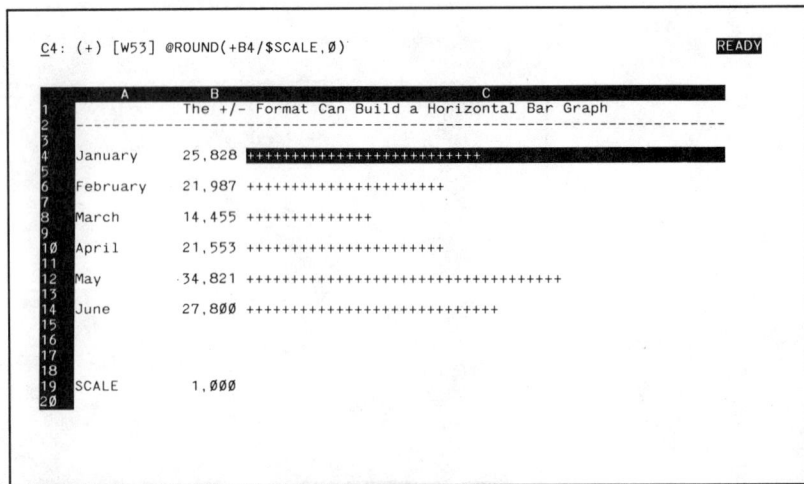

```
C4: (+) [W53] @ROUND(+B4/$SCALE,0)                                    READY

        A            B                          C
1                          The +/- Format Can Build a Horizontal Bar Graph
2   ---------------------------------------------------------------------------
3
4   January      25,828  ++++++++++++++++++++++++++
5
6   February     21,987  ++++++++++++++++++++++
7
8   March        14,455  ++++++++++++++
9
10  April        21,553  ++++++++++++++++++++++
11
12  May          34,821  +++++++++++++++++++++++++++++++++++
13
14  June         27,800  ++++++++++++++++++++++++++++
15
16
17
18
19  SCALE         1,000
20
```

Figure 9.7 ◆ *Using the +/− cell format to create a horizontal bar graph*

may be. Figure 9.8 demonstrates the difference between the two, and gives several examples of the @repeat function. The border design in the second row of the screen is made from repeating labels: \-*. Each column must be the same width, as well as an even number of spaces wide, for a two-character pattern to repeat properly. Since this worksheet has a variety of column widths, the pattern is irregular.

In row 3, the same pattern is used but this time it is perfectly even, the result of using the @repeat function:

@repeat("-*",40)

This creates a long label of 80 characters, long enough to stretch across the 72 characters of the Lotus worksheet. Since the text that is created is an overhanging label, the width of the columns does not affect the way it looks. The designs in rows 5 and 6 are simple variations with the @repeat function. They would most likely not be possible if the repeating label prefix were used in a typical worksheet with varying column widths.

Now look at the ruler lines in the lower portion of the screen—cells B14, B16, and B18. These practical formulas are based upon the @repeat function, and they repeat the text in cell B11, named RULER. The result is a fixed ruler line, the length of which depends upon the number in the cell to the left of each formula. This built-in ruler can be used to lay out worksheet ranges for printing with exact precision. This is the formula in B14:

@repeat($RULER,A14/10)&@left($RULER,@mod(A14,10))

```
B14: [W11] @REPEAT($RULER,A14/1Ø)&&LEFT($RULER,@MOD(A14,1Ø))          READY

              A         B         C         D      EFGHI J  K         L          M     N    O
 1
 2   _*_*_*__*_*_*_*_*_*_*__*_*_*_*_*_*_*_____*__*__*_*_*_*_*__*__*_*__*_*_*_*_
 3   _*_*_*_*_*_*_*_*_*_*_*_*_*_*_*_*_*_*_*_*_*_*_*_*_*_*_*_*_*_*_*_*_*_*_*_*_*_*_
 4
 5   [-!-]  [-!-]  [-!-]  [-!-]  [-!-]  [-!-]  [-!-]  [-!-]  [-!-]  [-!-]  [-!-]
 6   A=(πr²)  A=(πr²)  A=(πr²)  A=(πr²)  A=(πr²)  A=(πr²)  A=(πr²)  A=(πr²)
 7
 8
 9
1Ø
11   RULER   123456789_
12
13
14      23  123456789_123456789_123
15
16      41  123456789_123456789_123456789_123456789_1
17
18      55  123456789_123456789_123456789_123456789_123456789_12345
19
2Ø
```

Figure 9.8 ◆ *Creating borders with the @repeat function*

The formula is building a "ruler" that is divided into tenths. To calculate the number of full repetitions of RULER that should be displayed, the repeat value in A14 must be divided by 10. Since the value is 23, the formula displays two full repetitions of RULER:

@repeat($RULER,A14/10)

To complete the ruler line, additional characters must be appended to equal the number remaining after A14 is divided by 10. The second part of the formula returns the remainder of A14 divided by 10, and then extracts that many characters from RULER, using the @left function:

&@left($RULER,@mod(A14,10))

In the example, the remainder is 3, so the left three characters of RULER are appended to the first part of the formula, producing the 23-character result shown in the figure.

With a little imagination, you will find that the @repeat function can serve as a unique solution to many problems.

@length: COUNTING CHARACTERS

The @length function tells you how many characters there are in a string. Its single argument can be a string of text or a reference to a cell that contains text. This is a versatile and frequently used function. It can quickly tell you the number of characters in a formula, allowing you to find the shortest one among several different styles. Just turn the formula to text by prefacing it with a label prefix, and then refer to it with the @length function. If a long formula of 168 characters is in A4, this function will tell you its length:

@length(A4) = 168

A string formula cannot be justified in its cell by prefacing it with a label prefix—it would no longer be a formula, it would just be plain text. By using the @length function in tandem with @repeat and @cell, you can write a string formula that will center its result in the cell.

Column B in Figure 9.9 is 40 characters wide. Each of the four string formulas in that column refer to the text to its left in column A. The result is displayed centered within the column. The formula follows several steps to produce the result; here are the steps that build the one in B4. First, it must determine the width of the column in which it resides:

@cell("width",B3..B3)

```
B4: [W4Ø] @REPEAT(" ",(@CELL("width",B3..B3)-@LENGTH(A4))/2)&A4        READY
```

```
                    A                      B                     C
 1
 2                              Center - ^ - Center
 3
 4  Lotus 1-2-3                      Lotus 1-2-3
 5
 6  Tips                                Tips
 7
 8  and                                 and
 9
10  Tricks                             Tricks
11
12
13
14
15
16
17
18
19
20
```

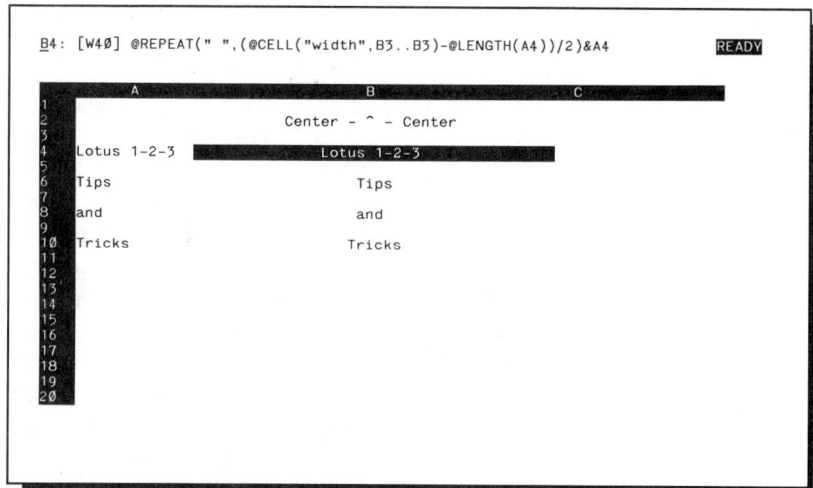

Figure 9.9 ◆ *Centering a string value*

TIP ◆ *The @cell function can refer to any cell in its column to determine the column width. If you were to use its current cell, a circular reference would be created. To avoid this, refer to a cell above or below it, as is done in Figure 9.9.*

Then, it finds the length of the text in A4 and subtracts it from the width of the column:

@cell("width",B3..B3) – @length(A4)

The result is the total number of spaces that should precede and follow the text to center it in the column. Therefore, half of that number should precede the text, so the result is divided by 2.

(@cell("width",B3..B3) – @length(A4))/2

The @repeat function can then produce the proper number of leading spaces:

@repeat(" ",(@cell("width",B3..B3) – @length(A4))/2)

Finally, the actual text in A4 must be displayed, and it will be preceded by the correct number of spaces:

@repeat(" ",(@cell("width",B3..B3) – @length(A4))/2)&A4

@value *AND* @string: STRINGS TO VALUES AND VALUES TO STRINGS

Lotus provides two functions that allow you to mix text and numbers in the same formula by translating one into the other, keeping the formula either all text or all numeric.

The @value function has already been mentioned in Chapter 7, and it is essential to the regular use of string arithmetic. Its purpose is to turn text that appears to be a number into the actual number. It is smart enough to know how to handle fractions (5/8), dollar signs ($1.25), percent signs (25%), and commas ($24,500,100).

Since you can never mix text with numbers, the @value function allows you to change text to numbers so that numeric calculations can be performed. The @string function, mentioned earlier in this chapter, performs the opposite task of turning numbers into text that looks like the number, so that string formulas can be created:

@value("$24,232 1/4")   = 24232.25
@string(@pi,3)   = 3.142

⊗ **CAUTION** ◆ *Although @string is similar to the @round function, you cannot round the integer part of the number. It will return an error if you try:*

@round(1234.123, – 2) = 1200
@string(1234.123, – 2) = ERR

Note also that the result of the @string function is no longer numeric and therefore cannot be given a format.

@exact: MATCHING STRINGS

This function compares two strings and returns 1 if they are exactly the same, 0 if not. You can also compare strings by creating a logical expression—"does this string equal that string"—but the expression is not case-sensitive. The strings do not have to be exactly alike. With the @exact function, capital letters do matter:

+ "tips" = "Tips"   = 1
@exact("tips","Tips")   = 0

If you ever need to test one string against another, remember this difference.

@n AND @s: NUMBER, STRING, OR BLANK

The @n and @s functions return the contents of the cell in the upper left corner of the range they address, but with a small twist. They simply return a blank if the cell is not a number (@n) or a string (@s). The main use for these functions was in the initial release of Lotus version 2.0. They provided a means of circumventing the problem of a formula referring to cells of mixed value. If A1 were the number 1 and A2 a string, then trying to mix the two cells in one formula would produce an error:

```
+A1+A2 = ERR
@if(A1>A2,5,10) = ERR
```

This seemed inconsistent because Lotus 1A simply assigned the value of 0 to any text cells in a numeric formula. Problems would develop when a Lotus 1A worksheet was loaded into Lotus 2.0, and any cells that referenced both text and numbers would result in ERR. These two functions provided the solution by allowing a formula to verify the type of cell it was addressing if that cell might be either text or number:

```
+A1+@n(A2..A2) = 1
@if(A1>@n(A2..A2),5,10) = 5
```

This created a lot of extra formula writing and more chances for formulas to result in ERR. With the release of Lotus 2.01, text cells once again had a numeric value of 0 when mixed with numeric cells in a formula. The @n and @s function then had a much smaller role to play.

They are still useful for preventing errors when building numeric or string formulas that refer to individual cells that may be either text or values. For example, if B1 is numeric and B2 is text, this string formula would, of course, return ERR:

```
+B1&B2
```

So, if you are not able to control the type of entry in either of the cells, the @s function will solve the problem:

```
@s(B1)&@s(B2)
```

If either cell is a numeric value, that portion of the formula will return a blank.

@trim AND @clean: SPRUCING UP TEXT

The @trim and @clean functions help to tidy up any text that contains extraneous spaces or unprintable characters. The @trim function removes all spaces that precede or follow a string, as well as any repetitions of spaces within the text (it allows only one space at any given point in the text).

The @clean function is similar to @trim, but this one strips out any unprintable (in Lotus) characters from the string. The @clean function is useful when importing "dirty" text, say from a word processor that cannot export straight ASCII documents, or data from a telecommunications session that was corrupted by static. The Lotus characters that have a LICS value of less than 32 will be stripped from the text, as well as the characters 151, 152, and 155.

Figure 9.10 demonstrates these two functions. Look at the text in B2, the cell that is being edited. Notice that the display in the control panel shows many extra spaces within the text. But these are not all spaces; some are unprintable characters that are revealed in the edit window. The @clean function in B4 refers to this cell and cleans out the unprintable characters. Only the usable text is left, which still includes the extra space characters.

The @trim function in B6 finishes the cleanup job; it refers to the partially repaired text in B4. It removes the spaces in front of the text, as well as the extra spaces between words. From this example, you can see that you would very likely want to nest these functions, one within the other, when cleaning up a range of text:

@trim(@clean(B2))

Generally, these formulas would not be left as formulas in the worksheet. You would write and copy them to the desired range, and then invoke the Range Value command to copy the formulas back onto the referenced cells to leave them in the corrected state. The formulas themselves would then be erased.

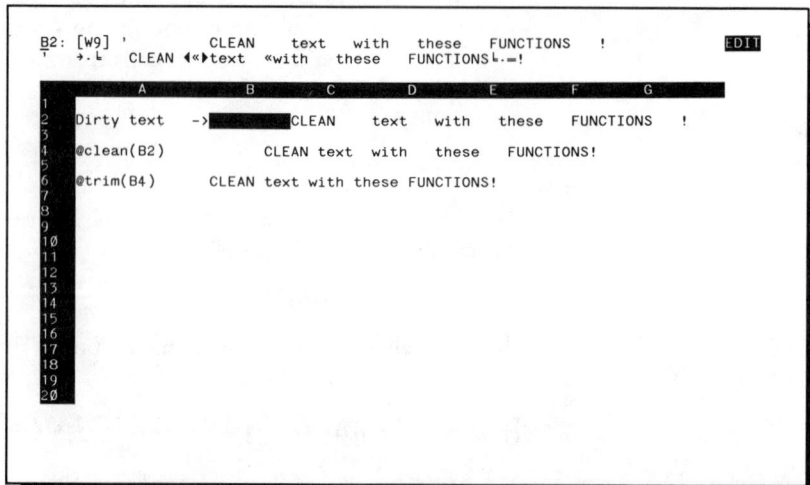

Figure 9.10 ◆ *Fixing corrupted text with @clean and @trim*

@upper, @lower, AND @proper:
BUILDING A CASE

The @upper, @lower, and @proper functions can help you to adjust the looks of a text cell. They do exactly what their names implies: change the text to all UPPERCASE, lowercase, or Propercase. Again, you can frequently use these with the @clean or @trim function to complete the job of correcting imported text. Figure 9.11 shows all three of these functions when used with the previous example.

Again, by nesting the functions into one formula, a text cell could be cleaned up with just the one formula:

@proper(@trim(@clean(B2)))

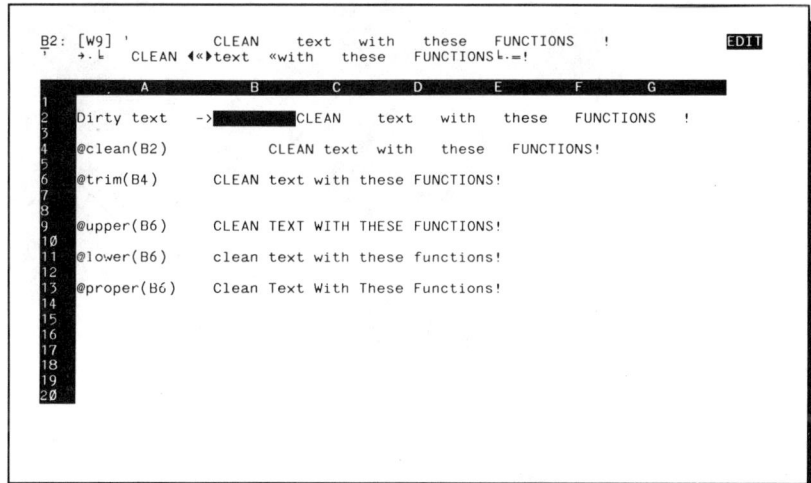

```
B2: [W9] '      CLEAN   text   with   these   FUNCTIONS   !          EDIT
      →.↳   CLEAN ◀«▶text  «with   these   FUNCTIONS↳.═!

         A           B         C        D       E       F       G
1
2  Dirty text    ->         CLEAN   text   with   these   FUNCTIONS   !
3
4  @clean(B2)          CLEAN text  with   these    FUNCTIONS!
5
6  @trim(B4)      CLEAN text with these FUNCTIONS!
7
8
9  @upper(B6)     CLEAN TEXT WITH THESE FUNCTIONS!
10
11 @lower(B6)     clean text with these functions!
12
13 @proper(B6)    Clean Text With These Functions!
14
15
16
17
18
19
20
```

Figure 9.11 ◆ *Adjusting the look of text with the @upper, @lower, and @proper functions*

◆ SUMMARY

This chapter has given you a look at string values, string arithmetic, and string functions, all essential tools in the Lotus toolbox. You have seen how to combine multiple step formulas into a single-cell formula, and how to split a long formula into more manageable units. The string functions, although used less frequently than the math functions, are extremely valuable. Among other things, they make it possible to build graphs within the worksheet and to center string formulas within a column.

The next chapter delves into the database features of Lotus, including the exceptionally powerful data functions, such as @dsum and @davg.

TEN:

Navigating a Database

10

◆ ◆ ◆

BECAUSE THE LOTUS WORKSHEET IS BUILT ON ROWS, COLUMNS, and cells, it is a convenient environment in which to perform database operations. But you should not confuse Lotus with a true database program and expect it to meet all your database needs. The program's database capabilities are most powerful when used in conjunction with the more usual data analysis techniques of the worksheet.

This chapter first reviews the structure and components of a Lotus database and the data commands that drive the operations. Then each command is discussed in more detail. Although records in a database may be sorted, the Sort command does not rely on the structure of a database, so it is covered in Chapter 13, rather than here.

You will learn how to structure the Input range so that it functions efficiently as the core of the Lotus database. Data entry routines and macros are demonstrated that will speed the process and ensure accurate results. The selection Criterion range is discussed as the key to the selection process. The use of text or logical expressions in this range is also covered.

The powerful data functions are described in this chapter, because they are so closely linked to a worksheet database. With them, you can build a reporting routine that will significantly enhance any database.

◆ _BUILDING A DATABASE_

A worksheet database is nothing more than a range of data that you define as a database. At the heart of its structure are the three ranges: input, criterion, and output. Both its structure and the data it contains must conform to certain physical constraints in order for you to access the data efficiently. The selection criteria must be written to accurately reflect both the structure of the data and the type of data being searched.

DEFINING A LOTUS DATABASE

When used as the source for a database, the rows in the data range are frequently called *records*. The columns within the data range create *fields* for each record, so that each cell is a separate field in that record.

A field must always contain the same type of data in each record, either numeric or text. For example, when entering zip codes in one column, make them either text or numeric, but do not mix the two among the records. The data within the field should also be of a similar category or scale. The data in a field named Length, for example, should not have some entries measured in inches, others in meters, and still others in fractions of a mile. If you used different units, you could not accurately select all records whose length is greater than 100 feet. And don't expect to get much information from a database if one field contains entries for cars, salaries, address, and diameter!

Although any inconsistencies in data may not be a problem when viewing a worksheet, they will corrupt the necessary structure of the data and prevent the effective use of any of the database utilities: searching, extracting, and so on.

THE INPUT, CRITERION, AND OUTPUT RANGES

The key to the structure of a Lotus database is the *column titles* for each field. When specifying a database with the Data Query command, the single row of column titles defines the top of the *input range*. The next row down is assumed to be the first record. Each column title must have a unique spelling, or Lotus will not perform the data operations as you would expect.

Besides the input range, you must also describe a *criterion range* where Lotus will find the selection criteria. This consists of at least two cells in one column. The first cell contains the column title of the field to be searched for matching records, and the second cell contains the data for which to search. You can include more columns to create a more precise search.

The search criteria can be either text or numeric entries that specify the match, or logical formulas that compare each record against the "truth" of the formula. The formula is usually written to compare the first record of the data, and therefore refers to the first row beneath the column titles.

For example, to search a database for all entries in the Age column that are equal to 32, all of the following criteria would serve the purpose. Assume that column A holds the ages and that the column titles of the database are in row 2, so the first record is in row 3:

Age	Age	Age
32	+A3=32	+A3>31#and#A3<33

When using a character-style criterion (nonformula) to search for text, you can specify the exact text or, by using wildcard characters, just close matches. The question mark stands for any one character, and the asterisk stands for any number of characters from that point on. The following criteria for the Name column demonstrate this; all will select the name Warren Jones:

Name	Name	Name
Warren Jones	Warr?n ??nes	War*

You can also search for records that do not match the criteria by prefacing it with a tilde. This criterion would find all records except for those that begin with *War*:

Name
~War*

With just the input and criterion ranges defined, Lotus can search the data for any records with a field containing data that matches the selection criterion.

You can also define an *output range* where Lotus can copy the records that match your criterion. This range consists of at least one row that contains the column titles of the fields that you wish to copy from the database input range.

> **TIP** ◆ *As with many other Lotus commands, the most recent settings for the Data Query command are retained internally. If you have more than one database or several different criteria in a worksheet, you should always use the Reset command before assigning new settings. This ensures that each range is precisely defined by you. Using macros to define the settings should eliminate any inconvenience that resetting involves.*

You can see the three ranges that make up a Lotus database in Figure 10.1. Remember that the data in the input range can have many other uses besides its role in the database.

The input range covers the range B5..F10; its column titles are, of course, in the first row (row 5). The Item and Tag_Color fields contain text data, and the other three fields are numeric.

The criterion range lies in the range B1..B2. B1 contains the column title in which the search will be made, in this case Tag_Color. The criterion shown will select all records that have the word *Blue* in the Tag_Color field.

Finally, row 13 contains the titles from three fields of the input range that make up the database output range. The records below the titles have all been selected because they match the criterion—they each have the word *Blue* in

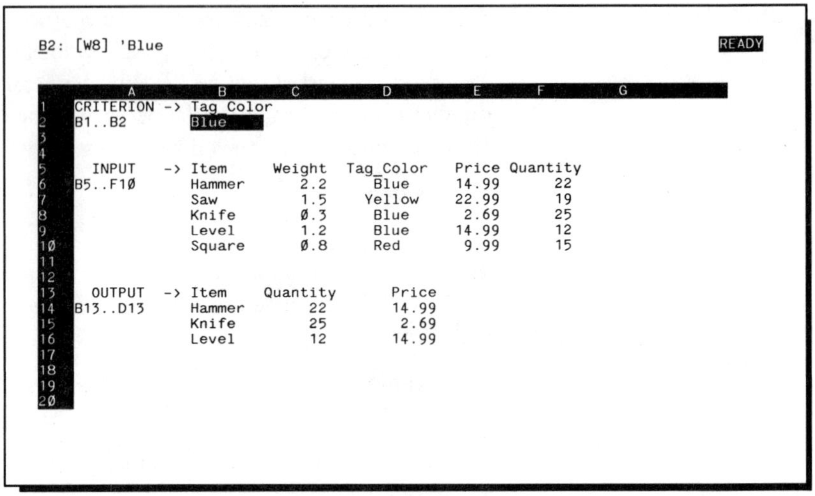

```
B2: [W8] 'Blue                                                    READY

          A         B         C         D         E         F         G
1  CRITERION -> Tag Color
2  B1..B2       Blue
3
4
5     INPUT   -> Item      Weight   Tag_Color   Price Quantity
6  B5..F1Ø      Hammer      2.2       Blue      14.99    22
7               Saw         1.5       Yellow    22.99    19
8               Knife       Ø.3       Blue       2.69    25
9               Level       1.2       Blue      14.99    12
1Ø              Square      Ø.8       Red        9.99    15
11
12
13    OUTPUT  -> Item     Quantity      Price
14 B13..D13     Hammer      22         14.99
15              Knife       25          2.69
16              Level       12         14.99
17
18
19
2Ø
```

Figure 10.1 ◆ *The basic structure of a Lotus database*

their Tag _Color field. Notice that in this case only three fields were used for the output range, and only those fields from the selected records are used by Lotus.

ACTING ON THE CRITERION: FIND, EXTRACT, UNIQUE, DELETE

When the input and criterion ranges have been defined under the Data Query command, you can search with the Find command. The cell pointer jumps to the first record in the database that matches the criterion. Pressing the ↓ or ↑ key moves the cell pointer to the next or previous matching record, until the last record is found. Pressing Escape returns the cell pointer to its previous position in the worksheet.

The Extract command does not move the cell pointer; it simply copies each matching record to the output range. The fields that are copied depend on the field titles in the first row of the output range. Since the data records are copied, the extracted data can be used for any purpose without affecting the original records. They can be printed, saved to a separate file, graphed, or even used as the input range for yet another database.

You can avoid duplicates in the extracted data by using the Unique command. If several records each have the same entry in the field being used in the criterion, only one record will be extracted. This command can give you a quick look at the variety of data in the input range. It also forms the basis for producing statistics on similar records in the input range, otherwise known as database reporting.

Instead of copying records to the output range, you can erase them from the database input range with the Delete command. This removes all records that match the criterion, and of course should be handled with care.

With the input, criterion, and output ranges defined, you can perform some sophisticated selection operations with the Data Query commands. However, Lotus is a spreadsheet, not a dedicated database program, and there are limitations on its power and flexibility in dealing with data.

CHOOSING THE APPROPRIATE DATABASE PROGRAM

The Lotus database capabilities can greatly enhance the power of the worksheet for analyzing data. On the other hand, if you try to use Lotus for complex database routines on a regular basis, you will most likely find the process to be self-defeating in the long run. There are several reasons for this.

A dedicated database program keeps the bulk of its records on disk while working with just a few of them in RAM. Lotus, on the other hand, stores the entire worksheet in RAM, so you can never work on a database that is larger than the available memory. With Lotus, if you want to change the information in just one record, you must still retrieve and then save the entire worksheet to make the revision. Lotus provides no basic tools for entering data into the worksheet, but database programs generally have input forms for that purpose. In Lotus, you must work in the row and column format, which can be inconvenient because you can never see an entire record on the screen at one time, except for small records of four or five fields.

You cannot view a field of more than 72 characters all at once, since that is the most that can be shown on the Lotus screen. Long text fields cannot be wrapped into several rows as an input form would do.

Once your data is in a database, you would normally want to start printing reports based on the data, and one of the biggest drawbacks of the Lotus database is its lack of any sophisticated reporting features. Even standard breakpoint reporting, where subtotals are printed for each category of data, is difficult to do in the worksheet. Macros and string functions can provide many tools for reporting on the data. But afterward, you may find yourself beaming with pride not so much for the results of the report as for the amazing feats of programming you performed to get there.

If you consider the Lotus database commands to be an adjunct to the worksheet, you will find their power hard to beat. Just be aware that with a 1-2-3 database, your needs at some point might better be served by a dedicated database program, and you should be prepared to transfer your worksheet data when the time comes.

◆ ENTERING AND MAINTAINING DATA

At the heart of a worksheet database is the input range, where the data is located. There can be many databases in a worksheet, but only one database is active for any one data operation. Much of the work that goes into constructing the database consists of entering the data in a fast, accurate, and consistent manner. Once established, the data must be maintained, with accuracy and integrity being the prime consideration.

THE INPUT RANGE

The input range of a worksheet database can have a maximum of 256 columns (fields), which is the number of columns in the Lotus worksheet. Its first row always has the unique column titles, with the first record being in the next row below. These titles cannot be formulas or have a numeric or string value; they must be straight text. A title can be any length up to the 240-character maximum in a cell, although short titles are much easier to work with when creating and manipulating the criterion and output ranges.

> **TIP** ◆ *Try to keep each title down to 15 characters or less. In that way, the titles can be used to create range names for each field in the first record of the database by using the Range Name Labels Down command. Then, any formulas in the criterion range can use those range names:*
>
>   + AGE = 32

Although the row below the titles is always the first record, you do not have to enter any data in that row. For clarity, you can use that row as a dividing line between the titles and the actual records. The dividing line can consist of repeating labels, such as hyphens or equal signs. Even though you will not be using the dividing row for any other purpose, it is still considered to be the first record for database purposes. Therefore, any logical formulas in your criterion range will still refer to that row in its role as the first record.

The spelling of the column titles is a critical issue because those in the three ranges—input, criterion, and output—must match exactly for the selection process to work. The program ignores capital letters, but a leading or trailing space in one title will make it distinctly different from the corresponding title in another range. Therefore, you should always use the Copy command to duplicate the titles. Enter the titles once in the input range, and then copy them to the other two ranges as needed.

> ★ **TRICK** ◆ *The column titles need not serve any other purpose than to define the columns of the database. With the one-line limitation, you may prefer to have two sets of column titles: one for visual display, and the other for the database input range. You can take advantage of the Hidden cell format to hide the database column titles just below the more descriptive and perhaps multiple row titles that you will view. The hidden row will still be defined as the top row of the database, and the row below it will be the first record.*

The top row of the range always contains the column titles, but you should make a point of anchoring the bottom row on something other than just the last record. The safest method is to create an end row below the last record. Enter an appropriate label into each field, such as <END>, and the row will stand out as the last row of the database. When printing all the records, you will always see the <END> flags in the last line of the printout, indicating that the last record was successfully printed. You can also include this row in your selection criteria so that it is always extracted whenever you perform an extract operation.

Range names can greatly simplify all the database operations. The input range should have a name that includes the first row titles and the end row below the last row of data. If you have more than one database in a worksheet, range names become essential. The names need not be descriptive, but should be such that the input, criterion, and output ranges for each one are somehow linked. The first database can consist of the names INPUT1, CRIT1, and OUTPUT1; the second can have INPUT2, CRIT2, and OUTPUT2.

The display of the cells in the input range does not affect the data selection process. The width of a column, the format of a numeric cell, or the alignment of a text entry may alter the display but does not affect the internal comparisons that are made by the Data Query commands. Text can be longer than the column is wide and Lotus will still accept it, since the actual contents of a cell are used. Remember that you can always adjust the display when printing, so arrange the look of the input range to suit your needs for entering or viewing the data.

The data within the input range must also be given consideration, and you might refer back to Chapter 3 for some hints on organizing the data efficiently. The number of columns used and the type of data in them can have a major effect on the operation of a database.

DATA ENTRY

Manipulating the data in a worksheet database may often be a short process that produces some important results. The results, though, are completely dependent on the accuracy and consistency of the data itself. In relation to debugging worksheet problems, Chapter 4 discussed the dangers of invalid data and the importance of keeping it consistent.

If you want to select all records whose City field is Washington, D.C., you will have a tough time doing so if that city is spelled differently throughout the database: Washington, D.C.; Wash.D.C.; WDC; Washington; or Washington D. of C. Whenever possible, standardize the data entry process so that data is always entered consistently. Chapter 3 emphasized the need for using data codes for regularly occurring items to keep the entries short and consistent. Chapter 4 described the best way to ensure the integrity of worksheet data: with the help of macros.

Using Macros for Efficient Data Entry

As usual, macros can play a key role in entering and maintaining data in a Lotus database. In fact, you can just about assume that without macros the data will become too varied, or corrupted, for the data commands to function properly. If you plan to make only text entries under the Zip column, for example, you must remember to preface each zip code with a label prefix. If you forget and enter one as a number, that entry will fall out of the proper order when you sort on the Zip field, and will never be selected because your criterion would be specifying text.

With a data entry macro such as the following, each zip code will always be entered as text. Moreover, you get the convenience of automatic cell-pointer movement for the entire data entry process:

```
{getlabel Enter State- ,CHOICE}
/cCHOICE ˜ ˜ {right}
{getlabel Enter Zip- ,CHOICE}
/cCHOICE ˜ ˜ {right}
```

You can validate data as it is entered when macros control the process. The preceding example used the {getlabel} command, which ensured that the zip code was entered as text. With a macro {if} statement you could also verify that the entry consisted of exactly five characters, and if it didn't, the macro could branch back and repeat the data entry macro:,

```
{getlabel Enter Zip- ,CHOICE}
{if @length(CHOICE)<>5}{beep 2}{branch \ENTER_ZIP}
```

A lookup table can serve as a list of valid data choices to which an entry can be compared for accuracy. The following two-line macro compares the data entered in cell CHOICE against a single column table, TABLE_VALID. If the data does not exist in the table, the lookup function returns ERR and the macro branches back to the input statement \DATA_IN:

```
{getlabel Enter data- ,CHOICE}
{if @iserr(@vlookup(CHOICE,TABLE_VALID,0))}
  {branch \DATA_IN}
```

If a field will have only a limited number of choices—whether just yes or no, or perhaps 10 or 15 job classification codes—a macro menu is the perfect solution. Chapter 1 demonstrated this technique in a menu that displayed several dates from which the user could choose. Here is a data entry menu that enters a standard abbreviation for one of several chemical names, and then moves the cell pointer. Notice that each menu item is prefaced with a letter of the alphabet. This prevents errors when a user is making a choice by typing the first letter of the menu item and more than one menu item starts with same letter, such as Calcium and Copper:

```
a)Sodium    b)Calcium    c)Boron    d)Iodine    e)Copper
Select a chemical to be entered
      Na ˜ {right}   Ca ˜ {right}   B ˜ {right}   I ˜ {right}   Cu ˜ {right}
```

Macros can make a tremendous difference in the time spent on entering new records, and the benefits of designing a macro data entry system cannot be overemphasized:

- ◆ Macro-controlled cell-pointer movement

- ◆ Tailored prompts for the user

- ◆ Automatic entry of numbers as text (zip, phone, and so on)

- ◆ Data validation

- ◆ More consistent data

- ◆ Menus for standard choices

◆ Increased speed of entry for difficult formulas, such as dates

◆ Conversion of formulas to values during entry to save memory and recalculation time

Restricting the Data Range

Once you determine the number and type of columns when creating a database, the natural tendency is to set aside a few thousand rows for the data and give each column the appropriate format for the numbers it will hold, and copy any necessary formulas into calculated fields. This has several drawbacks and should be avoided.

First, formatting a blank cell uses RAM that could otherwise be used for actual data, and also occupies disk space when the worksheet is saved. Trying to reserve hundreds or thousands of blank rows for the input range may prove to be a hidden danger when you forget that they are intended for data and use them for another purpose. The best way to set up the data range is to restrict it to only as many rows as currently needed.

As you know, the top row of the input range contains the unique column titles, and you can use an <END> row as the last row of the range. When you need to add another record, simply insert a new row above the <END> row and enter the data there. The database input range and any range name attached to it will expand to fit the new size.

Figure 10.2 shows a typical case of a restricted-range database. This small database covers eight rows, from the column titles to the <END> row. The input range shown is named INPUT1. Columns B and F contain text entries; while D and H are numeric. Column J consists of formulas that multiply the entry in column H by the variable cell MARKUP. The numeric cells each have their own format. All the columns are separated by a narrow dividing column that holds a dashed line—columns C, E, G, and I.

To enter a new record, you can insert a row at the <END> row. Unfortunately, the new row would not be formatted as the rows above it are, nor would it have the vertical dashed line in the divider columns. The formula in column J would also be absent. The quickest way around these obstacles is to create a template row that has all the necessary pieces of a typical row in the database. Figure 10.3 shows how this is done, and also contains a short macro to automate the process of inserting a new record.

A new row has been inserted above the <END> row. But notice that it already has the divider columns filled in, and the formula in column J is also present. Each cell has the proper format; you can see the format for cell J16 in the control panel. The trick resides in the range BLANK_ROW, B2..J2, the blank template row. It is an exact copy of a typical row in the database, but

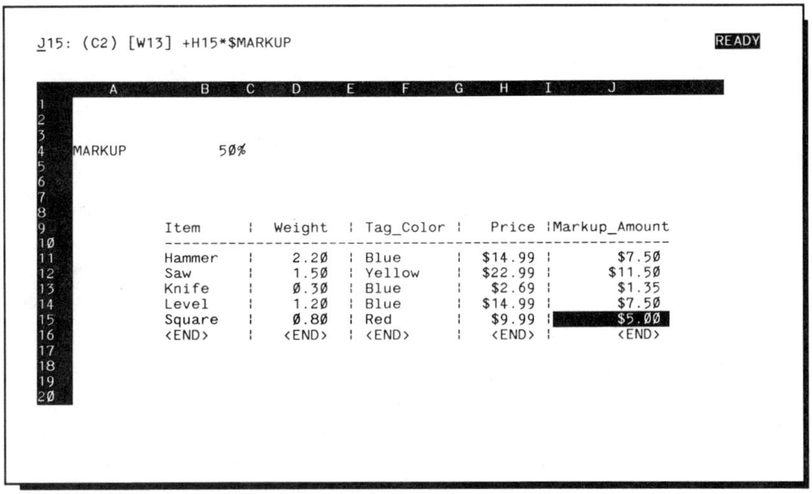

```
J15: (C2) [W13] +H15*$MARKUP                                    READY

         A        B    C    D    E    F    G    H    I        J
1
2
3
4  MARKUP          50%
5
6
7
8
9      Item     !  Weight  ! Tag_Color  !   Price !Markup_Amount
10     ----------------------------------------------------------
11     Hammer   !   2.20   ! Blue       ! $14.99 !      $7.50
12     Saw      !   1.50   ! Yellow     ! $22.99 !     $11.50
13     Knife    !   0.30   ! Blue       !  $2.69 !      $1.35
14     Level    !   1.20   ! Blue       ! $14.99 !      $7.50
15     Square   !   0.80   ! Red        !  $9.99 !      $5.00
16     <END>    !          ! <END>      ! <END>  !     <END>
17
18
19
20
```

Figure 10.2 ◆ *Restricting the range of the data*

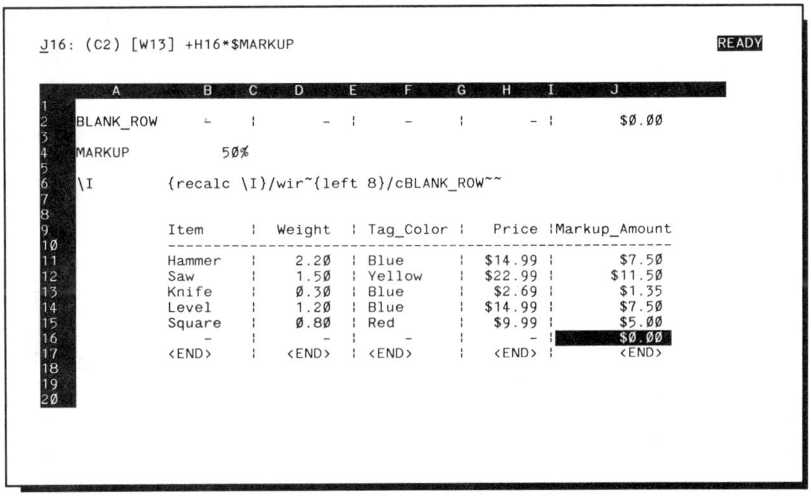

```
J16: (C2) [W13] +H16*$MARKUP                                    READY

         A        B    C    D    E    F    G    H    I        J
1
2  BLANK_ROW    └   !      -  !    -    !     -  !       $0.00
3
4  MARKUP          50%
5
6  \I          {recalc \I}/wir~{left 8}/cBLANK_ROW~~
7
8
9      Item     !  Weight  ! Tag_Color  !   Price !Markup_Amount
10     ----------------------------------------------------------
11     Hammer   !   2.20   ! Blue       ! $14.99 !      $7.50
12     Saw      !   1.50   ! Yellow     ! $22.99 !     $11.50
13     Knife    !   0.30   ! Blue       !  $2.69 !      $1.35
14     Level    !   1.20   ! Blue       ! $14.99 !      $7.50
15     Square   !   0.80   ! Red        !  $9.99 !      $5.00
16     -        !     -    !    -       !    -   !      $0.00
17     <END>    !          ! <END>      ! <END>  !     <END>
18
19
20
```

Figure 10.3 ◆ *Inserting a new row into a database*

without any data. A centered hyphen (-) has been entered into each of the empty data cells to serve later as a reminder that no data has yet been entered. When a new row is inserted into the database, this template row can be copied to the new location, which has been done in row 16. The Lotus Copy command copies not only the cell contents, but also its format.

In this case, the new row was inserted on the <END> row, but it could have been inserted anywhere in the database.

The process of inserting and copying the new row is short, but it can be made even shorter with a macro. The simplest macro would just insert the row and copy the template row:

```
/wir ~ /cBLANK_ROW ~ ~
```

It is especially important that the cell pointer be in the first column of the input range before BLANK_ROW is copied, otherwise it will be copied to the wrong cells in the row. The preceding macro cannot guarantee this, and it would be up to the user to invoke it only while in column B, the first column in INPUT1.

The macro \I in Figure 10.3 puts the cell pointer in the first column of the input range; it will work correctly in any database at any location in the worksheet. In the example, the macro was invoked with the cell pointer in column J, so the cell pointer had to be moved eight cells to the left:

```
{recalc \I}/wir ~ {left 8}/cBLANK_ROW ~ ~
```

Although the displayed macro appears to be short, it is actually built from a single, typically robust string formula, which is broken into several lines here:

```
+"{recalc \I}/wir ~"
&@if(@cellpointer("col")<@cell("col",INPUT1),
  "{right ","{left ")
&@string(@cellpointer("col") – @cell("col",INPUT1),0)
&"}/cBLANK_ROW ~ ~"
```

The first command recalculates the macro itself to update the @cellpointer functions which result in the cell pointer's address. Then it inserts a new row. This is followed by an @if function that determines where the cell pointer is in relation to the first column of the range INPUT1. If the cell pointer is to the left of the column, it returns the string {right ; otherwise, it returns {left .

The next part of the formula calculates the number of columns that the cell pointer must be moved in order to be positioned at the first column of INPUT1. It turns the result into a string value and concatenates it with the result from the previous @if function. The number will be a negative number if the cell pointer is to the left of the input range in the column, but that will not affect the cell pointer movement. For example, {right −1} works the same as {right 1}. The cell pointer is therefore positioned precisely in the first column of the input range. The last part of the formula simply copies the range BLANK_ROW, and the job is done.

The macro and the template row make an effortless task of adding new records, and they ensure that each row's structure is the same. If you generally add more than one record at a time, you could modify the macro to insert more than one new row and copy the template row to all of them. The job of positioning the cell pointer in the correct column would remain the same. Only the first and last parts of the macro would need to be revised, as this example shows for adding five new rows (the periods represent the previous macro code that positions the cell pointer at the proper column):

/wir{down 4} ˜ ....../cBLANK_ROW ˜ .{down 4} ˜

◆ SEARCHING AND EXTRACTING _____

The whole purpose of structuring your data as the input range of a worksheet database is to allow records to be selected with the Data Query commands. The following sections cover each of those commands and how they affect the query process, with the emphasis on the database criterion range.

CRITERIA: DEFINING THE SELECTION PROCESS

Once the input range has been labeled with its column titles and the data has been entered into it, you can set up the criterion range to define the searches to perform. Even though the input range can include up to 256 columns, the criterion range is limited to 32 columns. Usually, this is more than enough to set the necessary search delimiters. Remember that you should use the Copy command to copy the appropriate column title from the input range to the criterion range. This guarantees that there will be no spelling differences between the two.

> **TIP ◆** *If you regularly make a standard set of searches, you should create several criterion ranges that will always be available. To make a search, just specify the corresponding criterion. Then, specify an appropriate criterion for another search. Your range names can reflect the multiple ranges, so that for a database whose data is named INPUT1 you could have three criteria named CRIT1_A, CRIT1_B, and CRIT1_C.*

Of the two different styles of criterion ranges, logical formulas will most likely be used more frequently than text or numeric characters. Logical formulas can produce some extremely complex searches, as well as refer to other cells for their comparison values. Furthermore, they can use functions or formulas to calculate their comparison value. Entering a label or numeric value, though, is generally a less complex process.

Using Text or Numeric Criteria

A typical use for a database is to keep a list of names and addresses, whether it is a client list, personal phone directory, or list of references. Figure 10.4 shows an address list that fits the structure of a Lotus database. All the columns have text entries except for the Age column, which is numeric, and the Date_Last column, which is numeric but formatted as dates. To find all records where the entry under State is CA, the criteria would simply be as shown in B15..B16.

The cell pointer will move to each of the five records that meets the selection criteria—those in rows 5, 6, 7, 9, and 10. Two fields can be included in the criteria to form an AND statement, so that the record must meet the first criterion AND the second. For example, you could expand the criterion range and include the Zip column title to limit the search to all records where State equals CA AND Zip begins with 96—a total of three records, rows 5, 7, and 10.

```
A5: [W11] 'Smithen                                                    FIND

          A          B         C            D           E    F      G      H
1
2  Last       First     Address      City        State Zip    Age  Date_Last
3  ----------------------------------------------------------------------------
4  Kool       Elwood    7 Broadway   Tumbleweed  NV   87201   43   02-Jan-91
5  Smithen    Carol     46 Over St.  Cypress     CA   96802   32   11-Jul-90
6  Cody       Calvin    12-A West St. Seaside    CA   94025   22   24-Dec-90
7  Smythe     Gerald    123 4th St.  Cypress     CA   96803   59   29-May-90
8  Black      Sue       2021 4th Ave. Hard Rock  NV   87203   32   20-Nov-89
9  Shumway    Gordon    123 I St.    Seaside     CA   94022   27   12-Nov-90
10 Sebetta    Frank     656 Miguel   Cypress     CA   96803   36   04-Aug-90
11 Kenwood    Julie     P.O. Box 455 Red Pine    WA   82027   19   13-Mar-90
12 Schnapp    Iris      23 9th Ave.  Olive Hill  WA   82033   36   27-Sep-90
13 <END>      <END>     <END>        <END>       <END><END>  <END> <END>
14
15 Criterion  State
16            CA
17
18
19
20
```

Figure 10.4 ◆ *Using a character-based criterion*

The asterisk wildcard character is used to accept any characters that follow 96 in the zip code:

State	Zip
CA	96*

⊗ **CAUTION** ◆ *Be careful when you change a criterion by using extra rows and columns. Even if the text you have entered looks correct, you will not get the expected result if you have not redefined the criterion range with the Data Query command.*

To limit the search even more, add a third column to the criteria. Selection can be limited to records where State equals CA AND Zip begins with 96 AND Age equals 32. Only one record will be found, row 5:

State	Zip	Age
CA	96*	32

The criteria can be relaxed by creating an OR relationship among its items. This is done by putting the two elements of the OR criteria on separate rows. To search for all records where State equals CA AND Zip begins with 96 OR any other records where Age equals 32, put the Age criterion on its own row. Four records will be found—three as found in the previous search for State and Zip (rows 5, 7, and 10), plus one more in the eighth row whose state happens to be NV but whose age is 32:

State	Zip	Age
CA	96*	
		32

If you are extracting the selected rows to the output range, you may want to include the dashed line below the column titles as well as the <END> row at the bottom. Adding to the criteria from the example above, which found rows 5, 7, 8, and 10, you could pull out the two extra rows with this criterion:

State	Zip	Age
CA	96*	
		32
-		
<END>		

Notice that only one hyphen had to be entered to find the repeating text-dividing line in the third row. This is because the repeating text is actually just a hyphen with the repeating label prefix; the contents of the cell is still just a hyphen.

Creating True/False, Logical Expressions

A criterion can test each record in the input range against a logical expression. Remember that a logical expression is a formula that returns 1 if it is true or 0 if the expression is false:

@pi > 3 = 1
@length("Lotus") = 4 = 0

When you use such a formula in the criterion range, you are telling Lotus to make its selection by substituting the value from the corresponding field of each record into the formula. The record is selected only if the formula tests true. Most often, the logical formula is written so that it refers to just one cell in the input range. That cell would be in the first row below the input range's column titles, and in the column where the checking will be performed. Figure 10.5 is the same database that was used in the previous example, but the criterion range has been revised.

This time, the criterion is searching the Age column for all records where Age is greater than 35. Four records will be selected—rows 4, 7, 10, and 12:

+AGE > 35

The range name AGE is cell G3, directly below the input range's column titles. The Range Name Labels Down command has previously been used to

```
B16: [W8] +AGE>35                                            EDIT
+G3>35

       A          B         C            D          E    F      G       H
1
2  Last       First     Address      City       State Zip    Age   Date_Last
3  ---------------------------------------------------------------------------
4  Kool       Elwood    7 Broadway   Tumbleweed  NV   87201   43   02-Jan-91
5  Smithen    Carol     46 Over St.  Cypress     CA   96802   32   11-Jul-90
6  Cody       Calvin    12-A West St. Seaside    CA   94025   22   24-Dec-90
7  Smythe     Gerald    123 4th St.  Cypress     CA   96803   59   29-May-90
8  Black      Sue       2021 4th Ave. Hard Rock  NV   87203   32   20-Nov-89
9  Shumway    Gordon    123 I St.    Seaside     CA   94022   27   12-Nov-90
10 Sebetta    Frank     656 Miguel   Cypress     CA   96803   36   04-Aug-90
11 Kenwood    Julie     P.O. Box 455 Red Pine    WA   82027   19   13-Mar-90
12 Schnapp    Iris      23 9th Ave.  Olive Hill  WA   82033   36   27-Sep-90
13 <END>      <END>     <END>        <END>       <END><END>   <END>   <END>
14
15 Criterion            Age
16                        0
17
18
19
20
```

Figure 10.5 ◆ *Using a logical expression in the criterion*

create range names for each cell below the titles. This allows the range names to be used when writing the logical formulas. If you look in the control panel where the logical formula is being edited, you will see that it does indeed refer to cell G3.

It is important to note that the result that is displayed by the logical expression in cell B16 in no way relates to the selection process. The formula in this example is displaying 0 because the cell it is testing, G3, does not produce a result that is true.

A logical expression may also produce a result of ERR if the cell it is testing produces an invalid result. For example, if you wanted to find all dates in the Date_Last column that were greater than 1990, you would use this formula:

@year(DATE_LAST)>90

Since cell H3, DATE_LAST, contains text, the formula would return ERR but would still select the proper records. When your logical formula displays ERR, just double-check it to be sure it is written as you intended. You can even substitute a test value into the cell it actually references to verify that it returns an appropriate result.

Note that since the formula itself refers to a specific column in the database, Age in the above example, the column title in B15 in the criterion can be any one of the titles in the database. This may seem confusing, since the title is so critical in a criterion range that uses text or a number, but in this case the formula specifies the column to search. The only requirement is that the column title used in the first row of the criterion be valid. Because the title does not affect the search, you can combine expressions under one column title by using AND or OR operators. This will be discussed later in this chapter.

The most common mistake when using logical expressions is that of referring to the wrong cell when making the logical comparison. Remember that it is always the first record of the database that is used, which is always the first row below the column titles row. Lotus will adjust the formula down the column as it checks each record. In that sense, you can think of the one formula as a shorthand expression for a series of formulas, so that Lotus is really looking at the formula in this way in the above example:

As Lotus checks	*row 3*	+G3>35
	row 4	+G4>35
	row 5	+G5>35
	row 6	+G6>35

There may be times when you want to select a record based on the value in another record, the second record being above or below the first a certain number of rows. That is the one instance where your logical expression will not refer to the first record under the column titles. In the preceding example, you could pull out all records that sit just above a record whose Age is 32 by simply adjusting the cell reference in the expression. Instead of referring to cell G3, the first record, refer to the next cell down:

+G4>35

As Lotus checks down the column, it will not look at the value in the current record's Age column, but at the one below it. If the age in that record is greater than 35, then the current record will be selected. In Figure 10.5, rows 3, 6, 9, and 11 would be selected.

Although this may seem like an odd thing to do, it can at times be quite effective, especially in a sorted database. An example later in this chapter will use this technique to select all duplicate records in the database.

When the name and address database should have only text entries under the Zip heading, any numeric entries will be virtually lost among the records. The search criterion will not be able to locate a numeric zip code when it is searching for text. With the proper criterion, though, you can quickly spot the numeric cells. All you have to do is specify any records that are numeric (assume the first record in the Zip field has the range name ZIP):

@isnumber(ZIP)

Or you might want to search for any accidental text entries within an otherwise numeric field:

@isstring(AGE)

On the subject of zip codes, here is a logical formula that can be quite handy in a name and address list with many records. If the database is sorted on the Zip field, it allows you to jump the cell pointer not just to the records with the specified zip code, but to the last one with that zip code before the zip code changes to the next higher one. If the first record (with range name ZIP for F3) lies in row 3, as in the previous examples, then this criterion would select the last record with the zip code 95602:

+ZIP="95602"#and#F4>"95602"

Of course, using a variable cell for the search string would make the process more convenient if it were to be repeated for more than one zip code.

Referencing Other Cells

A logical expression in the criterion range can refer to outside cells, or variables, just as any worksheet formula can. Some powerful selection comparisons can be made that will dynamically change as the data in the variable cells change. However, the unique structure of the worksheet database can create many hurdles to the mixture of logical expressions and outside cell references.

To jump most of these hurdles, there is one and only one rule to remember when referring to other cells from within a criterion formula. As Lotus compares the formula against each record in the input range, it *adjusts* any cell references in the formula to the row position of each record. As you write the formula, you must decide whether a cell reference should be made absolute ($B$9) so it will not adjust, partially absolute (B$9 or $B9), or not absolute at all (B9).

The more common situation is a reference to a variable cell that is not within or otherwise associated with the database. For example, you could select records by date by referring to a variable cell that contained a valid Lotus date. Look at Figure 10.6, which is the previous names and addresses database. This time, the formula within the criterion range, cell B16, is selecting all dates greater than or equal to the date in the cell named CUTOFF_DATE:

+DATE_LAST> = $CUTOFF_DATE

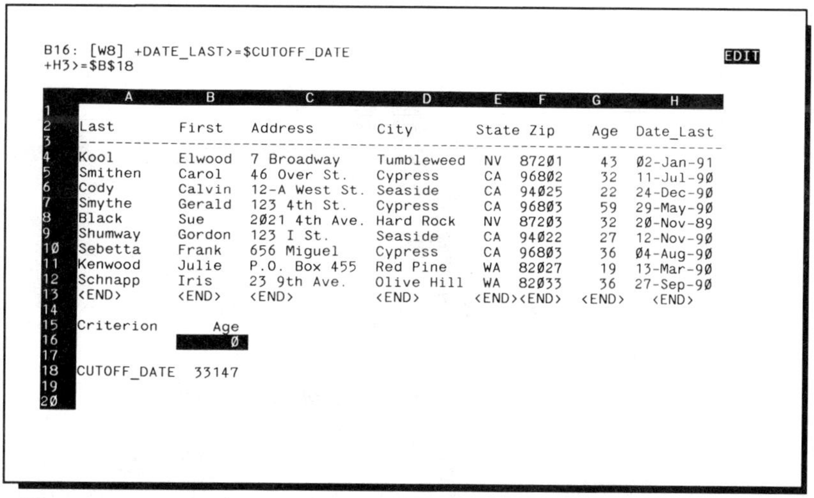

Figure 10.6 ◆ *Making an absolute reference to other cells in a logical expression in the criterion*

This formula is being edited, so you can see its actual cell references in the edit window. The cell CUTOFF_DATE, which has not been given a date format, contains a standard @date function that returns the date October 1, 1990.

The criterion formula simply compares the first cell in the DATE_LAST column against an absolute reference to the date in CUTOFF_DATE. Note that even though the Age column title is still being used in the criterion, it does not affect the workings of the search, now in the DATE_LAST column. The selection process is based solely on the logical expression. Using the date in CUTOFF_DATE, rows 4, 6, and 9 would be chosen.

Were the formula written without an absolute reference to CUTOFF_DATE, all of the records in the database would be chosen. This is because the formula would adjust as each record was checked; the second record would be compared against the empty cell B19, the third against B20 (which is also empty), and so on. Normally, the outside references are always absolute.

There are times, though, when you will want the formula to adjust its cell references. This is usually the case when you are referring to cells within the input range, and this technique allows you to select all records that have duplicates.

The database used in the previous example has had two records partially duplicated and has then been sorted using the Last field as the primary sort key, as shown in Figure 10.7. Because of the sorting, the duplicates can be seen one above the other—the duplication errors stand out clearly. However, in a large database you might not easily spot doubles among the records. But you could find them by writing a simple formula in the criterion to compare each record to the one below it.

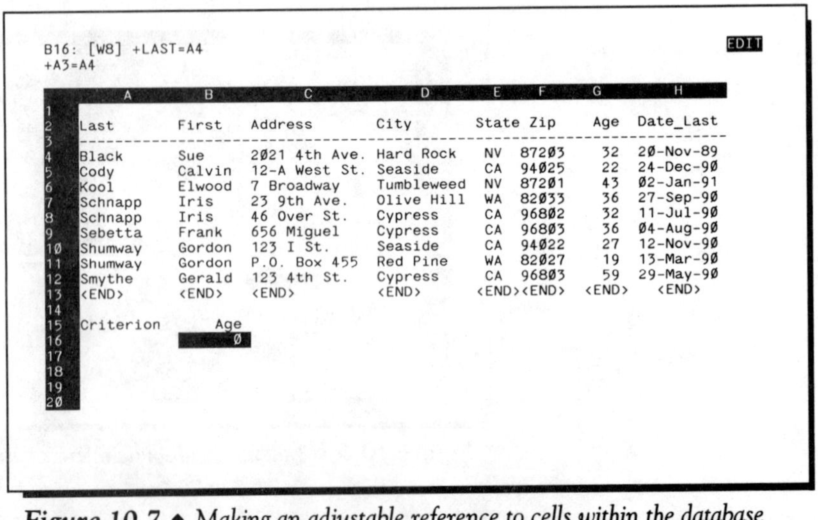
B16: [W8] +LAST=A4
+A3=A4
EDIT

	A	B	C	D	E	F	G	H
1								
2	Last	First	Address	City	State	Zip	Age	Date_Last
3	----------	----------	----------	----------	----------	----------	----------	----------
4	Black	Sue	2021 4th Ave.	Hard Rock	NV	87203	32	20-Nov-89
5	Cody	Calvin	12-A West St.	Seaside	CA	94025	22	24-Dec-90
6	Kool	Elwood	7 Broadway	Tumbleweed	NV	87201	43	02-Jan-91
7	Schnapp	Iris	23 9th Ave.	Olive Hill	WA	82033	36	27-Sep-90
8	Schnapp	Iris	46 Over St.	Cypress	CA	96802	32	11-Jul-90
9	Sebetta	Frank	656 Miguel	Cypress	CA	96803	36	04-Aug-90
10	Shumway	Gordon	123 I St.	Seaside	CA	94022	27	12-Nov-90
11	Shumway	Gordon	P.O. Box 455	Red Pine	WA	82027	19	13-Mar-90
12	Smythe	Gerald	123 4th St.	Cypress	CA	96803	59	29-May-90
13	<END>	<END>	<END>	<END>	<END>	<END>	<END>	<END>
14								
15	Criterion	Age						
16		0						
17								
18								
19								
20								

Figure 10.7 ◆ *Making an adjustable reference to cells within the database*

Here is the criterion formula in B16:

+ LAST = A4

Its actual cell addresses show up in the edit window. It compares the cell LAST, A3, to the cell below it, A4, without using absolute references. So as Lotus checks each record, it compares it to the one directly below it, adjusting the formula for each new record. In this case, the logical expression is comparing strings and is not case-sensitive. If you wanted to look for exact matches where the use of capital letters counts, you would have to use the @exact function:

@exact(LAST,A4)

Of course, the criterion in this example compares only the names in the Last field. There are many people who have the same last name, and you would not consider those records to be duplicates. But the odds of their having both the same first and last names are a lot slimmer. The criterion can therefore be made more restrictive by also checking the First field:

+ LAST = A4#and#FIRST = B4

Depending on how far you must limit the duplication checking, the criterion can be expanded to cover as many fields as you need:

+ LAST = A4#and#FIRST = B4#and#ADDRESS = C4#and#CITY = D4

Duplication of records is one of the most common sources of database problems, but because of typographical differences when the records are entered, two records may be duplicates but will not be exactly the same—the comparisons used so far will be too restrictive to find them. If you suspect that there may be several versions of some records, make sure the database is sorted on the fields you wish to check, and then relax the selection formula and search for only a few matching characters:

@left(LAST,3) = @left(A4,3)

What happens if a reference to a cell within the database is made absolute? The preceding example serves as a good model. You could write the formula using absolute references:

+ $LAST = $A$4

But the formula would never adjust and the comparison would never look at any other cells. If the formula were true, and the name in cell A3 was the same as the one in A4, then every record would be selected because the statement would always be true. If the formula were false, then no records would be selected. You can see that, in general, cell addresses in a criterion formula should be absolute if they refer to cells outside the database, and relative if they refer to cells within the database.

Taking the Search into a Cell

So far, when searching for text, the text criterion has looked at the first characters in each field when checking for a match. Wildcards can serve as a substitute for unknown characters, but you cannot search for characters that appear within a string, an unknown number of spaces from its start.

However, there is a technique that performs just such an internal search, and it is one of those tricks you won't discover until you have experimented with Lotus into the wee hours. Figure 10.8 demonstrates the problem and the solution.

The small database in the range A9..B15 contains several records with the last name of Jones. There are two sets of criteria: a text criterion in D2..D3, and a logical expression in D5..D6.

When using the text criterion, jones*, only one record will be located, the one in row 12. It is written with its last name first so that Jones makes up the first part of the Name field. None of the other records that has Jones as a last name will be found, because each has its first name first and the last name is buried within the field.

```
D6: [W1Ø] @FIND($F$6,NAME,Ø)+1                                    EDIT
@FIND($F$6,A1Ø,Ø)+1

                A            B        C        D        E        F
1
2   Text criterion will find 1 record    ->       Name
3                                                  jones*
4
5   @find criterion will find 4 records ->         Name
6                                                      7             Jones
7
8
9               Name              Age
1Ø  Susan Jones                   31
11  Terry Winn                    19
12  Jones, Ron                    33
13  Carol Pilz Jones              37
14  Alan Swank                    41
15  Ron Jones, Jr.                16
16
17
18
19
2Ø
```

Figure 10.8 ◆ *Selecting records based on an internal character string*

The second criterion, however, can dig into each record and find the characters that the first criterion could not. It is built from the @find function, and it uses the label in the variable cell F6 as its source string:

@find($F$6,NAME,0) + 1

Again, you can see all of its actual cell references in the edit window. All records that have any occurrence of the string Jones will be selected—rows 10, 12, 13, and 15.

This is a curious criterion formula because it is not a logical expression and there is no explicit comparison being made. You may wonder why the @find function has an extra +1 added to it. This allows the search to succeed even when the search string occupies the first character in the field, as in row 12. In that case, the @find function evaluates to 0, and without the additional 1, the 0 would indicate a failed search and the record would not be selected. By using the variable cell for the search string, you can quickly type in the text and find it anywhere within the field being searched.

You should note that this is one of those formulas that returns ERR if the label in the first record of the database, A10 in Figure 10.8, does not contain the search string. As usual, you should not let this bother you. Just be sure that the formula was written as intended.

OUTPUT: STORING THE SELECTED RECORDS

The first row of the output range may contain any of the column titles from the input range. Once the criterion is written, executing the Extract command will copy from all matching records those fields that are listed in the output range. For example, if Last (name) were the only field in the output range, only the data for that column would be extracted. This allows you to select just the fields you need from the input range.

Like the criterion range, the output range is limited to a maximum of 32 fields. Although this is usually more than enough, there is a simple way to produce more than 32 extracted fields; the method will be shown shortly.

The number of rows in the output range is determined in one of two ways. You can specify a range of rows, from the column titles down through the last row you need, and Lotus will use no more than that. If there are too many selected records to fit in those rows, Lotus will give you the *Too many records for output range* error message, and will copy only as many as will fit in the range.

The most flexible method of defining the output range is to simply specify the single row that contains the column titles. Using just that row, Lotus will take as many rows as it needs for the selected records, all the way to the bottom of the worksheet if need be.

⊗ **CAUTION** ◆ *This is a very important caution. Before the selected records are extracted, Lotus always deletes any entries within the output range. With a one-line output range, data will be deleted all the way to the bottom of the worksheet. Even if your one-line output range is in the first row of the worksheet and only a few records are extracted to it, a cell that contains data in row 8,192 in any of the output columns will nonetheless be blank after the Extract command is given.*

The advantage to this is that you do not have to limit the range for the selected records, nor do you first have to erase the output range in preparation for new records—Lotus does that for you. To avoid the danger of losing data simply put the output range below or away from any other ranges in the worksheet, and let it extend down as far as it needs to. Recall the worksheet layout described in Chapter 3, which outlined the benefits of separating the various data areas of the worksheet.

One frequent point of confusion is the relationship among the column titles in the three database ranges. The only link between the three is the input range. Any column titles used in the other two ranges must also appear within the input range, otherwise they will be ignored. The 1 to 32 columns of the output range can include any of those from the input range, and in any order. The criterion range will also be 1 to 32 columns taken from the input range, but those columns need not appear in the output range, nor must they be in the same order as those in the output range:

- ◆ Input range supplies the data to be searched

- ◆ Criterion range sets the search parameters

- ◆ Output range contains the fields that should be extracted from the selected records

Here is a simple solution for those occasions when you need more than 32 columns in the output range. For example, if your input range has 40 columns and you want to extract data from all of them, just perform two extract operations into two contiguous output ranges. The first range could be named OUT-PUT1_A and would have up to 32 columns, and the other could be named OUTPUT1_B and could have the remaining 8 columns of the input range. Here is a macro that would automate the two extractions:

```
/dqriINPUT1 ˜ cCRIT1 ˜ oOUTPUT1_A ˜ eoOUTPUT1_B ˜ eq
```

There may be times when you will want to extract the columns of divider lines between fields, but you will encounter the dilemma of those 1-character-wide columns being without column titles. The solution is simple: give each of them a unique title, but use the Hidden format. Copy the titles to the output range as usual, and the dividing columns will be extracted. You may want to use short titles for the divider columns, such as COL_B, COL_D, or COL_F for simplicity.

Finally, remember that any extracted data requires disk space when the worksheet is saved. If you will not be needing that data, erase the output range before saving.

> ★ **TRICK ◆** *You should remove any cell formatting that is carried over with extracted records. To clean up the entire output range, whether it is limited in rows or not, just change the criterion to one that selects no records. Give the Extract command one last time, and the entire range will be wiped clean. The data is not only erased, but the cell formats are also removed, just as though the rows were deleted. This operation can save quite a bit of time and leave your worksheet several pounds lighter.*

FIND: LOCATING THE SELECTED RECORDS

The Data Query Find command is much like a cell pointer "goto" command. With the input and criterion ranges set, selecting Find will jump the cell pointer to the first record that matches the criterion. The cell pointer expands to highlight all columns of the record. From there, it can be jumped to the next record by pressing the ↓ key or back up a record with the ↑ key. Pressing the End key jumps to the last row of the database, and pressing Home jumps to the first row.

By using the → or ← key, you can move the active cell pointer (with the blinking cursor) to any field in the database, allowing you to view the columns that might otherwise be off the screen as you move up or down the selected records.

A great feature of the Data Query commands is the ability to revise a selected record during the Find operation. The field under the cell pointer can be changed either by typing in a new entry, or by pressing F2 {edit} to change the existing one. This greatly simplifies the normal routines within the database, and makes finding and revising the data a one-step operation.

★ **TRICK ◆** *Here is a trick that often goes unnoticed. You probably know that function key F7, the {query} key, repeats the most recently executed Query command, whether it was Find, Extract, Unique, or Delete.*

But did you know that during a Find operation you can leave the cell pointer on the highlighted (found) record simply by pressing the F7 {query} key? You will be returned to the READY mode at the current record, which makes Data Query Find a true "goto" command.

If you are making extensive revisions to a database, such as searching and editing, changing the criterion, searching again and leaving the cell pointer on a record for more thorough revisions, you may want to split the display with the Worksheet Windows command to make the process easier. Position the criterion cells in one window, and put the input range in the other. Before you execute a Find command, put the cell pointer in the window with the input range where it can jump to the selected records and, if necessary, where it can be left for further editing. Then, a simple press of the F6 {window} key will put the cell pointer back into the first window, where a new search criterion can be specified. You can write a short macro to make the jumps even easier:

{window}{query}{?}{query}

EXTRACT: MAKING COPIES OF THE SELECTED RECORDS

If you do not have an output range defined, you cannot extract any records. That may be obvious, but if you get a beep when you try to extract, it may not be because there are no records to be found. Make sure you have defined all the ranges.

The Extract command copies the selected records to the output range, but not in the manner of the Copy command. It actually performs a Range Value operation—formulas are not duplicated, only their current values are. Along with the values, any cell format is also duplicated, so that the numbers are displayed in the same style.

✓ **TIP ◆** *You should always use the Find command at least once before performing an Extract, Unique, or, especially, a Delete command for the first time with an untested criterion. This can save you from some overwhelming consequences. If the criterion were* *written incorrectly, every record in the database could be copied to the output range, or even worse, deleted from the database. Use the Find command first to get a clear indication of whether the criterion is working as planned.*

Remember that only the fields shown in the output range will be copied from the selected records that match the search criterion, and those fields need not be in the same order of occurrence.

DELETE: REMOVING THE SELECTED RECORDS

When you invoke the Data Query Delete command, you are given another menu with the option of canceling your request. This is to ensure that you really do want to delete all the records that match the search criterion. In this spirit, you should always use caution when deleting records.

The Delete command can produce some quick results when maintenance is required in the database. For instance, to remove all records whose entry in DATE_LAST is beyond a year old, use this criterion:

```
+DATE_LAST<@now-365
```

You could first extract the records to the output range, where they could be saved to disk in a worksheet for old records. Then, using the same criterion, the records could be deleted from the worksheet, leaving only the newer records.

When records are deleted the result is similar to, but not quite the same as, the result of the Worksheet Delete Row command. It is similar to it in that the rows are actually removed from the input range, and that range is contracted by as many records as were removed. But the rows have not really been deleted.

Data cells in the same row as a deleted record, but outside the input range, will not be affected in any way by the deletion. Their position before and after the Delete command will be the same. The data input range will contract, but a range name that defined it will not adjust to the new size of that range, as it would if records had been deleted with the Worksheet Delete Row command. Even a range name that names a row that is deleted will not be affected by its removal, and will still refer to the exact same row.

Remember also that the entire record will be gone, not just the field or fields you have used in the criterion range.

UNIQUE: CHOOSING ONLY UNIQUE RECORDS

The Unique command can be powerful, because it can serve as the basis for more extensive database reporting. Of the records that match the criterion, only one of any duplicate records will be selected and copied to the output range.

The Unique command is a bit more dependent on the fields of the output range than is the Extract command. Both of these will copy data only from those fields that are listed in the output range, but the Unique command also uses those fields to decide whether a selected record is unique.

For example, if every field in the input range is represented in the output range, then all the fields of one record would have to match those of another before it would be excluded from the Unique command's selection as not being unique. If just one field is shown in the output range, then only that field will be used to judge whether a record is unique from all those already selected. Figure 10.9 provides an example of how this works. This is a simplified checking account worksheet, with columns for pertinent information on each check. The column named Code contains check-category codes that represent different expense classifications, such as mortgage payments, gas, electricity, food, taxes, or automobile expenses. You would probably have a column for description, too. The checks have been entered consecutively by date, with a random sprinkling of the check codes.

The criterion range, E1..E2, contains a formula to select all entries in the Code field:

+CODE>0

The actual address of CODE can be seen in the edit window.

The output range consists of the one-row title at G1, but as you can see, not every record has been extracted. Instead, the Unique command has extracted just one representative code for any code in that field. For example, although there are three instances of the code 8 in the input range, just one has been extracted. Notice that the extracted codes are in the same order that they appear in the database, but just one of each.

At this point, you have a clear representation of the variety of data in that field of the database. You also have the items necessary to create a table of subtotals for each category. When the Data Query Unique command is combined with the @d data functions, a data-summary sheet can be produced that is a snap to construct and produces an excellent data reporting tool. The data functions will be discussed next, followed by the reporting technique.

```
E2: +CODE>Ø                                              EDIT
+C5>Ø
        A         B         C        D        E        F        G       H
  1                                                   Code              Code
  2                                                     Ø                 1
  3                                                                       3
  4    Date    Check_#    Code    Amount                                 11
  5    --------------------------------------------                       8
  6    Ø1-Sep     521       1     8Ø5.ØØ                                   5
  7    Ø7-Sep     522       3      25.45                                   9
  8    1Ø-Sep     523      11      66.16
  9    1Ø-Sep     524       3      12.66
 1Ø    22-Sep     525       8      15.32
 11    24-Sep     526       5     142.ØØ
 12    25-Sep     527       5      49.76
 13    25-Sep     528       8      42.15
 14    29-Sep     529      11     154.91
 15    Ø1-Oct     53Ø       1     8Ø5.ØØ
 16    Ø2-Oct     531       8      32.16
 17    Ø3-Oct     532       5      52.6Ø
 18    Ø6-Oct     533       9      21.5Ø
 19    Ø6-Oct     534      11      77.Ø9
 2Ø
```

Figure 10.9 ◆ *Selecting records with the Unique command*

◆ *TAPPING THE POWER OF THE @d DATA FUNCTIONS*

The discussion of the data functions was not included in Chapter 8 because they are more closely linked to worksheet databases then to @ functions in general. These functions do not just work on a range; they select records based on a criterion and perform their work on only those records. For their power and flexibility, the data functions are perhaps the most underused of all the @ functions. As explained in Chapter 8, there are several reasons for this.

First, the data functions must operate on data that is structured as a database, with an input and criterion range. This immediately creates a basic source of confusion for those who are not fluent with the worksheet database. They also refer to a column of the database by its offset number, another source of confusion. Finally, if the data in the database is not organized in an efficient manner with consistent spelling, the data functions will work no better than the Data Query commands would under those circumstances.

After the discussion of the database structure, ranges, and commands, the data functions should be easy to master, and their value will be quite apparent.

WRITING AN @d FUNCTION

All data functions are built upon three components. These include an input and criterion range that are structured exactly like those ranges in a worksheet database, and an offset number of the column in the input range from which to summarize the result. With those three simple pieces, some strong statistical analyses can be made. The name and address worksheet used previously provides a quick demonstration of their power.

Figure 10.10 is the familiar name and address database, but this time there are no Data Query commands involved. There is still a range named INPUT1, A2..H13, and a criterion, CRIT1, in the two cells B15..B16. There are two other criterion ranges that will be discussed in a moment.

Look at the highlighted cell, G15. It contains the data average function, @davg:

@davg($INPUT1,6,$CRIT1)

The function is using the database range INPUT1, and it is averaging the ages in column G, which is offset six columns from the first column of the data range. It is selecting records to include in the average based on the criterion in the range CRIT1. If you look at CRIT1, you will see that the data function is averaging the ages of all those who live in California (CA).

Below the first function (cell G15) are two others that average the ages for people from Washington (WA) and Nevada (NV). The formulas are all the same

```
G15: [W6] @DAVG($INPUT1,6,$CRIT1)                                      READY

           A         B         C            D          E    F      G      H
 1
 2    Last      First     Address      City       State Zip    Age  Date_Last
 3    ---------------------------------------------------------------------------
 4    Kool      Elwood    7 Broadway   Tumbleweed NV   87201   43   02-Jan-91
 5    Smithen   Carol     46 Over St.  Cypress    CA   96802   32   11-Jul-90
 6    Cody      Calvin    12-A West St. Seaside   CA   94025   22   24-Dec-90
 7    Smythe    Gerald    123 4th St.  Cypress    CA   96803   59   29-May-90
 8    Black     Sue       2021 4th Ave. Hard Rock NV   87203   32   20-Nov-89
 9    Shumway   Gordon    123 I St.    Seaside    CA   94022   27   12-Nov-90
10    Sebetta   Frank     656 Miguel   Cypress    CA   96803   36   04-Aug-90
11    Kenwood   Julie     P.O. Box 455 Red Pine   WA   82027   19   13-Mar-90
12    Schnapp   Iris      23 9th Ave.  Olive Hill WA   82033   36   27-Sep-90
13    <END>     <END>     <END>        <END>      <END><END>  <END>  <END>
14
15    CRIT1 ->  State         Average age of those in CA -  35.2
16              CA                                  "        NV -  37.5
17    CRIT2 ->  State                               "        WA -  27.5
18              NV
19    CRIT3 ->  State
20              WA
```

Figure 10.10 ◆ *Analyzing a database with the data functions*

except for the criterion to which they refer. CRIT2 is used in the second formula, and the last formula averages the age of those in Washington, using CRIT3:

@davg($INPUT1,6,$CRIT3)

The advantages of these data functions are many. You could change any of the State entries, and the formulas would recalculate based on the selection of the new records. Deleting a record would never cause one of the functions to result in ERR, since they do not address any individual rows in the database. Once you have written a data function for a particular data range, writing others should be even simpler since the input and criterion ranges have already been established.

For example, to calculate the oldest date in the Date_Last column for the state of California, you would change the function to @dmin and change the column number to seven. The result would be 29-May-90.

@dmin($INPUT1,7,CRIT1)

To count the number of records whose state is Washington, use this formula, which refers to CRIT3 and counts all records whose state is WA. Its result would be 2:

@dcount($INPUT1,7,CRIT3)

Notice that the column number in the formula, 7, was left unchanged from the previous example. The column being counted is not necessarily relevant, as long as it is sure to be occupied for a selected record. If one of the Washington records did not have an entry in the Date column, then the count would have been 1.

You should try to use range names for the input and criterion ranges, just as you would with the ranges for the Data Query commands; the formulas become much more readable, too. If you are going to be copying a data function to many cells in a row to summarize those columns, you may want to build them to take advantage of a few shortcuts. First, always make the input range an absolute reference, since you will most likely always refer to precisely that range, as in the preceding example.

If the functions will be using the same criterion, then you should also make the criterion an absolute reference. Watch out for the offset number, though, as you can get into difficulties if you enter the offset column as a hard number in each function. First, you might type it in wrong by the time you count out to column 23 of the input range, and you might not recognize the fact that the functions are no longer summarizing the proper column. Moreover, if you ever insert or delete columns in the input range, the offset numbers in the functions will no longer be valid because the input range has expanded or contracted.

For an easy and flexible solution, look at Figure 10.11. This database has three numeric columns, C, D, and E, each of which has an @dsum function below it in row 12. Those functions are summing all the records in the input range named DATA, A1..E9, that match the criterion in CRIT1, B15..B16. In this case, the records being summed are those with a code that begins with G. If the formulas had been written in the style used previously, with hard numbers for the column offset, the one below column C would look like this:

@dsum($DATA,2,$CRIT1)

Both the input and criterion ranges would be made absolute. This prevents them from adjusting when the first formula in C12 is copied across that row.

But the trick is to allow the column offset number to adjust to any changes in the worksheet. So instead of entering a hard number, the @cell function is first used to return the column number of the column that should be summed, in this case the column in which the @dsum function resides:

@cell("col",C11..C11)

In Figure 10.11, this is column 3—the @cell function considers column A to be 1, B to be 2, and so on. Then, the column number of the first column of the input range DATA is calculated:

@cell("col",$DATA)

```
C12: (F2) @DSUM($DATA,@CELL("col",C11..C11)-@CELL("col",$DATA),$CRIT1)          READY

         A           B          C           D           E          F          G
1   Item        Code       Wholesale   Retail      Profit
2   -----------------------------------------------------------------
3   Hammer      G12             7.00      12.00        5.00
4   Saw         A16            18.00      22.00        4.00
5   Chisel      E22             4.00       8.00        4.00
6   Sledge      G70             9.00      18.00        9.00
7   Compass     A14             4.00       6.00        2.00
8   Ax          G10             3.00       7.00        4.00
9   <END>       <END>       <END>       <END>       <END>
10
11
12  Total for code G         19.00      37.00       18.00
13
14
15    CRIT1 =>   Code
16         >     G*
17
18
19
20
```

Figure 10.11 ◆ *Writing data functions that are easy to copy*

When the @cell formula refers to a range, such as DATA, it always uses the upper left cell of the range. This happens to be column 1 in this worksheet. Notice that the reference to DATA was made absolute so that the formula can be copied to other cells and still refer to the same cell.

The result is then subtracted from the column number that is to be summed, which was calculated previously, to produce the column *offset* number of the function's current column, 2. That number is then used in the @dsum function, shown here split into two parts:

```
@dsum($DATA,@cell("col",C11..C11)
 – @cell("col",$DATA),$CRIT1)
```

Written this way, the function can be copied to any column and it will always have the correct offset number for that column. You could delete or insert columns and rows and each formula would still return the proper result for its current column.

Next, you will see how the data functions can be combined with the Data Table command to produce an excellent database reporting tool.

◆ *REPORTING ON THE DATABASE* _____

If you were to sort the database in Figure 10.9 using the Code field as the primary sort key, you could view the data in groups by code. You could then put in some @sum functions to total each category of code. But this reporting procedure would be time-consuming, even if macro-driven. Furthermore, it would have to be repeated each time you wanted to produce the totals, as checks would have been added to the list and the size of each category would have changed.

A more efficient means of reporting can be built upon the output range that was produced with the Unique command. This technique will be demonstrated using the data in the output range, but the information there could easily be copied elsewhere to provide a more efficient or viewable location.

First, the output range is sorted to put the codes in numerical order, as you can see in the range G2..G7 in Figure 10.12. Then, an @dsum function is written in cell H1, which is one column to the right and one cell above the first entry in the output range. That cell has been given a Hidden format, since it does not need to be seen, but it still appears in the control panel. (Note that in Release 2.2, the cell contents would not appear in the control panel when Global Protection is enabled.) This function will form the basis for a *data table*, which will produce a total for each of the codes in the output range. Figure 10.12 shows the final result after the data table has been calculated.

```
H1: (H) @DSUM(A4..D19,3,E1..E2)                              READY

          A        B        C        D       E      F     G       H
1                                            Code              Code
2                                             Ø               1  1,610.00
3                                                             3     38.11
4      Date    Check_#    Code    Amount                      5    244.36
5     -----------------------------------                     8     89.63
6     Ø1-Sep     521        1     8Ø5.ØØ                      9     21.50
7     Ø7-Sep     522        3      25.45                     11    298.16
8     1Ø-Sep     523       11      66.16                          --------
9     1Ø-Sep     524        3      12.66                         2,3Ø1.76
1Ø    22-Sep     525        8      15.32
11    24-Sep     526        5     142.ØØ
12    25-Sep     527        5      49.76
13    25-Sep     528        8      42.15
14    29-Sep     529       11     154.91
15    Ø1-Oct     53Ø        1     8Ø5.ØØ
16    Ø2-Oct     531        8      32.16
17    Ø3-Oct     532        5      52.6Ø
18    Ø6-Oct     533        9      21.5Ø
19    Ø6-Oct     534       11      77.Ø9
2Ø
```

Figure 10.12 ◆ *Producing a database report built on the data from the Unique command*

The @dsum function uses the database input range, A4..D19, as its own input range. It sums the column that has an offset of 3, which is the Amount column (remember that the first column in the input range has an offset of 0). Finally, it uses the same criterion cells that were used for the extract, E1..E2, as its criterion. But this formula will simply total all the entries in the Amount field, since all records are being selected by the criterion. The Data Table command will produce the actual subtotals for each code.

This is a one-way data table, as there will be just one input cell for a variable. The data table covers the range G1..H7, which includes all the codes plus the column and row with the @dsum function. The input cell is E2, the cell below the column title in the criterion range.

With that information, the Data Table command substitutes each code in column G into the input cell E2, calculates the @dsum based on the new criterion, and places the result next to that code. The numbers you see next to each code are the result of that process being repeated automatically by Lotus for each code. Because both the Data Query Unique and Data Table routines are commands, these subtotals are hard numbers and will not automatically update when new checks are added to the list.

At the least, the Data Table command would have to be repeated; the F8 {table} key performs the last Table command. To be sure that all codes are represented in the list, the Unique command would of course have to be performed first. By adding a few range names to the worksheet, a macro could automate the process whenever you wanted to update the totals.

Below the subtotals, an @sum function returns a total for them all. To verify that all the codes have been represented in the table, the @sum function is written within an @if function. It compares both the sum of the table and the sum of the Amount column in the input range to be sure the totals are the same. That formula is shown here, split into two pieces:

```
@if(@round(@sum(D5..D20),2) < > @round(@sum(H2..H8),2),
    "Out of Balance!",@sum(H2..H8))
```

If the two totals are not the same, the function will result in the message *Out of Balance!*. Notice that each @sum is embedded in an @round function, with rounding to two decimal places. This ensures that any tiny internal calculation differences will not cause the @if function to act as if the sums are out of balance.

Obviously, this table could be created in a more pleasing style, and a description for each code could be placed to its left. But the reporting technique shown here can be used in countless worksheet databases, and it provides a flexible and easy-to-build reporting platform.

♦ SUMMARY

Lotus is a spreadsheet program and not a database, but you can use its database commands and functions to extend the scope of just about any data manipulation and analysis. This chapter has presented the ranges and commands of the worksheet database. You have seen practical routines for data entry, writing selection criteria, eliminating duplicates from the input range, and reporting on the database. You have learned about the database functions in light of their connection to a worksheet database.

The next chapter moves on to the subject of graphs. Presenting worksheet data in the form of a graph can provide quick glimpses into the significance of complex relationships. Three aspects of graphing are discussed: arranging the data to be graphed, using the graph commands, and printing graphs with the PrintGraph program.

Graphs That Speak
for Themselves

11

◆ ◆ ◆

THE 1-2-3 WORKSHEET IS ESSENTIALLY A TOOL FOR ANALYSIS,
and its graphs are intended to augment that activity. When Lotus was first
released, everyone considered its graphs first-rate aids to accompany reports or
oral presentations. Even though some improvements were made with the
release of Lotus 2.2, Lotus graphs are frequently not considered "presentation
quality" in most corporate settings. Their slipping status is partially a result of
changing definitions; to many people, *presentation quality* now seems to mean,
"Graphs that I have seen, but can't produce with my current software." In
fact, however, Lotus graphs are just as useful, if not as glamorous, as they've
always been.

In this chapter, the graphing process is viewed from three perspectives: the
worksheet data from which graphs are built, the graph commands that do
the building, and the PrintGraph program that produces the final product.

◆ STRUCTURING THE DATA

There is a close relationship between the layout of your worksheet data and
the success you will have when graphing it. A single graph can include as many
as 13 different worksheet ranges, all of which must contain the same number of
cells for the graph to be accurate. You can also include up to ten other worksheet cells that contain text for the graph titles and legends. (This will be covered shortly.) All of these cells must be carefully maintained to protect the
integrity of the graphs they produce.

FORMATTING THE DATA

Although you can include 13 different ranges in a graph, you need only a
single data range to produce any graph except for the xy graph (which requires
an x-axis range). Of course, that would be a pretty Spartan graph, but if you just
want a quick look at the data, that is all you need. As you add to the graph, you
can use five other data ranges, all of which are identified by the Lotus graph
command as ranges A through F.

> **TIP ◆** *There is no priority among the data ranges. The only differentiating features are each one's color, shading, or data point symbol in the graph. Therefore, you can specify your one and only data range as range D if that particular graph range has an appropriate color or shading.*

The data ranges for a graph need not be physically contiguous, even though Lotus will look at them as equivalent ranges. The linking factor among the ranges is not their location or their position to one another, but the number of cells each of them contains. The first cell in each data range always falls at the same left-hand position on the x-axis, no matter where those ranges reside in the worksheet. The last cell in each range, however, falls on the same point on the x-axis only if all the ranges have the same number of cells.

In line graphs, the data range with the largest number of occupied cells determines the working width of the graph. If the largest data range has 100 cells, then that many points will be shown on the graph. If another range has only 50 cells, then its last data point will fall on the fiftieth cell in the x-axis range. For a line or bar graph, this would be the middle of the x-axis in the graph. In an xy graph, every data point is linked to a value on the x-axis. Therefore, the number of values in the x range determines the width of the graph.

> **TIP ◆** *Since the number of cells in the graph ranges must remain consistent for a graph to do its job, it is often a good idea to keep a separate set of data just for graphing. In Chapter 3, you learned about using separate ranges for formatting printed output away from the source data. The same can be done for graphs.*
>
> *For all but the simplest of worksheets, you should not use your only set of data to build graphs. Instead, copy your data or use formulas to create a separate range for graphing, which contains all information relevant to creating a graph.*

CONDENSING AND SUMMARIZING THE DATA

If your graph data contains very large numbers, Lotus automatically divides them and shows them in thousands, millions, or as a factor of 10 raised to the appropriate power. This helps keep the numbers along an axis short and readable; the factor is shown next to the numbers for clarity, such as *Times 10E13*. You can turn off the display of the factor in the graph with the Graph Options Scale Y-Axis (or X-Axis) Indicator command.

There may be times, though, when the data in one graph spans a large range. The upper limits of the graph are so great that it simply dwarfs the smaller values, which hover close to the x-axis. To solve this visual dilemma, you can sometimes simply create more than one graph, and scale each one to effectively show its range of values. One graph might be scaled from 0 to 1000, and the other would run from 0 to 10,000,000. The graph-scaling option will be discussed a little later in this chapter.

If it is important to show the data on the same graph, you might produce three graphs. One would have all the data, although much of it would be hidden at the bottom of the graph. This graph would show you the trend that you wish to illustrate. The other two would each be scaled, as mentioned above, to display the detail of each section of the graph. There is yet another method that can provide a crucial view of data in just one graph. It uses the @log function to bring all the data into a reasonable scale.

The data used to illustrate the log graph is ideal for the job: the cumulative national debt over the last 100 years as reported by the U.S. Department of the Treasury. This is the type of information you would want to see in just one graph, with the years along the x-axis and the dollars along the y-axis. The problem is that the numbers span a tremendous range: the cumulative debt in 1987 was almost a thousand times greater than it was in 1870. Figure 11.1 shows the worksheet that will be graphed.

Column A holds the years that will form the x-axis, and column B shows the dollars. Remember that these represent the cumulative debt remaining to be

```
B4: (,Ø) [W21] 24ØØØØØØØØ                                    READY

         A              B              C           D
1       Year       Cumulative
2                     Debt
3    ----------  -------------------
4       187Ø       2,4ØØ,ØØØ,ØØØ
5       188Ø       2,ØØØ,ØØØ,ØØØ
6       189Ø       1,1ØØ,ØØØ,ØØØ
7       19ØØ       1,2ØØ,ØØØ,ØØØ
8       191Ø       1,1ØØ,ØØØ,ØØØ
9       192Ø      24,2ØØ,ØØØ,ØØØ
1Ø      193Ø      16,1ØØ,ØØØ,ØØØ
11      194Ø      5Ø,7ØØ,ØØØ,ØØØ
         A              B              C           D
19      198Ø     914,3ØØ,ØØØ,ØØØ
2Ø      1981   1,ØØ3,9ØØ,ØØØ,ØØØ
21      1982   1,142,ØØØ,ØØØ,ØØØ
22      1983   1,377,2ØØ,ØØØ,ØØØ
23      1984   1,572,3ØØ,ØØØ,ØØØ
24      1985   1,823,1ØØ,ØØØ,ØØØ
25      1986   2,125,ØØØ,ØØØ,ØØØ
26      1987   2,35Ø,ØØØ,ØØØ,ØØØ
```

Figure 11.1 ◆ *Cumulative national debt data to be graphed*

paid off. Notice that the values at the top of the list are in the low billions, and those at the bottom of the list, shown in the lower window, are in the trillions. The difference in scale becomes even more evident when the values are graphed.

As you can see in Figure 11.2, Lotus tries to scale the graph as best it can. In this case, it means dividing all the numbers by one trillion, and scaling the graph from 0.0 to 2.6. Lotus has labeled the y-axis accordingly, *Times 10E12*. Although the upward surge in the 1970s and 1980s is impressive, the values that are closer to one billion are unfortunately barely noticeable along the x-axis.

This graph is a good example of an xy graph. The years are evenly spaced along the x-axis, even though the data points are unevenly spaced; there are ten years between some points and five between others, and the last few points are consecutive years. The distinction between a line graph and an xy graph will be covered more thoroughly a little later in this chapter.

You may have noticed the one drawback to this graph: the data point identifiers along the x-axis. Since the years are values, not text, and are greater than 1000, Lotus scales them to smaller numbers. It divides them by 1000, just as it divided the large numbers along the y-axis by a trillion. Unfortunately, the

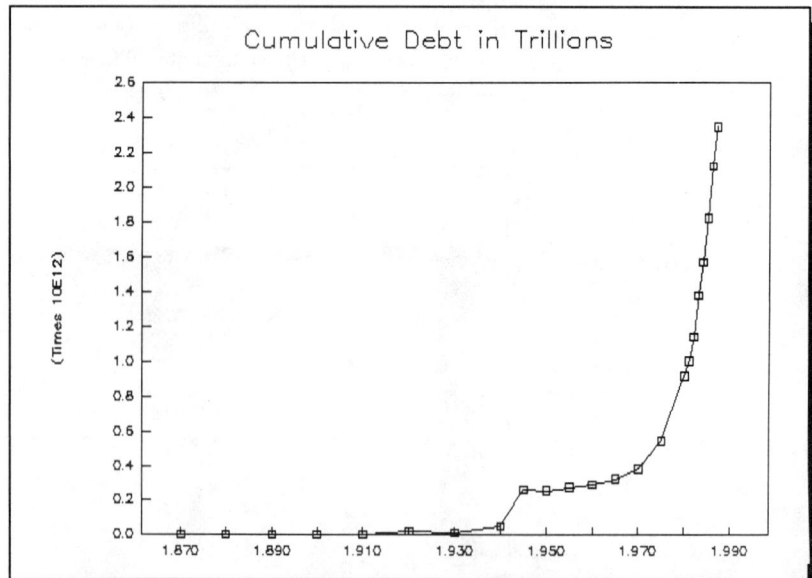

Figure 11.2 ◆ *Small numbers almost disappear in a graph that is scaled for large numbers*

results are quite unsatisfactory for displaying years and there is no manual control to turn off this scaling. Note also that Lotus date values could not be used in this case because there are years in the graph that precede 1900.

A Date format would not have helped, since Lotus does not deal with dates before 1900, and all Date formats display the date and/or month as well. So a rather simplistic solution is used: the x-axis is given a Fixed format with three decimals, making the numbers look almost like years.

Of course, this graph does leave a lasting impression, but it may not be sufficient if the values close to the x-axis need to be more closely examined. If this graph had data points for every year since 1870, the trend in those early years would perhaps be pertinent, and not being able to see them would be a real obstacle. This is where the log graph comes into play.

Using the @log function, a second column is created in the worksheet that returns the log of each value in column B, as shown in Figure 11.3. Remember that the log of a number is the power to which you would raise the value of 10 to produce the original number. The log of 100 is 2, because 10 squared is 100. The result in cell C4 (which is formatted with only one decimal) shows that 10 raised to the 9.4 power produces the number in B4. In this way, a value in the log column that is one greater than another in that column represents a number that is ten times greater than the other. That is why the number at the bottom, 12.3, which is about 3 greater than the one at the top, represents a number, cell B26, that is 1000 times greater than the one in B4.

```
C4: (F1) [W12] @LOG(B4)                                    READY
```

	A	B	C	D
1	Year	Cumulative	@log(DEBT)	
2		Debt		
3	-----	----------------	---------	
4	1870	2,400,000,000	9.4	
5	1880	2,000,000,000	9.3	
6	1890	1,100,000,000	9.0	
7	1900	1,200,000,000	9.1	
8	1910	1,100,000,000	9.0	
9	1920	24,200,000,000	10.4	
10	1930	16,100,000,000	10.2	
11	1940	50,700,000,000	10.7	

	A	B	C	D
19	1980	914,300,000,000	12.0	
20	1981	1,003,900,000,000	12.0	
21	1982	1,142,000,000,000	12.1	
22	1983	1,377,200,000,000	12.1	
23	1984	1,572,300,000,000	12.2	
24	1985	1,823,100,000,000	12.3	
25	1986	2,125,000,000,000	12.3	
26	1987	2,350,000,000,000	12.4	

Figure 11.3 ◆ *Creating a data column with the @log function*

Changing the graph data range to the log column, C, produces a graph in which all the data points are visible, since the lowest value is 9.4 and the highest is only 12.3. Figure 11.4 shows the new graph. Notice that it has had two other revisions. It is now appropriately titled *Cumulative Debt in Log Values*, and the y-axis is also titled *Log*. This ensures that the viewer will know that the relationship along the y-axis is not linear (1, 2, 3, 4, and so on), but exponential (10, 100, 1000, 10000, and so on), meaning that each increment on the y-axis is 10 times greater than the one below. The graph scale starts at 8.0, which allows the data points to extend over the better part of the graph.

In this case, manipulating the data before it was graphed produced a graph that could visually fulfill its purpose of summarizing a group of data. Note that the years in column A could serve as the x-axis while the log column could be located anywhere in the worksheet, and still serve its function as the data range. This would keep the original data available for printing or viewing.

KEEPING GRAPH TITLES IN THE WORKSHEET

Here is something that a lot of Lotus users never realize: you can enter the text for a graph title into a worksheet cell and refer to that cell in the Graph

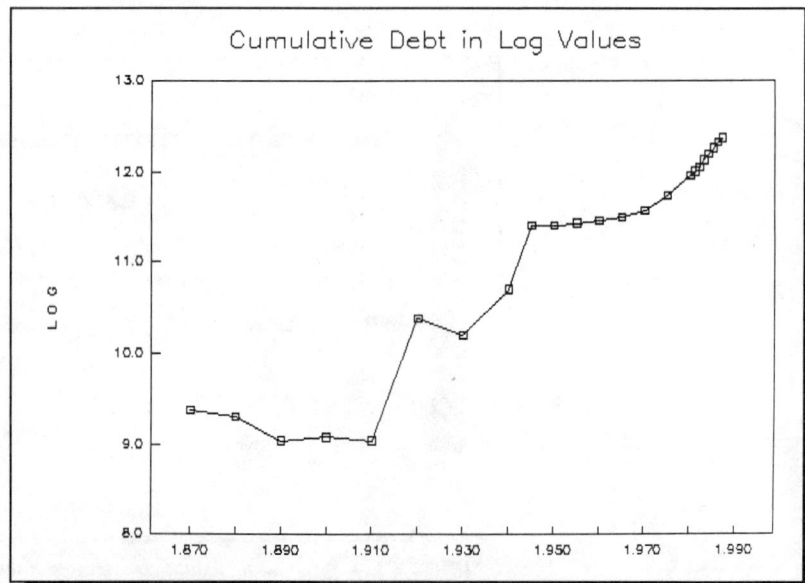

Figure 11.4 ◆ *Graphing with log functions*

Options Titles and Legends commands. At a Graph Titles command prompt, instead of typing the actual title you simply type a backslash followed by a cell address of the cell where the title is located:

\C29

Or, use a range name instead of a cell address:

\TITLE_X_AXIS

The backslash is not part of a range name; it just tells Lotus that the following text refers to a cell. This works with any of the four graph titles (first, second, x-axis and y-axis) and also for the six legends, A through F. By entering the titles directly into the worksheet, you can quickly scan the graphing range, where data pertinent to a graph is kept, and see all the graph data, including titles and legends. Otherwise, you would have to step through each graph command to see its setting, a tedious and eventually aggravating process. Moreover, you can easily change any of the titles simply by entering a new title into the proper cell.

The settings screens in Release 2.2 make graphing easier by allowing you to view all of the settings for the current graph at the same time. Don't forget that you can hide or redisplay a setting screen by pressing the Window key, F6.

The workings of these graph commands do not follow the consistent behavior of other Lotus commands, and they can be confusing as well as troublesome. This is the one set of commands in Lotus where you can specify the setting in one of two ways. You can either enter the information directly, as you do in the Print Options Heading command, or you can specify a cell address, almost as you do in the Print Range command.

The problem is that your title entry is always plain text, and it therefore never adjusts to a cell's movement in the worksheet. If you refer to a hard cell address, \G152, and that cell gets moved, your title will no longer reference the cell you want—it will still be looking at G152. The obvious way to circumvent this was also used when discussing the similar problem in macros: range names.

Of course, you can try to set up your graph data so that it will never move. Put it out of the way and plan to leave it alone. This would not only be difficult but it would go against the spirit of the worksheet, which is meant to be fluid and to encourage change. Once again, range names come to the rescue.

The Graph Options Legends Range command in Release 2.2 allows you to select the range of cells that contain the text for each graph legend. However, the addresses you choose are not kept as live references but converted into the \address format (such as \G13). Therefore, you are still stuck with the same problem of title entries not adjusting to changes in the worksheet.

The only way to refer safely to graph title cells is to use range names. Just as with macros, the cells of a named range can always be found, no matter where they have moved. Figure 11.5 presents a typical use of graph title cells, and also demonstrates the idea of keeping all graph data in one location in the worksheet.

Each title cell in column B has been given an appropriate range name by using the Range Name Labels Right command from the cells in column A. Notice that the data cell C13, under the cell pointer, is not a hard number but an @sum function. The entire table that will be graphed is actually built from formulas that summarize data that lies elsewhere in the worksheet. This whole range then, is strictly for graphing, but it will update as its source data changes.

To reference the secondary title (B2) in a graph command, you would enter its range name preceded by a backslash:

\TITLE_SECOND

The title in the graph would then be whatever was in the named cell.

Here is another notable trick: when referencing a cell for a graph title, the cell contents can be more than just straight text. This may be obvious, but it is amazing how easy it is to neglect the obvious.

Look again at the second title cell in Figure 11.5, which displays *Average for All is 691*. This cell is actually a string formula that will display the average of the graphed data (range named DATA) within the second title line of the graph:

+"Average for All is "&@string(@avg(DATA),0)

```
C13: (FØ) @SUM(R325..R4ØØ)                                    READY

        A            B         C        D        E        F        G
1   TITLE_FIRST   Monthly Totals for the Four Divisions
2   TITLE_SECOND  Average for All is 691
3   TITLE_X_AXIS  Month
4   TITLE_Y_AXIS  Amount
5
6   LEGEND_A      North
7   LEGEND_B      South
8   LEGEND_C      East
9   LEGEND_D      West
10
11                Month      North    South    East     West
12                -----------------------------------------
13                Jan         765      329      856      477
14                Feb         833      676      588      599
15                Mar         890      889      577      474
16                Apr         819      964      364      735
17                May         754      738      747      898
18                Jun         454      471      813      877
19                Jul
20                Aug
```

Figure 11.5 ◆ *Capturing graph titles from worksheet cells*

Suddenly, your graphs will not only display the picture of the data, but will also contain informative text to accompany it. The graph legends in the example worksheet are also formulas. They refer to the column titles of each data range, and will therefore always be accurate even if those titles are changed. It would be easy enough to include the average of each range in its legend, such as this formula for the range labeled North:

+C11&" ("&@string(@avg(C13..C24),0)&")"

For the given six months of data, the formula above would produce the legend

North (753)

By combining string and math formulas in graph title cells, and referring to them with range names, you can easily produce graphs that are flexible and remain accurate even as the data in the worksheet changes its value or position.

DISPLAYING GRAPHS WITH ALLWAYS

Allways is a 1-2-3 add-in program that was created by Funk Software of Cambridge, MA. It has been aptly described as a spreadsheet publishing program, and was so successful at bringing 1-2-3 spreadsheets to life that Lotus Development Corporation purchased the rights to Allways and included it with Release 2.2.

This 1-2-3 add-in allows you to enhance the appearance of your spreadsheet with:

◆ Different font sizes

◆ Boldfaced text

◆ Underlining

◆ Outlined and shaded cells

With Allways you can also include up to 20 graphs within the worksheet, and, if your hardware supports graphics, you can view the enhancements as you make them, so that you will know precisely how your printouts will appear.

There are two advantages to including graphs within the worksheet with Allways. First, you can add enhancements that are not available when creating graphs in 1-2-3. Second, by incorporating the graph into your worksheet data, you can create printed reports that are not only more professional looking, but also more informative, by placing a graph next to the data from which it is drawn.

ADDING GRAPHS TO THE WORKSHEET

To place a graph into the worksheet, you must first create it and save it to disk as a PIC file, using the 1-2-3 Graph Save command. Then invoke Allways and its Graph Add command, and specify the PIC file that you want to include in the worksheet and the range that you want the graph to occupy. Allways will insert a "snapshot" of the graph into that range and size it accordingly. But because you are pasting a picture of the graph into the worksheet and not the actual graph itself, it will not be automatically updated if you make changes to the data in the worksheet. If you enter new data for the graph, you must use 1-2-3's Graph Save command and save the graph to disk once more for the graph in Allways to reflect those changes.

> *TIP* ◆ *Although you must save the graph to disk again, you do not need to tell Allways that you have revised a graph's PIC file. This is because Allways looks at the graph PIC file each time you invoke the add-in, and draws the graph from the information contained in the file. Assuming you keep the name of the graph file the same when you revise it, Allways will automatically draw the graph with the revised picture.*

Once you have added one or more graphs to the worksheet, you have two options for displaying the graphs. If you are operating Allways in graphics mode, you can choose to have graphs displayed for viewing, so that they will look very much like they will when printed. The problem with this is that it puts a lot of stress on your computer's processor, and the response time for refreshing the screen may become uncomfortably slow.

To avoid this problem, use the Allways command Display Graphs No. Instead of seeing the graphs on-screen, you will see a rectangular box the same size as the graph, but filled with cross-hatching. This only conveys the size and placing of the graph but greatly alleviates the drag on processing speed.

> *TIP* ◆ *Before printing with Allways, you may want to display the graphs once again to be sure that each graph is the correct one for its position in the worksheet.*

Using the Display Mode Text command lets you operate Allways in text mode. In this mode a graph is signified by a box filled with the letter G; the Display Graphs command has no effect.

ENHANCING GRAPHS

The secret to enhancing your graphs with Allways relies on your first having created a graph with little detail. If you format the graph heavily within 1-2-3, practically anything else you add with Allways will make the graph cluttered. This is especially true if you plan to print your graph along with the worksheet data, because the graph will most likely be even smaller than the half-page graphs you produce with 1-2-3's PrintGraph.

If the graph you create in 1-2-3 is going to be less than half of a page when added to the worksheet with Allways, consider leaving out the titles at the top and along the x- and y-axes and using the Options Scale Skip command to avoid overcrowding along the x-axis. Even a horizontal or vertical grid might be too much for a small graph. Start with a simple graph, and see how it looks when you have placed it into the worksheet.

Once the graph is within Allways, you have several means of enhancing its appearance. The most obvious is adjusting its position and size in relation to its location in the worksheet, using the Graph Settings Range command. Also, you can create an outline box around the graph by using the Format Lines Outline command, add titles in Allways using any style or font, and shade the cells beneath the graph so that it stands out from the rest of the material on the page.

The ability to shade the cells under the graph demonstrates an interesting aspect of Allways: it makes graphs transparent. Any underlying cell entries in the worksheet will show through the graph, which allows you to add other types of information to the graph by entering it into the spreadsheet. For example, you could add a short explanatory note enclosed in a box within the graph, include the current date, or create a string formula that displays the total number of points on a line graph, such as:

```
@string(@count(DATA),0)&" total samples"
```

If you have already formatted a graph in 1-2-3, you can still enhance its text with the Graph Settings Scale command. Use it to scale the size of the 1-2-3 graph fonts, choosing a number from 0.5 (small) to 3.0 (big). You can scale the main graph title (Font 1) separately from the rest of the text in the graph (Font 2). Generally, your graphs will look better when you have increased the size of their fonts from the default size.

Whatever you do to enhance your graphs in Allways, just be sure to save your worksheet to keep the changes you have made in Allways.

◆ PRODUCING THE GRAPHS _____

The usefulness of a graph depends upon the data from which it is built and the graph settings that were used to produce it. The Lotus Graph menu is the largest of all in the worksheet, and just about every item on it can have a major effect upon the finished graph.

SIZING THE DATA WITH THE SCALE OPTION

By default, Lotus automatically scales a graph to the minimum and maximum values in the data being graphed. This allows the data to "expand" and fill the graph, avoiding the problem of a flat line at the top or bottom of the graph, or of bar graphs that barely leave the x-axis. When you are producing a series of similar but separate graphs, though, automatic scaling can cause viewers to misinterpret the relationship among the data in the various graphs.

Imagine that the owner of a small company is applying for a business loan and needs to present the company's sales figures in relation to those of its larger competitor. The wily applicant decides that a pair of graphs will present the information most advantageously, and Figure 11.6 shows why. In these two graphs it appears that the small company's sales increased sharply in the second half of the year, providing stiff competition for its rival. Of course, the illusion depends on the banker's failing to notice the values along the y-axis, which tell an entirely different story.

The point is that when you are graphing similar data to produce comparisons, you should always set the scaling factor to the same values in each graph. You can do this with the command Graph Options Scale Y-Scale. Choose Manual from the Scale menu, and then set the lower and upper limits. It is usually best to set the lower scaling limit to 0, unless you have a specific reason not to. In the example, the upper scaling limit should be the maximum value in the two columns of data for the two companies. A formula can be entered to produce that maximum value, for example:

@max(B6..C17)

Then both graphs could be plotted to that same scale, as though they were being plotted on the same graph. The comparisons become relevant, as shown in Figure 11.7.

The scaling option has other uses, too. You can manipulate the scale of a graph to emphasize a certain portion of it, in a sense expanding one section to fill the graph just as a photographer would blow up one portion of a photo.

In Figure 11.2, the cumulative deficits at the low end of the first graph were barely noticeable. But those smaller values could have been expanded into a graph of their own simply by setting the upper limit of the scale to exclude the larger values. For example, using 10E9 (ten billion) as the upper limit would have eliminated all the values that were over that amount. You could also expand the larger values and eliminate the smaller values by setting the lower limit to a value greater than the smaller values, again such as 10E9.

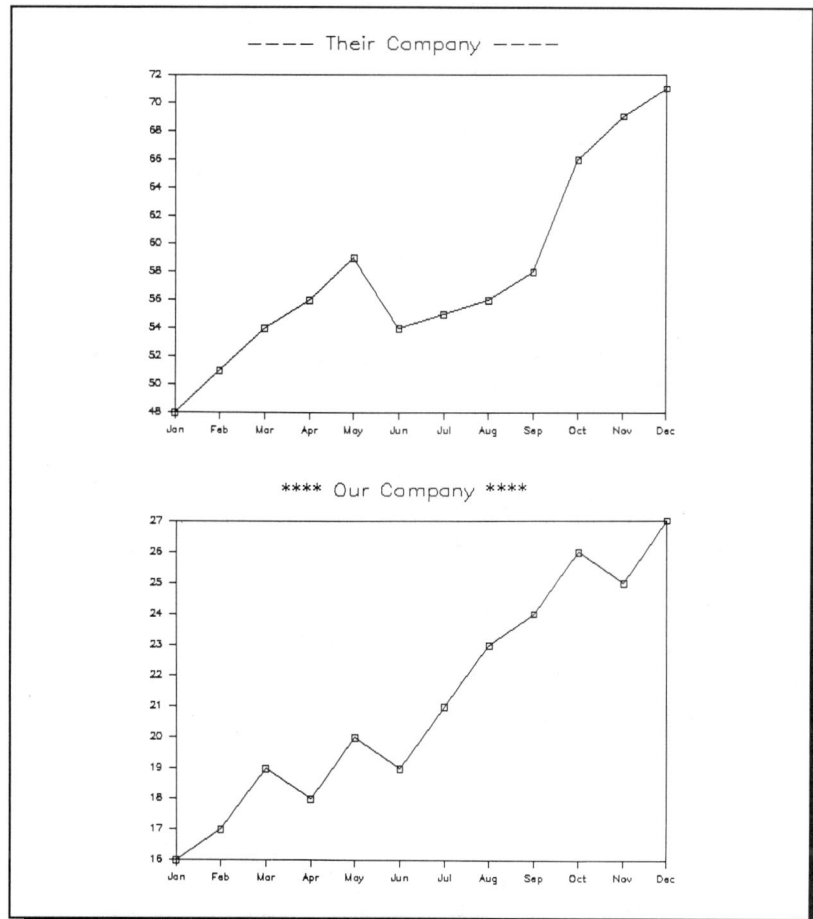

Figure 11.6 ◆ *Looking through the wrong end of the binoculars*

GETTING A PIECE OF THE PIE GRAPH

Pie charts make attractive graphs, in part because only one data range is being graphed, which eliminates the clutter that often muddles other types of graphs.

You must use the graph A range to specify the pie graph data range; no other graph range will work. Each wedge of the graph represents one cell in that range, and Lotus prints a wedge's percentage of the whole next to it in the displayed graph.

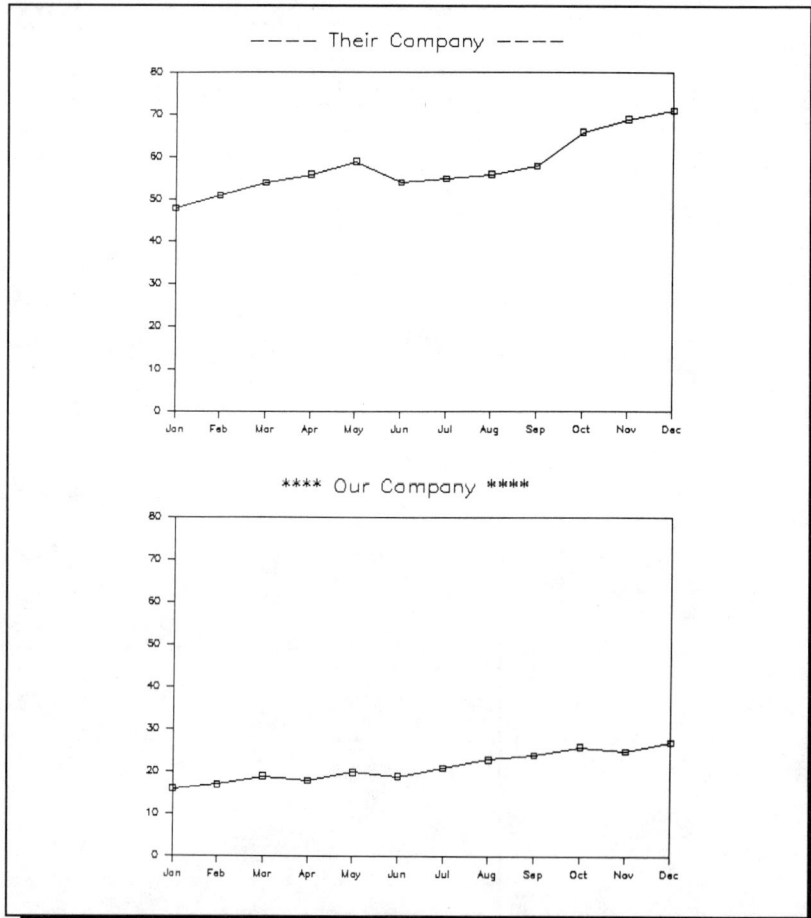

Figure 11.7 ◆ *Manually scaling graphs to the same lower and upper limits*

The x-axis range provides the text labels for each corresponding wedge of a pie graph. The fancy part comes when you color the pie by specifying a B range that contains Lotus color codes for each wedge. (Note that on a monochrome system, the wedges are shaded or given a cross-hatching.)

You have a choice of eight different colors, the codes for which are numbered 0 through 7, where 0 means no filling at all, a blank wedge. Again, on a monochrome system, the numbers represent different cross-hatching patterns. If you have more than seven wedges, you must repeat the patterns.

You can explode any or all wedges in the pie by adding 100 to its color number. A color code of 100 would explode the wedge but give it no filling. Using 103 would explode it and color it with the number 3 color. You can automatically explode pieces based on their value, as the next example will show.

In Figure 11.8, both the largest and smallest wedges—December and July—are exploded to call attention to them.

Of course, you could manually determine which pieces to explode if this were a one-time-only graph, but automating the process for regular use not only speeds the routine but also eliminates chances for error. Figure 11.9 shows the worksheet that produced the graph in Figure 11.8.

The month names in column A are the graph's x-axis, and the values in column B make up the A range data. Column C is the B range, which contains the color codes for each piece of the pie (the corresponding data cell in column B). These codes are built from @if functions that use the color codes that have been entered in column D, as this formula in C8 shows:

```
@if(B8<@max($A_RANGE)#and#
    B8>@min($A_RANGE),D8,100+D8)
```

This formula checks the value of the data cell in column B. If that cell is less than the maximum of all the data cells (named A_RANGE) and greater than the minimum, then the color code in D8 is used. Therefore, if the cell is equal to the maximum or minimum of the range, 100 is added to the color code to explode that piece of the pie.

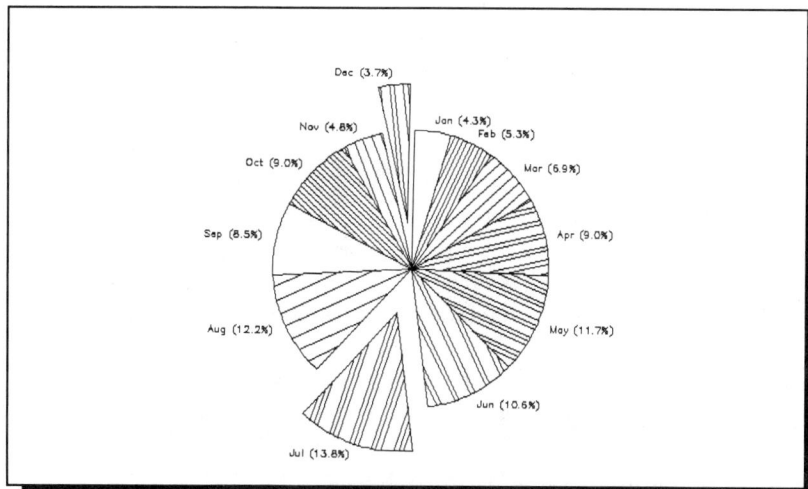

Figure 11.8 ◆ *Exploding the smallest and largest wedges in a pie graph*

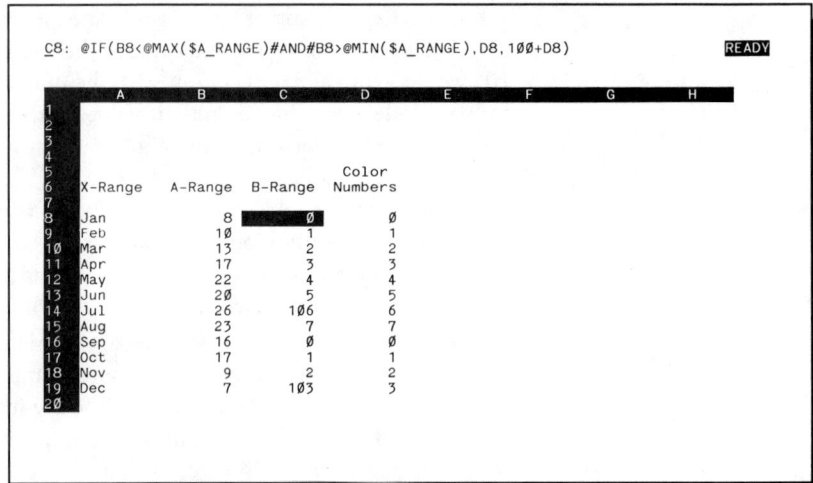

Figure 11.9 ◆ *Using @if functions to explode a pie graph*

SETTING THE X-AXIS

In all graphs except the xy graph, the x-axis consists of text labels that serve to identify the various data points in the data ranges. They are spaced along the x-axis according to their position in the range of labels, so that the tenth label out of 20 will be in the center of the x-axis in the graph. Remember that only the xy graph is required to have an x-axis.

Preventing Crowding on the X-Axis

A surplus of text along the x-axis is a common difficulty when using labels. The amount of text that can fit along the axis is limited, and it must be divided among the points you are plotting.

If you create separate data for graphing, you can then customize the text in the X range to better fit the graph. You can shorten or abbreviate the labels, or even use code identifiers to squeeze more labels along the x-axis. The source data, where the shortened labels might be undesirable, will be left unchanged.

One of the nice improvements in Release 2.2 is the way it staggers long labels on the x-axis instead of crowding them together. This produces a more readable graph and sometimes alleviates the need to shorten the labels.

There will be times, though, when overcrowding along the x-axis is inevitable. Both versions of 1-2-3 provide a graph option to alleviate this problem. This is the Skip command under the Options Scale menu, which allows you to set a "skip factor" for the labels along the x-axis. All data points will still be plotted, but the x-axis labels will be "pruned." You can use any number between 1 and 8192; the default is 1, where no labels are skipped (all are shown). If you set the skip value to 3, then only every third label will be displayed. Set it to 100, and every hundredth label will be shown. This effectively thins the text along the x-axis without causing any data points to be lost.

The Numeric X-Axis in an XY Graph

An x-axis must be specified in an xy graph because every data point is directly tied to a value along the x-axis. If the first 15 points on the x-axis have the values 1 through 15, but the last five are valued 101 through 105, then most of the data points will be squeezed into the far left side of the graph because the x-axis will be scaled evenly from 1 to 105. Experiment with this by alternating between a line graph (labels on the x-axis) and an xy graph (values on the x-axis) to see how Lotus treats the x-axis in the two different graphs.

In the xy graph, the points along the x-axis always have numeric value, and are spaced according to their value in a sorted order.

⊗ **CAUTION** ◆ *If you specify an xy graph when you have only text entries in the x range, the only point that will appear on the x-axis will be 0, because all text has a value of 0. You should use a line graph in this situation.*

A good example of the difference between a line graph and an xy graph occurs when the x-axis contains Lotus date or time values. In a line graph, each date would be treated as a piece of text, consisting of exactly what is shown on the screen. If the dates are formatted as dates, you would see dates along the x-axis. If they are not formatted, so that they display as numbers in the worksheet, you would see numbers along the x-axis.

In an xy graph, the dates are treated as values and spaced evenly, from the low value to the high value. The display of the values is not determined by what you see on the worksheet screen, since only their internal values are used. Instead, you must format the values in the graph's x-axis with the Graph Options Scale X-Scale Format command. You then choose from any of the usual cell formats, such as Date.

Since the X range is numeric, with a low and a high, it can be important to sort all the graph data by the values in that range before graphing. This is especially so when the x-axis represents time and there is a connection between the time and the data points. If not sorted by the X range values, the line connecting the data points can loop back on itself, making a crazy-quilt pattern. This is demonstrated using the data in Figure 11.10.

```
A5: (D9) @TIME(2,2Ø,Ø)                                              READY

        A        B       C        D        E       F        G        H
1
2
3  Line Graph, Unsorted          XY Graph, Unsorted       XY Graph, Sorted
4  ------------------------------------------------------------------------
5     Ø2:2Ø      6                Ø2:2Ø      6             Ø2:2Ø      6
6     Ø7:12     42                Ø7:12     42             Ø3:Ø1      8
7     14:35     42                14:35     42             Ø5:46     11
8     18:15     57                18:15     57             Ø7:12     42
9     2Ø:15     38                2Ø:15     38             Ø7:41     53
1Ø    Ø3:Ø1      8                Ø3:Ø1      8             Ø8:3Ø     58
11    Ø7:41     53                Ø7:41     53             Ø9:15     49
12    Ø9:15     49                Ø9:15     49             12:4Ø     4Ø
13    15:47     41                15:47     41             14:35     42
14    23:ØØ     11                23:ØØ     11             15:47     41
15    Ø5:46     11                Ø5:46     11             16:35     54
16    Ø8:3Ø     58                Ø8:3Ø     58             18:15     57
17    12:4Ø     4Ø                12:4Ø     4Ø             2Ø:15     38
18    16:35     54                16:35     54             22:Ø7     13
19    22:Ø7     13                22:Ø7     13             23:ØØ     11
2Ø
```

Figure 11.10 ◆ *Data for an xy graph may have to be sorted to be meaningful*

This worksheet could be the result of a car count on a highway over a period of time. As you can see, the time in column A runs over three days; the points were entered in the same order that they were measured. Column B contains the number of cars per minute that were recorded at each time in column A.

The data in columns A and B have been copied into two other ranges so that three graphs can be made. The first set of data will be plotted as a line graph. Columns D and E contain exactly the same data, but will become an xy graph, where the number of cars counted will be linked to a particular time of day. The last set of data in columns G and H is the same data, but sorted on the time values; it will also be graphed as an xy graph. Figure 11.11 shows the results of the three graphs.

The line graph plots the points in exactly the same order in which they occur in the worksheet. All the points are shown, but there seems to be little information gained by graphing the data. The second graph is again the same data, but plotted as an xy graph. This time, Lotus has arranged the times in a sorted order so that the x-axis runs from midnight to midnight (0 to 0 with its time format). Even though the times are now sorted, the data points are not. The line that connects each point does so according to the point's position in the worksheet, creating an unreadable blur of the graph. This can be corrected by sorting the data before graphing, as the last graph shows.

The two columns of the third set of data were sorted by the time values. The x-axis in the graph appears the same as in the previous graph, since both are

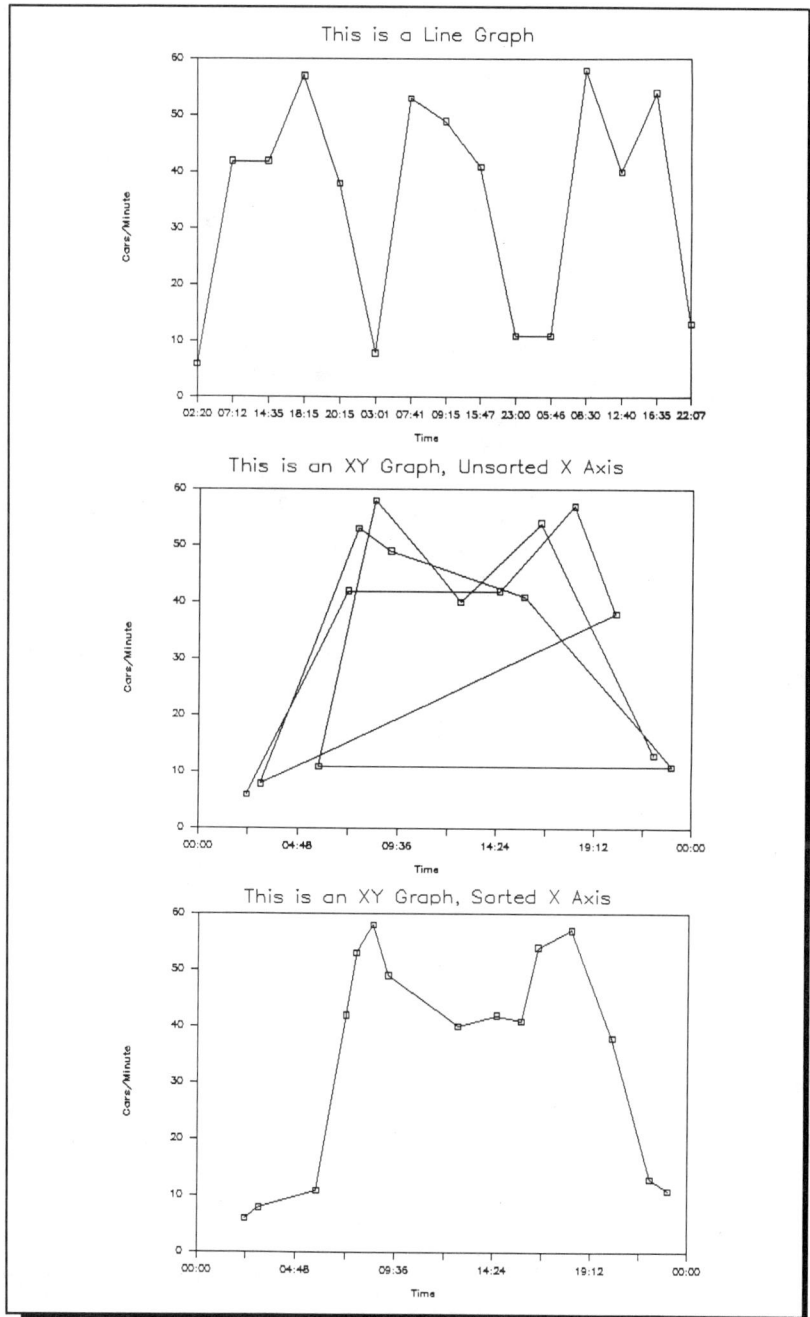

Figure 11.11 ◆ *Line, xy, and sorted xy graphs*

sorted by Lotus as they are graphed. However, this time the data in the worksheet also fall in the same sorted order, and a single line connects them in the graph. Now you can see a pattern among the data as the day progresses.

PLOTTING THE DATA AGAINST A BASELINE

Since graphs are a visual method of displaying data, it is often beneficial to plot the data in a line graph against a single baseline. That line might represent the average of all the data, a break-even point, the regression line for the data, or a value from outside the data to which you wish to compare the data.

The worksheet in Figure 11.12 contains monthly data for four individuals; data has been entered through July. All four ranges are to be plotted in one line graph, with the addition of a straight line across the graph that represents the average of all the data.

The appropriate range letter of each graph range has been entered above every column in row 2. The four individuals are graph ranges A through D, and the average is graph range E, column B. The first cell in the Average range, which is currently highlighted, is an @avg function that calculates the average of all the cells in the range DATA, D5..G16. Each of the cells in Column B simply refers to that first cell:

+$B$5

Each cell in this range will therefore always display the average for the data.

```
B5: @AVG($DATA)                                                    READY

        A          B          C          D        E        F        G
 1
 2    -X-        -E-     Data Labels    -A-      -B-      -C-      -D-
 3            Average    for E range    Winn     Ward    Tobler   Shields
 4    ------------------------------------------------------------------
 5    Jan       81                       92      102       71       52
 6    Feb       81                       77       92       67       55
 7    Mar       81                       72       95       82       50
 8    Apr       81                       77      106       72       57
 9    May       81                       99      103       84       64
10    Jun       81                       94      119       82       60
11    Jul       81                       91      112       78       71
12    Aug       81
13    Sep       81    <-Average-> 81
14    Oct       81
15    Nov       81
16    Dec       81
17
18
19
20
```

Figure 11.12 ◆ *A worksheet for plotting four ranges against their average*

> **TIP** ♦ *You might think that you could fill just the first and last cells of the average range and let Lotus tie them together in the graph with a line. But the graph line will only connect contiguous points in the graph (cells in the worksheet); to avoid gaps in the line, each cell must be filled with the same value—the average of the data.*

Column C contains one extra range for the data labels for graph range E, the average. Only one cell has an entry, and it will be used to flag the average line and also to indicate the actual average value using this formula:

$$+''<\text{-Average->}~''\&@string(B5,0)$$

You can see the results in the plotted graph, Figure 11.13. Each of the four data ranges has been plotted, and the legends indicate which line belongs to which individual. You can see the Average line cutting across the screen just above the 80 mark on the y-axis. The data label for the Average line sits just above it, and you can clearly see the actual value for the average.

NAMING AND SAVING GRAPHS

The graphs that you create can be printed, but they must first be saved to a disk file that will later be read by the Lotus PrintGraph program. You can also create numerous graphs in one worksheet, giving each graph a name of its own,

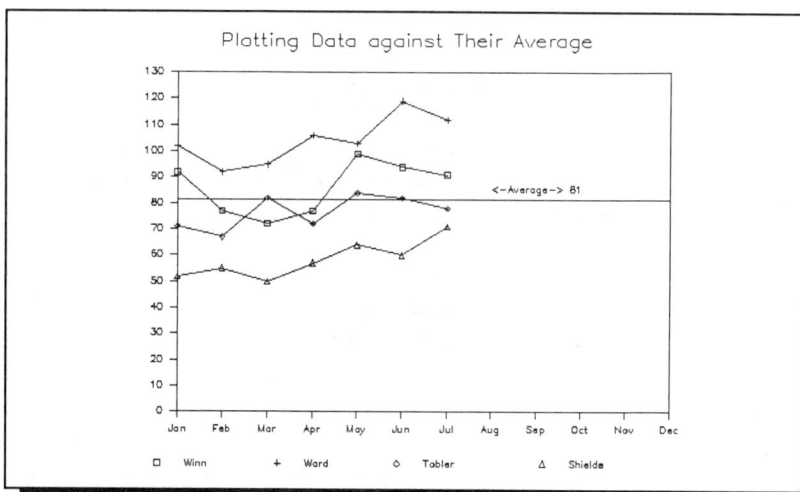

Figure 11.13 ♦ *Plotting data against the baseline of their average*

which can later be recalled for viewing. The distinction between *saving* a graph to disk for printing, and *naming* a graph for future viewing, is often cloudy. If you confuse one with the other, you may find yourself losing graphs you intended to keep.

Saving Graphs for Future Printing

To print a graph, you must first save it to disk with the Graph Save command. The current graph is the one that will be saved—the graph that you would see by invoking the Graph View command or by pressing the F10 {graph} key. You specify a graph file name, which is always given a .PIC extension unless you specify otherwise.

Once you have saved a graph to a file, that file is forever fixed and cannot be revised. In that sense, you should think of the Graph Save command as an immediate printout of the current graph settings, only the output goes to a file instead of the printer. Later, you can use the PrintGraph program to actually format and send that file to the printer.

> ⊗ **CAUTION** ◆ *A saved graph cannot be loaded back into Lotus. A graph file should never be confused with a graph that is kept within the worksheet, which can be revised and viewed again and again. If you save a graph but do not save the worksheet that created it, the source graph will be lost; all you will have is a picture of it in the .PIC file.*

The graph file can never be changed, so to make the printed graph an accurate representation of the worksheet graph, you must save the worksheet graph after making any changes to the worksheet. This will ensure that the graph file is completely up to date. In fact, the only time you will save a graph to disk is when you are ready to print it, whether printing will be done immediately or at some later time.

> ◰ **TIP** ◆ *There are numerous graphics programs, including other spreadsheet programs, that can read Lotus .PIC files and import them for revising, enhancing, and printing. This is the only operation other than printing that requires you to save a graph. Despite the popularity of its own graph file format, Lotus itself cannot retrieve one of its graph files back into the worksheet. You must use the Graph Name command if you want to keep multiple graphs in the worksheet.*

Naming Graphs for Future Viewing in the Worksheet

A single graph can be built from literally dozens of ranges and command options. There can be so many settings, in fact, that the developers of Lotus allow you to name and store within the worksheet all the current graph settings. You can create as many named graph settings as you need, any of which can later be called up for further viewing or revising as the current graph.

A named graph behaves just as the current settings do for the print and database commands. It does not remember the actual data that built the graph—just the data ranges and the options that were typed directly into its command prompts, as print headers are. If those ranges expand or contract through the insertion or deletion of rows, if they are moved, or if the data within them changes, the named graph will reflect those changes when called up for viewing.

Unfortunately, the idea of storing the current settings under a given name is not extended to the print or database commands, as it is in Symphony, and only one setting can be used at a time; hence the importance of macros for running multiple print or database routines.

When you invoke the Graph Name Create menu, you will be giving a name to the current graph settings. The name you enter can be up to 15 characters long. If you select an existing graph name from the menu, the current settings will overwrite whatever settings had been associated with that name. Be careful that the name you select is not of another graph that you also want to keep.

The named graphs are always saved along with the worksheet, as long as you remember to actually save the worksheet after creating and naming the graphs.

> **CAUTION** ◆ *If you want your named settings to be accurate, you must use the Name Create command to specify the current settings whenever you make a change to them that you wish to preserve. The Create command takes a snapshot of the current settings, so if you change any of them, such as the graph data ranges, type, titles, or legends, you must create the name again to take a new snapshot of the graph.*

The Graph Name Use command makes the chosen named graph the current graph, replacing all of the current settings with those from the given name. This can be devastating if you have neglected to name those current settings before making the other one current. Since so much work can go into the creation of a graph, caution is always advised before making another graph current.

The Use command makes another graph current, but it also immediately displays that graph. This is the one obstacle to using this command from within

2.2 ◆ ─────

macros—there is no way to get the macro to "press any key" to clear the display of the graph and return to the worksheet. This forces some user interaction (at least one finger's worth) when macros are designed to recall a named graph.

However, the macro commands {graphon} and {graphoff} in Release 2.2 eliminate this problem by automating the display of graphs. They also free you from having to press a key to clear the graph from the display. When you combine these new macro commands from the Graph Name Table command in Release 2.2, you have a simple tool for creating your own graphics slide shows within the worksheet. The next section discusses this useful method.

CREATING A SLIDE SHOW IN RELEASE 2.2

If you are using 1-2-3 Release 2.2, you can create a macro routine driven by a list of named graphs in the worksheet that displays each graph in the list for a specified amount of time. Once started, this macro runs without any operator assistance, something that cannot be done in Release 2.01. The layout of the macro worksheet consists of three sections, as shown in Figure 11.14.

At the top of the screen in Figure 11.14 is a four-column table listing the names of four graphs: Graph 1, Graph 2, Graph 3, and Graph 4. The last three columns were produced with the Graph Name Table command in Release 2.2, which enters the name, type, and main title of every graph in the current worksheet in three adjacent columns in the worksheet. Once you create a table of all your graphs with the Graph Name Table command, you can rearrange their

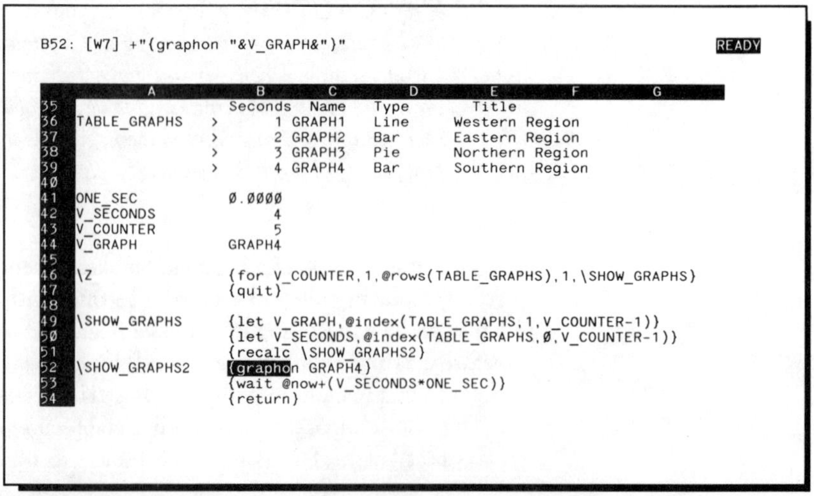

Figure 11.14 ◆ *Macros to present a graphics slide show*

order in the list by moving or copying rows, or delete those you do not want in the slide show. It's that easy to lay out the sequence of your "slides."

Each cell in the column labeled Seconds, situated to the left of the three-column graph table, contains a value for the length of time the graph should be displayed. In this example, the time is entered in seconds, and you can enter any number you want for each graph. When testing, however, note that a shorter duration is the quickest and easiest to test.

The four variable cells situated below the table are used by the macro. The first one, named ONE_SEC, contains a formula that evaluates to the Lotus time value of one second:

```
@time(0,0,1)
```

Below the variables is the macro code, beginning with \Z:

```
{for V_COUNTER,1,@rows(TABLE_GRAPHS),1,\SHOW_GRAPHS}
{quit}
```

This looping macro command can be paraphrased as follows:

> Using the variable cell V_COUNTER to hold the current loop number, start counting at 1 and continue looping until V_COUNTER is greater than the number of rows in TABLE_GRAPHS. Increment V_COUNTER by 1 for each loop of the macro. Finally, run the routine name \SHOW_GRAPHS for each loop.

No matter how many rows are in the table of graphs, this macro will loop once for each one.

The lines of macro code that follow actually display the graph, and are named \SHOW_GRAPHS:

```
{let V_GRAPH,@index(TABLE_GRAPHS,1,V_COUNTER-1)}
{let V_SECONDS,@index(TABLE_GRAPHS,0,V_COUNTER-1)}
{recalc \SHOW_GRAPHS2}
{graphon GRAPH4}
{wait @now+(V_SECONDS*ONE_SEC)}
{return}
```

The first line of \SHOW_GRAPHS uses an @index function to set the variable cell V_GRAPH to a name from the table of graphs, depending on the value in V_COUNTER. Because the @index function always treats the first row in the range as having an offset of 0, it is necessary to subtract 1 from the counter cell.

The second line places the number of seconds from the table for the current graph name into the variable cell V_SECONDS. The same @index function is used, but this time with a column offset of 0, so that it looks at the first column of TABLE_GRAPHS.

The third line simply recalculates the fourth line, SHOW_GRAPHS2, because that line is actually a string formula, which is shown here and can also be seen in the control panel in Figure 11.13:

+"{graphon "&V_GRAPH&"}"

This formula concatenates the graph name in V_GRAPH with the Release 2.2 macro command {graphon}. This macro statement displays the named graph, just as though you had used the Graph Name Use command. The difference is that the graph will remain on-screen until the macro determines it has been displayed long enough. This is done in the fifth line of the macro, eliminating the need for you to press any key to continue.

> ⊗ **CAUTION** ♦ *The {wait} macro takes a time parameter that specifies a given time of day (as a Lotus time value), not a given number of hours, minutes, or seconds. In other words, the syntax is not "wait five minutes," but rather "wait until five minutes from a given time (such as the current time)."*

This macro takes the current time, @now, and adds to that the result of multiplying the contents of the cell named V_SECONDS with the Lotus time value of one second from the cell ONE_SEC. The resulting value is a time of day a given number of seconds from "now," when the macro statement begins. Therefore, each graph listed will be displayed for the number of seconds entered in the cell to its left in the table.

When testing this macro with very short display times for each graph (as you should), you may notice some slight discrepancies between the time entered into the macro and the actual time that each graph is displayed. This is most likely due to variations in the amount of time that it takes to plot different types of graphs. When putting together a real slide show for a presentation, you can fine-tune the number of seconds you want for each graph. And keep in mind that you will undoubtedly be using longer display times, in which case the minor discrepancies won't affect your presentation.

♦ PRINTING WITH PRINTGRAPH

When you have saved a worksheet graph to disk as a .PIC file, you can print the file using the PrintGraph program. Remember that it is easy to use the System command to leave the worksheet to print a graph. When you are finished with PrintGraph, typing *EXIT* returns you to the worksheet.

There are two directory choices that must be set in PrintGraph. The first is the Graphs Directory, where Lotus can find the .PIC files to print. The second is the Fonts Directory, where the font files that PrintGraph uses to produce the graphs are kept. This is normally the 1-2-3 program directory. These directories and other PrintGraph settings can be made the defaults by using the Save command to store the current settings in the PGRAPH.CNF file.

★ *TRICK ◆ When you are selecting files from the Image-Select menu, you can display the highlighted graph file simply by pressing the F10 {graph} key. Although the Image-Select screen tells you that you can display the highlighted graph, this feature is frequently forgotten. By plotting a graph on the screen within Print-Graph, you get a preview of it before you go to the trouble of printing. Moreover, the image on the screen is closer to what will be printed than is the graph displayed in the worksheet.*

You can select more than one graph for printing by highlighting each graph name and tagging it by pressing the Space bar. A pound sign (#) is placed in front of each selected name. Something that is frequently overlooked is that the order in which you tag the graphs is the order in which they will be printed. This is extremely important when you want to group graphs together and print two or more graphs on a page.

Figure 11.15 shows the Image-Select menu. The files that are tagged with the pound sign will be queued for printing, and printed in the order in which

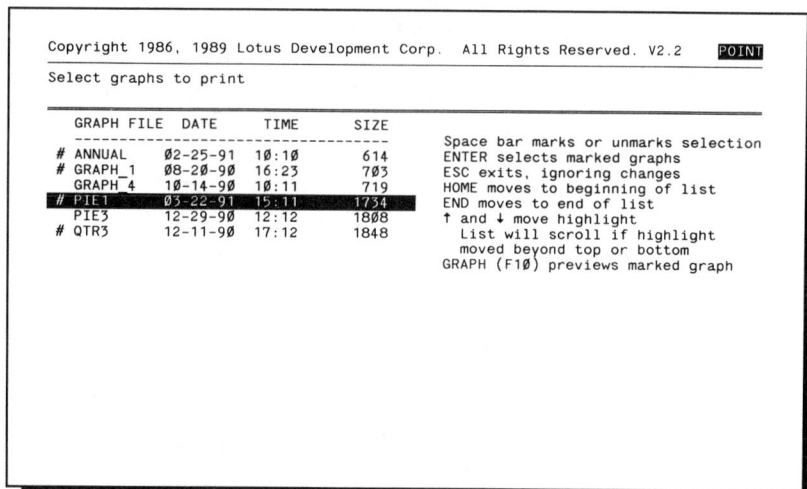

```
Copyright 1986, 1989 Lotus Development Corp.  All Rights Reserved. V2.2   POINT

Select graphs to print


   GRAPH FILE  DATE      TIME     SIZE
   ------------------------------------------   Space bar marks or unmarks selection
 # ANNUAL     02-25-91  10:10      614          ENTER selects marked graphs
 # GRAPH_1    08-20-90  16:23      703          ESC exits, ignoring changes
   GRAPH_4    10-14-90  10:11      719          HOME moves to beginning of list
 # PIE1       03-22-91  15:11     1734          END moves to end of list
   PIE3       12-29-90  12:12     1808          ↑ and ↓ move highlight
 # QTR3       12-11-90  17:12     1848            List will scroll if highlight
                                                  moved beyond top or bottom
                                                GRAPH (F10) previews marked graph
```

Figure 11.15 ◆ Selecting graphs from the PrintGraph Image-Select screen

they were tagged. The file name that is currently highlighted can be viewed by pressing the F10 {graph} key.

Before saving a graph file, you would have tested the graph in the worksheet as it was being created. You can also test it again by previewing it during the Image-Select process. But the printed graph is never exactly like either of these, and a graph must often be printed, revised, and then printed again. This is especially true when the graph will be included in a report and must meet the tough standards of its author. Therefore, if the look of the output is important, give yourself the luxury of a third "preview" by printing the graph in a low-density mode.

You choose the print density by selecting the appropriate printer driver from within the Settings Hardware Printer menu. Most printers have at least two drivers, labeled Low Density and High Density. The high-density graph will look superb, but may take many minutes to print, depending on the speed of your printer. The low-density graph has all the same features, fonts, and margins, but prints much more quickly. By taking a few extra minutes to print a low-density rough draft, you may save yourself from having to reprint a high-density graph.

You can also save time by printing a graph in a smaller than full-page size. The Settings Image Size Half command prints the graph across the top half of an 8½-by-11-inch page, in less than half the time it takes to print a full-page graph.

> ⊗ **CAUTION ◆** *Use caution when trying to fit three or more graphs on a single page. You can specify a Manual size for your graphs, but when graphs are printed smaller than half-size, they become difficult to read.*
>
> *If you want to produce small graphs, plan them as such when you create them in the worksheet. Eliminate the second line of the graph title; it is much smaller than the top line and may be too fuzzy to read when printed. Keep the x-axis uncluttered, either by using short abbreviations or by using the Options Scale Skip command. You should also keep the graph area itself uncluttered. If you try to include six data ranges, data labels, and horizontal and vertical grid lines, your small graph may resemble a road map of Manhattan.*

Remember that the colors you saw while playing with the worksheet graph are not necessarily the colors you will see when the graph is printed. You must set the color for each data range and the x-axis from within PrintGraph. Even then, though you have diligently set the colors for each range, the graph will not be printed in color—unless you have a color printer or plotter hooked up to the computer! That is blatantly obvious, but what is not so obvious is that the colors you select within PrintGraph have little to do with the colors that are used by your plotter or printer.

You should think of color selection more as a "pen selection" process, because it is the color of the actual pen in the plotter that determines the color of a range when it is printed. The first color on your PrintGraph Range-Colors menu represents the first pen in the plotter. The second color represents the second pen, and so on. So, if you choose Red for one range and select it again for another, both of those ranges will be the same color. Whether that color is actually red depends on how you have your printer or plotter set up.

> **TIP** ◆ *If you try to select colors and are only offered black, check the Printer Type PrintGraph is currently using. You may have neglected to select your color printer or plotter from the Settings Hardware Printer menu.*

When you create a pie graph, if you assign colors to the pieces of the pie with any of the seven color codes (1 through 7), PrintGraph will substitute each of those codes with one of its Range-Colors. Since there are also seven graph ranges (X and A to F), a pie wedge with the color code 1 is assigned the Print-Graph color for range X. Color 2 gets range B, color 3 gets C, and so on. The determining factor, therefore, for the printed color of the pie wedges is the color you have set, within PrintGraph, for each of the data ranges.

◆ SUMMARY

Creating a graph in Lotus can be as simple as specifying one data range. It can also be a complex process that relies on many worksheet ranges and numerous precise graph commands.

This chapter has covered the creation of graphs, from the layout of data within the worksheet, through graphing commands, to the PrintGraph program, which generates the final product. If you apply the many tips and techniques presented here (and heed the warnings) you can use the graphics features of Lotus to great effect in your data analysis.

Part 3 of *Lotus 1-2-3 Tips and Tricks* covers the process of transferring data. This includes sending worksheet data to a printer, to a print file, and to other cells, as well as transferring data between worksheets and between Lotus and the DOS environment.

PART THREE:

Making Connections

PART 3 EXPLORES THE MANY WAYS OF TRANSFERRING DATA IN the spreadsheet environment. In this dynamic arena, data movement is a critical aspect of every worksheet routine.

In Chapter 12, the topic is sending data from the worksheet to the printer. You will get a clear picture of the Lotus page format, and then learn how to structure your print range within those parameters. The often neglected powers and benefits of printing to disk files are also emphasized.

Chapter 13 covers the broader aspects of data transfer. It describes the many ways to transfer data within the worksheet as well as how to send data between worksheets. Of course, the ultimate transfer is between Lotus and the outside world—the DOS environment.

TWELVE:

Printing Your Worksheets

12

◆ ◆ ◆

EVERY WORKSHEET THAT YOU CREATE WILL UNDOUBTEDLY BE printed at least once, but will more likely be printed many, many times. A worksheet's format, size, and style often require that a unique set of options be arranged in an exact sequence for each printing routine. This chapter disassembles the printing process into its component parts, giving you the tools and tricks necessary to format your printouts exactly as you want them.

Macros are again emphasized as the perfect complement to all of your printing jobs, and several macros are demonstrated that will greatly enhance the control you have over the printing process.

The default printed page in 1-2-3 is examined piece by piece. Seeing how Lotus structures its output will allow you to lay out your printed pages exactly as you want them. A macro that prints a page header as *Page n of N* is included as a sample of what can be gained once the printed page is mastered. Then many of the common, obscure, and mysterious problems related to printing are discussed. Everyone will find something of interest here!

Various ways of adjusting the format of the output are presented, including the use (and problems) of border rows and columns, embedded printer commands, and global zero suppression. Also included are several methods for determining the width of a worksheet range before printing.

Finally, printing to a disk file is frequently ignored by Lotus users, who may be surprised at its ability to create batch files, send worksheet data to other programs, and serve as a fast debugging tool for print routines. When combined with the PRINT command in DOS, print files will free your computer from having to wait for the printer.

But first, two important points are discussed here, because they affect all print actions. If the results of a print routine are unsatisfactory and unpredictable no matter how you specify the print settings, you may have the wrong printer drivers installed in your copy of Lotus, or the wrong printer chosen as the default printer. You can use the Worksheet Global Default Status command to view the default printer settings, so be sure you have taken care of that if you continually have printer problems.

Another insidious problem is especially common on the original style IBM PC keyboard. If your printer is on but has been switched off-line, pressing the Print Screen key causes the computer to seemingly lock up as it waits for the printer to respond. So if your computer ever becomes frozen and can't be revived, you may have accidentally pressed the Print Screen key and you should check your printer. If it is off-line, either switch it on-line or turn its power off, and the computer will be free.

◆ MACROS: THE KEY TO SUCCESSFUL PRINTING

You may wonder why a chapter on printing is being introduced by a discussion of macros. The reason is quite simple: running your print routines through macros is the most important step you can take to enhance your printed output.

Printing is exactly the kind of chore for which macros are designed. A typical print job requires many steps that should be repeated in exactly the same manner each time it is run. A print job may be complex, with many different print ranges involved, numerous page settings for margins, headers, and borders, and various setup strings.

Most printouts can be run with simple keystroke macros, so if you are not yet using macros, incorporating them into your printing jobs is the best way to learn the basic macro techniques. Moreover, you will gain the overall benefits of macro-driven worksheet tasks. Macros provide several powerful enhancements to Lotus, as outlined in Chapter 1, and all of them are ideally suited to printing.

CONSISTENCY FOR REPETITIOUS OPERATIONS

Not only is every worksheet eventually printed, but there are usually several different print routines involved. When you build macros for your print routines, they can be printed by anyone at any time, and always with precisely the same results. Standard worksheet reports always have the same data presented in the same format, which adds a degree of confidence and professionalism to your work.

ACCURACY

Having to repeat a printing operation because it missed its mark is time-consuming. If the routine is etched into a macro, it will perform flawlessly every time it is run. By following good practice and including range names instead of cell addresses within a macro, the success of the print job is assured.

As with the data and graphing commands, the only safe way to print is to first issue the Clear All command. Once the settings have been reset to their default values, you can adjust them as necessary for a new routine. This prevents any settings from a previous print job from "hiding" within the Range or Options menu.

When a macro is used, the extra effort of clearing and then specifying the print parameters is not an issue. The macro describes the print routine completely and therefore always works as planned.

SPEED

Once a macro is written and debugged, it can be executed at macro speeds, generally in less time than it would take to type in the address of the print range. A macro can reduce the task of printing—so common but so tedious—to a quick flash of the screen.

SIMPLIFICATION AND CONVENIENCE

Since printing is a frequent and repetitious task, macros are an ideal way to relieve the tedium of carefully specifying each setting before issuing the Go command. People who are new to the worksheet application are spared the confusion of step-by-step print specifications, while those who are familiar with it can still avoid the trouble and simply zip through the print routines without having to remember each setting.

If a print routine must be modified, all that is needed is a quick edit of the macro. After that, anyone who prints the worksheet will be using the new format.

POWER FOR COMPLEX TASKS

Some print routines require nothing more than setting the print range. More typically, several of the print options must be set. In a large worksheet, the printing routines can become quite complex and virtually impossible to print successfully without the aid of a macro.

Imagine a print job that consists of several different ranges, each requiring specific margins, setup code, and header and footer. Each printed range might be separated from the one above by a specific number of blank lines. Perhaps a range is to be included in the printout only if it has been modified since the last printing. Hiding columns and revising column widths might be necessary to alter the worksheet format before printing; afterward, those settings would need to be returned to normal.

Without a macro to perform these tasks, the user would be swamped with the myriad details and would undoubtedly end up with a nagging headache by the time the print routine was finally completed.

WORKSHEET DOCUMENTATION

If a worksheet has more than one range to be printed, the print settings for each range must be noted somewhere, either in the worksheet or in a set of worksheet instructions. Why not use a macro instead? The benefits of macros discussed so far will be available at the touch of a key, and every print routine that is needed in the worksheet will be fully documented within the text of the macro. As with other macros, a print macro can replace a good deal of dialogue that might otherwise be placed in an instruction booklet:

> To print the database, first clear all the print settings. Then specify the range DATA as the print range. Set the left margin to 10, and the right margin to 132. If there are more than 56 rows of data, please include a footer on each page showing the date and page number.

This paragraph can easily be replaced with a simple macro:

```
/ppcarDATA ˜ oml10 ˜ mr132 ˜
{if @rows(DATA)>56}f ¦ Page # ¦ @ ˜
qagpq
```

The user is spared the effort of following detailed instructions, and the author of the application is assured of a first-rate printout.

CREATING MACROS TO DRIVE YOUR PRINTOUTS

Even the simplest print routine benefits from being incorporated into a keystroke macro. A macro named \P may be all that is needed in some cases:

```
/ppcarDATA ˜ agpq
```

Many worksheets will have more than one print routine, which can be included in one or more macro menus. Then, all the print routines that are needed in the worksheet can be displayed in one place, and the user need only choose one to complete the task. The main application menu might have these choices:

Enter   View   Sort   Print   Save   Quit

The Print choice from the main menu would then call the Print menu, which could have these choices:

Monthly   Quarterly   Annual   Summary

Besides giving the user instant access to the necessary printing macros, the Print menu also serves as a reminder of the reports that routinely need printing. Once your Print menu is established, you can expand on its features and convenience.

> **TIP ◆** *If your worksheet has Recalculation set to Manual, be sure to include a {calc} command in your macro before it prints. This will ensure that all formulas are updated before being printed. Even if you are printing manually, without a macro, do not forget to press F9 before printing.*

Here are two macro examples that demonstrate the power and convenience of macro-driven print routines. You can incorporate these macros or similar ones into any worksheet.

Setting the Page Length with a Macro Menu

Your macro Print menu provides choices for several print routines, but you can provide other menus for various print options. For example, you can create a macro menu that lets the user choose different paper sizes depending on the intended use of the printout. The macro automatically specifies the appropriate page length, top and bottom margins, and setup codes. The necessary macros are shown in Figure 12.1.

The main macro menu is not shown, but it would have a Print choice that calls the Print menu, \MENU3, which starts at B4. It has four print routines listed; the macros for the second and third choices have been left blank so that the first and last can be seen clearly. This is the macro under the first choice, Monthly, in \MENU3:

```
{let CHOICE,0}
{menucall \MENU4}
{if CHOICE<>1}{restart}{branch \M}
{\PRINT_MONTHLY}{branch \M}
```

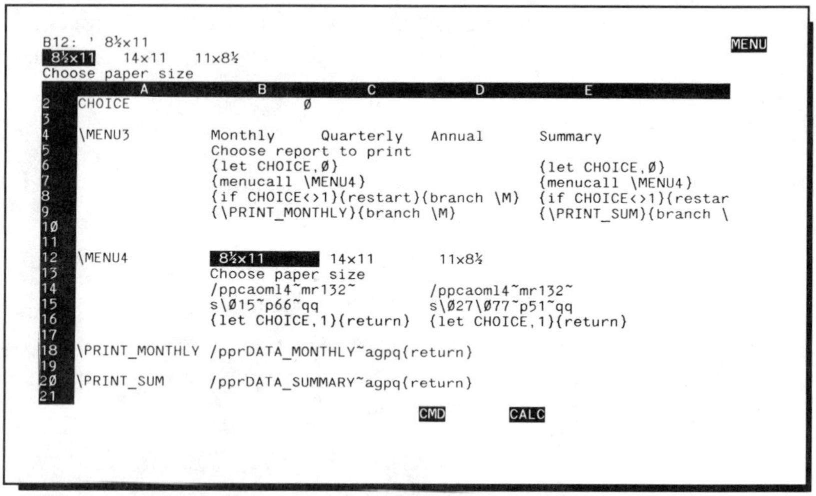

```
B12: ' 8½x11                                                          MENU
  8½x11    14x11    11x8½
Choose paper size
           A             B         C         D         E
2  CHOICE                          Ø
3
4  \MENU3         Monthly    Quarterly  Annual      Summary
5                 Choose report to print
6                 {let CHOICE,Ø}                    {let CHOICE,Ø}
7                 {menucall \MENU4}                 {menucall \MENU4}
8                 {if CHOICE<>1}{restart}{branch \M}  {if CHOICE<>1}{restar
9                 {\PRINT_MONTHLY}{branch \M}        {\PRINT_SUM}{branch \
10
11
12 \MENU4          8½x11         14x11      11x8½
13                Choose paper size
14                /ppcaoml4~mr132~          /ppcaoml4~mr132~
15                s\Ø15~p66~qq              s\Ø27\Ø77~p51~qq
16                {let CHOICE,1}{return}   {let CHOICE,1}{return}
17
18 \PRINT_MONTHLY /pprDATA_MONTHLY~agpq{return}
19
2Ø \PRINT_SUM     /pprDATA_SUMMARY~agpq{return}
21
                                          CMD        CALC
```

Figure 12.1 ◆ *Setting the page length from a macro menu*

When this report is selected for printing, a {let} statement in row 6 sets the cell named CHOICE to 0. This is done for programming reliability, and will be discussed in a moment. Then a subroutine call is made to \MENU4, the menu of paper sizes, which starts at B12.

There are many ways to handle the process of choosing and then setting the necessary print options. The one shown here is simple, and it is easy to edit. The menu has choices for three different paper sizes, the macros for two of which are shown. Here is the macro that starts in cell B14 that is used when 8½-by-11-inch paper is selected:

```
/ppcaoml4 ~ mr132 ~
s\015 ~ p66 ~ qq
{let CHOICE,1} {return}
```

The first two lines of the macro clear the print settings to their default values, and then set the appropriate margins and page length for the given paper size, in this case using compressed print (setup code is for an Epson-compatible printer). The macro then quits the Lotus Print menu.

You can see that for the 11-by-8½-inch paper, a setup code for elite type is used (again for Epson-compatible printers), which allows for a 132-character right margin on the 11-inch paper. The page length is set to 51, as shown in cells D14..D15:

```
/ppcaoml4 ~ mr132 ~
s\027\077 ~ p51 ~ qq
{let CHOICE,1} {return}
```

★ **TRICK** ◆ *In \MENU4, the common difficulty of making the first letter of each menu item distinct from those of the other choices is avoided by prefacing each entry with a space. The user can make a selection only by moving the highlight and pressing Enter. Alternatively, you could solve the problem by prefacing the choices with consecutive numbers or letters: 1), 2), 3), or A), B), C).*

After the print settings are made, another {let} statement, row 16, sets the cell CHOICE to a value of one. Then the {return} command returns control to the calling macro, row 8. The macro in B8 is shown here again:

```
{if CHOICE<>1}{restart}{branch \M}
{\PRINT_MONTHLY}{branch \M}
```

There, an {if} statement checks the value of CHOICE before proceeding. The combination of this {if} statement and the previous {let} statements allows the user to follow the natural inclination to press Escape to cancel the paper selection process in \MENU4 and return to the main menu. Without them, an Escape would immediately return control to the cell after the calling macro, causing the print routine to continue without the print options being set. By setting and then checking the value of CHOICE, the macro can cancel the print routine if CHOICE is not set to 1. In that case, the {restart} command is given, and control is returned to the main menu.

If CHOICE is set to 1, the macro continues in the next cell, B9, which calls the actual print routine, \PRINT_MONTHLY. You can see this macro in cell B18, as follows:

```
/pprDATA_MONTHLY ~ agpq{return}
```

If the menu option Summary had been chosen from \MENU3, the print macro at B20, \PRINT_SUM, would have been run:

```
/pprDATA_SUMMARY ~ agpq{return}
```

Notice that they do not invoke the Clear All command, since the Lotus Print command has already been initialized in \MENU4. When the printing is finished, the {return} statement sends control back to the calling macro in \MENU3, which returns control to the main menu.

This type of Print menu structure has many uses. It can select a printer by subsequently accessing the Worksheet Global Default Printer Name command. Setup codes could also be chosen from a menu, with the appropriate margins being set by the macro. A particularly helpful Print menu is one that allows the user to cancel the print routine and return to the main menu, as described next.

Providing a Safety Net before Printing

Some Lotus commands, such as Quit and File Erase, provide a no/yes menu that allows you to back out of menu selections that have irreversible results. Since the menus and macros you develop for printing are your own custom creations (and therefore not familiar to all users), a "safety net" menu can be a real convenience and timesaver.

A simple no/yes menu provides you or other users with an opportunity to back out of the decision to print a report. A typical set of print macros for a no/yes menu is shown in Figure 12.2. The macro structure shown should look familiar, as it mimics the paper size menu in Figure 12.1. This time, only one item is shown on the Print menu, \MENU3, in order to maintain clarity, and the submenu \MENU5 is called. Again, the {let} and {if} statements are used to allow the user to press Escape while in the submenu:

```
{let CHOICE,0}
{menucall \MENU5}
{if CHOICE<>1}{restart}{branch \M}
{\PRINT_MONTHLY}{branch \M}
```

The submenu \MENU5 has the two choices, No and Yes, shown below. If the printer is not on-line, or the paper is not properly adjusted, the user can choose No to immediately return control to the main menu:

```
{restart}{branch \M}
```

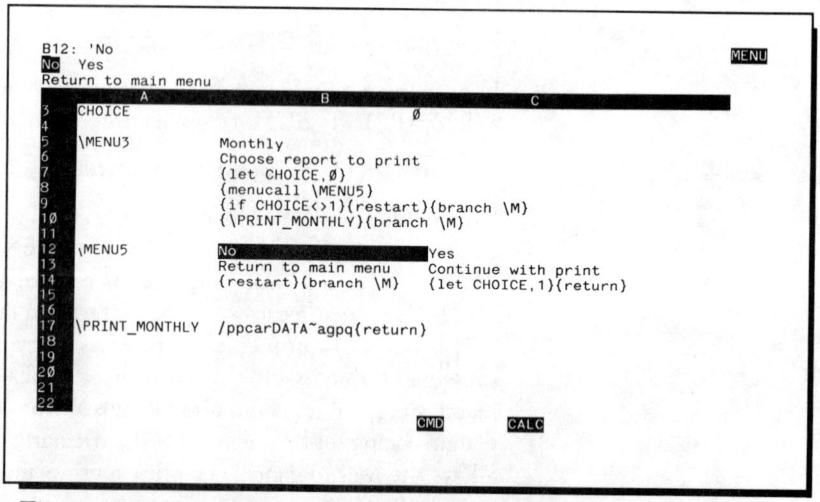

```
B12: 'No                                                    MENU
No  Yes
Return to main menu
            A                  B              C
3  CHOICE                              Ø
4
5  \MENU3             Monthly
6                     Choose report to print
7                     {let CHOICE,Ø}
8                     {menucall \MENU5}
9                     {if CHOICE<>1}{restart}{branch \M}
10                    {\PRINT_MONTHLY}{branch \M}
11
12 \MENU5             No                 Yes
13                    Return to main menu   Continue with print
14                    {restart}{branch \M}  {let CHOICE,1}{return}
15
16
17 \PRINT_MONTHLY     /ppcarDATA~agpq{return}
18
19
20
21
22
                                  CMD        CALC
```

Figure 12.2 ◆ *A macro menu to cancel a selected print operation*

If the printer is ready, choosing Yes returns control to the macro in cell B9:

{let CHOICE,1}{return}

There, the value of CHOICE is checked as in the previous example. If all is well, the print routine continues in B10.

You can easily include this safety net following the paper size menu shown in Figure 12.1, to provide a final selection before printing begins. It will prove invaluable as a means of control in all your worksheet print macros.

◆ CONTROLLING THE PRINTED PAGE

It so often seems that every program has a different way of formatting its output to the printer. Where Lotus puts the header just below the top margin, another program might put it within the margin. A word processor prints an entire line of text no matter how wide it is. In the Lotus worksheet, only the specified portion of the row is printed.

These discrepancies, although minor, can add confusion to otherwise simple routines. If you thoroughly understand the printed page layout, you can control the format of any worksheet printout.

PAGE LAYOUT

If you're having a bad day, it may seem that Lotus applies a different format every time you try to print. In fact, Lotus follows a simple formatting structure to which your worksheets must be adapted.

You can adjust the various options that control the printed page for each print routine. When the print command Clear All is issued, each setting is returned to its default value. You can view the default settings with the Worksheet Global Default Status command. You can create your own default values by modifying the settings on the Worksheet Global Default Printer menu, and then saving the current default settings to the 123.CNF file with the Worksheet Global Default Update command.

⊗ **CAUTION** ◆ *Think carefully before you decide to create your own default print settings. You could run into trouble when you take one of your worksheets to a computer that has another* *copy of Lotus running. Worksheets designed to rely on your own default print settings will not work on a system that has a different set of defaults.*

When your worksheet is first loaded into another version of Lotus, initially the print settings remain as you set them. But as soon as you issue the Clear All command, the options return to the current default settings installed on that copy of Lotus, and the trouble begins. (You would encounter similar difficulties if you retrieved a worksheet designed on someone else's system into your version of Lotus).

It may be safer in the long run to leave the default settings at their initial values, and rely on macros to make the necessary changes to your print routines.

Left and Right Margins

Some spreadsheet and word processor programs require you to include the left margin within the print area, so that the margin you see on the screen is what will appear on the printed page. In the Lotus worksheet, you need not include a blank column at the left of the print range to have a left margin on the printout. The left margin is specified at the time of printing and appears as blank spaces to the left of the first printed column.

The right margin determines the position of the last character at the right side of the printout. It is measured from the left edge of the paper. The number of characters that will be printed between the margins is therefore determined by subtracting the left margin from the right margin.

TIP ◆ *The initial default settings for the left and right margins are 4 and 76, which leaves room for 72 characters to be printed. This also happens to be the maximum number of characters that can be displayed on the Lotus screen.*

Top and Bottom Margins

The top and bottom margins are the number of blank lines between the top edge of the paper and the header, and the bottom edge of the paper and the footer. If the top margin is set to 0, the header will print on the first line of the page. With the margins set to their default of 2, there are two blank lines between the edge of the paper and the header or footer.

If you want to print on as much of the paper as possible, you can set the left, top, and bottom margins to zero, and the right margin to 240. In Release 2.2, you can set all of these margins with just one Print command, Options Margins None.

2.2 ◆ ———

The top and bottom margins can range between 0 and 32, but the total of the top and bottom margins plus header and footer cannot exceed the page length. If they do, you will receive the error message *Margins, header and footer equal or exceed page length.*

Page Length

A standard printer prints at 6 lines per inch, so a standard 8½-by-11-inch sheet of paper can hold 66 printed lines, which is the default page length in Lotus. Remember that you are responsible for telling Lotus the length of the paper your printer is currently using. If you change to paper that is 11 inches wide by 8½ inches high, you must reset the Lotus page length to 51 (8½ inches times 6 lines per inch).

If you are printing 8 lines per inch by sending the appropriate setup code to the printer, then you must also inform Lotus of the "longer" page size. Instead of 66 lines on the standard 11-inch page, you can now fit 88 lines.

Most laser printers, including the Hewlett-Packard series of LaserJets, cannot print to the very edge of the page; they must leave a small margin of about ½ inch. At 6 lines per inch, this means that there are only 60 lines available to laser printers on 11-inch paper.

If a laser printer is your primary printer, you may want to use the Worksheet Global Default Printer Pg-Length command to set the default page length to 60 (although you should still follow the safe path and specify the page length of 60 in your print macros). Then use the Update command to save this new print setting as the default for all future sessions with 1-2-3. Note that the default printer settings, such as margins and page length, are not related to the printer you choose with the Worksheet Global Default Printer Name command. If you choose another printer, you may have to change the default settings to make them compatible with the new printer.

Note that the page length can range between 1 and 100. Specifying a short page length can be convenient when printing labels or other short forms where a paged format is required.

★ **TRICK** ◆ *A short page length can also provide a practical means of testing print routines. A page length of 12 allows the header, text, and footer to print in just two inches of paper when using the default top and bottom margins of 2. If you are having trouble formatting a print routine, you will certainly appreciate being able to test it four or five times on one sheet of paper.*

Header and Footer

Only one line each is allowed for the header and footer on the printed page. The header always falls between the top margin and the beginning of the text, and the footer falls between the end of the text and the bottom margin.

> **TIP** ◆ *Even if you do not specify a header or footer, a blank line is still reserved for each and inserted into the printed page. Therefore, using a header or footer does not take up extra room on the page. Note, however, that the add-in Allways does not follow this rule. When defining your print settings in Allways, if you do not specify a header or footer, no extra blank lines are used. You therefore have six extra lines available on the page when printing with Allways.*

You are allowed a maximum of 240 characters for a header or footer, although the amount that will be printed depends on the left- and right-margin settings. With the default margins of 4 and 76, a maximum of 72 characters can be printed, even if the header or footer is longer than that. Within a header or footer, there are three symbols that are given special consideration: #, @, and ¦. They are interpreted by Lotus as follows:

Page number

@ *Current date in the form 04-Jul-76*

¦ *Determines text justification*

The page number is calculated by Lotus, based on the page length, top and bottom margins, and the number of rows that have already been printed. Issuing the Align command automatically resets the page count to 1.

The date displayed when the @ symbol is used is taken from your computer's system date. As with the other current date and time functions in Lotus, your computer's internal clock must be set correctly for them to be correct in Lotus.

The vertical bar character (a shifted backslash, ¦) tells Lotus how to justify the text within the header or footer. It is not used as a label prefix in this case. With no vertical bars in the header or footer, the text is by default left justified. If Lotus encounters one bar in the header or footer text, the text following it is centered. A second bar causes the remaining text to be right justified. Here are several examples of headers (or footers), followed by the output each will produce:

```
@¦Center Section¦Page #
¦¦This is right justified
< Left¦¦Right >
¦(#)
```

<pre>
20-Jan-88   Center Section   Page 1
                                               This is right justified
         < Left   Right >
                              (1)
</pre>

⊗ **CAUTION** ◆ *You might be inclined to ignore the current right-margin setting if the width of your print range fits within the margin limits. Remember, though, that the justification of the text within the header and footer is determined by the left and right margins. A centered header is centered between the left and right margins, and a right-justified header prints exactly up to the right margin.*

Consider what would happen if the left margin were 10 and the right margin were allowed to remain at 240 from a previous wide printing. A narrow print range can print successfully with an overly wide right margin, but imagine what happens to a header or footer.

If you leave the right margin at 240 but switch to 8½-inch paper, a centered header or footer will be centered all the way out on space number 125, the position halfway between margins of 10 and 240, plus 10 spaces for the left margin. A right-justified header will be printed so far to the right that it will probably miss the paper entirely.

The text for a header or footer must be typed in directly from the keyboard. You cannot enter a formula and expect it to automatically update, because Lotus will simply treat it as text characters. In Release 2.01, you cannot refer to the contents of a worksheet cell as you can when specifying graph titles. But you can do just that in Release 2.2, by prefacing a cell address or range name with a backslash:

2.2 ◆ ────

    \G19

As with graph titles, it is better to refer only to range names:

    \PRN_HEADER1

Arrange the text in the cell exactly as you would for the Options Header or Footer command on the Print menu. You can enter up to 240 characters, and include the @ sign for the date and # for the page number. You can also justify the text by using the vertical bar, ¦. Note that the ¦ character is also a special label prefix, so if you begin the header or footer text in a cell with that character, be sure to precede it with a normal label prefix, such as an apostrophe.

Even though a header or footer cannot refer to a cell for its text in Release 2.01, a flexible solution (that is also very handy in Release 2.2) is once again provided by macros. With them, you can trick Lotus into accepting characters that were not entered from the keyboard.

Lotus does not differentiate between keystrokes and keystroke macros. By executing your print routines through macros, you can create headers and footers that will dynamically change with the worksheet. For instance, here is a macro that would create a header that prints the current number of records in the database named DATA. The first and last lines are straight text, and the second line is built from the string formula shown. That line would actually display the current number of rows in DATA:

```
/ppcarDATA ˜ ohTotal Number of Records–
@string(@rows(DATA),0)
˜ qagpq
```

If the range DATA had 1,271 records in it, then the header would show this:

Total Number of Records – 1271

Using a similar method, you can number each page of a printout as *Page n of N*, so that in an eight-page report the first page header (or footer) would show *Page 1 of 8*, the second would show *Page 2 of 8*, and so on. To determine the total number of pages that a given range will require, you first need to know the number of rows in the range. Second, you must determine the number of lines that will be printed on each page. This is discussed next, after which you will see a simple but dynamic macro for creating the page-numbering header.

> **TIP** ♦ *One point that is frequently forgotten is that the footer does not print until the last line of text on the page is printed. To print a footer on a partially full page, you must issue the Page command to force a final form feed, at which point the footer will be printed.*

No-Man's-Land

There is a phantom zone at the top and bottom of every formatted Lotus page that is often neglected. This is the two blank lines between the header and the start of the text, and the end of the text and the footer. No matter how you set your top and bottom margins, or whether you use a header or footer, these blank lines are always included in the printout. The exception, of course, is when you use the print option Other Unformatted to print continuously, without page breaks, or when you are printing through Allways, which includes the extra blank lines only when a header or footer is specified.

Text Area

The print range is printed in the available text area of the page. The text area consists of those lines that are left after subtracting from the page length the top and bottom margins, header and footer lines, and the four blank "phantom" lines. The width of the text is, of course, determined by the right margin minus the left margin.

> ☑ **TIP** ◆ *Since printing is a frequently repeated task, any ranges that will be printed should have their own range names. If you are printing manually (without a macro), you need only press the F3 {name} key when prompted for a range to be printed, and select the range name from the list. If you are playing it smart and using macros for all your print jobs, then range names become even more necessary to ensure the reliability and readability of the routines.*

With the Lotus printed page neatly split into its component parts, you should now be able to determine exactly how many lines will be printed when the Lotus default print settings are used.

DETERMINING THE NUMBER OF LINES PER PAGE

Given the page length and top- and bottom-margin settings, you can determine the number of lines of text that will be printed on each page. Figure 12.3 graphically demonstrates the entire Lotus page layout: margins, header and

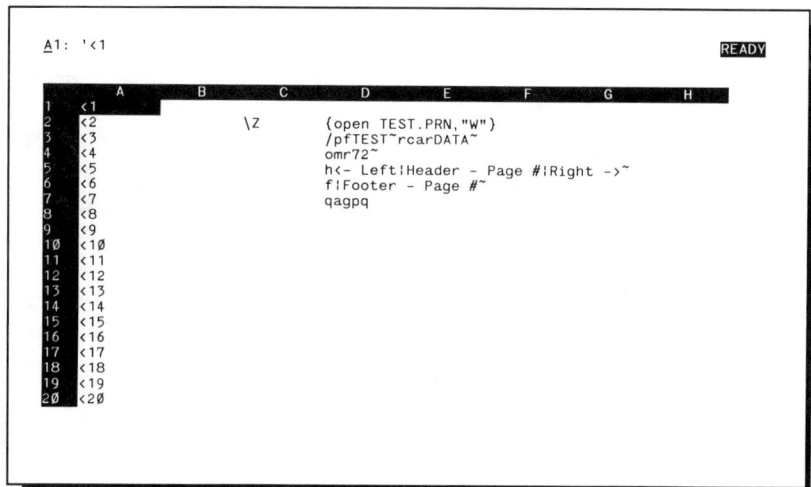

```
A1: '<1                                                          READY

        A          B       C      D        E        F        G        H
1   <1
2   <2                     \Z      {open TEST.PRN,"W"}
3   <3                             /pfTEST~rcarDATA~
4   <4                             omr72~
5   <5                             h<- Left!Header - Page #!Right ->~
6   <6                             f!Footer - Page #~
7   <7                             qagpq
8   <8
9   <9
10  <10
11  <11
12  <12
13  <13
14  <14
15  <15
16  <16
17  <17
18  <18
19  <19
20  <20
```

Figure 12.3 ◆ *A worksheet to demonstrate the Lotus page layout*

footer, page length, and page breaks. Column A of this worksheet has been filled with enough numbers so that several pages will be needed to print them all; the column is named DATA. The numbers are prefaced with a < character, which makes them text entries. When printed, the arrows will point to the left margin.

The macro named \Z at D2 will print the range DATA to a disk file named TEST.PRN:

```
{open TEST.PRN,"W"}
/pfTEST ~ rcarDATA ~
omr72 ~
h <- Left ¦ Header - Page # ¦ Right -> ~
f ¦ Footer - Page # ~
qagpq
```

The {write} statement in the first line of the macro creates text TEST.PRN, so that the print command Replace can always be used in the macro to replace the file that already exists.

The second line names the print file to which the output will be sent, clears all print settings to their default values, and specifies the range DATA as the print range.

The next line sets the right margin to 72. This was used instead of the default of 76 so that the entire printout would fit within 72 spaces. You will see why shortly.

Then, a header is specified with arrows at the left and right edges, and the page number in the center. The footer prints centered page numbers.

Finally, the Align and Go commands are given, followed by a Page and a Quit command. With the file successfully printed to disk, you can use the File Import command to bring it back into a blank worksheet at cell A1, as shown in Figure 12.4.

This one worksheet screen, windowed to show rows 1 to 72, shows the complete layout of the printed page. The cell pointer is on cell A3, which contains the header from the printed text. Notice that it is one long string of text. It is preceded by four blank spaces, which is the default left margin that was used for the printing. You can now see why the right margin was set to 72: it conveniently places the right edge of the header exactly at the right edge of the screen. The following table describes each row of the printout.

Row	Description
1–2	Margin top, page 1
3	Header, page 1
4–5	Blank rows between header and text

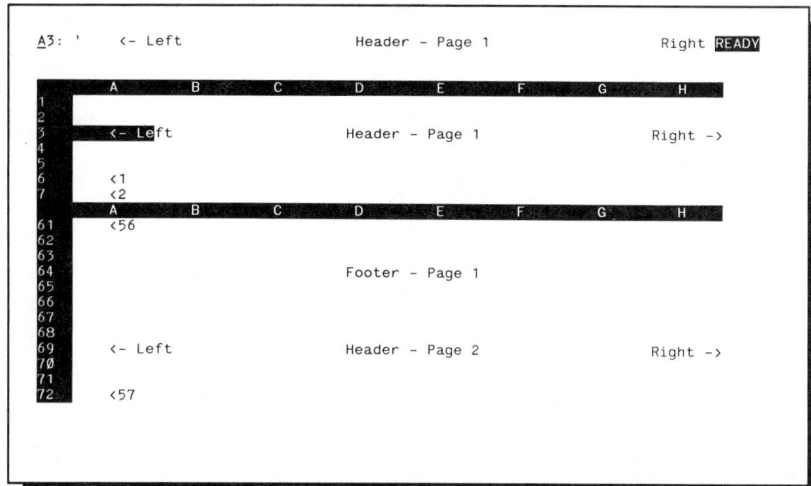

Figure 12.4 ◆ *The structure and layout of a Lotus printed page*

6–61	Text area, 56 lines total
62–63	Blank rows between text and footer
64	Footer, page 1
65–66	Margin bottom, page 1
67–68	Margin top, page 2
69	Header, page 2
70–71	Blank rows between header and text
72	Text area begins, page 2

If the output had been sent to the printer instead of to a file, the paper perforations between the first and second page would fall precisely between rows 66 and 67 (assuming your paper had been inserted correctly into the printer).

As you can see, with the Lotus default settings there are 56 text rows printed on a page. For other page lengths or margins, you can determine the number of rows that will be printed by first subtracting 6 from the page length, for the header, footer, and "phantom" rows. From the remainder, subtract the top and bottom margins. The result is the number of text lines that will be printed.

On 11-inch paper, by setting the top and bottom margins to 0, you can therefore print a maximum of 60 text rows in a paged format. Note that with the Options Unformatted setting, you can print without any page breaks and use the entire page length for text.

> ▨ **TIP** ◆ *Even though the unformatted printout spans the breaks between the pages, Lotus still counts the lines left on the page. This means that you can issue a Page command at the end of a printout and the paper will feed to the top of the next sheet.*

Building a Dynamic Header: Page n of N

Knowing how to calculate the number of printed lines on a page gives you an edge when you are printing data that should not be split between two pages. Suppose the data in your print range is arranged in groups of five rows, such as the quarters of the year and a total. To avoid splitting a group between two pages, you will want to determine how many full groups fit exactly on one page, and adjust the top, bottom, or both margins accordingly.

With the default margins, you have 56 lines available. Dividing 56 by 5 leaves one extra row on the page, placing four rows from that last group onto the next page. Therefore, you will need to set the top or bottom margin to 3 in order to print exactly 55 lines of text—just enough for 11 groups of 5.

Once you determine the available lines per page, you can also calculate the number of pages that a given print range will require. This is how you can write a macro to create a header or footer that prints *Page 1 of 8*.

All you need is an @row formula to count the number of rows in the print range, named DATA here, and then divide the result by the number of printable lines on each page. If you are using a standard 11-inch page with the default margin settings, you will have 56 text lines, so you will need to divide the number of data rows by 56. The result would be made into a string to be incorporated into the header or footer in the print macro.

But you also must consider the case when there is a fraction of a page left over from the division. This means that there will be one extra page in the printout, even if there is only one line of text on it. Therefore, you must force any fractional answer to result in the next higher page number. Adding 0.49 to the division allows the @string function to properly round any result:

```
@string(@rows($DATA)/56 + 0.49,0)
```

The result of this formula is the total number of pages that DATA will require when printed. It is a string value and can be built into the print macro to create the header, shown here on the second line of the macro:

```
/ppcarDATA ˜ oh ¦ ¦ Page # of
8
˜ qagq
```

This macro produces a right-justified header. Note that there must be a space after the word *of* in the first line, otherwise there would be no space between it and the page number.

WHEN LOTUS AND YOUR PRINTER ARE OUT OF SYNCH

Many printing problems can arise when Lotus and your printer are not synchronized. By understanding the relationship between Lotus and the printed page, you will avoid many of these problems and be able to control every aspect of the printing process.

Using the Page, Line, and Align Commands

Lotus can count the number of lines it sends to the printer. If you tell it that your page length can hold 66 lines, it will know exactly where to print the bottom margin on one page and the top margin of the following page.

Once the paper is properly aligned in the printer at the first line of the page, you can control the paper from within Lotus and never have to touch the printer again. This is not only convenient, but it saves you from some of the problems mentioned next.

When you issue the Page command, Lotus will advance the paper to the top of the next page. If you have just printed a page and a half of text, you can start the next printout on a separate page by first pressing P for Page. The paper will be at the start of a new page, and the Lotus line count will be reset to 1. If you include the Page command before the final Quit command in a print macro, the paper will always be sent to the top of the next page when the printing is finished:

```
/ppcarDATA ˜ agpq
```

You can advance the paper a line at a time with the Line command. This allows you to insert some blank space on the page between two separate print ranges. Here is a short macro that prints two different ranges and inserts five blank lines between them:

```
/ppcarRANGE_1 ˜ agllllrRANGE_2 ˜ gq
```

The Align command is used to notify Lotus that the printer paper is now precisely aligned at the top of a page, and Lotus should reset its line count to 1. The command should not be confused with the physical act of aligning the paper. The Align command does not send any signals to the printer, as do the Page and Line commands.

When your printer paper jams and spoils a printout, you must fix it and manually reset the paper to the top of a page. That is the time when you must always issue the Align command. This lets Lotus know that, wherever it was in its line count during the printout, it should now start over at line 1.

The Align command also resets page numbering back to 1, so you should not use it during the printing of a series of ranges or the pages will not be numbered consecutively. Note that quitting the Print menu also resets page numbering to 1.

★ **TRICK** ◆ *You cannot specify a beginning page number for your printouts, so once you quit the Print menu you cannot continue printing starting at the last page number. There is a way around this, though. Although it wastes a small amount of paper, it does allow you to resume printing at a chosen page number.*

Assume you have previously printed an 11-page report and you now want to continue with page 12. First, issue the Options Other Unformatted command to eliminate headers, footers, and page breaks. Then set the page length to 1. Now press P for Page as many times as you need page numbers advanced, in this case 11 times. The printer will advance one line for each Page command as the Lotus page count also advances by one.

Then manually reset the paper to the top-of-form position. Reset the print options to Formatted printing and to the proper page length. Don't press Align before printing, or the page numbering will return to 1. Just issue the Go command, and your header or footer on the first page will show page 12.

Curing the Mysterious Blank Rows Syndrome

Have you ever had a printout that had several blank rows appear somewhere in each page, and the printed text ran right across the page perforations? Every Lotus user has had this happen at least once, and has probably been asked about it many more times by others with the problem. It is the classic example of the user causing Lotus and the printer to get out of synch.

The problem arises because Lotus is not aware of the actual position or size of the paper in the printer. It is printing just as it is supposed to, but the blank lines for the bottom margin of one page and the top margin of the next are not being printed precisely on either side of a page perforation. Although this unusable result is the same, the problem can come from several sources.

The first thing to consider is that the Lotus Page Length option may not match the actual size of the paper in the printer. For instance, the problem will show up on the second page of the printout if you switch the paper in the printer to 11-by-8½-inch but forget to change the Lotus page length from 66 to 51. Or, if you are new to laser printers, you may have neglected to set the page length to 60, the maximum on an 11-inch page when printing 6 lines per inch.

Second, if the page length seems to be set correctly for the current paper size, consider the printer setup code you are using. If you send a setup code to the printer to switch to 8 lines per inch printing, you must also adjust the Lotus page length to 88 (11-inch paper) or 68 (8½-inch paper). If you set the printer for double-spacing, then you must set the page length to only half the number of lines usually available on the page.

Third, when the page length is set correctly for the page size and setup codes being used and the problem still persists, there is only one other possibility left. You have realigned the paper in the printer without advising Lotus of your action.

Suppose you print a report that is a little over one page long. Before you print the next one, you go to the printer and roll the paper up to the top of the next page. If you then specify a new print range and issue a Go command, Lotus will print to the end of what it considers the current page, print the bottom and top margins, and so on. Unfortunately, your paper is not where it is supposed to be.

When you must manually align the paper in the printer, be sure to press Align before choosing Go in the Lotus Print menu. This will reset the line count to 1. But the only time you should ever need to touch the paper is when you have a printer problem. In most other situations, if you want to set the paper to the top-of-form position, you can simply select the Page command from the Lotus Print menu. It automatically sends the paper to the top of the next sheet, determined by the Lotus line count of how many lines were left on the current page.

Adjusting Margins That Are Too Wide or Too Narrow

If you are finding that the margins on either side of the text are not as they should be, there are two things to check. First, be sure you are using the correct margin setting for the character size you are printing. In a condensed mode of 17 characters per inch, a left margin of 4 will produce a skinny, quarter-inch margin. To print with a one-inch left margin, you would have to set the left margin to 17.

If you think the margins are set appropriately, suspect that the paper is not properly aligned left and right in the printer. Perhaps someone moved the paper for a peculiar print job and forgot to return it to its correct position.

What is the correct position for the paper in the printer? Set the Lotus left margin to 0, and print a few cells that contain a left-aligned capital M. If the paper is set properly, the left leg of the M will be just about at the left edge of the paper. If it falls too far to one side of the edge, adjust the paper until it prints in the proper spot.

⊗ **CAUTION** ◆ *Whatever you do, you should always avoid moving the established left edge of the paper in the printer. When changing to wider paper in a continuous-feed, tractor-driven printer, adjust only the right-hand tractor for the new width. The left-hand tractor should remain locked at the proper "zero margin" position. Then you can set the appropriate margin from within Lotus and expect it to print at exactly the right place.*

Handling Excess Print Characters

There are two unique results when the print range is too wide:

1. Margins OK, printer too narrow

2. Printer OK, margins too narrow

For example, imagine a print range that includes 15 columns that are each 12 characters wide, for a total of 180 characters.

Consider the case where the margins are set correctly but the printer is too narrow. Setting the print margins to 10 and 200 will provide an adequate width of 190 characters for the 180-character line. However, printing this range will cause problems on a typical 8½-inch printer because most printers of that width can handle a maximum line length of about 132 characters, in compressed mode. When a line of 180 characters is sent to the printer, it will print its maximum of 132 and then dump the rest on another line. Each row of the print range will therefore require two printed lines. Thus, the printed lines will alternate between 132 and 48 characters.

⊗ **CAUTION** ◆ *The results of sending too many characters to your printer are not always obvious when the excess characters in the print range are blank. This can occur when you accidentally include a blank column at the right edge of the range. The excess secondary rows in the printout are blank, which makes the printout appear to be double-spaced. In fact, though, your print range is still too wide for your printer and needs to be narrowed.*

Now consider the second case, where the printer is wide enough but the print margins are too narrow. When the print range is too wide for the Lotus margin settings, Lotus prints the excess columns on a new page. In the given example, you could print the 180-character print range on a wide 232-column printer in compressed mode with the left and right margins set at 10 and 200, respectively. If you neglected to set the right margin wide enough, Lotus would be forced to print as much as it could fit within the margins, and print the rest on another page.

So if your printouts are being unexpectedly chopped off at the right margin with the remainder showing up on a separate page, make sure you have specified an adequate left and right margin. Remember that you must subtract the left from the right margin to determine how many characters of text will actually be printed.

◆ FORMATTING THE OUTPUT

The flexibility of the worksheet environment provides an infinite number of ways to format your worksheets for printing. With the help of some built-in Lotus tools including, once again, macros, you can design your printouts without restricting the look or practicality of the worksheet itself. When you print with Allways, the spreadsheet publishing add-in, your printouts will be absolutely first rate and require minimal effort on your part.

USING BORDER ROWS AND COLUMNS

The print commands for Borders Rows and Borders Columns do for printing what the Worksheet Titles command does for the display screen. You can specify a range of rows (or columns) that will be printed at the top (or the left side) of each page.

By specifying a group of rows for the print border, you can print a long range of many rows and have its column titles printed on each page. This prevents you from having to manually insert rows and a new set of titles for every 56 rows in the range. Setting border columns allows you to print the columns of a very wide range on several pages while maintaining the same left-hand columns on each page.

The worksheet in Figure 12.5 demonstrates the use of borders. The column titles for the print range lie in rows 1 through 4 in columns A through F. By specifying the four title rows as Borders Rows, those titles will be printed at the top of each page, no matter how many pages are printed. The print range starts at row 5, just below the border rows.

TIP ◆ Here is the first and foremost rule when specifying border rows or columns. If those border cells serve as column or row titles as in the example (this is usually the case), do not include

```
A1: [W17] \=                                                    READY

            A        B        C        D        E        F        G
1   ==================================================================
2   City of Origin &  :  Account and  :  Percentage
3   Primary Contact   :  Group Number :  Gross Factor :
4   ==================================================================
5   New Orleans       :  AN-2868-N    :     88.0% :
6   Santa Monica      :  EA-4403-R    :     58.0% :
7   Philadelphia      :  AF-9223-S    :     98.0% :
8   Trenton           :  FN-1154-E    :     25.0% :
9   Reno              :  YA-5809-S    :     29.0% :
10  Sacramento        :  RA-9467-Y    :     27.0% :
11  San Francisco     :  AR-4437-A    :     24.0% :
12  San Antonio       :  SA-4477-Y    :     90.0% :
13  St. Paul          :  RY-5533-A    :     62.0% :
14  Los Angeles       :  NE-7908-A    :     68.0% :
15  Pasadena          :  YE-9109-A    :     78.0% :
16  Salt Lake         :  EY-3116-E    :     54.0% :
17  Chicago           :  AS-1689-R    :     87.0% :
18  Miami             :  EE-4894-F    :     39.0% :
19  St. Louis         :  SS-9506-E    :     65.0% :
20  Atlanta           :  NR-6087-N    :     40.0% :
25-Oct-89  01:10 PM
```

Figure 12.5 ◆ *Printing border rows on each page*

them in your print range. If you do, those cells will be printed twice—first as the border cells, and again as part of the print range. If the print range in Figure 12.5 started at row 1, which includes the four border rows, then the first page of the printout would start with the border rows, and would be followed immediately by the first rows of the print range, which would again be rows 1 through 4.

Although there may be a rare occasion when you will want the border cells printed as part of the print range, under most circumstances you will want to exclude them.

You do not have to specify an entire border range over or next to your data; you need only specify the relevant rows or columns. For example, in Figure 12.5 you might be inclined to specify the range A1..F4 as the border rows. This is not a problem, but you only need to refer to any four cells that contain those rows. You could therefore use A1..A4, C1..D4, or IV1..IV4.

When you are printing with Allways, the same rules apply, but you are also allowed to specify rows as a bottom border. With border rows at both the bottom and the top of your print range, you can now create what are in effect multilined headers and footers. Just specify in which the two sets of rows you want the header and footer text to appear, and they will be printed at the top and bottom of each page.

Remember that if you are always going to print a range with the same borders, not only the data range but also the border cells deserve their own range name.

The border cells print in the normal text area of the page, and therefore take room that would otherwise be available for the print range. When calculating the number of lines available on each page, or the number of characters in a line, be sure to include any border rows or columns in your calculations. In Figure 12.5, for example, the four border rows would leave only 52 rows per page instead of the default 56 rows.

> ⊗ **CAUTION** ◆ *You may sometimes run into the problem of border rows or columns printing when you do not want them to. You cannot cancel the borders by pressing Escape when prompted for the border range, as you can a header or setup code. Instead, you must use the Clear command on the Print menu, from which you can clear the Borders option.*

MODIFYING THE DISPLAY FOR PRINTING

In the early stages of the Lotus learning curve, most users arrange the data so that it can be conveniently printed. Column and row titles, column widths, cell formats, and the layout of formulas and other process cells are all arranged so that the data can be printed as one unit. Unfortunately, maintaining an appropriate appearance can restrict the usefulness of the data for data entry, maintenance, and processing.

In Chapter 3, you learned why input, process, and output ranges should be considered as distinct units. When constructing a worksheet, you should therefore take advantage of its flexibility and, when necessary, create output cells for printing.

There is, however, another option for formatting a range for printing that is a snap if you use macros. With the speed and reliability of macros, you can alter the display of a range prior to printing it, and then reverse the changes when the printing is finished.

2.2 ◆ ——

The Worksheet Global Zero command allows you to turn off the display of any numeric cell that has a value of 0. You have quite a bit more flexibility in Release 2.2, where you can not only turn off the display of zeroes but also specify the characters to display in place of any zeroes in the worksheet. Use the Worksheet Global Zero Label command, and enter the text that you want to see in place of zeroes. Your entry will always be taken as text by this command, and you can also include a label prefix if you want the text to be other than left justified (if that is your default). So, to display a centered hyphen in place of a zero, enter ^—. Or, enter the word ZERO, and that word will appear instead of the number.

The ability to display text in place of zeroes is strictly for creating a pleasing display, and it is frequently needed only for printing. Therefore, your print macro can turn off the display of 0s before printing, and turn them back on again when the printing is finished:

/wgzy/ppcarDATA ˜ agpq/wgzn

This macro solution can also assign a new format to a given range, and then change it back when the printing is done. Column widths might also need adjusting, and they too can be reset when finished. Remember that you can completely hide columns with the Worksheet Column Hide command.

When changing the width of columns or hiding them before printing, you can shorten the routine if you first split the screen with the Worksheet Windows command. Then adjust the columns in the lower (or right-hand) window. When the printing is done, just clear the windows and it will be as though the columns had never been changed.

This works because column changes are not permanent unless they are made in the "dominant" window. This is either the upper window when the screen is split horizontally, or the left-hand window when it is split vertically. The worksheet used in the previous example serves to illustrate this, as shown in Figure 12.6. The upper window, rows 1 through 8, is the worksheet as it might appear when used for data entry or strictly as process cells. Columns B, D, and F have been hidden, and the other column widths have been adjusted for optimum viewing on the screen. In the format shown, it is not suitable for printing.

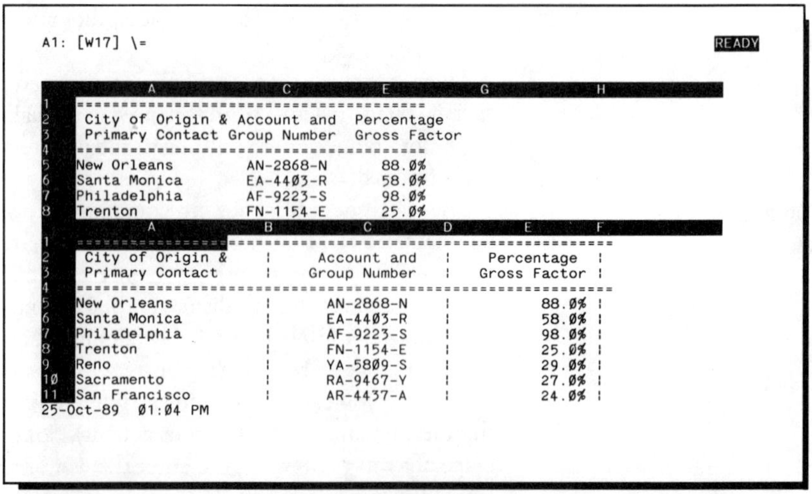

```
A1: [W17] \=                                              READY

         A            C           E           G          H
1  =========================================================
2  City of Origin & Account and  Percentage
3  Primary Contact Group Number  Gross Factor
4  =========================================================
5  New Orleans      AN-2868-N       88.0%
6  Santa Monica     EA-4403-R       58.0%
7  Philadelphia     AF-9223-S       98.0%
8  Trenton          FN-1154-E       25.0%
         A            B           C           D          E          F
1  =========================================================
2  City of Origin &    ¦     Account and  ¦   Percentage  ¦
3  Primary Contact     ¦     Group Number ¦   Gross Factor ¦
4  =========================================================
5  New Orleans         ¦     AN-2868-N    ¦      88.0% ¦
6  Santa Monica        ¦     EA-4403-R    ¦      58.0% ¦
7  Philadelphia        ¦     AF-9223-S    ¦      98.0% ¦
8  Trenton             ¦     FN-1154-E    ¦      25.0% ¦
9  Reno                ¦     YA-5809-S    ¦      29.0% ¦
10 Sacramento          ¦     RA-9467-Y    ¦      27.0% ¦
11 San Francisco       ¦     AR-4437-A    ¦      24.0% ¦
25-Oct-89  01:04 PM
```

Figure 12.6 ◆ *Altering column widths in the lower window before printing*

In the lower window, you can see rows 1 through 11, but they do not appear the same as those rows in the upper window. Here the hidden columns are displayed, and the other columns have been expanded to an appropriate width for printing. You can also use a different global format in each window, although changing the format of a range will affect both windows.

With the screen split horizontally, you can easily create the desired layout in the lower section by invoking a macro before printing. After printing, the macro can clear the window, leaving only the layout seen in the top section, as this macro would for Figure 12.6:

```
/wwh{window}{home}
/wcs17 ˜ /wcdB1 ˜ {right}
/wcs9 ˜ {right}
/wcs13 ˜ /wcdD1 ˜ {right}
/wcs5 ˜ {right}
/wcs13 ˜ /wcdF1 ˜ {right}
/wcs3 ˜
/ppcarDATA ˜ agpq
/wwc
```

2.2 ◆ ———

TIP ◆ *If you are using Release 2.2 and need to set several adjacent columns to the same width, don't forget the Worksheet Column Column-Range command, which allows you to adjust a group of columns to a new width with just the one command.*

EMBEDDED PRINTER COMMANDS

You can send a set of control sequences to the printer with the Options Setup command in the Print menu. You can also include these print commands directly in the worksheet. The codes are entered as text, just as you would enter codes for the Setup option in the Print menu. Each code must be prefaced with the vertical bar label prefix, ¦.

All printer control codes must be entered within the first column of the print range, otherwise their special meaning will be ignored by Lotus and they will be printed as text. When Lotus encounters a code in the first column of the print range, it sends the code to the printer and ignores the other cells in that row. No line feed is sent to the printer, so on the printout it appears as though that row did not exist.

One distinct advantage of embedded printer control codes is that they can be as long as 240 characters. You are not limited to the 39 characters offered by the Print command's Setup option. Unfortunately, even 240 may not seem that large when you are dealing with printers (such as laser printers) that require some pretty complex setup codes.

⊗ CAUTION ◆ *The vertical bar label prefix does not serve as a setup code prefix in the add-in Allways. In fact, setup strings are irrelevant in Allways, which handles all print attributes itself. In Allways the ¦ character serves as a special label prefix that forces the text to be flush-right aligned in the cell. It does not leave a space to the right of the text, as the double quote label prefix does. When using the ¦ character in either Allways or 1-2-3, just remember the different effect it has in each environment.*

The Worksheet Page command inserts the page break code, two colons, in a blank row in the worksheet. Lotus automatically inserts a new row in the worksheet before entering the code, allowing you to break a range of data without losing any of the data on the printout:

¦ ::

You can enter your own page break command by typing the label prefix and two colons into a cell in the first column of the print range. The Worksheet Page command simply saves you the step of inserting a row and then entering the characters.

The page break code is prefaced with one vertical bar, but other printer control codes must have two vertical bars. To send a printer control code that turns on emphasized printing to an Epson-compatible printer, you would type in these characters in a cell in the first column of the print range:

¦¦\027\069

Note that the first vertical bar would not be displayed on the screen, since it serves as a label prefix. You would see only the second bar and the setup code. You should also know that you cannot disable an embedded printer control code by giving it a Hidden format. Although you would not see other characters that are hidden when the worksheet is printed, Lotus uses the printer codes whether they are visible or not.

Since a row will not be printed when it begins with a cell that has a vertical bar label prefix, you can create nonprinting comment rows to annotate your work:

¦Cell entries with the vertical bar label prefix can
¦serve as nonprinting comments within the worksheet.

Just be sure that the comments begin in the first column of the print range. Any cells in the print range to the right of a comment in that column will also not be printed, and can therefore be used for comments as well.

You can selectively eliminate rows from the printout by entering "null" cell entries in an extra column at the left-hand edge of the range you are printing.

The null code is a single vertical bar at its simplest, but you should add some text after it so that the entry will be visible on the screen:

¦No Print

The result is that each row with a null entry in its first column will be skipped in the printout.

Here is a double trick: that extra column can be hidden before printing so that it will not add extra spaces in the printout. Figure 12.7 shows how the system works. The data range lies in column B. Several null entries have been entered in column A. Before printing the range A1..B18, column A was hidden. The result of the printing can be seen to the right, which was imported from a print file. Every row that had a null code in it was skipped.

KEEPING SETUP CODES AT THE READY

Using setup codes to control your printer can be a very lively art, and one that you may tire of rather quickly. This is especially true if you have a laser printer, which can go through setup codes at a furious rate. Of course, if high-quality output is your ultimate goal, using a spreadsheet publishing add-in such as Allways is certainly the answer. At the other extreme, if draft quality is usually adequate for your work, you may get by with just a few setup codes to handle most of your printing needs.

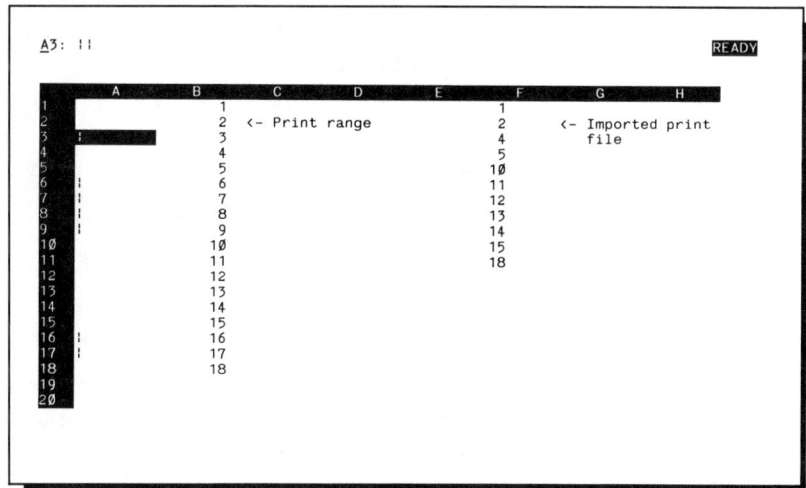

Figure 12.7 ◆ *Using null cell entries to eliminate rows from the printout*

But there is a lot of territory in between, and finding a convenient means of controlling your printer via setup codes can pay big dividends. Once again, a little imagination combined with the power and convenience of macros supplies the answer.

Maintaining a List of Setup Codes

The solution lies in keeping a list of setup codes in a separate worksheet. Give the worksheet an obvious name such as SETUP, and enter the setup strings in the cells down column C, remembering to preface a string with a label prefix if it begins with a backslash. You can enter each code into a separate cell and also combine codes to provide a single setup code to handle multiple printer commands. For example, to provide the maximum amount of text on a page for a laser printer, you might combine into one cell, such as C2, the codes for landscape orientation, compressed print, and line spacing of 8 lines per inch.

Give each setup code's cell a descriptive range name. For the example discussed above, you could give cell C2 the name LAND_17_8. Another cell in column C might be named PORT_17_6, for portrait orientation, 17 characters per inch (cpi), and line spacing of 6 lines per inch. Type in the range name you use in column B next to each setup string, so you will know what each cell is named. A typical list of codes for an HP LaserJet printer might look like this:

```
RESET           \027E
COPIES          \027&l#X
PORT            \027&l0O
LAND            \027&l1O
LAND_17_8       \027&l1o8d\027(s16.66H
```

In column A, enter a description of each setup string in column C. This might be as simple as "Landscape, 17 cpi, 8 lpi", or you may need to be more descriptive. At some point in the future when you are looking through your list of codes, you will be glad you explained each one.

Save this worksheet in a convenient subdirectory, where it will be easy to find when you need it. Now when you build a worksheet and need a setup code, the right code is no farther away than your SETUP worksheet file.

Accessing Your List of Setup Codes

The easiest way to find the setup code you need is simply to bring in that cell from the SETUP worksheet. For example, suppose you want to print multiple copies of your worksheet on your laser printer, and the setup code in your SETUP worksheet is named COPIES (as shown in the previous section). Just move the cell pointer to an empty cell, invoke the File Combine command, and specify the name COPIES as the range to bring in from the worksheet named SETUP. The command is shown here in macro form:

/fccnCOPIES ˜ SETUP ˜

In this example you would also need to replace the # sign in the setup code with the number of copies you want printed. With that done, there are several ways for you to use the code in the print command.

The most direct method is the manual approach. Simply call up the print menu and type in the setup string while referring to the copy in the cell (in Release 2.2, you can turn off the settings screen by pressing the F6 key). By using the code this way, the SETUP worksheet serves only as a convenient, electronic reminder of your setup codes. To extend its utility as a reminder sheet, you could bring in the entire file to the current worksheet so that you could refer to any of the codes listed there.

You could also bring the appropriate code into the worksheet to be used as an embedded code. Just be sure to place the code in a cell in the first column of your print range, and to replace its normal label prefix with the two vertical bars that tell 1-2-3 it is a setup code.

Another alternative for macro users is to automate the process of accessing these codes. Suppose you are building a print macro for a worksheet, and you want to include the laser printer setup code named LAND_17_8 in the SETUP worksheet. Create a variable cell named SETUP_CODE, and bring in the code to that cell with the File Combine command, as discussed above. Now your macro can refer to the new variable cell for the setup code, shown here in a short macro that prints a range named DATA:

/ppcarDATA ˜ os{SETUP_CODE} ˜ qagpq

Be sure to place the {return} command under the cell named SETUP_CODE so that there will be no chance of the macro continuing down that column.

DETERMINING THE WIDTH OF A PRINT RANGE

Before printing, you must decide whether a print range will fit within the width of the printed page. Without a few tools and tricks, it can be a time-consuming process.

For example, in the following discussion, a typical 8½-inch wide page is used. This width supports a maximum of 132 characters when printing in compressed mode. With the left margin set at 10, 122 characters remain for the text.

Rough Calculations: Cell Widths Minus Print Margins

If all the columns in the range to be printed are the same width, it should be a simple matter to add their widths. So if columns A through J are each 9 characters wide, then their total width would be 90, leaving 42 characters for the margins on each side of the text. If the columns are not the same width, the width of the range is more difficult to determine. If there are many columns of varied width, then the job gets tougher still.

> **TIP** ◆ *If the right margin is not wide enough to contain the entire print range, Lotus does not break the print range at the last available margin space, as you might expect. Instead, it stops at the last column before the margin edge is reached.*
>
> *For instance, if you have 14 columns and each is 9 characters wide, you will need 126 spaces. But with the margins set at 10 and 132, Lotus will not print all 122 characters for which it has room. It will print 13 full columns, 117 characters, and then break the range onto another page. Since the last column didn't print, you might think that you need to add another 9 spaces to your margin, but that is not the case. Adding just the 4 characters will do.*

You can always perform a test print of just one line of the range to see if it fits within the print margins. If the line is too long for your margins, be prepared to turn the printer off to prevent Lotus from wasting a page by going to the next page to print the excess. Or, you can print to a disk file, a procedure that is described later in this chapter, and then view the file. This trial and error method was really all that was available in Lotus 1A, but Lotus now has several tools for determining the exact width of a range.

Precise Calculations: @repeat and @cell

The @repeat function, discussed in Chapter 9, repeats one or more characters a given number of times. If you know your maximum page width is 132 and your left margin is 10, you can enter the function in the first column of the print range in a blank row:

```
@repeat("-",132--10)
```

Using the hyphen as the text character produces a dashed line of 122 characters, the maximum width that can be printed. You can then scroll to the right to see in which column the line ends, indicating the maximum right edge that can be printed on a page. This function is used in cell A3 in Figure 12.8 to create a line above a print range, which is bordered in asterisks.

```
A3: [W2Ø] @REPEAT("-",132-1Ø)                                           READY

        A               B           I       J           K
  1
  2                                          2       End of @repeat line ->
  3    -------------------------------------  3    -------------------------------
  4                                          4
  5    * * * * * * * * * * * * * *   5   * * * * * * * * * * * *
  6    *                           6                             *
  7    *                           7                             *
  8    *                           8                             *
  9    *       <-  Print Range  ->   9                            *
 1Ø    *            A5..J13          1Ø                            *
 11    *                          11                             *
 12    *                          12                             *
 13    * * * * * * * * * * * * * *  13   * * * * * * * * * * * *
 14                               14
 15                               15
 16                               16
 17                               17
 18                               18
 19                               19
 2Ø                               2Ø
```

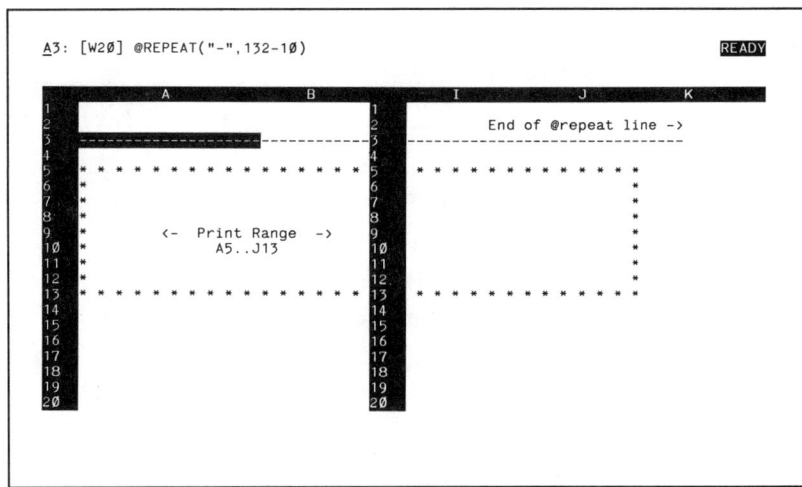

Figure 12.8 ◆ *Using @repeat to determine the width of a print range*

Remember that the row for the function must be blank so the dashed line can overhang as far as necessary. With a line like this, you can quickly compare it to the size of the print range, but you will not necessarily know the exact width of the range. For that, you can use the @cell function.

You again need a blank row in the print range. Row 16 was used in Figure 12.9, which shows the same print range from the previous example. In each cell in that row, the @cell function was entered to return the width of the column:

@cell("width",A17..A17)

Remember to refer to a cell above or below the function's cell to avoid getting a circular reference. The formula was copied across the row to column J, and the result is a range of numbers representing the width of each column in the print range. In cell A15 an @sum function was used to total the column widths, as you can see in the control panel. Again, the left-margin value of 10 was added to the actual width of the print range to provide the total number of characters needed on the page—the right margin setting.

The advantage to this method is that you can vary the width of any column at any time, and the formulas will still return the width of each one, which makes the system very flexible.

To further refine both the @repeat and @cell function methods, create a variable cell for the left margin named LEFT, and create another cell for the maximum width of the page, named MAX_WIDTH. Then refer to these

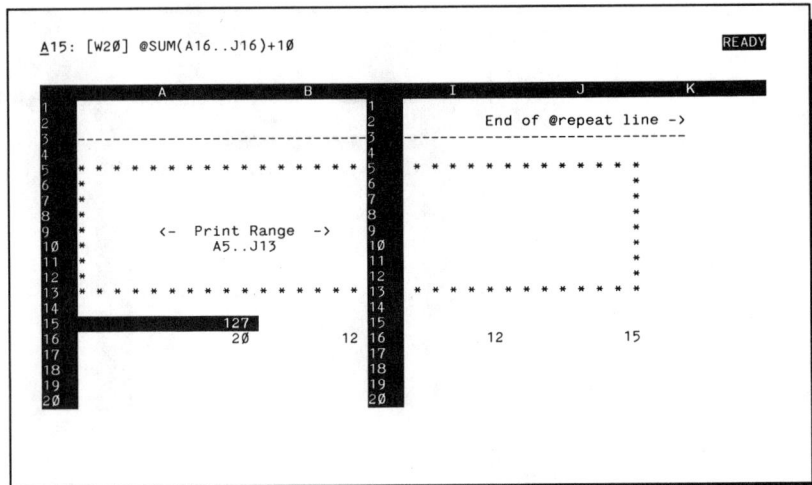

Figure 12.9 ◆ *Totaling @cell functions to determine the width of a print range*

cells in the formulas, vary the values, and check the resulting width. If MAX_WIDTH were 132 and LEFT were 10, then this formula would return a line 122 characters long, as in the previous example:

@repeat("-",MAX_WIDTH--LEFT)

The sum of the @cell functions would incorporate the left-margin variable cell to return the total width needed for the printout:

@sum(A16..J16) + LEFT

PRINTING WITH ALLWAYS

If you own a laser printer, you may feel a bit cheated when you use it to print your 1-2-3 spreadsheets. At best, you have been happy with the laser printer's very crisp output in either the standard 10 cpi typeface or the 17 cpi line printer style. At worst, you have tried to master your printer by feeding it setup codes from 1-2-3. No doubt the stack of paper that fills your wastebasket is a monument to this frustrating trial-and-error approach to creating attractive printouts. If you really want to take advantage of your printer, especially if it's a laser printer, then Allways is for you.

In Chapter 11, you already discovered that the enhancements Allways can add to your spreadsheet are first-rate, but there is another, less obvious, class of benefits to consider as well. These are the features that don't enhance the printed page, but instead enhance the manner in which you produce the print-outs by giving you many of the tools found in first-rate word processors.

Publishing with Ease

Unlike 1-2-3, Allways measures the left and right margins in inches, not characters. This allows you to change font sizes without adjusting the margins in order to maintain an even left-hand margin. You also specify the top and bottom margins and the page size in inches. This way, you can actually pin-point where a particular line will fall on a page, without having to use a calcu-lator to divide the inches by the number of characters or lines per inch.

Like a word processor, Allways shows page breaks right on the screen. It shows not only the horizontal breaks between pages, but also the vertical break at the last column in the print range that will fit within the side margins. This feature can eliminate a lot of print testing that you would otherwise have to perform.

Since page breaks are shown on-screen, Allways gives you the option of printing from one specified page number to another. You can also choose the number of copies you want printed, and whether to print in portrait or land-scape mode.

The most refreshing aspect of Allways is that it is a lot "smarter" about your printer than 1-2-3 is. For example, if you tell Allways you have an HP Laser-Jet printer, it knows exactly how many lines it can fit on a page, and that it can print in both landscape and portrait modes. It knows what built-in fonts the printer has, and, if you have a font cartridge, it lets you choose the cartridge from a long list in its Print Configuration Cartridge command.

All of these features combine to make printing in Allways an effortless treat compared to the guesswork that often accompanies printing in 1-2-3. How-ever, all of these benefits don't come without a price, and there are several rea-sons why you will not want to use Allways every time you print.

Precautions for Publishing

The most important reason for using Allways with discretion is its memory requirements, which add up to about 125K of RAM. This is no small amount when your worksheet must also be stored in RAM. If you have expanded memory, Allways will divide itself between that (45K) and your conventional memory (80K). For many users, the memory requirement may not be a problem, but for those who create large spreadsheet applications, Allways will be a specialized tool not practical for daily use.

Creating just the right look with Allways is a never-ending task: just when you think the job is done, you realize you should probably try a different font or row height, and the job begins anew. Like any subjective endeavor, you can spend a lot of time enhancing your spreadsheets without ever producing any output. Spend enough time working with Allways so that you master its features, but don't try to make every report look like a pricey magazine layout.

When you run Allways in its graphics mode, you pay a rather stiff penalty in speed. If you find that Allways runs too slowly on your hardware, you should try running it in text mode by toggling its Display Mode command to Text. Then, the screen will look and react just as it does in 1-2-3, but you can still add your Allways enhancements; the enhancements that you apply to a cell will be visible as special codes in the first line of the control panel at the top of the screen. For example:

FONT(3) Triumvirate 14 pt Bold Underline, LINES:RB

Once you have formatted a worksheet with Allways, you must be careful not to make changes to the worksheet when Allways is not attached. This is because Allways must be active in order to link its own formatting with the movement of cells in the worksheet. If you insert or delete rows or columns or move cells to new locations when Allways is not attached, your worksheet and Allways will be out of synchronization the next time you attach Allways to print the worksheet. This will result in its formatting no longer applying to the correct cells in the worksheet. Obviously, you should not begin enhancing your spreadsheet with Allways until after the initial construction phase, and only when you feel that the worksheet is close to its final layout and ready for its first printing.

> **TIP** ◆ *You can arrange your worksheet so that only one area need be printed with Allways, leaving the other areas free to be moved or changed without Allways being attached. This is the same idea as that of keeping certain data strictly for output purposes, as discussed in Chapter 3. You could use formulas or macro-driven copy routines to update the data in the Allways print area, but the only time you would rearrange the Allways area is when Allways was active.*

Finally, you should realize that formatting a worksheet with Allways must proceed in a step-by-step fashion, and does not lend itself to automation with macros (although you can certainly drive Allways with macros in 1-2-3). Use your judgement when it comes to enhancing your worksheets, and don't try to use every Allways feature in every printout.

◆ *PRINTING TO DISK FILES* _____

Many Lotus users have worked for years without ever reading the first Print menu, Printer or File. But sending the print output to a file instead of the printer can open up many opportunities. Many examples throughout this book use printing to a file for purposes of documentation and debugging. By printing a range to disk using the Cell-Formulas option, you can easily scan the resulting file for error cells, nonformula cells, and misreferenced formulas. Print files have other uses, too, such as testing print routines, eliminating the inevitable delay caused by slow printing, and sending data to other programs.

SENDING THE PRINT OUTPUT TO A FILE

Lotus worksheet files can only be read by Lotus unless another program is specifically designed to read them. Most programs have their own proprietary way of saving their data, and rarely does a program save to a purely text file. But just about every program has an option to create a text file from its data in memory. Word processors usually have a way of saving the current document in a text format. Lotus does it by allowing you to print to a file.

When printing to a file, the file will receive exactly what would have been sent to a printer, including all margins, headers, footers, and page breaks. The file will be a pure text file, often referred to as an ASCII file. Note that the file is stripped of any printer control codes that you may have used in the print routine or within the worksheet. Only the printable text is written to disk.

> ⊗ *CAUTION* ◆ *The Print File command erases the contents of the destination file even if the Go command is never given. When you select the name of an existing file and then issue the Replace command, that file is essentially emptied in anticipation of new data. So even if you decide to cancel the print operation by pressing Escape or Ctrl-Break, the file will already have been destroyed. This procedure has the same effect as the "open file for writing" command: {open "FILENAME","w"}.*

The text in the print file will appear just as it would have if printed on paper, but you may often find this formatting undesirable. For instance, if you are exporting the worksheet data to a word processing document, you will probably not want a left margin, since the word processor can position the text once it has been imported. You will certainly not want page breaks included within the print file, as that is definitely a chore for the word processor to perform. In those cases where the output should not be formatted, you should use these "null" print settings:

- ◆ Options Margin Left to 0
- ◆ Options Margin Right to 240
- ◆ Options Other Unformatted

2.2 ◆ ———————

If you are printing in Release 2.2, you can set the left margin to 0 and the right margin to 240 with the single command Options Margins None. That command also sets the top and bottom margins to 0, but that is not important because those margins are ignored when the Unformatted option is selected.

Printing with these settings will eliminate any blank margin spaces on the left, allow as much room as possible for the right margin, and eliminate page breaks (top and bottom margins, headers, and footers). The "generic" output will then be suitable for use in batch files, for export to database programs that can import text files, and for combining into word processor documents.

STOP THE WAIT WITH THE DOS PRINT COMMAND

If you frequently print large worksheets or have Lotus applications that produce many printouts, you may find that the DOS command PRINT provides you some respite from the Lotus Wait light. Installing a print buffer, as described in Chapter 6, can also speed up the printing process, but you may not be able to spare the memory necessary to buffer all the output when printing large volumes of material.

You invoke the PRINT command from the DOS prompt and include the names of the files you want printed. Once the command is accepted you can return to Lotus, or another program, and continue working while the files are being printed. Here is the command to print all files with a .PRN extension in the subdirectory Work on drive C:

```
Print C:\Work\*.PRN
```

You should consult your own DOS manual for specifics on this command, because they vary with different DOS versions and machines. Practice on your system to familiarize yourself with its workings.

A small amount of memory is reserved by the PRINT command when it is run for the first time after booting your computer. You can tell it which printer to use, or accept its default of LPT1 (parallel port number one). Once it is loaded, you can invoke the command again at any time to add or delete files from the print queue, or empty the queue entirely.

To take advantage of the waiting PRINT command from Lotus, instead of printing to the printer you print to a file, which is then available for adding to the print queue. With the Lotus System command, you can jump to DOS, specify any files to be printed, and return to Lotus, all in a split second:

```
/s
print C:\Data\FILE1.PRN
Exit
```

⊗ **CAUTION** ◆ *Do not use the System command to leave Lotus to run PRINT for the first time during a session. The PRINT command must be initialized from the DOS prompt before starting another program. Otherwise, if you run it for the first time while Lotus is active, the memory required by the command will overwrite some of the memory that is used by Lotus. This not only prevents you from returning to Lotus, but also ties up the memory that Lotus had been using. You would generally have to reboot the system and start over to free that memory. Until you are familiar with the routine, you should take the precaution of saving your worksheets before using the System command to access the PRINT command.*

Remember that the print files created by Lotus do not include any print enhancements, such as compressed or double-strike printing. This may rule out the use of the PRINT command if you have sprinkled various enhancements throughout your printouts. If all your files have the same type style, however, you can send the proper control code to the printer from DOS before printing the files. You can use the DOS COPY command for simple codes, such as this one for compressed printing on an Epson-compatible printer:

```
copy con: prn:
^O
^Z
```

Although you will not want to use the PRINT command for small printouts or for those with many enhancements, it can be a valuable tool for printing large, multipage jobs.

TESTING PRINT ROUTINES WITHOUT PAPER

Computers can save paper, but they can also waste a lot of paper when print routines need to be tested and debugged. By printing to files instead, you can test a print routine many times without ever turning the printer on. The print file used to demonstrate the Lotus printed page in Figure 12.4 was a perfect example of the speed and practicality of printing to disk. Not only was the use of a printer avoided, but by importing the file back into the worksheet the lines of the printout were conveniently numbered by the worksheet rows in which they fell.

You can easily test short printouts on the printer, as well as those with print enhancements. However, if you want to see where the page breaks fall, the layout of the headers and footers, and whether all the rows of a range will fit within the margins, then printing to disk is the way to go.

You can easily view the print file outside of Lotus; you do not have to import it back into the worksheet. Use the System command to jump to DOS, and then view the file with one of the several methods available. You could even use your word processor as a reasonable viewer if it loads quickly and can import ASCII files. The DOS TYPE command is always available, and the MORE command can be accessed quickly, but neither is a practical viewing tool.

The best tool for the job is one of the many file viewer programs, such as Browse or List. When these programs are used to view a Lotus print file (or any other text file), you can page through the document in either direction, find specified text, scroll to the right for wide printouts, and get a line count. The programs tend to be small and therefore load quickly. If you keep one of them in a subdirectory that is on your DOS path, it will always be available when you leave Lotus to view a print file.

2.2 ♦ ——————

If you are using Release 2.2, you can facilitate the viewing of your test print files with the macro command {system}. You can use a variation of the following macro to eliminate the manual process of invoking the System command and then calling up your file-viewing program:

{system "LIST C:\TEST.PRN"}

Depending on your computer's setup, just substitute the name of the viewing program (here named List), the name of the print file (TEST.PRN), and the drive on which it will be found (C:\). You could include this macro right after the print macro that you are testing, so that you will view the printed output immediately after it is created.

♦ SUMMARY

Printing a worksheet is a regular but often complex and tedious procedure. That is why this chapter started with a discussion of macros and how they can benefit every worksheet print routine. The Lotus page layout was covered, including margins, header and footer, the number of printed lines per page, and problems that can arise between Lotus and your printer.

Formatting the worksheet before printing is important; this chapter showed you how to use macros to make changes before printing and then undo them after the printout is made. Finally, printing to disk was discussed. Although many Lotus users never take advantage of them, print files are a valuable addition to the Lotus toolbox. Printing to disk can aid your normal worksheet tasks in many ways, including exporting data to other programs, testing print routines, and printing files in the background by using the DOS PRINT command.

The next chapter discusses the ways in which data can be moved into, out of, and around the worksheet. A variety of Lotus commands are used, including Copy, Move, Range Value, Data Sort, Data Parse, File Import, and File Combine.

THIRTEEN:

Transferring Data Where You Need It

13

◆ ◆ ◆

THE WORKSHEET ENVIRONMENT IS ANYTHING BUT STATIC.
Formulas set up dynamic links between cells, allowing one cell to change its value based on another in the current file or, in Release 2.2, on a value in another file on disk. There is also a wide assortment of Lotus commands and techniques for exchanging data between cells, worksheets, and the environment outside of Lotus. This chapter covers those commands, starting with the frequently used cell-to-cell transfer commands: Copy, Move, Range Value, and Range Transpose.

Sorting is then discussed in the context of this chapter. Although data that is sorted may often be within a Lotus database, the Sort command seems more closely related to generalized data movement, the topic covered in this chapter, than to the formal structure of a database with its column titles, input, and criterion ranges. Numerous cautions are discussed, as well as a simple means of sorting on internal characters in a cell.

File operations can be used within the worksheet. (An example is the technique for resetting a range to zero that is presented in this chapter.) But Lotus file operations are generally used for interworksheet data exchange. The File Xtract and File Combine commands are covered extensively, including discussions of worksheet cloning, combining, and consolidation.

The linking formulas of Release 2.2 are covered next. These formulas serve as a powerful means of getting data from one worksheet to another, and fulfill a function similar to the File Combine command.

Importing and exporting external text data provides a powerful link to the outside world. The Data Parse command can become an intelligent filter when it is used to extract the file names from a directory listing for use in a consolidation macro.

◆ USING THE TRANSFER COMMANDS

Lotus provides four commands for relocating a cell or range within the worksheet: Copy, Move, Range Value, and Range Transpose. These are "freeform" commands in that they can act on any cell or range; no structure is required, unlike the database operations.

DEFINING THE SOURCE AND DESTINATION RANGES

All of these cell movement commands require just two pieces of information: the source and destination ranges. These can be either one cell or a contiguous block of cells (a range). When you are prompted by one of these commands, there are three ways to specify the source and destination ranges:

- ◆ Cell address

- ◆ Range name

- ◆ Pointing

You can always choose to type in the actual cell address of each range, but this is probably the least efficient method because it requires that you know the exact coordinates of each one in advance.

You should assign range names to ranges that are referred to frequently, and using names is probably the fastest of the three techniques. It is certainly the preferred method for use in macros. Copying the cells of a named range is as simple as specifying two unique names, such as FROM_CELLS and TO_CELLS. No matter where those ranges are located, the operation will be performed as expected.

Pointing is probably the method most frequently used to specify the source or destination range, although when you are writing a linking formula in Release 2.2, you are limited to using either a cell address or range name. Using the cell pointer to highlight the range is a mechanical method, which provides absolute visual assurance that both ranges have been properly specified.

The cell pointer is not moved when you specify cell addresses or range names. You simply type in the locations of the two ranges. When pointing, though, there are several points to remember that can save time and avoid frustration.

The cell pointer need not be at the upper left corner of the source range when you initiate one of these Lotus commands. When you are prompted for the source range, just press Escape to unlock the current range, move the cell pointer to the range you wish to select, press the period key to lock in that corner of the range, highlight the necessary cells, and press Enter.

This technique is especially helpful when you start the command at the destination cell (or the upper left corner of the destination range). After you've specified the source range, the cell pointer always returns to the cell from which the command was initiated. If that cell is the destination range, you can simply press Enter to complete the command.

When highlighting a range by pointing, you can use the period key to switch the active corner cell to the next corner around the range. The active corner cell is identified by the blinking cursor. This allows you to expand or contract the high-light in any direction when you move the cell pointer. By alternating the corners around a large range, you can view each of the four corners without having to cancel the command and double-check the locations of those cells.

> CAUTION ◆ *Be careful if you plan to switch the active corner of a highlighted range within a macro. The active corner may move either clockwise or counterclockwise around the range, so you will not be able to predict which corner will be active after pressing the period key.*

When pointing to a range for any Lotus command, you are never prevented from moving to any cells in the worksheet. If you have set the screen titles with the Worksheet Titles command, you can still point "past" the titles to include either the title cells or any cells above them or to their left. If you have hidden any columns with the Worksheet Column Hide command, those columns will always be expanded when you are in POINT mode, which allows you to include them in the range. If you find this continual game of peekaboo with hidden columns irritating, you should refrain from hiding columns during the construction phase. Instead, wait until the worksheet is substantially completed.

One final word on the data transferring commands. Only the Move command causes dependent formulas and range names to follow a moved cell. The other commands simply transfer the cell contents without "dragging" along any formulas or range names. This will be discussed again as each command is covered, since it is an important factor to consider when you are moving data around the worksheet.

THE COPY COMMAND

The Copy command duplicates a cell's contents in another cell or range in the worksheet. Along with the actual text, number, or formula that make up the contents, the cell's format and protection status are also transferred.

One important use for the Copy command stems from the fact that a formula is evaluated in its new location as it is copied. This allows you to copy a range of formulas back on top of themselves to force a "range recalculation." Just remember that each formula is evaluated independently in the order that it is copied, so its value may not reflect the current state of the entire worksheet.

When copied, formulas always adjust their cell references to their new locations, as discussed in Chapter 3. That is, the references will adjust if they were written as relative addresses. When cell addresses or range names are absolute, they do not adjust when copied. For instance, a formula that refers to a variable cell named INTEREST_RATE would be made absolute to refer to the same location when copied:

@sum(A4..A33)*$INTEREST_RATE/12

2.2 ◆ ─────

When you copy a file linking formula in Release 2.2, it follows the same rules as those for regular formulas. Relative addresses adjust to their new location in the worksheet, and absolute addresses do not. Of course, all file references in linked formulas will remain unchanged. These formulas are also evaluated to their new position when copied, so there will be disk activity after the copy command is invoked, as 1-2-3 gets the new values from any linked files on disk.

There are times, though, when you will want to copy a formula without having it adjust, even though you must use relative addresses within the formula. For example, suppose you have written a formula with relative cell references that you want to copy into other cells in the same column. But you also want to duplicate the same formula in a cell in another column, and then copy it within that column, too. In other words, you need to copy the formula once to each column without its adjusting, and then let it adjust as you copy it within each separate column.

The easiest way to copy a single formula without its adjusting is to simply turn it into text, copy it, and then turn it back into a formula in the destination cell. To make the formula into text, you must edit the formula and preface it with a label prefix. The formula can then be duplicated in its new location, and later the label prefix can be removed. A macro to perform the copy would look like this:

{edit}{home}'~/c~{?}~

Here is a sneaky technique for copying cells to alternating rows or columns, such as every third cell in a column. This also works for the Range Value and Transpose commands.

Figure 13.1 shows a worksheet with data in every third row. Columns A through C contain numbers, and there is a formula in E1 that sums the numbers in the first row. With this technique, it is simple to duplicate that formula in each occupied row down the range E1..E19. All you need do is copy the range E1..E18 to cell E4. The formula will be copied to every third cell, ending on E19. In the example shown, column F was included in the copy to display the labels for each row. You can see the result in Figure 13.2.

This works because a "rolling" copy was created by overlapping the source range (E1..E18) and destination range (E4). As the copy proceeded, Lotus was like a dog chasing its own tail. The first cell, E1, had a formula in it and was copied to E4. The second cell copied was E2, a blank cell, and it was copied to E5.

```
E1: @SUM(A1..C1)                                                POINT
Enter range to copy FROM: F18..E1
          A         B         C    D    E         F            G
 1        1         2         3  ! !      6     <- Formula
 2                                 ! !          <- Blank
 3                                 ! !          <- Blank
 4        4         5         6  ! !
 5                                 ! !
 6                                 ! !
 7        7         8         9  ! !
 8                                 ! !
 9                                 ! !
10       10        11        12  ! !
11                                 ! !
12                                 ! !
13       13        14        15  ! !
14                                 ! !
15                                 ! !
16       16        17        18  ! !
17                                 ! !
18                                 ! !
19       19        20        21  ! !
20                                 ! !
```

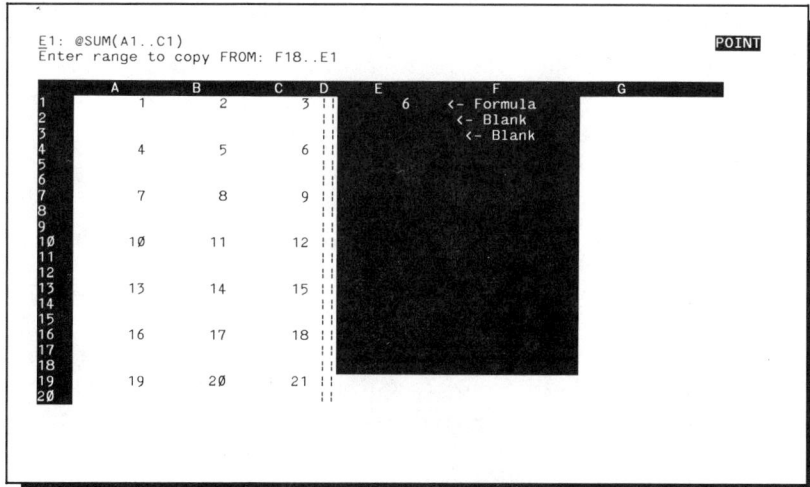

Figure 13.1 ♦ *Copying a formula to alternate rows*

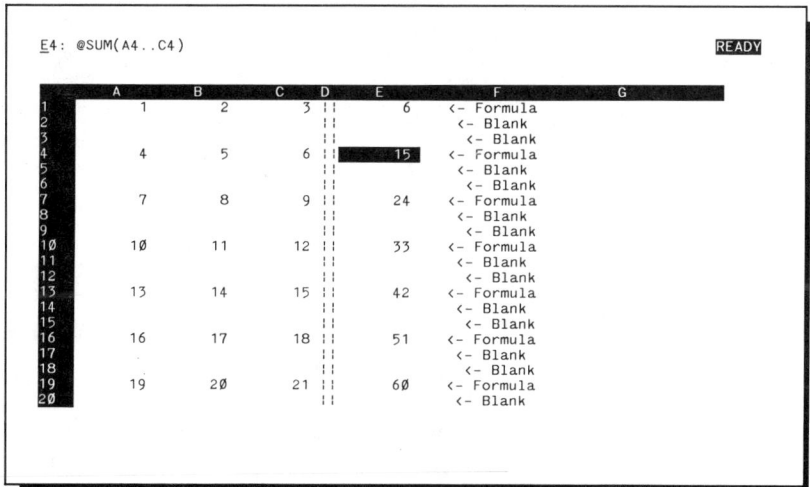

```
E4: @SUM(A4..C4)                                                READY

          A         B         C    D    E         F            G
 1        1         2         3  ! !      6     <- Formula
 2                                 ! !          <- Blank
 3                                 ! !          <- Blank
 4        4         5         6  ! !     15     <- Formula
 5                                 ! !          <- Blank
 6                                 ! !          <- Blank
 7        7         8         9  ! !     24     <- Formula
 8                                 ! !          <- Blank
 9                                 ! !          <- Blank
10       10        11        12  ! !     33     <- Formula
11                                 ! !          <- Blank
12                                 ! !          <- Blank
13       13        14        15  ! !     42     <- Formula
14                                 ! !          <- Blank
15                                 ! !          <- Blank
16       16        17        18  ! !     51     <- Formula
17                                 ! !          <- Blank
18                                 ! !          <- Blank
19       19        20        21  ! !     60     <- Formula
20                                 ! !          <- Blank
```

Figure 13.2 ♦ *The result of the copy with a formula in every third row*

Cell E3, another blank, went to E6. Then Lotus encountered cell E4, already occupied with the formula from E1, which it proceeded to copy to E7. And so on down the column.

This technique works across columns as well, and for any spacing between the formulas.

THE MOVE COMMAND

Moving a cell is a unique process that has its own set of rules and cautions. There are three critical aspects of the Move command that distinguish it from the other cell transfer commands:

1. Everything relating to a moved cell moves with it.

2. A moved cell can destroy a range that occupies its target cell.

3. A formula in a moved cell does not adjust to its new location.

When a cell is moved, formulas in other cells that refer to it adjust their references to its new location. A formula that refers to a range may or may not be affected by a cell or cells being moved from that range. To cause the formula to adjust, the moved cell or cells must occupy one of the two corner cells addressed in the formula. For example, moving cell B9 or F19 would redefine the range in this formula:

@sum(B9..F19)

Moving any other cells, such as B10 or F16, would not change the reference. However, if the formula referenced the other two corners, F9 and B19, moving either of them would cause the formula to change its reference:

@sum(F9..B19)

Range names may also be redefined when the moved cell or cells occupies either the upper left or lower right corner of the range. Refer back to Chapter 2 for more about the effect of moving cells on range names and formulas.

A range that has been specified in a Lotus command, such as the print range or data sort range, will also be redefined if the upper left or lower right corner is included in the move.

Although the result of redefining a range by moving one of its corner cells may sometimes surprise you, even more treacherous is the fact that moving a cell can destroy a range that lies under the destination cell or cells.

Chapter 2 discussed the danger of "popping" a range by deleting a row or column or by moving a cell or range onto one of its named corners. Unfortunately, there is no warning when a range is about to be destroyed by such an action, so use caution when moving cells.

The third point to remember about the Move command is that a formula in a moved cell remains unchanged even as the formulas and ranges that refer to it adjust their references. The entire cell is picked up, including its format and protection status, and is placed in its new location. A formula within that cell, however, addresses the same cells it did before the move.

▨   *TIP ◆ Moving one cell can theoretically force each formula and range name in the worksheet to adjust its reference. For this reason, using the Move command in a large worksheet may produce a long pause (not very long, perhaps, but it can be irritating). If no formula cells depend on the cell you want to move, you can copy the cell instead of moving it, and then erase the source range to produce the desired relocation. Don't forget that the cell format and protection status remain after a cell is erased, and they need to be reset.*

THE RANGE VALUE COMMAND

The Range Value command behaves just like the Copy command, with one difference. Any formulas in the source range will not be duplicated in the destination range; only their values will be placed there. A cell's format and protection status are duplicated along with the value, just as with the Copy command.

Being able to copy just the values avoids the two slower alternatives for turning formulas into values. You can edit a formula, press F9 to evaluate it, and then press Enter. Or, you can invoke the File Xtract Values command and then use the File Combine Copy Entire command to bring the file back into the worksheet, replacing the formulas with their values. In connection with this, refer to the discussion in Chapter 3 on the importance of avoiding formulas when hard numbers will do.

The Range Value command greatly simplifies the process of creating multiple solution tables from one work area of formulas that operate on one set of data. When the formulas are evaluated for the current data, you can use the Range Value command to copy them to another area where they can be stored for later use. New data can then be brought in, the worksheet calculated, and the formulas again copied as values to another location.

When you are using the Range Value command to replace a range of formulas with their corresponding values, remember that a formula that has been turned into its value is gone forever.

THE RANGE TRANSPOSE COMMAND

Like the Range Value command, the Range Transpose command also behaves like the Copy command, but the rows and columns of the source range are transposed in the destination range. As in a copy, cell formats and protection status are brought along, and all formulas adjust to their new location. And here lies the one large caution to observe when using this command in Release 2.01.

After a range is transposed, the result of some formulas may look outrageous. There are two reasons for this. First, a formula within the transposed range adjusts to its new position, just as though it had been copied there. The cells to which it now refers may be totally unrelated to those to which it previously referred, and its result will therefore be meaningless. Second, a formula that resides outside of a transposed range but refers to cells within that range will no longer refer to the same values after the transposition. Its references do not adjust, but the cells to which it once referred are relocated. For this reason, the Range Transpose command is best used to shift data only, either numbers or text.

2.2 ◆ ——————

The Range Transpose command is handled a bit differently in Release 2.2. It transposes the rows and columns as it does in Release 2.01, but any formulas in the transposed range are copied as values, not formulas. This effectively eliminates the first problem mentioned above (by eliminating any formulas), as shown later in this section.

Here is an interesting use for the Range Transpose command. You can use it to circumvent Lotus's inability to sort by columns across a range of rows (it can sort only the rows down a range of columns).

Figure 13.3 shows a small table of numbers, A1..E8, each column of which is summed in row 8. The goal is to arrange the columns in descending order, based on their sums. Thus, column B should be first, column C second, and so on.

The routine requires several steps, the results of which appear in Figure 13.4. First, the Range Value command is used to copy just the formulas to row 9; this

```
A8: @SUM(A1..A7)                                                    READY

        A        B        C        D        E       F      G      H     I
1       A        B        C        D        E
2      86       76       75       89       79
3      85       99       82       80       73
4      75       72       74       70       87
5      70       91       90       71       62
6      84       89       84       66       86
7    -----    -----    -----    -----    -----
8     400      427      405      376      387
9
10
11
12
13
14
15
16
17
18
19
20
```

Figure 13.3 ◆ *Sorting by columns with the help of the Range Transpose command*

```
H12:  @SUM(H5..H11)                                                      READY

          A         B         C         D         E         F         G         H         I
1         A         B         C         D         E
2        86        76        75        89        79
3        85        99        82        80        73
4        75        72        74        70        87
5        70        91        90        71        62
6        84        89        84        66        86
7       -----     -----     -----     -----     -----
8       400       427       405       376       387
9       400       427       405       376       387
10
11
12        B        76        99        72        91        89      -----         0       427
13        C        75        82        74        90        84      -----         0       405
14        A        86        85        75        70        84      -----         0       400
15        E        79        73        87        62        86      -----         0       387
16        D        89        80        70        71        66      -----         0       376
17
18
19
20
```

Figure 13.4 ◆ *The transposed table after sorting on column I*

preserves their current values in that row during the transposition. The discussion that follows applies specifically to Release 2.01. For Release 2.2, be sure to modify the method as described after this discussion.

Next, the entire table, A1..E9, is transposed to a blank area of the worksheet, in this case cell A12. Note that the values in row 9 are included.

You can now sort this new transposed table in the usual fashion. The range A12..I16 is the data range, and the values in column I make up the primary sort key. The sort will be in descending order for this example. A secondary sort key was not needed in this case, although if you needed one, the column titles in column A would have been a reasonable choice.

Notice the formula in H12 that is displayed in the control panel of Figure 13.4. All the formulas in that column have adjusted to their new locations after being transposed, and now they simply sum the seven cells above them as they originally did in row 8. Since those cells are empty, the formulas evaluate to zero, hence the need for the values that appear in column I.

Once the sorting is done, the table A12..I16 can be transposed back to its beginning position at A1, and then erased. The values in row 9 can also be erased, leaving the finished, sorted table as shown in Figure 13.5.

If you use Release 2.2, you can eliminate the first step in which you use the Range Value command to copy the formulas to row 9. This is because the Range Transpose command in Release 2.2 copies formulas as values. Therefore, the range that you will transpose is simply the table you see in Figure 13.3, cells A1..E8.

2.2 ◆ ───────

```
A8: @SUM(A1..A7)                                                    READY

         A        B        C        D        E        F    G    H    I
1        B        C        A        E        D
2       76       75       86       79       89
3       99       82       85       73       80
4       72       74       75       87       70
5       91       90       70       62       71
6       89       84       84       86       66
7      -----    -----    -----    -----    -----
8      427.     405      400      387      376
9
10
11
12
13
14
15
16
17
18
19
20
```

Figure 13.5 ◆ *The table after sorting by columns*

When you sort the transposed table, the data range will be A12..H16 in Figure 13.4, and the totals in column H will serve as the primary sort key. Remember, in Release 2.2 these are transposed as values, not formulas. After you have sorted the table, use the Range Transpose command to copy the table back to its original position—but be careful! This time, you absolutely do not want to include the "formulas" in column H.

To finish, transpose only the range A12..G16 back to A1 (you don't need the dotted divider rows in column G, but you can include them if you want). If you were to include the numbers in column H, they would be transposed over the formulas in row 8, replacing them with meaningless values.

> **TIP** ◆ *With any major and irrevocable data transfers, such as the one shown in Figures 13.3 to 13.5, it is always a good idea to save your worksheet before proceeding with the routine.*

◆ SORTING IT ALL OUT

Sorting data is generally considered a database activity. But sorting is not dependent on the rigid structure of a database, and in fact the only similarity is that the command works on entire rows within a range, just like the data commands do. Sorting has much in common with the Copy and Range Transpose commands already discussed in this chapter, and for that reason it can be viewed as another way of rearranging the data in the worksheet.

THE ESSENTIALS OF SORTING

To perform a sort, you must define the data range of rows and columns that are to be sorted. If you are thinking of this range in terms of a database, you could describe it as having records and fields. Then you must select a primary and (optionally) a secondary sort key column. These are the columns whose entries will determine the sort order of the rows in the data range. You can choose either ascending or descending order for each key column. The Go command invokes the sort.

Sorting Sequence

The sorting sequence that Lotus applies is determined when you install your copy of Lotus. There are three sequences from which to choose, but note that no matter which method you install in your Lotus driver set, numbers that are actual values (and not just text that looks like numbers) are always sorted last. Figure 13.6 shows how each method sorts the same column of data.

The default sort order is Numbers First, shown in column A. The word *numbers* in this description refers to numerals used in text, such as in addresses. Again, value cells always come last. Notice that the letters of the alphabet in rows 7 through 14 are not sorted according to case—neither uppercase nor lowercase carries a sorting priority.

```
 F4:  @CODE(E4)                                                        READY
              A          B          C          D          E           F            G
  1    Numbers              Numbers                              @code of
  2    First                Last                    ASCII        Column E
  3    ─────────────────────────────────────────────────────────────────
  4         1                    a                     .              46
  5         2                    A                     1              49
  6         3                    B                     2              50
  7         a                    b                     3              51
  8         A                    ×                     A              65
  9         b                    X                     B              66
 10         B                    Z                     X              88
 11         X                    z                     Z              90
 12         ×                    1                     [              91
 13         Z                    2                     a              97
 14         z                    3                     b              98
 15         .                    .                     ×             120
 16         [                    [                     z             122
 17                 Ø                    Ø                     Ø
 18                 1                    1                     1
 19                 2                    2                     2
 20                 3                    3                     3
```

Figure 13.6 ◆ *The three sorting sequences, one of which can be chosen when you install Lotus*

Column C has been sorted using the Numbers Last sequence, where text that has numerals is sorted after letters of the alphabet. Once again, the case of a letter has no bearing on the sort order.

The data in column E was sorted with the ASCII sort order. Here, the order is determined by the ASCII code value of each character. This is similar to the Numbers First method, except that the case of a letter has bearing on the sort—uppercase is sorted before lowercase. The corresponding cells in column F contain an @code function that displays this value for each entry in column E; you can see the formula in F3 displayed in the control panel. Note that the characters displayed in column E are from the Lotus International Character Set (LICS), and do not necessarily match the more widely accepted ASCII set.

Remember that each of these three columns was sorted with what was essentially a different version of Lotus. To duplicate this worksheet, you would sort one column, save the worksheet, and exit from Lotus. Then you would again call Lotus, but this time with a different driver set, one that had been installed with another of the three sorting sequences, such as this one named ASCII.SET:

123 ASCII

Retrieve the worksheet, sort the second column, save the worksheet, and exit from Lotus. Repeat the process for the third column, using a driver set with the third sorting sequence. Realistically, you will always be using just one sorting sequence; you cannot change to another one without reloading Lotus along with another driver set. There is no way to determine what the sequence is from inside the worksheet, so be careful if you are sharing worksheets. Sorting data under several versions of Lotus may produce different results.

Sorting with Safety

Of the utmost importance when sorting is ensuring that all the columns to be sorted together are included in the sort data range. If you leave a column out of that range, the sorted data will no longer be tied to the entries in that column. If you do not discover your mistake before saving (and the results are not always obvious), you will probably be forced to rearrange the data manually, if even that is possible.

Sorting can have such disastrous results that most of the tricks involved with sorting are intended simply to avoid those disasters.

★ **TRICK** ◆ *You should always save your worksheet before performing an untried sort routine. If the sort goes awry, your worksheet will still be safe on disk. This is not really a trick, of course, but you will feel like a wizard if a sort fails but you have recently saved your worksheet.*

One common mistake arises because sorting is often considered a database chore. A Lotus database always starts with the field column titles, but you will regret the error if you include these titles within your sort data range. Include only the rows that you wish to sort within that range, and the column titles will remain safely untouched at the tops of the columns.

If you plan to sort a range on a regular basis as part of your normal worksheet routine, you should give the sort range its own range name. This is especially important if you regularly sort more than one range in a worksheet. You can also assign names to the primary and secondary sort key columns. The combination of the three names allows you to perform the sort through a macro:

```
/dsrdDATA_RANGE ~
pKEY_COL1 ~ a ~
sKEY_COL2 ~ d ~ g
```

One way to increase the security of your data is to include an index column within the sort range. This column is filled with consecutive numbers, so that each record in the range has a unique number assigned to it. The column is included in any sort. If you ever want to sort the records back into their original order, you can use the index column as the primary sort key.

To further protect your data against bad sorts that don't include all the required columns, you can include a second index column at the opposite side of the sort range. With this "sandwich" around the data, you will be able to tell if the data has ever been scrambled in a sort—the numbers in any row of the index columns will not match.

A sort is similar to a copy. Formulas and range names that refer to any cells being sorted will not follow those cells to their new location. Formulas within the sorted data will adjust to their final locations as if they were copied.

WATCH THOSE FORMULAS

One difficulty frequently encountered while sorting involves formulas. This is because two situations occur in which a formula can be affected by the sort: if the formula is inside the sort range, or if it is outside the sort range but refers to cells that are within it.

The cell references in a formula that resides within the sort range are always adjusted when the formula's position is changed due to a sort, just as though the formula had been copied to the new position. This means that a formula's value (result) may change whenever a sort is performed, since it will refer to different cells after the sort.

The only time that you will see no change in a sorted formula's value (that refers to cells within the sort range) is when the formula refers to data in its own row. The formula in that case is linked to its own record, so no matter where that record is transferred, the formula still refers to the same data.

If a formula within a sort data range refers to a variable cell (or cells) outside of the sort range, then that formula should have an absolute reference to the variable cell. If such a reference doesn't exist, the formula will adjust when sorted and lose its reference to the desired cell.

A formula that is outside the sort range and refers to cells inside the range will not be affected by the sort—it will still refer to the same cells in the worksheet even after the data is sorted. If it refers to cell L16 before a sort, and the data in L16 is sorted to L44, the formula will still address L16. Therefore, the value that an external formula displays will probably change after a sort, when new data has been sorted into the cells to which it refers.

SORTING ON INTERNAL CHARACTERS

Normally, a sort arranges rows based on the first characters in the cells in the sort key columns. A cell that begins with A will always precede one that begins with B. Sometimes, though, it is necessary to sort on internal characters within the sort key column cells.

For instance, suppose the sort key column is a list of codes that are made up of two components, such as *C232-CK580*. The characters to the left of the hyphen indicate one category of information, and those on the other side of the hyphen have some other meaning. You might want to sort on the second half of the codes, which would be a simple matter had the codes been split into two separate columns. So you need a method to pull out those characters, and the string functions provide an easy, flexible, and powerful solution.

Look at Figure 13.7. In column A is a list of hyphenated codes of nine characters each. They have been previously sorted; the first code begins with A and the last begins with Z. The problem is how to sort on the characters to the right of the hyphen. That is where the formulas in column B come into play.

The string formula in cell B5, displayed in the control panel, pulls out the five characters from the right side of the text in A5:

   @right(A5,5)

The formula has been copied down column B for each of the code entries. The trick now is to use this new column as the primary sort key column, so that the data will be sorted on those internal characters after the hyphen.

Before sorting, though, the formulas must be turned into hard values, otherwise their relative adjustments will negate the effort to sort them. (Try it and see what happens.)

The formulas in column B of Figure 13.8 have been turned into values with the Range Value command, the evidence of which can be seen in the control panel. The sort data range includes two columns, Codes and String Formulas, A5..B14. The primary sort key is column B, and the Codes column is used as the secondary sort key to break any ties encountered in the primary column. The result of the sort is as shown in the figure.

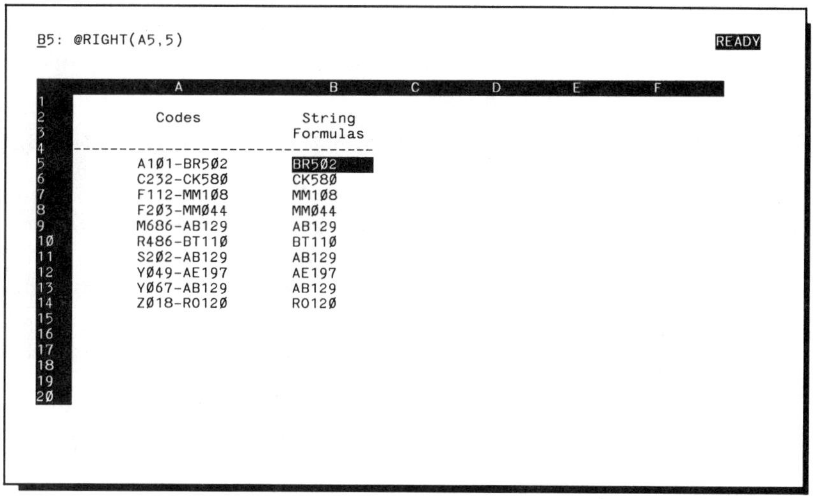

```
B5: @RIGHT(A5,5)                                                    READY

              A              B           C       D       E       F
1
2             Codes        String
3                          Formulas
4          --------------------------------
5          A101-BR502      BR502
6          C232-CK580      CK580
7          F112-MM108      MM108
8          F203-MM044      MM044
9          M686-AB129      AB129
10         R486-BT110      BT110
11         S202-AB129      AB129
12         Y049-AE197      AE197
13         Y067-AB129      AB129
14         Z018-R0120      R0120
15
16
17
18
19
20
```

Figure 13.7 ♦ *Using string functions to sort data on internal characters*

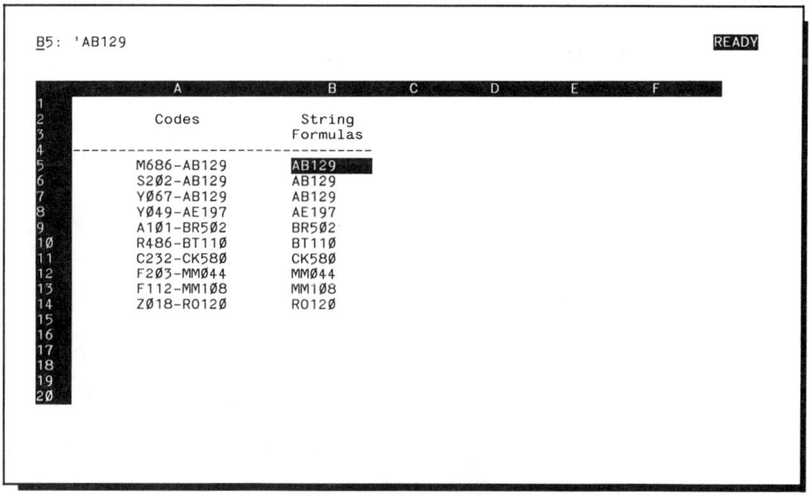

```
B5: 'AB129                                                          READY

              A              B           C       D       E       F
1
2             Codes        String
3                          Formulas
4          --------------------------------
5          M686-AB129      AB129
6          S202-AB129      AB129
7          Y067-AB129      AB129
8          Y049-AE197      AE197
9          A101-BR502      BR502
10         R486-BT110      BT110
11         C232-CK580      CK580
12         F203-MM044      MM044
13         F112-MM108      MM108
14         Z018-R0120      R0120
15
16
17
18
19
20
```

Figure 13.8 ♦ *The codes after sorting on the extra column of string formulas previously turned into values with the Range Value command*

You can see that column B has determined the sort order. The first three entries in that column are duplicates, but the ties were broken in the Codes column. At this point, you can erase the temporary entries in column B, leaving just the sorted codes.

The data you wish to sort may not be arranged as consistently or predictably as were these codes, but the string functions can usually provide a formula that will pull out the characters you need.

For example, if there were a variable number of characters on either side of the hyphen in the codes shown above, you could use the following formula to pull out all characters to the right of the hyphen, no matter how many there might be:

@right(A5,@length(A5) − @find("-",A5,0) − 1)

This formula finds the position of the hyphen in the text, position 4, subtracts that from the length of the string (10−4), and pulls out that many characters less 1 (5), because string positions always start at zero.

Or, suppose you wanted to sort on the first character of the code plus the first two characters that follow the hyphen. In other words, since the code in A5 is M686-AB129, you would want to sort on M-AB:

@left(A5,1)&&@mid(A5,@find("-",A5,0),3)

In this case, the first character is extracted with the @left function. Then an @mid function pulls out three characters from the hyphen position, determined with the @find function.

◆ FILE OPERATIONS WITHIN THE WORKSHEET _____

Most file manipulation routines are done to combine external worksheets into an active worksheet. But there are times when file operations can perform useful tasks just for the current worksheet. This creates temporary files, which can be erased once the job is done.

SETTING A RANGE TO ZERO WITH THE FILE COMBINE COMMAND

The most obvious example of "internal" file operations was frequently needed in Lotus 1A, before the Range Value command was available. A file routine was required to change a range of formulas into hard numbers. The range was first extracted as values, and the File Combine command was used to bring those values back into the worksheet, either to a new range or on top of the formulas, overwriting and replacing them. A macro to turn a range of formulas named DATA into hard values might look like this:

```
/fxvTEMPFILE ~ DATA ~ r{esc}
{goto}DATA ~
/fcceTEMPFILE ~
/fewTEMPFILE ~ y
```

Although this routine is no longer needed in Lotus 2, file routines are still useful within the worksheet. Suppose you have a range of data that you want to reset so that all are zeros. Simply erasing them would be easy, but what if formulas, text, or other entries are mixed within the range that you want to leave untouched?

You say that you would unprotect the data cells, turn on global protection, and then erase the entire range, leaving only the protected cells? Forget it. When global protection is enabled, Lotus cancels the erasing of a range as soon as it encounters one protected cell. But the short macro in Figure 13.9 achieves the desired results.

The worksheet shown has text entries in column A and numeric entries in column B, with @sum formulas producing subtotals at various points in the column. These all make up the range named DATA, A1..B17. The goal is to perform one operation that will reset the numbers to zero, while leaving the formulas and text untouched.

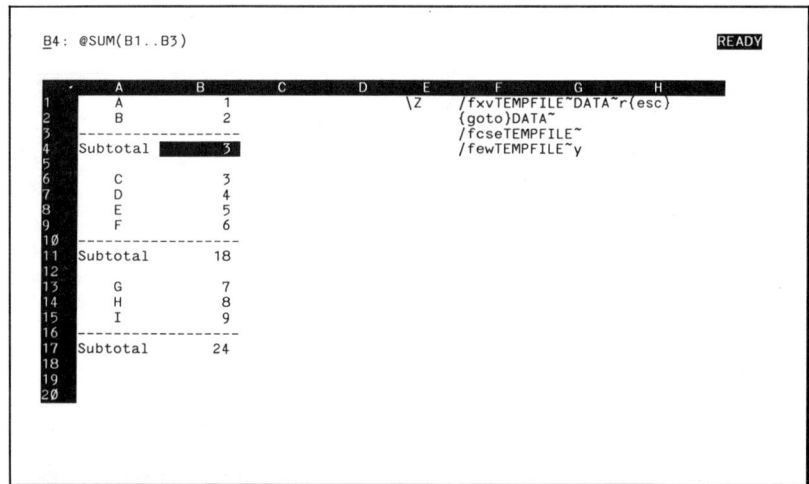

```
B4:  @SUM(B1..B3)                                                          READY

         A         B         C         D    E       F          G          H
1        A         1                          \Z    /fxvTEMPFILE~DATA~r(esc)
2        B         2                                {goto)DATA~
3   --------------------                             /fcseTEMPFILE~
4   Subtotal       3                                /fewTEMPFILE~y
5
6        C         3
7        D         4
8        E         5
9        F         6
10  --------------------
11  Subtotal      18
12
13       G         7
14       H         8
15       I         9
16  --------------------
17  Subtotal      24
18
19
20
```

Figure 13.9 ◆ *A range of data that will be reset to zeros*

The macro named \Z in F1, which looks similar to the previous macro, will quickly perform this task:

```
/fxvTEMPFILE~DATA~r{esc}
{goto}DATA~
/fcseTEMPFILE~
/fewTEMPFILE~y
```

Its first command extracts the range DATA to the file named TEMPFILE. Then the macro moves the cell pointer to the range DATA and uses the File Combine command to copy TEMPFILE back on top of the range—but with subtraction. Since the extracted values are equal to the entries in the worksheet, each numeric cell is effectively reset to zero, as shown in Figure 13.10.

Text is left unharmed, as are the formulas, which are never touched by the File Combine Add or Subtract command. Only value cells are affected. The last line of the macro erases the temporary file.

PRINTING TO A FILE

Throughout this book you have seen examples where printing to a file provides a simple solution to an otherwise difficult problem.

In Chapter 4, for example, printing a worksheet or range of cells to disk and then importing the print file back into a worksheet was recommended as one way to search those cells for specific references, errors, or hidden cell formats.

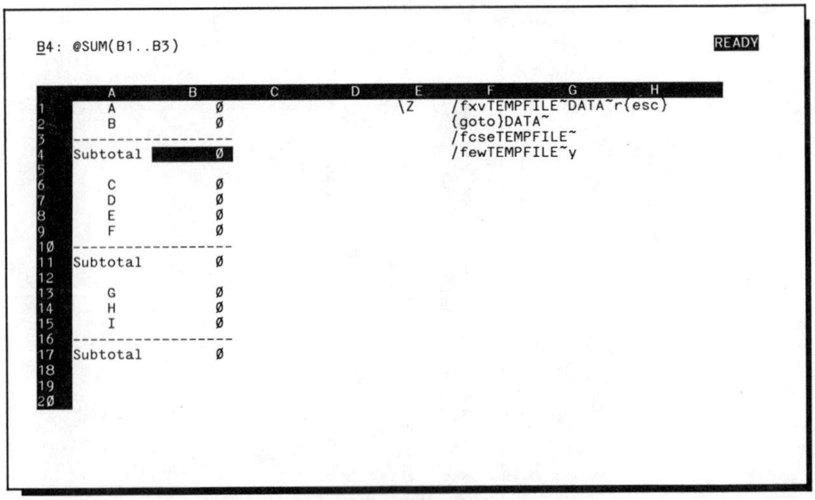

Figure 13.10 ◆ *Data cells that have been reset to zero with the File Combine Subtract command*

Chapter 8 described how dates that are entered as text can be printed to a file and then—using the File Import command—imported as numbers back into the worksheet. This split their day, month, and year components into separate columns, which can be referenced by valid date functions.

Although it is usually less efficient than using string formulas, it is possible to concatenate text in adjoining cells by printing the cells to a file, and then using the File Import Text command to bring the file back into the worksheet, making each row one long string of text.

The ability to turn worksheet data into pure ASCII text, as printing to a file does, is a powerful adjunct to the usual tools of the Lotus worksheet and should not be overlooked. Refer to Chapter 12, which described the process of printing to a file in more detail.

♦ CLONING WORKSHEETS WITH THE FILE XTRACT COMMAND

The File Xtract command (spelled with an X on the Lotus menu) allows you to pull a range or an entire worksheet into a new worksheet file. Extracting some or all of the cells from a worksheet is often the first step in combining the data it contains into another worksheet with the File Combine command. An extracted file retains all the settings of its parent file, such as column widths, range names, cell formats, default settings, and the remembered ranges of the print, graph, and data commands.

The File Xtract command has two options, Formulas and Values. Extracting a range with the Values option means that the resulting file will have no formulas in it, just text or numeric (value) cells. This is one of the methods that can be used to turn formulas into hard values, as described earlier.

If you choose the Formulas option, all cells in the resulting worksheet will be duplicates of the parent—formulas will remain formulas.

> **CAUTION ♦** *When you retrieve a newly extracted worksheet, you may find that the displayed values of the formulas are not what you expected, even though the formulas are the same as they were in the original. This happens when you extract only part of the first worksheet, and the extracted range contains formulas that reference data outside of that range. In the new worksheet the formulas will address the same cells, but those cells will be blank. Although logical and consistent, this result may be confusing at times.*

Deciding whether to extract as formulas or as values depends on the intended use of the new worksheet file. If you want a permanent record of a range or worksheet, then you should definitely choose the Values option. The extracted file will be a frozen image of all the cells in the first worksheet. If you want to preserve the dynamic structure of the original, then the Formulas option is the right choice. The new file will still be "active," allowing you to manipulate data and have the formulas in it reevaluate after the changes.

⊗ CAUTION ◆ *When ranges are extracted from a worksheet, the result can be confusing and sometimes dangerous. As an example, assume there is a range name or reference in a formula that defines the range A1..C5. If you extract the range B1..C5 and a formula that refers to it to a new file, when you retrieve that file you will find that the range reference in the formula is IV1..C5—254 columns have been added!*

This occurs because the upper left corner of the extracted range, cell B1 in this case, always ends up in the home position in the new worksheet. That forces the reference to column A to wrap around to the other side of the worksheet by one column, to column IV. This is a dangerous situation that may be difficult to detect.

When creating a clone of a worksheet, exercise caution in the extraction procedure. If necessary, include extra rows above or columns to the left of the extracted range to keep any range references in the proper context. This creates extra rows or columns in the home position of the new worksheet.

The File Xtract command can help clean up a cluttered worksheet. You may at times find that a worksheet has grown beyond what seems to be the active (occupied) work area, when pressing End Home jumps the cursor miles to the right and miles below what you would expect to be the lower right corner of your worksheet.

Use the File Xtract command to pull just the active part of the worksheet into a new file. Retrieve that secondary file, and End Home should take the cell pointer just to the last occupied row and column. Save the new file under the name of the original file.

◆ USING DATA FROM OTHER WORKSHEETS

In 1-2-3 Releases 2.01 and 2.2, the File Combine command allows you to bring data from a worksheet file on disk into the current worksheet in memory.

With this command, you have the option of either bringing in the data so that it overwrites any data already in the cells, or adding to or subtracting from the entries in the current worksheet. You can also opt to bring in the complete worksheet from disk, or just a range from it.

In Release 2.2, you may use linking formulas to perform a similar function. Formulas have several advantages over the File Combine command, but there are times when you will prefer the command over the formulas. For further discussion on linking formulas, see the section entitled "Linking Formulas in Release 2.2" later in this chapter.

THE FILE COMBINE COMMAND

The command File Retrieve replaces the worksheet in memory with a worksheet from disk. To bring the data from one worksheet into another, you must combine them with the File Combine command.

Only the contents of the cells and their formats and protection status are brought into the worksheet in memory from the worksheet on disk. The column widths, range names, and other remembered ranges are all ignored. The upper left cell from the incoming worksheet is placed at the current cell pointer position; the rest of the cells flow to the right and down from that cell. There are three methods for combining worksheets: Copy, Add, or Subtract.

The Copy, Add, and Subtract Options

Choosing File Combine Copy replaces any cells in the parent worksheet with the incoming cells from the child worksheet on disk. It makes no difference whether a cell in the parent is blank or contains text, numbers, or a formula. An incoming cell from the child worksheet will replace the contents, format, and protection status of that cell.

CAUTION ♦ *Although similar, the File Combine Copy command is not quite like the Copy command. If a cell in the child worksheet is blank (even though it may be formatted or unprotected), then the corresponding cell in the parent worksheet will not be affected. The Copy command would replace an occupied cell with a blank cell.*

Therefore, if you want to replace a range in the parent worksheet with data from a worksheet file, you should first erase the parent's range before invoking the File Combine command. Otherwise, a blank cell in the incoming file will not create a blank cell in the parent worksheet if that cell already has an entry.

> *A second point to note is that within a worksheet, you cannot copy a cell to a protected cell when global protection is enabled. This is not true with the File Combine command. An incoming cell will overwrite a protected cell without any warning.*
>
> *A final but important note is that formulas always adjust when they are brought into a parent worksheet, even if they have absolute references.*

The other two File Combine options, Add and Subtract, behave in a similar way. Instead of replacing the cells in the parent worksheet, the incoming cells are either added to or subtracted from them. The Subtract option was used in an example earlier in this chapter to reset a range of values to zero by subtracting that range from itself.

These two options differ from the File Combine Copy option in two major ways. First, all text cells in the child worksheet are ignored during the Add or Subtract combine; only numeric cells and the values of formula cells are brought in. Second, a text or formula cell in the parent worksheet is not affected by an incoming cell from the child worksheet.

Choosing All or Part of the File

Whichever way you decide to combine one worksheet into another, you must specify whether you want the entire file brought in, or just a range from it: Entire File or Named/Specified Range, as the Lotus menu describes the choices.

You would think that pulling out a small part of a large file would take almost no time, but that is not the case. In fact, if it takes ten seconds to retrieve all of a worksheet, it may take about eight seconds to combine just a small part of that worksheet, even if the incoming range is from cell A1. This can be frustrating when you have pieces of many worksheet files to bring into the active worksheet.

The simple solution is to have already used the File Xtract command to pull out the relevant ranges from the other worksheets. Then, you can bring in each smaller worksheet in the blink of an eye with the File Combine Copy Entire command. The extra work involved for this routine is slight, and the increase in speed will be well worth it.

If a child worksheet from which the range needs to be pulled is macro-driven, you can modify the macro that saves the worksheet so that it first extracts the necessary data:

```
{calc}
/fxvXTRACT_1 ˜ DATA_RANGE ˜ r{esc}
/fsFILENAME ˜ r{esc}
```

This macro first calculates the worksheet to ensure that everything is up to date. The File Extract command then pulls out, as values, the range DATA_RANGE to the file named XTRACT_1. The worksheet itself is then saved as FILENAME. The extracted data could then be accessed from the parent worksheet at any time by bringing in the file XTRACT_1.

LINKING FORMULAS IN RELEASE 2.2

2.2 ◆ ─────

The linking formulas in Release 2.2 are by no means a substitute for the File Combine command, but there are many times when they provide a faster and easier method of bringing data from a worksheet file into the current worksheet.

Ease and Speed

Perhaps the best feature of linking formulas is that they require little or no maintenance. The File Combine command, however, must be invoked in the correct sequence of steps while the cellpointer is in the correct cell (although using macros alleviates much of this worry). Once you write your linking formulas, you can leave them alone and treat them pretty much as you would any other formula in the worksheet. Every time you retrieve the worksheet, the linking formulas will be automatically updated. Plus, there is little danger when using a linking formula that you will bring in a tremendous amount of the wrong data to the wrong location in the worksheet, as can happen with the File Combine command.

To write a linking formula, simply enclose within angle brackets the name of the worksheet to which you want to link, and follow that with a cell address or range name in that worksheet:

    + < <FILENAME > >A1

If it is not in the current default directory, you can include the file's drive and path. A file name extension is not necessary unless it is something other than WK1.

⊗ **CAUTION** ◆ *The cell addresses referenced in a regular formula will update automatically as those cells are moved about the worksheet. A linking formula, however, is completely static, and is not aware of any changes you make to cells in the linked file.*

Once you create a link to another worksheet, when you are later working in that other worksheet you must be careful not to move a cell that is linked. If you do, you will have to go back to the first worksheet and rewrite your linking formula to address the new location. The same rule applies to worksheet files. If you copy a worksheet to a new subdirectory or disk and erase the original, any worksheets containing linking formulas that were linked to that file will no longer be able to locate it, and the formulas will result in ERR. You will have to rewrite your linking formulas to refer to the file's new location.

You can, however, completely avoid the problem of linked cells being moved in the source worksheet file by trying to refer only to range names. As always, range names will be found no matter where the range may be. But how do you refer a linking formula to a range when you have a multicelled range in the file, such as B11..D16, and the linking formula can only refer to a single cell? Fortunately, the answer involves something much simpler than naming every cell in that range.

First, the range B11..D16 in the source worksheet (the one to which you will link) should already be named before you begin; assume it is named THE_RANGE. Then write the first linking formula so that it refers to that range name:

+ < <FILENAME > >THE_RANGE

Even though the formula refers to a multicelled range, its result will be that of just the upper left cell of the range, cell B11. This is the same manner in which the @cell function behaves.

Now that you are linked to the upper left cell of THE_RANGE, you can simply copy the formula to enough cells in the current worksheet so that all the cells in the range in the file are covered. If you wrote the first formula in cell A1, you would copy it so that it covers the range A1..B6. The addresses in the formula will adjust as each is copied, so that the formula in A2 will refer to B12 in the other file, the one in B2 will refer to C12, and so on. The range name not only allows you to find the correct range (or at least its upper left hand cell), it also lets you update the addresses of all the linking formulas that refer to that range to ensure their accuracy.

Suppose you have been working in the FILENAME worksheet, and have inserted rows or columns so that THE_RANGE is in a new location. Back in your original worksheet with the linking formulas, you will find that only the first formula will be correct, because it still refers to the range name. The others will still be referring to the same hard cell addresses, which are no longer correct. It is easy to fix them all in one operation. Just copy the first formula to those other cells once more, and let the cell addresses adjust according to the new position of THE_RANGE in the other worksheet. The formulas will once again have the correct references.

As mentioned earlier in this chapter, the File Combine command takes about as long to bring in cell A1 from a large worksheet file as it takes the File Retrieve command to load the entire file. This is not the case with linking formulas. Although a linking formula must also read data from a worksheet file, it gets to that data many times faster than the File Combine command. This is an obvious advantage when you must bring in just a few cells from a very large worksheet, and you have not previously extracted those cells to separate files with the File Xtract command (a method that was recommended earlier in this chapter).

> ⊗ **CAUTION** ◆ *Although bringing in a single cell via a linking formula is faster than bringing in that cell with the File Combine command, you will find that bringing in a range of cells is much slower. This is because each linking formula is evaluated separately, so that using ten formulas to bring in a range of ten cells will take about ten times longer than bringing in just one cell.*
>
> *The File Combine command, however, takes about the same amount of time to bring in a range of ten cells as it does to bring in one. Once it finds the upper left cell of the range within the file, it simply continues reading the worksheet data until it has all ten cells.*

Single-Cell Linking

There is one very important difference between a linking formula and a normal 1-2-3 worksheet formula that you should be aware of: the linking formula can reference only one cell in a file and cannot be combined with any other formula elements. For example, suppose you want to add the sum of a range in the current worksheet to the sum of a range in a worksheet on disk. You might think that the formula would look like this:

@sum(B1..B10) + @sum(< <C:\FILENAME > >G21..G30)

Unfortunately, this formula is invalid. It not only refers to a multicelled range, but it is also part of a larger compound formula.

To perform this task, you can choose between two other approaches to accessing the data in the file. You could simply write ten linking formulas, each one referring to a single cell in the range you want to sum in the worksheet file. The first formula would look like this:

+ < <C:\FILENAME > >G21

You would copy this formula down a column to nine more cells, for example from C1 to C10, and you would then have the values from the range you want.

Remember that linking formulas adjust their cell references when they are copied, just as regular formulas do. Your summing formula would now refer only to cells within the current worksheet:

@sum(B1..B10) + @sum(C1..C10)

The other way to get the sum of the range from the worksheet file is to refer to a cell in that file that already contains the @sum function to sum the desired cells. Again, a little planning makes the whole process a lot easier. If the total were contained in cell G31 in the worksheet on disk, you would create one linking formula in the current worksheet, say in cell C1, which would look like this:

+ <<C:\FILENAME>>G31

To get your total, you would now refer to cell C1:

@sum(B1..B10) + C1

This is the preferred method, as only a single linking formula is needed.

Updating Links

As a worksheet is loaded into memory, all linking formulas in it are updated; you will notice disk activity beyond what is needed to load the worksheet. Once the Ready mode indicator appears, you normally will no longer need to worry about the linking formulas. This is because the other files on disk will remain unchanged while you are working on the current worksheet, and there will be no reason to update the links.

However, if you are working on a network where other users may be changing the worksheet files to which you are linked, you must remember to use the File Admin Link-Refresh command from time to time to update all the linked formulas in your worksheet. Do this, for example, before printing, just as you would press the F9 key to update all the worksheet formulas.

If your current worksheet has links to other worksheets, and still other worksheets have links to the current one, be especially careful to update the links before saving the current worksheet. Otherwise, the other worksheets will be referring to cell entries that may not be up to date.

◆ WORKSHEET CONSOLIDATION _____

The process of consolidating one or more worksheets into a master worksheet can extend the scope of Lotus applications while keeping the component pieces smaller and more manageable. The File Combine command and, to a lesser extent, linking formulas in Release 2.2 are the tools you need to build one worksheet from others. You might compile 12 monthly worksheets into one annual one. You could consolidate 75 district income reports into 15 regional worksheets, and then bring the regional files into a master corporate worksheet.

There are two variations of worksheet consolidation, one or both of which can be applied to any given worksheet. First, you can use the File Combine Copy command to copy all or part of several worksheets into various locations in the parent worksheet, to be printed together or as the source data for further calculations. Or, you can use the File Combine Add (or Subtract) command to add one child file on top of another, creating a grand total in a single range when the last file is brought in.

In Release 2.2, linking formulas provide another means of consolidation, which closely parallels the File Combine Copy method. Since most consolidations tend to grow rather large, it may generally prove wiser to use the File Combine Copy command than linking formulas.

2.2 ◆ ———

CONSOLIDATING WITH THE FILE COMBINE COMMAND

By applying the techniques discussed in this chapter, you can safely link many worksheets and automate the entire routine with macros. And macros are the key to successfully linking worksheets with the File Combine command.

Several difficulties are commonly encountered when combining files:

- ◆ Parent worksheet combine range is not erased before proceeding

- ◆ You forget which files are supposed to be brought in

- ◆ Not all the files are brought in

- ◆ Misspelled file names cause the routine to fail

- ◆ Files are combined into the wrong location

These problems can be avoided when macros are used to perform the consolidation. Not only will the process run faster, but the macros you write to control the routine will serve as very visible, easy to understand documentation, and they are easy to revise as well. When macros are at your beck and call, the need for linking formulas in worksheet consolidations is greatly diminished. The routine shown in Figure 13.11 demonstrates the power and simplicity of macro-driven consolidations.

```
B7: +"{recalc \COMBINE}~/fcae"&@INDEX($FILE_LIST,0,$COUNT-1)&"~"                    READY

         A              B            C            D           E          F          G
1   COUNT                        1
2
3   \Z             /reDATA_COMBINE~{goto}DATA_COMBINE~
4                  {let COUNT,1}{recalc \COMBINE}
5                  {for COUNT,1,@count(FILE_LIST),1,\COMBINE}
6
7   \COMBINE       {recalc \COMBINE}~/fcaeDATA010~
8                  {return}
9
10  FILE_LIST      DATA010
11                 DATA011
12                 DATA012
13                 DATA013
14                 DATA014
15                 DATA015
16                 DATA016
17                 DATA017
18                 DATA018
19                 DATA019
20                 DATA020
```

Figure 13.11 ♦ *Using macros to consolidate worksheets*

This example should look familiar, because you have already seen the one in Chapter 1 that printed many ranges of a worksheet from a list of range names. Instead of printing from a list of range names, this worksheet uses the File Combine Add Entire command to bring in each worksheet named in the list of worksheet files.

Later in this chapter, you will see how to create the list of file names with a DOS command and also with a Release 2.2 File command.

Notice that the first command in macro \Z erases the range DATA_COMBINE in which the files will be combined, and then the cell pointer is moved to that range in preparation for the consolidation:

> /reDATA_COMBINE ~ {goto}DATA_COMBINE ~
> {let COUNT,1}{recalc \COMBINE}
> {for COUNT,1,@count(FILE_LIST),1,\COMBINE}

The next line sets the value of the variable cell count to one, and then recalculates the macro named \COMBINE. This is the macro that actually does the file operations, and it refers to the cell COUNT. The third line of the \Z macro uses the {for} command to execute \COMBINE the number of times that there are file names in the range FILE_LIST. That macro is built from a string formula, as was the print macro in Chapter 1. The control panel shows the contents of \COMBINE, which is shown here divided into two lines for clarity:

> +"{recalc \COMBINE} ~ /fcae"
> &@index($FILE_LIST,0,$COUNT − 1)&" ~ "

The first thing this macro must do each time it is called is recalculate itself. This allows it to pick up the value in COUNT for the @index function that produces the file name in the macro. After the {recalc} command, the command File Combine Add Entire is initiated, with the file name being provided by the @index function. On the first iteration of this routine, when COUNT equals one, it picks up the first name in FILE_LIST. Remember that the @index function is based on offsets, which explains why the formula subtracts one from COUNT, because the first item on the list has an offset of zero.

The macro finishes with an Enter and a {return} to send control back to the {for} statement, which executes the next loop. No matter how long the list of file names might be, this macro will race through them without forgetting one or misspelling a name. You are assured of an accurate tally in the parent worksheet.

CONSOLIDATION THROUGH LINKING FORMULAS IN RELEASE 2.2

2.2 ♦ ————

You can see that the simple macro-driven routine in Figure 13.11 is very short, reliable, and easy to revise. So would you need to use linking formulas in Release 2.2 to perform the same consolidation? Probably not, because then you would have to face the monumental job of writing a separate set of formulas in separate ranges to refer to each file's data, and then summing each cell in each file to get the total for all of them. Also, the formulas would take many times longer to do the same job as the macros and the File Combine command. If your list of files ever changed, macros could handle them without being revised, but if you used linking formulas, you would have to create a new range of linking formulas for a new file, or delete a range that referred to a file that no longer exists.

All in all, the File Combine command is a very straightforward solution to this type of consolidation. However, you may occasionally need to create a consolidation that is not as direct as the one shown here—for example, one that involves bringing in many individual cells, as opposed to the entire worksheet or one large range of cells.

In this case, you would benefit from the speed of linking formulas, and you would not have to write many lines of macros to bring in all the unique cells. When you copy linking formulas to other cells in the worksheet, their cell references automatically adjust to the new locations, which may also prove convenient. Your own needs for consolidation will dictate whether you use an automated File Combine routine or linking formulas.

◆ IMPORTING AND EXPORTING TEXT DATA

Transferring data between the Lotus environment and the world outside of Lotus is most easily accomplished through the use of plain text. Whether called ASCII files, text files, flat files, or—as in Lotus—print files, this data is a universal commodity that just about every program can read and write.

USING TEXT FILES AS THE UNIVERSAL EXCHANGE

Chapter 12 described the process of printing to a disk file in Lotus. This produces output that can be imported into a word processor or other program that can import text files. It is a fast, easy method of transferring data, and should not be thought of as a difficult process. Just remember that you generally want the left print margin set to zero and the right margin as wide as possible (240). Choose Options Other Unformatted, and the data sent to disk will be one long block of text ready for your word processor to format.

You can also import text from a word processor or other program that can produce strictly text output. There are two options for using the Lotus File Import command: Text and Numbers.

Importing a file with the Text option in column A, for example, creates rows of long labels in that column. In that form, data is not suitable for worksheet calculations, but it can either be left as text or split into separate columns as needed.

If the incoming data is structured appropriately, you can use the File Import Numbers command. This splits each element of the incoming data into separate columns. As Lotus reads a new element, it places it into a new cell in a new column to the right in the same row. When it finds a carriage return, it starts a new row. Elements are either text or numbers.

Text must be enclosed in quotes. When Lotus first encounters a quote, it starts entering the text that follows in a new cell in the column to the right. It keeps entering text there until it finds another quote, at which point the next element begins in another new cell to the right.

Numbers cannot contain commas, because a comma is seen as a text character that splits two elements. Dollar signs are ignored. However, if a number is followed by a percent sign, Lotus assumes it should be a percent and divides the incoming number by 100. Fractions are not handled as individual elements, so the fraction 2/3 would be split into two separate cells.

If this discussion sounds familiar, then you already know about the generic and widely used "comma-separated file" format, sometimes known as a comma and quote delimited file. Many programs (including the BASIC language, but unfortunately not including Lotus) can export data in this format. Lotus can import this type of data and neatly place it into separate columns in the worksheet.

The consolidation macro shown earlier in Figure 13.11 started with a known list of file names, but you could expand the scope of that macro to handle a variable list of names, a list that might change with each running of the worksheet. The next example shows how macros, the File Import command, and the Data Parse command can be used to create a consolidation file list from the directory of files that are currently on disk.

IMPORTING AND PARSING A DIRECTORY LISTING

In the example in Figure 13.11, a known list of files was combined into the master worksheet. But suppose the list of files could differ each time the routine is run? So you can be sure the macro will adapt to changing conditions, the following discussion shows you how to capture a directory listing of the worksheets on disk, and use that as the basis for the consolidation list. The process that is shown is by no means the most direct, but it demonstrates a very typical situation in a flexible manner that is easy to revise.

2.2 ◆ ─────

In Release 2.2, the File Admin Table command, which is demonstrated at the end of this section, provides a shortcut to the steps in this routine. Even with that command available, you will still find the following discussion valuable, especially in the use of the Data Parse command.

Using the Data Parse Command

Recall that in Chapter 5, the DOS command TREE was used to collect a list of all subdirectories on the hard disk as preparation for building the Lotus hard disk Gateway program. The output from TREE was sent to a file, which was then imported into Lotus. This time, a directory listing of all the worksheets that are needed for the consolidation will be made from DOS. In this example, the files reside in a subdirectory named COMPILE. The following DOS command will produce the file LISTING.PRN in that same subdirectory:

```
dir C:\COMPILE\*.WK1 > C:\COMPILE\LISTING.PRN
```

The greater-than symbol, >, redirects the output of the command (normally sent to the screen) to the file. The .PRN extension on the file is not required, but it is in keeping with the Lotus convention for naming print (text) files. To automate this DOS routine, you could include it in a batch file that also loads Lotus:

```
dir C:\COMPILE\*.WK1 >C:\COMPILE\LISTING.PRN
cd \123
123
```

2.2 ◆ ————

To perform this task in Release 2.2, you could take advantage of the {system} macro command (although the File Admin Table command is still the ultimate tool for this task, as will be discussed shortly). The following macro will create the text file of the directory listing automatically:

```
{system "dir C:\COMPILE\*.WK1 > C:\COMPILE\LISTING.PRN"}
```

The worksheet routine consists of three steps:

1. Import the directory listing file.

2. Parse the listing to pull out the worksheet names.

3. Consolidate the worksheets.

The last step, the consolidation, is basically the same as the one that was demonstrated in Figure 13.11.

Figure 13.12 shows the worksheet after the directory listing file, LISTING.PRN, has been imported at cell A1 with the File Import Text command.

```
A1:                                                            READY

         A         B        C         D         E    F    G    H
1
2    Volume in drive C has no label
3    Directory of  C:\COMPILE
4
5    .                <DIR>        5-30-90   11:30p
6    ..               <DIR>        5-30-90   11:30p
7    DATA010   WK1     3955        9-10-90    9:57a
8    DATA011   WK1     3656        9-04-90    7:37a
9    DATA014   WK1     3951        9-01-90    8:27a
10   DATA016   WK1     3419        9-08-90    8:04a
11   DATA017   WK1     3411        9-09-90   11:28a
12   DATA022   WK1     3906        9-05-90    8:37a
13   DATA025   WK1     3029        9-08-90   10:47a
14   DATA026   WK1     3988        9-07-90    8:04a
15   DATA029   WK1     3262        9-06-90    7:46a
16   DATA030   WK1     3796        9-02-90   11:39a
17   DATA034   WK1     3143        9-05-90   10:12a
18   DATA035   WK1     3055        9-05-90   11:51a
19   DATA036   WK1     3629        9-02-90    9:45a
20         19 File(s)    1384000 bytes free
```

Figure 13.12 ◆ *Importing a text file of a directory listing*

Only worksheets are listed in the directory. You can see that all the files have similar names, prefaced with DATA and followed by a unique three-digit number, which allows for up to 1,000 worksheets. These are all the worksheets that were extracted from the child worksheets for the consolidation, and then copied into the COMPILE subdirectory.

Whether the files came from the same computer, the same office, or the same state is not significant. The only thing that matters is that the data in them represent similar ranges in each worksheet so that the ranges will lay neatly one on top of the other when consolidated. Each file name must, of course, be unique. Here is the short macro that imports the directory listing and prepares the list of files for the consolidation macro:

```
{home}{down}
/re{down 3}{end}{down} ~
{home}/fitLISTING.PRN ~
{down 5}/cFORMAT_LINE ~ ~
/dpri.{end}{down}{up} ~
oFILE_LIST ~ g
```

This macro first erases the import area to ensure that the range is blank and therefore ready to receive the new file. The macro uses {end}{down} to mark off the erase range, so the length of the previously used file listing is not important.

In the third line, the cell pointer moves back to A1, where LISTING.PRN is imported as text, as was shown in Figure 13.12.

The cell pointer then moves down five rows, stopping just above the file names in the list. There it copies the range FORMAT_LINE to the current cell. The result is shown in Figure 13.13, which has a Data Parse format line in place in row 6.

This format line has been set up ahead of time and stored in the range FORMAT_LINE. The Data Parse command was used in Chapter 7 to turn numbers that were mistakenly entered as text back into actual values. In this case, the data being parsed is quite consistent. File names are never more than eight characters, and because these were expected to have the .WK1 extension, only the first eight characters of each row in the list are needed. They are identified by the first part of the format line (L>>>>>>), and the rest of the format line (SSSS...) "skips" the other characters:

```
L>>>>>>SSSSSSSSSSSSSSSSSSSSSSSSSSSSSSSS
```

Once the parse line is in place, the Data Parse command is invoked in the last two lines of the macro, shown again here:

```
/dpri.{end}{down}{up} ~
oFILE_LIST ~ g
```

```
A6:  !L>>>>>>SSSSSSSSSSSSSSSSSSSSSSSSSSSSSSSSSS                    READY

       A         B          C          D        E       F        G        H
1
2      Volume in drive C has no label
3      Directory of  C:\COMPILE
4
5      .                <DIR>        5-30-90   11:30p
6      L>>>>>>SSSSSSSSSSSSSSSSSSSSSSSSSSSSSSSSSS
7      DATA010   WK1       3955      9-10-90    9:57a
8      DATA011   WK1       3656      9-04-90    7:37a
9      DATA014   WK1       3951      9-01-90    8:27a
10     DATA016   WK1       3419      9-08-90    8:04a
11     DATA017   WK1       3411      9-09-90   11:28a
12     DATA022   WK1       3906      9-05-90    8:37a
13     DATA025   WK1       3029      9-08-90   10:47a
14     DATA026   WK1       3988      9-07-90    8:04a
15     DATA029   WK1       3262      9-06-90    7:46a
16     DATA030   WK1       3796      9-02-90   11:39a
17     DATA034   WK1       3143      9-05-90   10:12a
18     DATA035   WK1       3055      9-05-90   11:51a
19     DATA036   WK1       3629      9-02-90    9:45a
20           19 File(s)    1384000 bytes free
```

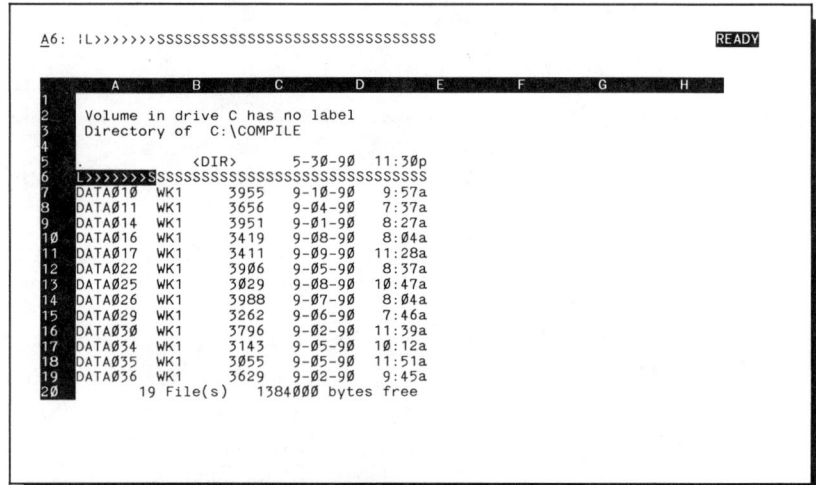

Figure 13.13 ◆ *A format line that will be used by the Data Parse command*

The cell pointer is moved with {end}{down} so that the entire file list will be highlighted as the input range, no matter how long it is. The cell pointer moves back up one row to eliminate the last line of the list, which shows the number of files and bytes. The parse output range is the cell FILE_LIST (which would have been erased previously), where the extracted file names will be copied by the command. Note that the Data Parse Reset command is given first to clear any existing settings, always a good practice.

Figure 13.14 shows the parsed file list, the cell FORMAT_LINE, and the macro that drives the routine. The macro would then continue with the file combine routine described in Figure 13.11.

The Data Parse command is a powerful tool for manipulating text that is brought into the worksheet environment. But it is not the only tool that could have been used for this example. String formulas, too, would work nicely to pull out the eight-character file names. Expertise with many tools allows you to build diverse applications.

Importing a List of Files in Release 2.2

2.2 ◆ ——————

The File Admin Table command creates a four-column table in the worksheet of a directory listing of files on your disk. You can select the file type from the 1-2-3 menu, choosing among Worksheet (WK?), Print (PRN), Graph (PIC), and Other (*.*). You can also create a list of all worksheets to which the

```
J54:  'DATAØ1Ø                                                          READY

         I              J          K          L          M          N          O
45  FORMAT_LINE   L>>>>>>SSSSSSSSSSSSSSSSSSSSSSSSSSSSSSS
46
47  \Z            {home}{down}
48                /re{down 3}{end}{down}~
49                {home}/fitLISTING.PRN~
50                {down 5}/cFORMAT_LINE~~
51                /dpri.{end}{down}{up}~
52                oFILE_LIST~g
53
54  FILE_LIST     DATAØ1Ø
55                DATAØ11
56                DATAØ14
57                DATAØ16
58                DATAØ17
59                DATAØ22
60                DATAØ25
61                DATAØ26
62                DATAØ29
63                DATAØ3Ø
64                DATAØ34
```

Figure 13.14 ◆ *The parsed file names and the accompanying macro*

current worksheet is linked, a valuable asset that allows you to keep track of the worksheets on which the current one is dependent.

To create the directory listing of worksheets used in Figures 13.11 through 13.14, invoke the File Admin Table Worksheets command, and specify the range FILE_LIST as the destination for the table. You could easily include this step in the macros:

    /fatw ˜ FILE_LIST ˜

The result is shown in Figure 13.15, where you can see the range FILE_LIST and the short macro that created the list.

With the File Admin Table command, the file list is created in four columns. The columns in Figure 13.15 have been widened so that each column's contents are visible. The first column is in the range FILE_LIST, and holds only the file names. You can see the first entry in the control panel in Figure 13.15. The second column contains the date each file was created, the third the time of creation, and the fourth the file size in bytes.

The dates and times are created as Lotus date and time numbers, not text. The last four dates and times in the list have been formatted as date and time to demonstrate this.

For the purposes of the macro routine for which this list was created, only the first column will be used; the other three can simply be ignored. On the other hand, you can see how easy it would be to use the entries in the date column to verify that each worksheet is current and was created after a given date.

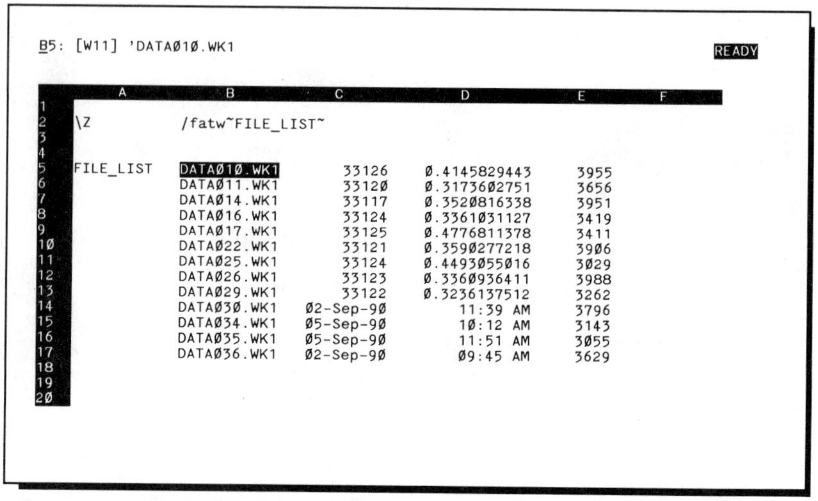

Figure 13.15 ◆ *Creating a list of files with the File Admin Table command*

⊗ **CAUTION** ◆ *The File Admin Table command is not quite as selective as the DOS command DIR. If there are any subdirectories below the one where your worksheets are stored, those subdirectories will be included in the generated table, and you will have to write your macro to skip these entries in the list.*

This behavior is very much the same as other 1-2-3 File commands, where subdirectories are always shown on the list of files. Because of this, you also benefit from the fact that the list is generated in a sorted order, based on each entry's file extension and name in the first column.

◆ SUMMARY

This chapter has dealt with the commands and techniques for transferring data into, within, and out of the Lotus environment. The first part of the chapter dealt with the Lotus commands for moving data around the worksheet, including Copy, Move, Range Value, and Range Transpose.

Sorting was discussed as a means of rearranging data within the worksheet. The sorting sequence that Lotus uses is established when you install the program, and the three choices it offers were demonstrated. Several safety tips for sorts were recommended, and a technique for sorting on internal characters was shown.

The Lotus file commands have uses even for chores within a single worksheet. Examples of changing a range of formulas to values and resetting a data range to zero were shown. You can use the File Combine and File Xtract commands in concert to develop extensive worksheet consolidation applications, demonstrated here by a macro-driven worksheet. Linking formulas in Release 2.2 provide another method for accessing data in other worksheets. Their benefits and shortcomings were discussed and compared to the File Combine command.

Finally, text data was discussed as the universal form of exchange. Lotus can export data via the Print File command to a word processor or other program that accepts pure text files. Text can be imported into Lotus with the Text or Numbers option. The Data Parse command can be used to extract pieces of text from long strings of text. The final example in this chapter used that command on an imported file directory listing, which was then used in a consolidation macro. The File Admin Table command in Release 2.2 provided a practical shortcut for this last example.

Throughout this book, the phrase *Lotus environment* has occurred repeatedly. The more you use Lotus, the more you'll come to appreciate the full meaning of those words. Powerful tools, a fast but simple interface, context sensitive help, and speed combine to make the Lotus worksheet an amazingly productive and supportive environment in which to work. But there is more.

There are dozens of add-in programs available, which taken together affect virtually every aspect of the Lotus environment. To cover them all would be too large an undertaking for this book. But Appendix A provides a brief overview of the subject, introducing the variety of programs that are available, and discussing some important points to remember as you use add-ins.

If you are outgrowing the Lotus 2 environment, you should read Appendix B, which looks at the highlights of Lotus 3 and the issues that need to be considered as you decide whether the upgrade is for you.

APPENDICES:

THE ABILITY TO WORK WITH ADD-IN PROGRAMS GIVES LOTUS an entirely different look, and stretches its boundaries far beyond that of a spreadsheet program. Every Lotus user will have at least one or two of the three add-ins discussed in this book: Speedup and Learn for Release 2.01, and Allways for both releases.

A full discussion of add-ins and the many ways they can interact with Lotus is well beyond the scope of this book, but Appendix A provides the basic information you need to continue exploring add-ins on your own. It covers their installation and use, and briefly describes the wide variety of add-ins that are available for Lotus 1-2-3.

For those of you who are pushing the Lotus 2 spreadsheet to its limits, Appendix B discusses Release 3 of 1-2-3. If you already have or are willing to purchase the necessary hardware, and are willing to live with some of the obstacles involved in the upgrade, Lotus 3 may provide you with the extra power you need.

A

Using Add-ins to Expand the Lotus Environment

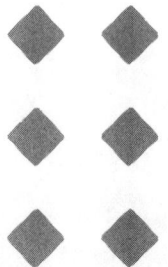

A
◆ ◆ ◆

THE CAPABILITIES AND TREMENDOUS POPULARITY OF THE
Lotus spreadsheet have spawned dozens of third-party programs that further
increase its usefulness. These programs fall into several distinct categories. The
most widespread is the *worksheet template*, which is a prefabricated set of worksheets designed for a specific application. These include tax packages, checking account managers, and financial analysis tools.

Some programs do not work with Lotus, but are *file compatible*. This means
that they can read from, and sometimes write to, Lotus worksheet files, thereby
providing a convenient means of transferring your Lotus worksheet data to
other programs. There are graphics programs that can read Lotus .PIC files,
and database programs that can read worksheet files. Other than working with
the files, these programs have no direct connection with Lotus.

Lotus *add-on* programs run separately from Lotus, but understand the workings of the spreadsheet. These are generally terminate-and-stay-resident programs that run concurrently with Lotus, but are invisible to it. They work with
1-2-3 without the benefit of any formal linking. For instance, an add-on program must have its own methods for accessing data in the worksheet. Then, it
can import data, perform a calculation with that data, and export a result back
into the worksheet, all without the help or approval of Lotus.

The fourth category of Lotus-related products consists of *add-in* programs.
These take advantage of the add-in capabilities that are built into Lotus, and
provide a convenient means of expanding the scope of the 1-2-3 worksheet in a
tightly integrated and stable manner.

◆ THE NATURE OF ADD-IN PROGRAMS

Since Lotus was specifically designed to accept add-in programs, add-ins
have many advantages over add-ons, which work "outside" of Lotus.

First and most important, you can attach (load) add-in programs while working within 1-2-3. This allows you to pick and choose those ancillary programs

that you wish to run during your 1-2-3 session. You can also detach (unload) add-ins, giving you control over memory usage.

You can choose to have 1-2-3 automatically attach selected add-ins each time you run it.

Add-in programs have an intimate knowledge of the worksheet and can use all of its features. An add-in can access worksheet data by address or range name. It can create range names as well as ranges for the print, data query, or other commands. In general, an add-in acts as a seamless extension to the 1-2-3 environment.

Because they are so closely linked, your Lotus macros can control any attached add-in program, allowing you to build applications with capabilities far beyond those of the worksheet alone.

An add-in program can have its own set of menus and commands, or it can simply be a messenger that brings new @ functions to the worksheet. These new functions can be used by Lotus as though they were its own.

An add-in program is generally written in assembly language, and it is no small task. The programmer has access to a variety of subroutines in the Lotus Developer Tools, a library of worksheet routines provided by Lotus Development Corporation just for this purpose. Ideally, the add-in program is designed to have a look and feel that closely matches that of the 1-2-3 spreadsheet, and will therefore present few hurdles in the learning process. The market for add-ins is extensive, and they cover a wide variety of applications.

◆ ADD-INS FOR ALL PURPOSES

The most well-known add-in has to be Allways, the spreadsheet publisher that lets you enhance the printed output of your worksheets. (See Chapters 11 and 12 for more information on Allways.) When it was first released by Funk Software for 1-2-3 Release 2.01, it was quite well received among Lotus users. Later, its inclusion with Release 2.2 assured it a place at the top of the list of add-ins. Since most people are more than willing to improve the quality of their printed output, add-ins such as Allways are assured of a bright future.

> ⊗ **CAUTION ◆** *Note that if an add-in program was written for Release 2.0 or 2.01, it should by design also work in Release 2.2. However, you may occasionally find an "ill-behaved" add-in that cannot exist in the Release 2.2 environment. In that case, you should call the company that wrote the add-in program to see if they have issued an upgrade that works under Release 2.2.*

The other add-in Lotus supplies with Release 2.2 is the Macro Library Manager. (See Chapter 1 for a discussion on this add-in.) Where Allways works in graphics mode and is very visible to the user, the Macro Library Manager is quite subtle and barely noticeable when it is active—a good example of the internal power of 1-2-3 that add-ins can access, manipulate, and enhance.

Perhaps the most frequent overuse (and sometimes abuse) of the Lotus worksheet is when it is used as a word processor. So it is not surprising that a very popular type of add-in program is the *word processor*. At the touch of a key, a powerful word processor is at hand for any writing task. As an add-in, it is immediately available for small tasks such as writing a short memo. A word processor that is an add-in can access worksheet data, making it the ideal tool for writing a monthly report that must include data from one or more worksheets. For those who use 1-2-3 intensively, the add-in word processor is no doubt the primary add-in for extending the Lotus environment.

The *database add-in* program serves to alleviate the crunch caused by the second most common overuse of the worksheet. Performing complex database routines on thousands of records can quickly deplete the memory and overextend the capabilities of the worksheet. Some database add-ins allow you to access data from disk, much as stand-alone database programs do, which takes a tremendous pressure off the worksheet. Other add-ins work on data within the worksheet and extend the 1-2-3 database commands. Most database add-ins allow you to create data entry forms and print sophisticated reports.

A handy add-in that doesn't fulfill the role of another program, such as a word processor or database program, is the *cell annotator*. With one of these add-ins, you can attach text notes to cells in the worksheet via a pop-up window. These notes can provide documentation or instructions in an unobtrusive way that meshes nicely with the style of the worksheet. A note stays with a cell if that cell is moved, and a menu of noted cells allows you to jump quickly to a cell with a specific note. Notes can be printed to serve as part of the worksheet's permanent documentation.

There are add-ins for extending the *graphics* of 1-2-3, something everyone has wanted at one time or another. This type of add-in allows you to create graphs from worksheet data, just as you do within 1-2-3, but offers a wide variety of graph types and styles, such as 3-D, high-low, area, or combination line and bar. You save your graphs as .PIC files, which can be printed in the usual way with PrintGraph.

Many different add-ins support extended *data analysis* within the worksheet. These include goal-seeking, forecasting, risk analysis, and general statistical packages. The add-ins in this category provide tremendous calculating power to the worksheet, and avoid an otherwise extensive series of data transfers and the use of outside programs. They can allow you to use the 1-2-3 worksheet without giving up the processing capabilities that you require.

A large category of *add-in utilities* extend the worksheet in a thousand different directions. Some are barely noticeable, such as *@ function add-ins* that simply provide new @ functions in the worksheet. Lotus' own add-in for Release 2.01, Speedup, is quite unobtrusive once it is attached (see Chapter 6). Some are quite conspicuous, such as *worksheet display add-ins* that change the 1-2-3 display, allowing you to view more rows and columns on one screen.

Other add-ins provide *file management* tools. With these, you can sort the list of worksheets and other files on your disk, peek into the contents of the worksheet files, and back up your files. You can perform file operations such as creating a new directory and copying, moving, renaming, or deleting a file. Some can compress worksheet files as they are saved, so that they take up less than half as much room on disk.

One popular feature in an add-in utility for Release 2.01 is *search and replace*. This allows you to search through the worksheet for text or numbers, much as you might in a word processor.

You can even get a *spell checker add-in* to check the spelling of any labels in the worksheet. This may not be at the top of the list of add-ins, but when you combine it with an add-in word processor that stores its text within the worksheet, its value becomes apparent.

With such a multitude of add-ins, you will surely find several that could enhance your use of 1-2-3. Whether it is printing your worksheet sideways or recording your keystrokes with the Lotus add-in Learn (discussed in Chapter 1), you can tailor your Lotus environment to suit your own requirements and habits.

◆ USING ADD-IN PROGRAMS

Because they work in conjunction with 1-2-3, add-in programs are generally pretty easy to master. Their menus, function keys, and command sequences should follow the pattern found in 1-2-3, allowing you quick access to them.

An add-in's documentation should explain both how to install it and how to use it with 1-2-3. Installation frequently requires nothing more than copying one program file and one help file to your 1-2-3 subdirectory.

1-2-3 Release 2.2 can accept add-in programs from the moment you first run it. If you use Release 2.01, however, you must first install the Add-in Manager to your 1-2-3 driver set before you can use any add-ins.

CONFIGURING YOUR RELEASE 2.01 DRIVER SET

All add-in programs come with instructions and the necessary programs for configuring your copy of Release 2.01 to accept add-in programs. The configuration process consists of running the ADD_MGR.EXE program to append the ADD_MGR.DRV drivers to your 1-2-3 driver file, 123.SET (or whatever name you are using if not this default name), using the following command:

ADD_MGR 123.SET

Once you have configured your driver set, you are ready to run any add-in program. This means that the installation procedure for a new add-in may consist simply of copying its program file to your Lotus subdirectory, or to a floppy disk that you use for add-ins.

The Lotus file 123.DYN must be available at startup in order for Lotus to accept add-ins. It resides on the 1-2-3 PrintGraph disk, so be sure to copy it to your 1-2-3 subdirectory or to your System disk.

Making changes to your driver set with the Lotus Install program destroys the add-in drivers, and you will have to run the ADD_MGR program again. One way to tell if your 123.SET file is configured for add-ins is to check its file size. The ADD_MGR.DRV file adds more than 20K to the file, expanding it from about 35K to about 60K.

When your driver set is configured for add-ins, your copy of Lotus will require about 20K more RAM, so keep that in mind if some of your worksheets are pushing the limits of your memory.

There may come a time when you absolutely must have that extra 20K of RAM in order to work on your spreadsheet. You can remove the Add-in Manager from your driver set by using the DEL_MGR program, which accompanies the ADD_MGR program on the add-in program's disk. Getting rid of the add-in capability under these circumstances may not be a great loss when you consider that add-ins require conventional memory for their program code (although most can use expanded memory for any data they must store), and that you would not be able to run one in the limited memory anyway.

If your Lotus driver set file has the default name of 123.SET, issue the following command at the DOS prompt from the 1-2-3 subdirectory:

DEL_MGR 123.SET

If your driver set has another name, simply substitute that name in the place of 123.SET. Now you will save about 20K when you run 1-2-3, but you will not be able to run any add-ins. Later you can use the ADD_MGR program to once again configure your copy of 1-2-3 to accept add-ins.

TIP ◆ *If you expect to run into this problem in the future, you will find it most convenient to create a new driver set that does not have the Add-in Manager. Before you run the DEL_MGR routine, first copy your existing driver set under a new name:*

copy 123.SET NOADDIN.SET

Now run DEL_MGR and remove the Add-in Manager from the new driver set, NOADDIN.SET. When you now run 1-2-3, you will by default be using the 123.SET driver file. But when you want to save memory, run Lotus without the Add-in Manager by loading 1-2-3 with this command:

123 NOADDIN

2.2 ◆ —————

TIP ◆ *Although the ADD_MGR program is unnecessary if you use Release 2.2, you may still find a need for the DEL_MGR program. The installation routines for many add-in programs will automatically append the Add-in Manager to your Lotus driver set, no matter which version of 1-2-3 you have. This won't hurt anything in Release 2.2, but it will take up about 20K of RAM when you run 1-2-3, and that much disk storage space as well. If you suspect that an add-in program has changed your 1-2-3 driver set, use the DEL_MGR program to remove the Add-in Manager from it, with the command:*

DEL_MGR 123.SET

ACCESSING ADD-INS FROM THE WORKSHEET

To access add-ins in Release 2.01, you press the Alt-F10 key to bring up the Add-in Manager menu. In Release 2.2, you have the choice of using the Alt-F10 key or the Add-In command on the 1-2-3 menu.

CAUTION ◆ *In general, an add-in program cannot be used unless it resides within the 1-2-3 subdirectory, which must also be the default subdirectory when you load 1-2-3. This means that if you are using both 1-2-3 Release 2.01 and Release 2.2 on your system, you may have to keep two copies of your add-ins, one in each of the 1-2-3 subdirectories. Also, even though you can take advantage of the PATH command to start 1-2-3 from a different subdirectory, you will not be able to use any add-ins. The best approach here is to change to the 1-2-3 subdirectory and then load 1-2-3.*

When you issue the Invoke command from the Add-in menu, you can choose to assign a *hot key* to the add-in—either Alt-F7, Alt-F8, Alt-F9, or, in the case of Release 2.2, Alt-F10.

Later, you can press the hot key and the add-in will pop up. You can always choose to invoke an add-in by name with the Invoke command on the Add-in Manager menu. Both methods produce the same result—the add-in is invoked and ready to use.

With the ability to run add-ins comes the need to check for the existence of any add-ins that may be attached to 1-2-3. You can see which add-ins are currently attached by invoking the Lotus Add-in menu and choosing Detach. All the attached add-ins will be displayed on its menu. Just press Escape to leave the menu without detaching any of them.

You can also use the built-in @ function @isapp to check for the existence of an add-in. It returns 1 if the named add-in is attached, and 0 if it is not. So if there is a program named CELL_BIT attached to Lotus, the following formula would return 1:

```
@isapp("CELL_BIT")
```

Another @ function, named @isaaf, checks for the existence of an add-in @ function. Again, it returns 1 if the named @ function is in the Lotus environment, and 0 if it is not.

Both of these functions play a critical role when a worksheet that uses add-in programs is macro-driven. The macro must know whether an add-in or @ function is attached before it proceeds. For instance, this macro checks to see whether the add-in CELL_BIT is attached. If it is not, a call is made to the routine named \ATTACH:

```
{if @isapp("CELL_BIT")<>1}{\ATTACH}
```

The \ATTACH routine makes use of the macro keyword {appn}, which calls an add-in's hot key or the Add-in menu, depending on the value of *n*. A value of 1, 2, or 3 represents one of the three hot keys, and will invoke the corresponding add-in. The value 4 calls the Add-in menu, just as though you had pressed Alt-F10. Here is the routine named \ATTACH, which attaches the add-in named CELL_BIT to the hot key Alt-F7:

```
{app4}aCELL_BIT~7q
```

2.2 ♦ ——————

⊗ CAUTION ♦ *If you are using Release 2.2, you might think that you could just as easily have your macro call the Add-In command from the 1-2-3 menu:*

```
/aaCELL_BIT~7q
```

But without offering any advantage in return, this macro would be incompatible with Release 2.01. It is better to use the {app4} command to call the Add-in menu, knowing that the macro and its worksheet will run under each version of 1-2-3.

The add-in CELL_BIT can have its own menus, perhaps with a command named Worksheet Cell Collapse. That command could easily be invoked with this worksheet macro:

{app1}wcc

The ability of Lotus to reside concurrently with add-in programs is one of its strongest features. Whether or not you attach an add-in to 1-2-3 depends on your work requirements and routines. But with the add-in capability, the boundaries of the worksheet environment are dissolved, allowing 1-2-3 to be customized to meet the needs of any user.

B

*Upgrade
Considerations*

B
◆ ◆ ◆

WHEN LOTUS 2.0 WAS RELEASED IN LATE 1985, IT WAS IN ONE
sense a small upgrade of Release 1A—little extra RAM was needed to run it,
and a hard disk was not required. Most work habits that users had learned
while using Lotus 1A could be continued with Lotus 2.0. But in its features list,
Release 2.0 went far beyond its predecessor.

Worksheets could be much larger with Release 2.0's support for expanded
RAM and sparse matrix memory management. Support for math coprocessors
speeded up worksheet recalculation. The macro language, already a great success, was enhanced with the Command Language. String arithmetic was also
supported, and came with a wealth of string functions. The System command
extended the power of the spreadsheet by making the DOS environment readily
available, and the Data Parse command made it easy to import and analyze
external sources of data. The ability to accept add-in programs opened up the
Lotus environment to third-party products.

The list goes on, but the point here is that the Lotus spreadsheet reached a
new level of sophistication without demanding too much from its users. For
many, the decision to upgrade to Release 3 will be more difficult than the one to
upgrade to Release 2.01 or 2.2. You will have to determine whether the benefits
of Release 3's new features offset its hardware requirements, speed, and minor
incompatibilities with Releases 2.01 and 2.2.

◆ NEW FEATURES IN LOTUS 1-2-3 RELEASE 3

Lotus 1-2-3 Release 3 will handle *multiple worksheets and files* in memory at
the same time, but don't confuse a worksheet with a file—they are now separate issues. A Release 3 file can have from 1 to 256 worksheets, labeled A to
IV, that together create the third dimension that many users have requested.
You can have multiple files active in memory during a Lotus session, provided
the total number of worksheets in all active files does not exceed 256. Worksheets within a single file can be used independently, or they can be grouped so
that a change in the formatting of one is reflected in all.

You can create *formula links* between worksheets that are much more flexible, and therefore more powerful, than the single-cell links available in Release 2.2. A linking formula can be as complex as any other formula you can write, and they can refer to worksheets in the current file, in another file active in memory, or in files that reside on disk. Ranges may span rows, columns, and worksheets in three dimensions, so you can easily write a formula that uses a 3-D range as its parameter. The transition to three dimensions is quite logical and should require little relearning.

Release 3 is a large program that requires more RAM than Release 2. On top of that, the ability to hold multiple files in memory also implies that you will use more RAM for your Lotus 3 applications. To circumvent this memory problem, Release 3 requires 640K of conventional memory, plus a minimum of 384K of *extended* memory in which to run. This means that you cannot run Release 3 on an 8088-based computer; you must have an 80286, 80386, or 80486 processor.

Fortunately, once Release 3 is up and running, it can utilize much more memory than earlier releases. Your spreadsheets can be as large as 16M without your computer running out of conventional memory before its expanded memory is even partially used. This is because Release 3 accesses all available memory—conventional, expanded, and extended—as one large block of *contiguous* RAM. You can see this when you invoke the Worksheet Status command, which displays just one number for available memory.

Because Release 3 uses extended memory to run its program code, much more conventional memory is left unused than in Release 2. Therefore, if you have approximately 500K or more of extended RAM for 1-2-3, you will find that it uses only about 50K of conventional RAM. This leaves plenty of room for memory-resident programs or other applications that require conventional RAM.

Besides running under DOS, Release 3 is also *OS/2 compatible*, so that if you make the jump to that operating system, you will be ready to run 1-2-3 immediately.

Release 3 automatically spools your print jobs to a *print queue*, and then prints from the disk file while you continue to work in the spreadsheet. You can print graphs along with spreadsheets, and Lotus will paginate as necessary for the text and graphs that are printed.

The worksheet has some new additions, too. Cells can now contain 512 characters, and the edit window will expand to show them all. By adding a semicolon after a formula, you can append a *formula note* to it, up to the 512-character limit. You can also attach *range name notes*; the command Range Name Table displays the notes to the right of the names and addresses. The command Worksheet Window Map sets all columns to a width of one character, and clearly identifies all text, formula, and value cells.

There is an *Undo* command, with one level of undo, that is much more memory efficient than the Undo command in Release 2.2. You can sort on up to *256 sort keys*. The database commands have been extended so that external databases can be accessed. There is *automatic cell formatting*. If you enter *1-Jan*, Lotus will guess that you really mean the date value for January 1 of the current year. It will enter that value and give it the proper date format as well.

The future of Lotus 3 will be determined not just by the features in the spreadsheet, but also (and perhaps more so) by two products that work along with it: the Lotus Add-in Toolkit and DataLens.

THE LOTUS ADD-IN TOOLKIT

The Lotus Add-in Toolkit for Release 3 is the successor to the Lotus Developer Tools, and like them, it is a separate product that is used to write add-in programs for 1-2-3 Release 2. The Toolkit is a structured, high-level programming language for developing add-in programs for Release 3. Its style has been compared to Pascal, although it is tailored to the job of accessing worksheet data and routines. The Toolkit is designed to pick up where the macro language leaves off, and gives Lotus applications developers a much more extensive set of tools for programming in 1-2-3.

The program consists of a text editor for creating the source code (although any ASCII editor will do), a compiler that creates the add-in program file, and a program debugger. Along with the program are a group of add-in library files, to which your programs can refer to gain access to 1-2-3 spreadsheet data and commands.

When you compile your source code, the result is not a ready-to-run machine-language program, but a pseudo-code that must be interpreted by 1-2-3 at run-time. When you attach your add-in to Lotus, all the necessary run-time libraries are loaded, and the resulting code is interpreted and executed.

There is an extensive range of applications that you can develop under the Toolkit, and they fall into three main categories: new @ functions, new macro keyword commands, and turn-key applications.

Although the Toolkit is by no means a simple extension to the macro language, anyone who is familiar with the basic concepts of programming should be able to write their own @ functions and macro commands in a short amount of time. Obviously, the sky is the limit when it comes to developing extensive spreadsheet applications with the Toolkit.

On the other hand, developers of high-end add-in programs, such as Allways, will still use assembly language for its speed and compactness, and the Toolkit will serve only as an interface between the programmers and Lotus. In the right hands, the Lotus Add-in Toolkit will do much to extend the Lotus environment.

EXCHANGING DATA VIA DATALENS

Another key to the success of Lotus 3 lies in DataLens (originally known as Blueprint), a device driver specification for accessing external data from within the Lotus spreadsheet.

DataLens formalizes what has already been established in the market for Lotus 2 database add-in programs that allow Lotus to read from or write to external data files.

DataLens drivers are something like add-in programs, in that you must first attach one to 1-2-3 before you can use it. Then, you can invoke the Data Query External command, and use a specified external file as the input or output range for the Lotus data commands. Depending on the DataLens driver, you can extract from, delete, or write to the database file, just as though it were a data range within the worksheet. The DataLens driver acts like a translator between 1-2-3 and the database file, providing the key to the data access. Release 3 comes with a driver for dBASE III. The DataLens Toolkit will allow developers to write DataLens drivers for virtually any file format, operating system, or hardware environment, and many other drivers will be written by third parties as time goes by.

With the combination of multiple worksheets, the Add-in Toolkit, and DataLens, Lotus 3 has the potential for being far more powerful than Lotus 2. With that prospect established, you must decide if you can utilize that power and if you are ready to make the adjustments necessary to live with Release 3.

◆ *MAKING THE TRANSITION FROM RELEASE 2 TO RELEASE 3*

The upgrade to Release 3 is by no means the simple step that the move from Release 2.01 to Release 2.2 is. As their version numbers imply, Release 2.2 is just a minor upgrade that is almost completely compatible with Release 2.01. But there are many things you should consider before you make the move to Release 3.

First are the *hardware requirements*. It was mentioned earlier that this version requires a processor such as the 80286 that can address *extended* memory. You must have at least 384K of *extended* memory in order to run Release 3.

Many Lotus users already have *expanded* memory cards in their computers, which can be switched to serve as *extended* memory. This makes it possible to configure your computer for Release 3, although you will have to go through the gyrations of making the change, which may involve opening your computer and setting switches on the memory card. Then you will have to reset the ROM switches in your computer that tell it how much memory it has installed.

Once you have changed to *extended* memory, you might find that you no longer have enough *expanded* memory in which to run other applications, such as large Release 2 spreadsheets. As long as you must reconfigure your hardware settings, you should consider adding more memory to your computer if you switch to Release 3, so that you have at least 2M above your conventional memory. You will most likely want this memory anyway as soon as you start to take full advantage of the Release 3 spreadsheet's size and capabilities.

Release 3 runs noticeably slower than Release 2, so the upgrade will actually set you back in terms of speed. If you can give the program more than 384K of *extended* memory, it will run a bit faster and not access the disk as frequently to swap code in and out of memory.

None of your Release 2 add-ins will work under Release 3, although you might find that some will no longer be needed. You may also find that the company that sells the add-in has an inexpensive upgrade that runs under Release 3.

If you have been craving more spectacular graphs and printing capabilities, your wishes will most likely not be answered by moving to Release 3. While those aspects of the program are improved, they are still more in the realm of Lotus 2 than of the stand-alone presentation graphics programs that are available. However, add-ins that greatly enhance Release 3 in these areas will undoubtedly be developed someday.

Although Release 3 is a powerful spreadsheet programming environment, it is noticeably missing a macro debugger. Its Step mode is essentially the same as that in Release 2.01.

In terms of compatibility, you will find that there are numerous small differences between Release 3 and Release 2. This will probably not be a problem while you are working in Release 3, but will be an issue when you want to use your Release 2 worksheets in Release 3. Extensive, macro-driven routines from Release 2 will definitely need to be thoroughly tested under Release 3, and numerous small adjustments will more than likely have to be made.

For example, during certain command routines the cell pointer will end up in a different cell when moved across a window than it would in Release 2. Range names in formulas do not change to their actual cell addresses when you edit the formula. When writing a formula, if you reference the actual cell address of a range that also has a name, only the cell address will appear; the name will not be shown in its place. Since Release 3 automatically converts text entries that look like a date into the actual date value, you may find yourself or your macros entering the wrong information (you must preface such entries with a + in order for it be taken as a formula and not as a date). Range names behave differently in Release 3, and can produce some very different results than would appear in Release 2. Finally, and definitely at the bottom of the list of importance, is the fact that the macro {beep} command produces different tones in each version of the spreadsheet.

While many of these differences are discussed in the Release 3 reference manual, the multitude of problems that may arise from simply retrieving and then running a Release 2 worksheet under Release 3 can be quite aggravating. Therefore, you should be somewhat cautious if you plan to use Release 3 along with other people who use Release 2.

Finally in this same vein, a Lotus 2 user should have no trouble moving to Release 3, and will require little retraining to make the transition. But realize that "little retraining" can cover a lot of ground, and you should be prepared for a period of disruption during the changeover.

If you decide to stick with Release 2.01 or 2.2, rest assured that Lotus 2 will continue to be sold and supported. There are millions of copies of Lotus 2 in use throughout the world, and a tremendous number of templates, add-in programs, books, and training materials available for it. Lotus 2 may very well continue to be the spreadsheet of choice for users of 1-2-3 for years to come.

INDEX
◆ ◆ ◆

Selections from The SYBEX Library

SPREADSHEETS AND INTEGRATED SOFTWARE

Visual Guide to Lotus 1-2-3
Jeff Woodward
250pp. Ref. 641-3
Readers match what they see on the screen with the book's screen-by-screen action sequences. For new Lotus users, topics include computer fundamentals, opening and editing a worksheet, using graphs, macros, and printing typeset-quality reports. For Release 2.2.

The ABC's of 1-2-3 Release 2.2
Chris Gilbert/Laurie Williams
340pp. Ref. 623-5
New Lotus 1-2-3 users delight in this book's step-by-step approach to building trouble-free spreadsheets, displaying graphs, and efficiently building databases. The authors cover the ins and outs of the latest version including easier calculations, file linking, and better graphic presentation.

The ABC's of 1-2-3 Release 3
Judd Robbins
290pp. Ref. 519-0
The ideal book for beginners who are new to Lotus or new to Release 3. This step-by-step approach to the 1-2-3 spreadsheet software gets the reader up and running with spreadsheet, database, graphics, and macro functions.

The ABC's of 1-2-3 (Second Edition)
Chris Gilbert/Laurie Williams
245pp. Ref. 355-4
Online Today recommends it as "an easy and comfortable way to get started with the program." An essential tutorial for novices, it will remain on your desk as a valuable source of ongoing reference and support. For Release 2.

Mastering 1-2-3 Release 3
Carolyn Jorgensen
682pp. Ref. 517-4
For new Release 3 and experienced Release 2 users, "Mastering" starts with a basic spreadsheet, then introduces spreadsheet and database commands, functions, and macros, and then tells how to analyze 3D spreadsheets and make high-impact reports and graphs. Lotus add-ons are discussed and Fast Tracks are included.

Mastering 1-2-3 (Second Edition)
Carolyn Jorgensen
702pp. Ref. 528-X
Get the most from 1-2-3 Release 2 with this step-by-step guide emphasizing advanced features and practical uses. Topics include data sharing, macros, spreadsheet security, expanded memory, and graphics enhancements.

The Complete Lotus 1-2-3 Release 2.2 Handbook
Greg Harvey
750pp. Ref. 625-1
This comprehensive handbook discusses every 1-2-3 operating with clear instructions and practical tips. This volume especially emphasizes the new improved graphics, high-speed recalculation techniques, and spreadsheet linking available with Release 2.2.

The Complete Lotus 1-2-3 Release 3 Handbook
Greg Harvey
700pp. Ref. 600-6
Everything you ever wanted to know about 1-2-3 is in this definitive handbook. As a Release 3 guide, it features the design and use of 3D worksheets, and

improved graphics, along with using Lotus under DOS or OS/2. Problems, exercises, and helpful insights are included.

Lotus 1-2-3 Desktop Companion
SYBEX Ready Reference Series
Greg Harvey
976pp. Ref. 501-8

A full-time consultant, right on your desk. Hundreds of self-contained entries cover every 1-2-3 feature, organized by topic, indexed and cross-referenced, and supplemented by tips, macros and working examples. For Release 2.

Advanced Techniques
in Lotus 1-2-3
Peter Antoniak/E. Michael Lunsford
367pp. Ref. 556-5

This guide for experienced users focuses on advanced functions, and techniques for designing menu-driven applications using macros and the Release 2 command language. Interfacing techniques and add-on products are also considered.

Lotus 1-2-3 Tips and Tricks
Gene Weisskopf
396pp. Ref. 454-2

A rare collection of timesavers and tricks for longtime Lotus users. Topics include macros, range names, spreadsheet design, hardware considerations, DOS operations, efficient data analysis, printing, data interchange, applications development, and more.

Lotus 1-2-3 Instant Reference
Release 2.2
SYBEX Prompter Series
Greg Harvey/Kay Yarborough Nelson
254pp. Ref. 635-9, 4 ¾" × 8"

The reader gets quick and easy access to any operation in 1-2-3 Version 2.2 in this handy pocket-sized encyclopedia. Organized by menu function, each command and function has a summary description, the exact key sequence, and a discussion of the options.

Mastering Symphony
(Fourth Edition)
Douglas Cobb
857pp. Ref. 494-1

Thoroughly revised to cover all aspects of the major upgrade of Symphony Version 2, this Fourth Edition of Doug Cobb's classic is still "the Symphony bible" to this complex but even more powerful package. All the new features are discussed and placed in context with prior versions so that both new and previous users will benefit from Cobb's insights.

The ABC's of Quattro
Alan Simpson/Douglas J. Wolf
286pp. Ref. 560-3

Especially for users new to spreadsheets, this is an introduction to the basic concepts and a guide to instant productivity through editing and using spreadsheet formulas and functions. Includes how to print out graphs and data for presentation. For Quattro 1.1.

Mastering Quattro
Alan Simpson
576pp. Ref. 514-X

This tutorial covers not only all of Quattro's classic spreadsheet features, but also its added capabilities including extended graphing, modifiable menus, and the macro debugging environment. Simpson brings out how to use all of Quattro's new-generation-spreadsheet capabilities.

Mastering Framework III
Douglas Hergert/Jonathan Kamin
613pp. Ref. 513-1

Thorough, hands-on treatment of the latest Framework release. An outstanding introduction to integrated software applications, with examples for outlining, spreadsheets, word processing, databases, and more; plus an introduction to FRED programming.

The ABC's of Excel
on the IBM PC
Douglas Hergert
326pp. Ref. 567-0

This book is a brisk and friendly introduction to the most important features of

Microsoft Excel for PC's. This beginner's book discusses worksheets, charts, database operations, and macros, all with hands-on examples. Written for all versions through Version 2.

Mastering Excel on the IBM PC
Carl Townsend
628pp. Ref. 403-8
A complete Excel handbook with step-by-step tutorials, sample applications and an extensive reference section. Topics include worksheet fundamentals, formulas and windows, graphics, database techniques, special features, macros and more.

Excel Instant Reference
SYBEX Prompter Series
William J. Orvis
368pp. Ref.577-8, 4 ¾" × 8"
This pocket-sized reference book contains all of Excel's menu commands, math operations, and macro functions. Quick and easy access to command syntax, usage, arguments, and examples make this Instant Reference a must. Through Version 1.5.

Understanding PFS:
First Choice
Gerry Litton
489pp. Ref. 568-9
From basic commands to complex features, this complete guide to the popular integrated package is loaded with step-by-step instructions. Lessons cover creating attractive documents, setting up easy-to-use databases, working with spreadsheets and graphics, and smoothly integrating tasks from different First Choice modules. For Version 3.0.

Mastering Enable
Keith D. Bishop
517pp. Ref. 440-2
A comprehensive, practical, hands-on guide to Enable 2.0—integrated word processing, spreadsheet, database management, graphics, and communications—from basic concepts to custom menus, macros and the Enable Procedural Language.

Mastering Q & A
(Second Edition)
Greg Harvey
540pp. Ref. 452-6
This hands-on tutorial explores the Q & A Write, File, and Report modules, and the Intelligent Assistant. English-language command processor, macro creation, interfacing with other software, and more, using practical business examples.

Mastering SuperCalc5
Greg Harvey/Mary Beth Andrasak
500pp. Ref. 624-3
This book offers a complete and unintimidating guided tour through each feature. With step-by-step lessons, readers learn about the full capabilities of spreadsheet, graphics, and data management functions. Multiple spreadsheets, linked spreadsheets, 3D graphics, and macros are also discussed.

ACCOUNTING

Mastering DacEasy Accounting
Darleen Hartley Yourzek
476pp. Ref 442-9
Applied accounting principles are at your fingertips in this exciting new guide to using DacEasy Accounting versions 2.0 and 3.0. Installing, converting data, processing work, and printing reports are covered with a variety of practical business examples. Through Version 3.0

DATABASE
MANAGEMENT

The ABC's of Paradox
Charles Siegel
300pp. Ref.573-5
Easy to understand and use, this introduction is written so that the computer novice can create, edit, and manage complex Paradox databases. This primer is filled with examples of the Paradox 3.0 menu structure.

Mastering Paradox
(Fourth Edition)
Alan Simpson
636pp. Ref. 612-X
Best selling author Alan Simpson simplifies all aspects of Paradox for the beginning to intermediate user. The book starts with database basics, covers multiple tables, graphics, custom applications with PAL, and the Personal Programmer. For Version 3.0.

Quick Guide to dBASE:
The Visual Approach
David Kolodney
382pp. Ref. 596-4
This illustrated tutorial provides the beginner with a working knowledge of all the basic functions of dBASE IV. Images of each successive dBASE screen tell how to create and modify a database, add, edit, sort and select records, and print custom labels and reports.

The ABC's of dBASE IV
Robert Cowart
338pp. Ref. 531-X
This superb tutorial introduces beginners to the concept of databases and practical dBASE IV applications featuring the new menu-driven interface, the new report writer, and Query by Example.

Understanding dBASE IV
(Special Edition)
Alan Simpson
880pp. Ref. 509-3
This Special Edition is the best introduction to dBASE IV, written by 1 million-reader-strong dBASE expert Alan Simpson. First it gives basic skills for creating and manipulating efficient databases. Then the author explains how to make reports, manage multiple databases, and build applications. Includes Fast Track speed notes.

Mastering dBASE IV
Programming
Carl Townsend
496pp. Ref. 540-9
This task-oriented book introduces structured dBASE IV programming and commands by setting up a general ledger system, an invoice system, and a quotation management system. The author carefully explores the unique character of dBASE IV based on his in-depth understanding of the program.

dBASE IV User's
Instant Reference
SYBEX Prompter Series
Alan Simpson
349pp. Ref. 605-7, 4 ¾" × 8"
This handy pocket-sized reference book gives every new dBASE IV user fast and easy access to any dBASE command. Arranged alphabetically and by function, each entry includes a description, exact syntax, an example, and special tips from Alan Simpson.

dBASE IV Programmer's
Instant Reference
SYBEX Prompter Series
Alan Simpson
544pp. Ref.538-7, 4 ¾" × 8"
This comprehensive reference to every dBASE command and function has everything for the dBASE programmer in a compact, pocket-sized book. Fast and easy access to adding data, sorting, performing calculations, managing multiple databases, memory variables and arrays, windows and menus, networking, and much more. Version 1.1.

dBASE IV User's
Desktop Companion
SYBEX Ready Reference Series
Alan Simpson
950pp. Ref. 523-9
This easy-to-use reference provides an exhaustive resource guide to taking full advantage of the powerful non-programming features of the dBASE IV Control Center. This book discusses query by example, custom reports and data entry screens, macros, the application generator, and the dBASE command and programming language.

dBASE IV Programmer's Reference Guide
SYBEX Ready Reference Series
Alan Simpson
1000pp. Ref. 539-5

This exhaustive seven-part reference for dBASE IV users includes sections on getting started, using menu-driven dBASE, command-driven dBASE, multiuser dBASE, programming in dBASE, common algorithms, and getting the most out of dBASE. Includes Simpson's tips on the best ways to use this completely redesigned and more powerful program.

The ABC's of dBASE III PLUS
Robert Cowart
264pp. Ref. 379-1

The most efficient way to get beginners up and running with dBASE. Every 'how' and 'why' of database management is demonstrated through tutorials and practical dBASE III PLUS applications.

Understanding dBASE III PLUS
Alan Simpson
415pp. Ref. 349-X

A solid sourcebook of training and ongoing support. Everything from creating a first database to command file programming is presented in working examples, with tips and techniques you won't find anywhere else.

Mastering dBASE III PLUS: A Structured Approach
Carl Townsend
342pp. Ref. 372-4

In-depth treatment of structured programming for custom dBASE solutions. An ideal study and reference guide for applications developers, new and experienced users with an interest in efficient programming.

Also:
Understanding dBASE III
Alan Simpson
300pp. Ref. 267-1

Advanced Techniques in dBASE III PLUS
Alan Simpson
454pp. Ref. 369-4

A full course in database design and structured programming, with routines for inventory control, accounts receivable, system management, and integrated databases.

Simpson's dBASE Tips and Tricks (For dBASE III PLUS)
Alan Simpson
420pp. Ref. 383-X

A unique library of techniques and programs shows how creative use of built-in features can solve all your needs—without expensive add-on products or external languages. Spreadsheet functions, graphics, and much more.

dBASE III PLUS Programmer's Reference Guide
SYBEX Ready Reference Series
Alan Simpson
1056pp. Ref. 508-5

Programmers will save untold hours and effort using this comprehensive, well-organized dBASE encyclopedia. Complete technical details on commands and functions, plus scores of often-needed algorithms.

dBASE Instant Reference
SYBEX Prompter Series
Alan Simpson
471pp. Ref. 484-4; 4 3/4" × 8"

Comprehensive information at a glance: a brief explanation of syntax and usage for every dBASE command, with step-by-step instructions and exact keystroke sequences. Commands are grouped by function in twenty precise categories.

Understanding R:BASE
Alan Simpson/Karen Watterson
609pp. Ref.503-4

This is the definitive R:BASE tutorial, for use with either OS/2 or DOS. Hands-on lessons cover every aspect of the software, from creating and using a database, to custom systems. Includes Fast Track speed notes.

Command Language Keywords

{?} Pause; waits for user to press Enter

{appn} Calls an add-in program's hot key when *n* is 1, 2, or 3; calls the Add-in Manager menu when *n* is 4

{beep n} Computer beeps using tone *n* (1–4)

{blank *range*} Erases *range*; similar to the Range Erase command

{bordersoff}/{borderson} Turns off/on display of column letters and row numbers (can also use {frameoff} and {frameon})

{branch *loc*} Continues with the macro at *loc*

{breakoff}/{breakon} Disables/enables the Ctrl-Break key during macro execution

{close} Closes a file that was opened with {open}

{contents *target,source,[w],[f]*} Places contents of *source* in *target* as text; can also specify width *w* and format *f*

{define *loc1:t1,loc2:t2....*} Denotes location for storing arguments passed from a subroutine call; type *t* can be number or string

{dispatch *loc*} Continues with the macro named in *loc*; macro command equivalent to the @@ function

{filesize *loc*} Enters size (number of bytes) of currently open file in *loc*.

{for *counter-loc,start-n,stop-n,step-n,loc*} Invokes the subroutine at *counter-loc*; repeats for each *step-n* between *start-n* and *stop-n*; stores the current loop count in *counter-loc*.

{forbreak} Aborts a {for} loop prematurely; macro continues after {for} statement

{get *loc*} Pauses and waits for keystroke; stores keystroke character at *loc*

{getlabel *prompt,loc*}/{getnumber *prompt,loc*} Pause; displays *prompt*, stores text/number entry in *loc*

{getpos *loc*} Enters file pointer's current position in file (in bytes) in *loc*

{graphon *[name],[nodisplay]*}/{graphoff} In Release 2.2, displays/cancels current graph or graph with specified *name*; use with {wait} macro to display for a specified amount of time. Use *nodisplay* to make named graph settings current without displaying the graph

{if *condition*} Macro continues in same cell only if *condition* is true

{indicate *text*} Displays *text* in indicator (5 characters maximum, or 240 in Release 2.2); without *text*, indicator is reset to its default display

{let *loc,i,[t]*} Places *i* in *loc*; *i* can be text or value; or specify type with optional *t*

{look *loc*} Checks keyboard buffer for keystroke; if a key has been pressed, enters the character in *loc*

{menu} or / or < Calls the 1-2-3 menu

{menubranch *loc*} Continues with the macro at *loc*, and executes it as a macro menu

{menucall *loc*} Like {menubranch}, but after execution, control is returned to macro after the {menucall} statement

{onerror *macro-loc,[message-loc]*} If error occurs, branches to *macro-loc*; error message can be entered into *message-loc*

{open *file-name,access-mode*} Opens the text file *file-name*; *access-mode* can be W, R, or M

{paneloff}/{panelon} Disables/enables the control panel display during macro execution

{put *loc,col-n,row-n,n or t*} Enters number *n* or text *t* at row/column offset in *loc*

{quit} Ends macro execution, returns to READY mode

{read *n,loc*} Copies *n* bytes from currently open file to *loc*

{readln *loc*} Copies one line from currently open file to *loc*

{recalc *loc,[c],[i]*} Recalculates *loc*; repeats if optional condition *c* is true; recalculation repeats the number of times specified in optional iteration count *i*

{recalccol *loc,[c],[i]*} Same as {recalc}, but calculates column-by-column

{restart} Aborts subroutine; resets macro subroutine stack

{return} Ends macro subroutine, returns control to calling macro

{setpos *n*} Sets a new position in the currently open file at byte *n*

{system *"command"*} In Release 2.2, temporarily exits to DOS, executes *command*, and returns to 1-2-3, where macro continues

{wait *n*} Pauses macro for time value *n*

{windowsoff}/{windowson} Freezes/returns the display to normal during macro execution

{write *text*} Writes *text* to the current position in the currently open file

{writeln *text*} Same as {write}, but adds a carriage-return line-feed